# Introduction to Macroeconomics

Kenny Christianson

**Custom Publishing**

New York   Boston   San Francisco
London   Toronto   Sydney   Tokyo   Singapore   Madrid
Mexico City   Munich   Paris   Cape Town   Hong Kong   Montreal

Printed in the United States of America

10 11 12 13 14  V0ZU  16 15 14 13 12


2009400022

BW/LP


**Pearson**
**Custom Publishing**
is a division of

www.pearsonhighered.com

ISBN 10: 0-558-40180-5
ISBN 13: 978-0-558-40180-1

# CONTENTS

To my parents, Kenneth and Frances Christianson

# PREFACE TO THE PRELIMINARY EDITION

Why write a textbook with the dozens of economics textbooks out there? I didn't like them. First, they were too expensive. Second, they didn't cover all of the material I thought important in a Principles of Macroeconomics text. Each had a different way of looking at the world. Third, the industry was becoming more concentrated as mergers gobbled up many of the publishers. So, fortunately, I was able to put together a book on my own at about 40% of the price of a typical macroeconomics textbook. It lacks the frills, but it has a lot of substance.

With the current sub-prime lending crisis, rising price of gasoline, credit crunch, and falling value of the dollar, it is certainly an interesting time to be studying macroeconomics. The ideas and concepts presented in these pages will help to guide you through this complicated world.

There are many, many individuals to thank and acknowledge for their contributions to this textbook. I owe a sincere debt of gratitude to the thousands of students at Binghamton University and Ithaca College who have been the Guinea pigs for the rough drafts of this textbook. Their comments, suggestions, and blank stares have been invaluable to my own learning process.

I must acknowledge all of the textbook authors that have influenced my own thinking in macroeconomics. I started learning principles from the tenth edition of Paul Samuelson's textbook, and the memories of my first models in economics still resonate. I also learned much from Dornbusch and Fisher, Taylor, Gordon, and Stiglitz. My teachers, especially James Price, my first principles professor, and Roy Bahl from graduate school, are held in very high esteem.

This textbook itself borrows much from the ideas of others. I started teaching from the Mansfield textbook, and was introduced to Boyes and Melvin with a new teaching assignment. From them I borrowed the ideas of automatic stabilizers and the importance of the international sector. My treatment of the classical model is derived from Miller and Van Hoose's intermediate macroeconomics textbook. The neo-Keynesian model is derived from Tucker, while the neo-classical model comes from several sources, including Hubbard and O'Brien and Parkin. In this textbook I try to synthesize the thinking of many of these economists in presenting the history of economic thought.

The staff at Pearson Custom, especially Karen Guerette, has been instrumental in getting this project off the ground. I couldn't have done it without them, and I am grateful.

Finally, I must thank my family. I dedicate this book to my parents, who taught me the work ethic and social responsibility that guided me in writing this book. I must thank my wife and kids for putting up with me while working on this project, and for weeks at a time of losing both me and the family computer.

Any errors, omissions, and goofs remain the responsibility of the author.

I hope you enjoy your journey through macroeconomics.

Kenny Christianson
Ithaca, NY
June 2008

# PREFACE TO THE FIRST EDITION

After using the preliminary edition of this textbook for two semesters and eight classes at Binghamton University and Ithaca College, I must admit that I am satisfied with the results. The feedback from the students has been both positive and gratifying. It aids the learning process when the material from the book is the same as that covered in lectures each week. Recent economic events have made the study of macroeconomics even more relevant than ever. The debates in Congress over the bail out bills and stimulus packages are reflected in the text's discussions of the different theories of macroeconomics. My hope is that the present text can adequately cover the many changes in the global economy in the ten short months since the preliminary edition was published.

I must thank my many students from the 2008–2009 academic year who put up with the preliminary edition for all of their suggestions and comments, and especially for pointing out all of the typos and mistakes from that edition. I hope that this new edition (which is being called the first edition) will correct these mistakes without creating too many new ones. My publishing representatives, Beth Wood from Pearson Custom and Marc Sawyer from Kendall Hunt, were both helpful in the preparation of the second volume, and I am sorry that I could not use both. Besides the teachers mentioned in the preliminary preface, my professors James Price and Roy Bahl, I must also acknowledge and thank some of the many others who worked tirelessly on my behalf over the years. These include my elementary school teachers Miss Welch, Miss Loper, Mrs. Shevitz, Mr. Mitchell, and Ms. Smith, high school teachers Mr. Prescott and Mr. Lutes, and professors Robert McClure, Jeffrey Stonecash, and Ralph Ketcham. All of them played a role in developing my intellectual skills and love of learning. I especially would like to thank Julian Schlusberg, my eighth grade drama and English teacher, who taught me how to speak and write and most importantly, how to believe in myself.

I am indebted to my Graduate Assistant, Timothy Haase, for his careful review of the preliminary edition and his timely preparation of the index for the book. I would also like to thank my friend Walter Hartman, and my wife Caryn Christianson for their assistance with the preliminary manuscript.

As I sit here writing this preface the United States economy faces its greatest challenges since at least the Great Depression. In the midst of a global recession and credit crisis, GDP is falling by over 6% annually, unemployment is at 8.9% and probably heading to double digits in the near future, and the CPI actually declined for the last three months of 2008. Newly-elected President Obama has introduced over $3 trillion in fiscal stimulus, while the Fed has taken unprecedented actions to maintain financial stability and increase the money supply. Since taking office in February 2006, Federal Reserve Chair Ben Bernanke has altered the Fed's monetary policy tools and the size of its balance sheet so drastically that texts and chapters on monetary policy written before his time are now obsolete.

In the midst of this economic chaos surrounding us, there is probably no better time to be studying macroeconomics. The field has seldom been more relevant or interesting. I hope that this book will be a good beginning in your lifetime of learning about the economy.

Kenny Christianson
Ithaca, New York
May 2009

# 1

# INTRODUCTION TO ECONOMICS

Welcome to the world of economics! Essentially, economics is the study of choices that arise from scarcity. In the process of living our daily lives, we are faced with a myriad of choices every day. Where do I go to college? What occupation is best for me? What should I have for lunch? These are all decisions that we must make in the face of scarcity. Economics studies the principles and rules for improving the ways that we make choices. We have limited resources with which to satisfy unlimited human wants.

In these pages, you will discover the methods and models that economists use to study the world. In the process, you will never look at the world in the same way again.

## WHY STUDY ECONOMICS?

Economics is a social science, meaning that it is involved with the study of human behavior, interactions, and relationships. We try to build models to help understand the patterns of production, distribution and consumption that we see around us every day. Economics provides tools to measure and analyze the costs and benefits of different actions. In this way, it can help to improve the decisions made by individuals, businesses, and governments.

Politicians and policy makers use economic tools and concepts to advance their sides of a debate or issue. Without knowledge of basic economic ideas, it is difficult to meaningfully contribute to public debate and support your side of an argument. Economics provides the tools for more effective civic participation.

Businesses hire economists for many reasons, such as forecasting the economy to better predict future costs and revenues for the firm, or to analyze the trends in the particular markets in which that company is involved. Financial institutions hire economists to analyze risks, to track the macroeconomy, and to judge the performance of specific stocks and bonds. The Federal Reserve System hires economists to improve the implementation of monetary policy and to increase financial literacy in the country. Government agencies hire economists to study relevant markets, to judge the competitive effects of mergers, and to determine the costs and benefits of proposed programs. Colleges and universities hire economists for teaching and research.

As you can see, the talents and skills of economists seem to be in high demand by many sectors of the society, public, private, and non-profit. For this reason, the starting salaries of economics majors tend to be among the highest for college graduates, behind only engineering and computer science majors. Data for starting salaries from fall 2008 are shown in Table 1-1. As shown in the table, economics majors enjoyed the highest starting salaries of all social science and business majors in the fall of 2008.

Besides the pecuniary rewards of studying economics, there are also many psychic rewards. The methods of economics provide ways of understanding the world and analyzing problems that enable more effective public debate and improved public decision-making and program design and implementation. With economic weapons in your arsenal, you are better able to defend and advance your side of an issue. In short, economics provides the tools to help make the world a better place.

Some of the many issues addressed by economics include:

- What are the effects of free trade on the US economy?
- How much should be spent to control global warming?
- How do we reduce air and water pollution at the lowest cost?
- Does the minimum wage increase unemployment?
- Should the Fed raise interest rates?
- Do income taxes reduce the incentive to work?
- Is our budget deficit harmful to the economy?
- Is our trade deficit harmful to the economy?
- Is government spending inflationary?

**Table 1-1**  Starting Salaries by Discipline, 2008

| | |
|---|---|
| Chemical Engineering | $63,773 |
| Computer Science | $61,110 |
| Electrical Engineering | $57,603 |
| Mechanical Engineering | $57,024 |
| Information Sciences | $52,322 |
| Civil Engineering | $51,780 |
| **Economics** | **$51,062** |
| Finance | $48,158 |
| Accounting | $48,020 |
| Business Admin/Mgmt | $46,171 |
| Marketing | $41,506 |
| English | $35,453 |
| Sociology | $35,434 |
| Visual and Performing Arts | $35,073 |
| Psychology | $34,095 |

Source: Fall 2008 Salary Survey, National Association of Colleges and Employers accessed at *www.career.vt.edu.* Used with permission.

- What are the costs of the war on terror?
- Should we allow China to keep the value of its currency artificially low?
- Is the WTO a force for good or evil?
- What are the connections between the War on Iraq, military contractors, and the federal government?
- What are the causes of economic growth?
- How do we reduce poverty and increase the standard of living around the world?
- Why are some countries rich and some poor?
- How did predatory lending contribute to the global recession of 2008–2010?
- Can fiscal and monetary policy rescue the US economy from its own excesses?

These are some of the many questions that can be understood and analyzed using the tools of economics.

## WHAT IS ECONOMICS?

As mentioned on the last page, economics is the study of choices that arise from scarcity. We all constantly face decisions that must be made in the existence of scarcity. We have limited time, money, skills, and resources with which to try to satisfy our needs and desires. Because our resources are limited, we have to choose how we put those resources to their best uses.

For example, what will you do next Friday night? Whether you realize it or not, when you decide what to do on a Friday night, you are making an economic choice. You are making a choice that arises from scarcity. There are only a limited number of hours on a Friday night. If you spend the night going to a movie, you cannot use the same time to play video games. If you spend the night drinking at a party, you cannot spend those same hours studying economics. Because there are a scarce number of hours on a Friday night, you are forced to make choices about how you allocate those hours among various activities. If the number of hours on a Friday night was unlimited, you would not be forced to make such choices. You could do everything you wanted. But because the number of hours on a Friday night is scarce, when you decide how to use those hours, you are making an economic choice.

For another example, suppose there is a little boy in a candy store with a dollar. Since he has a limited amount of funds, he must make choices over how those funds are allocated. Money spent on lollipops cannot be spent on bubble gum, and vice versa. If lollipops are 10¢ and bubble gum is 5¢, then with $1.00 the little boy can buy ten lollipops, twenty pieces of bubble gum, or some combination in between. He cannot walk off with the whole candy store. He faces choices that arise from scarcity.

As a third example, consider the case of Microsoft. Even though the company was founded by the man who became the richest person in the world, Microsoft still must make choices over how its resources are allocated. Computer engineering skills that are devoted to improving internet browser software, for instance, cannot be used to develop media player software at the same time. Even Bill Gates must make choices that arise from scarcity.

As a final example, consider the federal government. There is a finite amount of public resources at the disposal of the government. It faces choices that arise from scarcity. The resources used to fight the war on Iraq cannot be used for domestic purposes such as health care or education. When thousands of people were stuck on the roofs of New Orleans during Hurricane Katrina, almost 40% of Louisiana's National Guard troops were in Iraq (Boston Globe, September 11, 2005). With a limited number of troops, those in Iraq cannot be used to help citizens in need at home.

When I was growing up, I often heard the phrase "If we can put a man on the moon, then how come we can't educate our children? Or provide decent mass transit? Or better health care?" The question misses the point. Because the government devoted the resources to putting a man on the moon in the 1960s, it could not use those same resources for education or mass transit or health care. In a very real sense, we could not educate our children *because* we put a man on the moon. The federal government made a choice that arose from scarcity. The resources used to put a man on the moon could not be used for other, perhaps more worthy, social purposes.

So economics is the study of choices that arise from scarcity. Individuals, consumers, producers, corporations, and governments all must make choices concerning how to allocate scarce resources. Economics studies a broad range of decision-making, not just businesses. It also applies to your individual leisure choices and consumption decisions. It also applies to the decisions made by non-profit institutions such as the Red Cross or National Rifle Association. It also applies to government decision-making. Economics provides the tools to study a wide diversity of social phenomenon.

## ECONOMIC GOODS AND FREE GOODS

Economists often distinguish between two types of goods, economic goods and free goods (Boyes and Melvin). *Economic goods* are goods that are scarce; because they are scarce, they have a positive price. You have to sacrifice something to obtain an economic good. *Free goods,* on the other hand, are abundant; because they are abundant, they have a zero price. You do not have to sacrifice anything to obtain a free good. Since there is no sacrifice, there is no choice. Economics has little to say about our consumption of free goods since we do not need to make choices about them.

Consider the example of oxygen, or air in general. For most of us the consumption of clean air is a free good individually. Although society as a whole may spend billions of dollars per year in pollution control equipment to increase air quality, personally we can consume clean air or oxygen for free. We do not have to make sacrifices when we consume oxygen, so there is no reason to be conscious of our oxygen consumption. We do not have to economize on our use of oxygen. There are no choices to be made.

While consuming oxygen, I do not have to worry about how much others are using compared to myself. If we are both in the same room, I am not concerned with how much you are breathing compared to my breathing. I don't have to think to myself "I better start breathing harder so that you don't get all of the oxygen." Similarly, I do not have to be concerned about my own rate of consumption over time. I do not need to think "I better not breathe so hard now, so that I have more oxygen for later." There is plenty of oxygen for both now and later. I do not have to make choices about how I use oxygen. So while biology may have much to contribute about how I use oxygen, economics has little to say.

Compare oxygen to a peanut butter sandwich. A peanut butter sandwich is an economic good. It is scarce, and it has a positive price. There are not peanut butter sandwiches flooding the streets. Since it is scarce, I have to be conscious of my consumption. If you eat the sandwich, then there is nothing left for me. If I eat the sandwich now, it is not available for later. It has a positive price. I have to make choices about my consumption of a peanut butter sandwich. So, as we will see, economics can contribute much more to our understanding of peanut butter sandwich consumption than to our understanding of oxygen consumption.

The point is, the concept of scarcity is central to the existence of economics. Without scarcity, there are no choices. Without choices, there is nothing for economists to study.

## A MORE FORMAL DEFINITION

As we have discussed, economics can be defined as the study of choices that arise from scarcity. A more complete definition is provided below.

*Economics is the study of how individuals and organizations allocate scarce resources among alternative uses to satisfy unlimited human wants.*

This definition contains many ideas important in economics. We will take each in turn.

- Economics concerns the decision-making of many types of "individuals and organizations," not just businesses.
- "Allocating scarce resources among alternative uses" implies that choices must be made due to scarcity.
- There are many types of resources, including land, labor, capital, and entrepreneurship. We examine each of these below.
- The basic economic problem is that while human wants are unlimited, the resources with which to satisfy those wants are limited. As the Rolling Stones have been singing for over forty years, "you can't always get what you want."
- Economics often takes human wants as given, or outside the scope of the analysis and inherent to the individual. At the same time, we should realize that in a consumer society, wants are often created through advertising and the introduction of new technology. Advertising often tries to convince us to desire a product by tying that product to some more basic instinctual human need. The right mouthwash will find you a desirable mate, or the right toy will make you a great parent. The advertising agencies of Madison Avenue want us to believe that happiness comes from the possession of material goods, namely their clients' products.

## RESOURCES

As mentioned above, the allocation of scarce resources is at the heart of economics. Resources include land, labor, capital, and entrepreneurship.

*Land* is the physical topography used for production. It includes not only the real estate where businesses are located, but also all of the timber, mineral, fossil fuel and other resources that are extracted from the land and utilized in production. By clumping all of these natural resources into an input called "land," simple economic models often ignore the environmental consequences of economic activity. Land is just another resource that is used to produce goods and services. Land provides raw materials.

As we will discuss in Chapter Five, the *Global Footprint* tries to measure all of the consequences of economic activity on the land and water by including all of the costs of extraction, use and disposal in determining our use of land. It is a resource accounting tool that tries to measure the full effects of human activity on the environment, rather than clumping all of these important natural resources into a concept called "land." In simple models, economic activity occurs in a vacuum without concern for the environment. The Global Footprint is an attempt to remedy such weaknesses of simple economic analysis.

*Labor* is the time and physical and mental efforts spent by humans in the production process. Simply put, labor is the time we spend producing. Labor can be enhanced through improvements in *human capital*, or the education, training, knowledge and experience of human beings used in the process of production.

*Capital* includes the physical objects that are actually used for production. Capital includes tools, machinery, equipment and factories. Most people think of money when they hear the word "capital." Economists mean something different. They mean physical capital, or the tangible entities that do the producing. In a factory, capital consists of the machinery and tools used by workers. For a carpenter, capital includes hammers, saws, cordless drills and tape measures. In a classroom, capital includes blackboards, chalk, erasers, and spiral notebooks. To economists, capital is not stocks and bonds, which are types of financial capital, but the things that produce, or *physical* capital.

*Entrepreneurship* is the willingness to take risks to combine resources in new ways, to invent original products, to find new ways of manufacturing old products, or to combine old products in new ways. A country could be resource rich, but if no one is willing to take the risk to combine resources to produce goods and services in new ways, the standard of living may be extremely low. Risk-taking by some allows all of us to be wealthier.

As a college student, you are an entrepreneur in developing human capital. You are taking risks to improve your education, talents, and abilities, increasing both your own productivity and the productivity of the economy as a whole. What would life be like if no one took the risks to become a college student?

A simple model of the use of resources can be illustrated as follows:

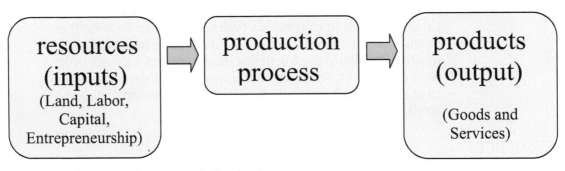

Figure 1-1   The Use of Resources in Production

Resources (or inputs) are used in production processes throughout the economy to produce goods and services (output). The amount of goods and services produced in the economy is an important determinant of the standard of living. The increase in the amount of output per person over time, known as per capita GDP, is a common measure of economic growth.

## THE METHODOLOGY OF ECONOMICS

How does economics study the world? What sets economics apart from other disciplines? We explore these questions in this section.

Economics studies the world through a process of model-building. The real world is very complex; there are many different factors which might influence a variable, event, or issue that we are trying to understand. Rather than including as many variables as possible in trying to explain human behavior, economists seek models with the fewest possible variables. We simplify the world through the use of assumptions.

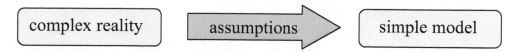

Figure 1-2    How Economists Study the World

Starting with the complex reality of our everyday existence, economists make assumptions to simplify the world. This is accomplished through the process of model building. This conscious effort to reduce the number of variables considered is what sets economics apart from other disciplines in the social sciences. Anthropology, sociology, and political science, for example, often seek the greatest number of explanatory variables, rather than the fewest.

Let's look at some examples of model-building. First, think of a road map. As a thought experiment, consider this question:

How useful is a full-scale, life-size road map?

As you can imagine, a full-scale, life-size road map would be useless. It would be too big and cumbersome to gain any information from it. By the time you unfolded it and traced out your route, you would already be there.

Maps are useful because they simplify the world. They are models of the topography of the world. Maps reduce the scale of the world. They also simplify the world by excluding unnecessary information. A map does not include every single tree, rock, house, alley, and shrubbery that you will pass along the way. If it did, it would be so cluttered as to be worthless. Maps teach you how to get from one place to the other because they are models of the world.

Different maps are useful for different purposes. The problem of navigating around campus is much different from the problem of getting from campus to Los Angeles. You would not ask for the same maps in either situation. In the same way, economics studies different types of models. Some models focus on the big picture, while other models are concerned with questions on a smaller scale. This is the difference between macroeconomics and microeconomics that we explore in the next section.

Second, visualize a small plastic model of a 1965 Ford Mustang, such as one that might be purchased in a hobby store. Once the "model" is adequately finished, it provides a good representation of the real automobile. You do not need to see every single spark plug, radio dial, foot pedal, and headlight bulb to gain an understanding of what a real 1965 Ford Mustang looks like. The simple model enables you to learn about the car without all of the unnecessary details that may make the model too difficult to build in the first place.

Third, imagine a paper airplane compared to a plastic toy airplane that you might purchase in the toy aisles of a department store. Which provides a better model of what a plane looks like? Which provides a better model of how a plane flies? It all depends on what you are trying to understand.

In sum, economics helps us to understand the world by building models to simplify the world. By taking the complexity of our everyday existence and reducing it to basic models, economics can help us to understand human behavior and social relationships, in much the same way that a map can help us to find our way home.

## THE SCIENTIFIC METHOD

To improve the accuracy and learning capabilities of the model-building process, economists seek to employ the scientific method. We try to study the world objectively, to build models to analyze social problems and make predictions about the effects of changes in policy. The problem is that the real world lacks the laboratories of the natural sciences. We cannot just increase the temperature or establish control groups in the same way that a chemist or physicist can in the lab. We lack the ability to conduct natural, verifiable experiments. In its place, we mimic the scientific method by attempting to find comparisons in the real world.

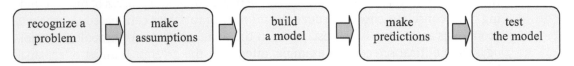

Figure 1-3   The Scientific Method

To study the world, economists practice the scientific method. First, researchers or policy makers will recognize a problem, such as growing trade deficits or the rising cost of health care. To understand the problem, the next step is to make assumptions and to build a model. By manipulating different variables in the model, economists can make predictions about the real world. How well the predictions actually hold in the real world is a test of the validity of the model. If it works, you use it again. If it fails you build a different model. The scientific method continues until, hopefully, economists can provide others with a better understanding of the world around them.

## MACROECONOMICS VS. MICROECONOMICS

One important distinction made in economics is between macroeconomics and microeconomics. As the prefixes suggest, macroeconomics studies the big picture, while microeconomics looks at the little picture. More specifically, macroeconomics is the study of aggregate economic variables, such as Gross Domestic Product, unemployment, and inflation, and how these variables affect each other and, ultimately, our standard of living. Microeconomics is the study of individual decision-making by households and firms, and how these households and firms interact in markets. All of economics is the study of choices that arise from scarcity, but microeconomics studies the choices made by individuals, while macroeconomics studies the choices made by government policy makers.

## NORMATIVE VS. POSITIVE ANALYSIS

Another distinction made in economics is between positive and normative analysis. Simply put, positive analysis is concerned with what is, while normative analysis is concerned with what ought to be. Positive statements are just descriptions of fact. They are often causative, as in "If A, then B." Since they are facts, they are either true or false. They are testable in the real world. If you tell me that your height is five-foot-ten, I can check whether this statement is true or false with a tape measure. If I say that it is 80 degrees outside, you can check the accuracy of my statement with a thermometer. Positive statements are descriptions of fact that can be tested to be true or false, without any value judgments involved.

Normative analysis, on the other hand, involves statements of opinion. It is concerned with what ought to be, or with what the beholder believes the world should be like. Normative statements are prescriptive rather than descriptive. They make the values of the author explicit. Because normative statements involve opinions, they cannot be true or false. They are not testable in the real world. If you think that I am too short or if I think it is too hot outside, these are opinions that would involve personal preferences and cannot be determined to be true or false. Normative statements imply that the world could be changed for the better somehow.

In general, economics strives for positive analysis. Economists try to be as objective as possible in describing the world, and leave the opinions to others. Many professional economists are hired to assist private or public policy makers in making decisions by describing and predicting the world as accurately as possible. The prescriptions are left to those who make policy, while economists describe the costs and benefits of various alternatives as objectively as possible. Of course, no matter how objective you try to be, normative concerns will always creep in. We cannot separate ourselves from the values, experiences, backgrounds and beliefs that we bring to the study of a subject, no matter how objective we attempt to be. But as economists, we try.

As an exercise, determine whether each of the following statements is normative or positive:

- Barack Obama was elected President of the United States in 2008.
- Barack Obama is doing a good job as president.
- The temperature outside is 70 degrees Fahrenheit.
- It is too cold outside.
- Marijuana should be legalized.
- If marijuana is legalized, consumption of marijuana will increase.
- US real GDP declined by 6.3% in the fourth quarter of 2008.
- The Obama Administration should cut taxes even further to help stimulate GDP growth.
- Overall, gasoline prices increased significantly during 2005 due to the effects of Hurricanes Katrina and Rita.
- Prisons should be reserved only for violent criminals.
- Gasoline prices should be higher to encourage conservation and promote alternative energy sources.

## A MATH REVIEW

To finish this chapter, let's end with a basic review of the mathematical concepts you will need throughout the course. As we have seen, economics is the process of model-building. The primary models of economics use mathematical analysis. There are three ways to represent a mathematical relationship:

1. Tables
2. Graphs
3. Equations

We will examine each of these in turn. The level of mathematics expected for the course is a basic knowledge of ninth-grade algebra. If you can understand equations for straight lines and draw their graphs, you should be well on your way to learning how to use models in economics.

We will start with a model of a relationship between two variables that is negative or indirect, so that the line of the graph between the two variables will be downward-sloping.

The equation for a straight line can be given by:

$$Y = a + bX$$

where a = vertical intercept
b = slope of line

If b is less than zero, then the line will slope downward, as shown in Figure 1-4.

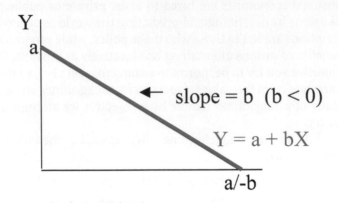

Figure 1-4   The Graph of a Straight Line

As shown above, for a graph of the equation Y = a + bX, where b < 0, the vertical intercept in equal to a, and the horizontal intercept is equal to the vertical intercept divided by the negative slope, or a / –b.

By convention, Y is considered the dependent variable and is placed on the vertical axis. X is the independent variable. Values of Y depend on the values of X.

As an example, consider the following equation:

$$Y = 20 - 2X$$

In this equation, the vertical intercept = 20 and the slope = –2.

To find the horizontal intercept, set Y = 0:

since   Y = 20 – 2X
then    0 = 20 – 2X
        2X = 20
        X = 10

So the horizontal intercept is 10, or the vertical intercept of 20 divided by the minus slope of 2.

The equation can be shown by Figure 1-5.

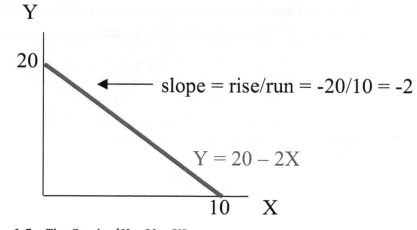

Figure 1-5   The Graph of Y = 20 – 2X

The equation can also be represented by a table, as shown in Table 1-2.

**Table 1-2**   The Table for $Y = 20 - 2X$

| X | Y | |
|---|---|---|
| | | To derive the table, plug in different values of X to find the values for Y |
| 0 | 20 | |
| 1 | 18 | |
| 2 | 16 | |
| 3 | 14 | |
| 4 | 12 | |
| 5 | 10 | |
| 6 | 8 | |
| 7 | 6 | |
| 8 | 4 | |
| 9 | 2 | |
| 10 | 0 | |

Another important skill is to know how to solve two equations simultaneously: Suppose that

$$Y = 20 - 2X$$

and

$$Y = 4 + 2X.$$

The easiest way to solve these equations is to set them equal to each other:

$$20 - 2X = 4 + 2X$$

so
$$16 = 4X$$
$$X = 4$$
$$Y = 20 - 2(4) = 12$$
$$Y = 4 + 2(4) = 12 \text{ (check)}$$

If you have the correct answer for X, then you should get the same value for Y from either equation. This is a way of checking your work.

Graphically,

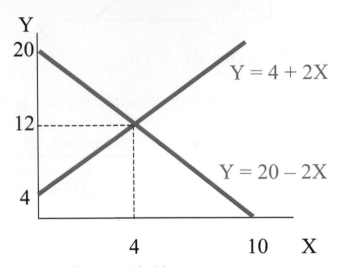

Figure 1-6  Intersection of Two Straight Lines

If you are comfortable with expressing simple two-variable relationships through tables, equations, and graphs, then you are well on your way to building models in economics.

# 2

## MODELS OF SCARCITY AND CHOICE

The first chapter explored two basic themes: (1) economics is the study of choices that arise from scarcity, and (2) economics uses a process of model-building to simplify the world so that we can understand it. In one sense, economics consists of a toolkit of models that can be used to help solve many types of problems, from social issues to personal finance. In another sense, economics provides a paradigm for understanding the world. In this chapter, we begin to examine some of the models in the economists' arsenal. We will look at the ideas of opportunity cost, production possibilities curves, and comparative advantage.

### OPPORTUNITY COST

Every time you make a decision that arises from scarcity, you give up the opportunity to make a different choice. You give up the next best alternative use of the resources devoted to your choice. What you sacrifice is known as the opportunity cost.

> *Opportunity cost* is the benefit foregone from not choosing the next best alternative.

Every action that uses scarce resources has an opportunity cost. If we return to the examples in the first chapter, what is the opportunity cost of studying economics on a Friday night? Opportunity costs are different for different people, which is why we make different choices. For some, the opportunity cost of studying economics on a Friday night might be not seeing a movie. For others it may be a date or video games. For some it may be drinking or smoking. Some students may have such low opportunity costs that they actually do study economics on a Friday night. But for most of us, the opportunity cost is too high. We are better off doing other things on a Friday night besides studying economics.

Using our other examples, what is the opportunity cost of the lollipop purchased by the little boy in the candy store? It is the quantity of bubble gum that cannot be purchased with the same amount of money. If bubble gum is 5¢ and lollipops are 10¢, then the opportunity cost of a lollipop is the two pieces of bubble gum that could have been purchased instead.

For Microsoft, the opportunity cost of using computer engineers to develop new browser software is the media player software that never gets developed. Once employees are put to work on one project, a company gives up other projects that the employees might be working on instead.

The federal government faces many opportunity costs. The opportunity costs of the War on Iraq, for example, are excessive. National Guard troops stationed in Iraq cannot be used for disaster relief at home. Soldiers killed in Iraq will no longer produce goods and services at home. The raw materials used to produce bombs and tanks could be devoted to building hospitals, schools, mass transit, or space exploration. In analyzing public policy choices, it is important to be aware of the opportunity costs of government actions.

Your decision to go to college faces many opportunity costs. First, there are the opportunity costs of the time spent in college. For many of us, the best alternative use of our time would be working in the labor force, so an important opportunity cost of college for many of us is the foregone wages sacrificed by not working. The time spent with friends and family, or a boyfriend or girlfriend, may be an opportunity cost of college for some of you. The time spent in college could also be used to take a trip around the world or lie on a beach in southern California. We all face different opportunity costs for our time.

Another important opportunity cost of college involves the money spent. That money could have sat in a bank and earned interest, so the foregone interest that could have been earned on the money spent on college expenses is also an opportunity cost of college. For some of you, that money may have been used to buy a new car, to make a down payment on a house, or to start your own business.

As you can see, the idea of opportunity cost is a valuable concept. In fact, it is one of the most important ideas in all of economics. The consideration of opportunity costs is one of the factors that set economists apart from others who study the world.

## PRODUCTION POSSIBILITIES CURVES

The first model to be introduced in economics is often the production possibilities curve. It is a model of choice. After making assumptions to simplify the world, we can use the production possibilities curve (PPC) to describe the choices available to us. PPCs are usually shown as graphs or tables.

> A *production possibilities curve* is a model that shows the maximum combinations of two goods that can be produced, given a certain quantity of resources and state of technology.

We will begin with an illustration. Let's examine the choices faced by a typical college student. In reality a student faces many opportunities, but we will assume that a student has two choices—to study or to play video games. We assume that there are only two choices so that we can draw two-dimensional graphs of the options available. We also have to make assumptions about the resources available. (Remember that economists make assumptions to simplify the world.) Assume that during the semester, you have class for six hours a day during the week, and work and church for six hours a day on the weekends. If you sleep for eight hours, this means that you have 14 hours per day devoted to sleep and classes. This leaves ten hours per day that must be divided between schoolwork and play, between your academic life and your social life. If there are seven days per week and fifteen weeks per semester, then we have

10 hours/day × 7 days/week × 15 weeks/semester = 1050 hours/semester.

So given our assumptions, we have 1,050 hours per semester of leisure time to devote to studying or game playing. An hour of studying takes, obviously, one hour's worth of time. To determine how many video games can be played, we have to make an assumption about technology, or how many video games can be played per hour. We will assume that two video games can be played per hour, or 2 × 1050 = 2,100 per semester. We also must assume that you cannot study and play video games at the same time.

We can derive the following graph:

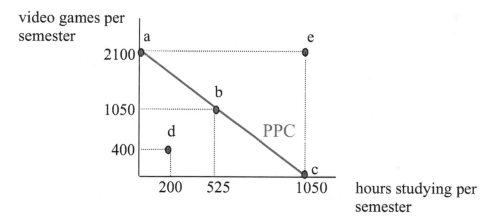

Figure 2-1    A Production Possibilities Curve

The graph above depicts the maximum combinations of video games and hours of studying that can be achieved throughout the semester. If all time was spent playing video games, then 2100 video games could be played. This is represented by point (a). You may enjoy yourself at this point, but you probably will not be back next semester because you are not spending any time studying. If all time was spent studying, then 1050 hours of studying could be achieved. This is point (c). Here, you will do very well in school, but you have no time to relax. Besides points (a) and (c), you could also produce at any point which lies along the PPC, such as point (b), or at points inside the PPC, such as point (d).

At any point which lies along the curve, such as points (a), (b) and (c), you are making the best use of your time at college. You cannot gain any more of one activity without giving up some of another activity. Economists call these points which lie along the PPC *efficient*. At any point on the curve, you are making the maximum use of your resources. You cannot gain any video games without giving up some studying, and you cannot gain more studying time without giving up some video games. These points are efficient.

A point such as (d) is *inefficient*. You are not making the best use of your time at college. You can increase one activity without giving up any of the other activity. From point (d), it is possible to increase video games without giving up any studying, or to increase studying without giving up any video games.

Point (e) is *unattainable*. There are insufficient resources and technology to produce at such a point.

Finally, the slope of the PPC shows how many video games must be given up to obtain one more hour of studying. The slope of the PPC shows the opportunity cost of one unit of the good on the horizontal axis. Here, the slope of the PPC is equal to (moving from point a to point c):

$$\text{slope} = \text{rise/run} = -2100/1050 = -2.$$

The slope of the PPC is –2. This means that the opportunity cost of one hour of studying is the two video games that must be sacrificed.

In this simple example, we assume that opportunity costs are constant. If opportunity costs are constant, then the PPC is a straight line, as shown above. On the other hand, more realistic models, and especially models of the economy as a whole, may exhibit PPCs with bowed-out shapes. This implies that opportunity costs increase as output is increased. We turn to this complication in the next session.

## GUNS AND BUTTER

One of the early economics texts by Nobel Laureate Paul Samuelson, first published in 1948, contained a PPC with the example of guns and butter. Since this is an example that generations of economists have learned, the phrase of "guns and butter" has entered the common parlance, even being used by former President George W. Bush in a speech or two.

Assume that a country can produce two goods, guns and butter. Guns represent military production, while butter represents civilian production. The maximum quantities of guns and butter that can be produced are given by the following table.

**Table 2-1**   Production Possibilities Curve for Guns and Butter

| Butter | Guns | Opportunity Cost of 1 Ton Butter |
|--------|------|----------------------------------|
| 0 | 42 | — |
| 1 | 40 | 2 guns |
| 2 | 36 | 4 guns |
| 3 | 30 | 6 guns |
| 4 | 22 | 8 guns |
| 5 | 12 | 10 guns |
| 6 | 0 | 12 guns |

By plotting the points from the table, the graph in Figure 2-2 can be derived. Note that the shape of the PPC in Figure 2-2 is different from the one in Figure 2-1. Here, the PPC is bowed away from the origin, a shape that is known as concave. As the production of butter increases, the opportunity cost of the next ton of butter also increases. This is shown in Table 2-1, and is known as the Law of Increasing Cost.

*The Law of Increasing Cost:* As production of a good is increased, the opportunity cost of additional units of that good will also increase.

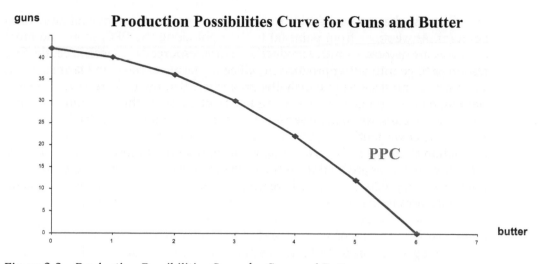

**Production Possibilities Curve for Guns and Butter**

Figure 2-2    Production Possibilities Curve for Guns and Butter

Opportunity cost increases as production increases. For example, in Table 2-1, the opportunity cost of the first ton of butter is two guns, the opportunity cost of the second ton of butter is four guns, the opportunity cost of the third ton of butter is six guns, and so forth.

Why does the law of increasing cost hold? The reason is due to the specialization of resources.

## SPECIALIZATION

Specialization exists everywhere in modern society. Some resources are more suitable for certain purposes than others. Some land is better suited for agricultural uses, while other land may be better as a site for industry. Some people are good at carpentry, while others excel at ballet. Some machines can produce gasoline, other machines burn gasoline. Land, labor, and capital resources are extremely varied and specialized in different tasks. This specialization leads to the Law of Increasing Cost.

Consider the production possibilities curve shown in Figure 2-3, a typical concave PPC between guns and butter. Look at point (a). What is society like at point (a)? At point (a), all resources are devoted to military activity, regardless of how well they can produce military goods. Not only are soldiers used for military production, but so are the farmers. All of the land is being used for military purposes, not only strategic sites, but also the fertile plains of the Midwest. All machines are being used for military production, not only machines that produce guns but also machines that produce butter. Since the cows are not being used for butter production, they must be being used for target practice instead.

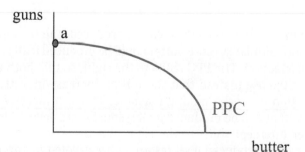

Figure 2-3   A Typical PPC

Suppose that we now decide to begin butter production, moving away from point (a). As we move from point (a) to the right along the PPC, more and more resources are devoted to butter production. Since resources are specialized, the first resources to go into butter production will be the farmers, cows, and farmland that are best at (or most specialized in) butter production. Because these resources are specialized in butter production, we gain a lot of butter. Since these resources are not specialized in guns, we do not lose a lot of guns. So at first the PPC is flat. We can gain a lot of butter without giving up many guns. But as we continue to increase butter production along the PPC, we eventually start to run out of those resources that are specialized in butter production. As we begin to use the resources that are more specialized in gun production instead, we have to give up more and more guns to obtain equal increases in the amount of butter produced. The PPC becomes steeper.

The Law of Increasing Cost exists because of the specialization of resources. As we increase production of a good, we start to run out of resources that are specialized in that good. As we begin to use resources that are specialized in the production of the other good, then the opportunity cost of the first good increases.

How do people discover where they are specialized? As we will see, the principle of comparative advantage provides an answer. Briefly, people specialize where their opportunity costs are lowest. We explore this idea in the next section. But first we must look at the effects of shifts in the PPC.

## SHIFTS IN THE PPC

The PPC can shift for two reasons, either a change in resources or a change in technology. Resources and technology are held constant along a given PPC.

If resources that can produce both goods increase, then the PPC shifts outward. For example, suppose that there is an increase in labor resources through immigration. Now, more of each good could be produced if all resources are devoted to that good. Both intercepts increase, and the PPC shifts outward. Graphically:

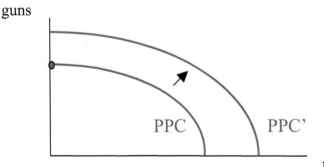

Figure 2-4   An Increase in Labor Resources

With more labor, more guns can be produced if all resources are devoted to gun production. Similarly, more butter could be produced if all resources are devoted to butter production. The PPC shifts to the right, so that both intercepts increase.

Suppose instead that there is an increase in butter technology through the invention of a new milking machine. This will increase the maximum quantity of butter that can be produced if all resources are devoted to butter production. So the butter intercept shifts to the right. But there is no change in the amount of guns that can be produced if all resources are devoted to gun production. The gun intercept remains unchanged. The PPC shifts as shown in Figure 2-5.

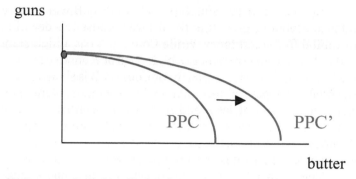

Figure 2-5   An Increase in Butter Technology

An increase in butter technology will leave the guns intercept unchanged, while the butter intercept increases. The PPC rotates to the right.

Production Possibilities Curves can describe the choices available to individuals, firms, and the economy as a whole. They provide a model of choice. Before we go on, we will explore how PPCs can be used to illustrate economic growth.

## AN APPLICATION OF PPCs: ECONOMIC GROWTH

One way that production possibilities curves can help us to understand the economy is to examine the problem of economic growth. Suppose that the economy's output is divided into two sectors, capital goods and consumption goods. Capital goods represent the tools, equipment, and machinery that are used in production. Consumption goods are those goods that are used up for the current enjoyment of consumers. For example, if a ton of steel is used to make an automobile, it is producing a consumption good. If a ton of steel is used to build an automobile factory, it is producing a capital good. If a farmer eats his seed corn in the middle of the winter, it is a consumption good. If he saves it to plant next spring, it is a capital good.

Figure 2-6 shows the choices that an economy faces between capital goods (K) and consumption goods (C). Suppose that there are two countries, Country A and Country B. Country A devotes its resources to consumption goods at Point A so its households have a high standard of living today. Country B devotes more of its resources to capital goods at point B, so it consumes less today but devotes more resources to building capital for the future. Which economy will grow more?

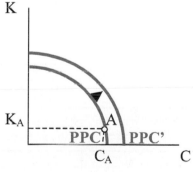

**Country A**
**Low Capital**

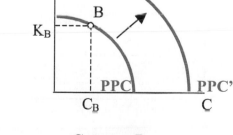

**Country B**
**High Capital**

Figure 2-6   PPCs and Economic Growth

Economic theory suggests that Country B will be able to experience higher rates of economic growth in the future because it is devoting more of its resources to capital formation today. While Country A has a high standard of living today, it will not be able to experience as high rates of economic growth in the future as Country B. The higher rate of growth for Country B is shown as a greater outward shift in the production possibilities curve so that its output potential in the future is improved. Suppose that Countries A and B start with identical PPCs, but Country B devotes more of its resources to capital formation at point B compared to Country A at Point A. Since Country B devotes more of its resources to capital formation today, it will experience higher rates of economic growth in the future.

There is a substantial body of evidence to support these assertions. For example, since World War II Asian countries have had higher rates of saving and less consumption spending, so more resources have been devoted to capital compared to many western nations. As a result, Asian countries have experienced greater rates of economic growth since World War II compared to the west.

The saving rates and GDP growth rates for different countries since 1971 are shown in Figure 2-7. Note that in general the trend line is upward. Those countries with high saving rates, such as China and Korea, also have exhibited the highest rates of economic growth in the past forty years. Those countries with the lowest savings rates, such as Greece and New Zealand, also have lower rates of economic growth. The evidence suggests a strong link internationally between saving rates and economic growth rates.

## Saving and GDP Growth Rates 1971–2007

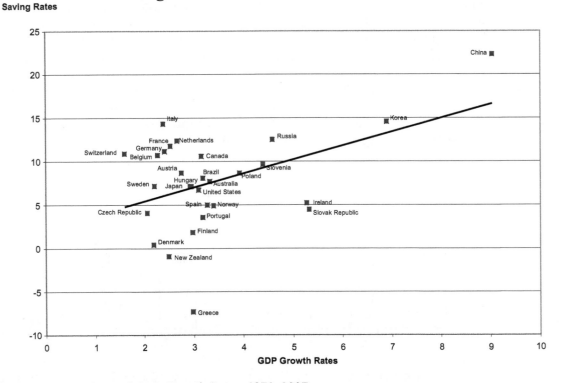

Figure 2-7   Saving and GDP Growth Rates, 1971–2007

Source: OECD and World Bank

## COMPARATIVE ADVANTAGE

How do individuals, companies, and countries discover what activity in which to specialize? Economic theory suggests that they are guided by the principal of comparative advantage to specialize where they are relatively more efficient.

*The Principle of Comparative Advantage:* Each party to a trade should specialize in the production of that good in which it is relatively more efficient (or has a lower opportunity cost).

Corollary: Mutual benefits arise from specialization and trade.

The principle of comparative advantage is the economist's main argument in favor of free trade. By specializing where we are most productive, and then trading with others who have specialized where they are most productive, we are all made better off. Economists distinguish between absolute advantage and comparative advantage.

*Absolute advantage:* when one party has a lower resource cost than another.

*Comparative advantage:* when one party has a lower opportunity cost than another.

For example, Tiger Woods may have an absolute advantage in mowing the lawn, since he may be able to mow faster than anyone else. However, he does not have a comparative advantage in mowing the lawn, since his opportunity costs are too high. He is better off hiring someone else to mow his lawn, even if it takes that individual more time. (Thanks to Greg Mankiw for this example.)

Example I: College Roommates (Absolute advantage)

Suppose that during a two-day weekend, you and your roommate must do laundry and make popcorn. The amount that each of you can produce in a day is given by the table below:

**Table 2-2**  A Case of Absolute Advantage

|  | You | Roommate |
|---|---|---|
| POPCORN / DAY | 8 | 3 |
| LAUNDRY / DAY | 4 | 6 |

You have an absolute advantage in making popcorn; your roommate has an absolute advantage in doing laundry.

To find where comparative advantage lies, first determine opportunity costs. This is easiest by setting up ratios.

You:                    Roommate:

8P  = 4L                  3P = 6L
*1P = ½L                   1P = 2L
1L  = 2P                 *1L = ½P

Here, you can produce eight bags of popcorn in the same amount of time that you can do four loads of laundry. So the opportunity cost of eight bags of popcorn is the four loads of laundry you could do instead. Through division, the opportunity cost for you of one bag of popcorn is one-half of a load of laundry, and the opportunity cost of one load of laundry is two bags of popcorn.

The analysis is similar for your roommate. She can produce three bags of popcorn in the same amount of time that she can do six loads of laundry, so the opportunity cost of three bags of popcorn is six loads of laundry. Proportionally, the opportunity cost of one bag of popcorn is two loads of laundry, and the opportunity cost of one load of laundry is one-half of a bag of popcorn.

The principle of comparative advantage states that you should specialize where your opportunity costs are lowest. Since you have a lower opportunity cost in popcorn (½L v 2L), you should specialize in popcorn production. Since your roommate has a lower opportunity cost in laundry (½P v 2P), then she should specialize in laundry production.

To show that more goods can be produced with specialization, first assume that we have a two-day weekend. We can compare the output without specialization to the output with specialization:

**Table 2-3**  The Gains from Specialization

|  | Two-Day Weekend | |
| --- | --- | --- |
|  | without specialization:<br>**You – 1 day at each activity**<br>**Roommate – 1 day at each** | with specialization:<br>**You – 2 days at popcorn**<br>**Roommate – 2 days at laundry** |
| POPCORN | 8 + 3 = 11 | 2 × 8 = 16 |
| LAUNDRY | 4 + 6 = 10 | 2 × 6 = 12 |

Without specialization, 11 bags of popcorn and 10 loads of laundry are produced. With specialization, 16 bags of popcorn and 12 loads of laundry are produced. So we can produce more of both goods through specialization. But are both parties made better off? This depends on the terms of trade.

*Terms of trade:* The rate at which both parties would be willing to make a trade. The terms of trade depend on opportunity costs.

For example, you are specializing in popcorn. On your own, you could give up the time to make one bag of popcorn and do ½ of a load of laundry. So you will be willing to trade that one popcorn only if you obtain more than ½ of a load of laundry, since if you do not obtain more than ½ of a load of laundry you will be no better off through trade.

Your roommate is specializing in laundry. On her own, she could give up the time it takes to do one load of laundry and produce ½ of a bag of popcorn. So she will only be willing to trade one load of laundry if she can obtain more than ½ of a bag of popcorn. Conversely, your roommate would have to give up two loads of laundry on her own to obtain a bag of popcorn. So if she can obtain a bag of popcorn for less than two loads of laundry, she will be better off.

You—are willing to trade one popcorn for anything greater than ½ of a load of laundry.
Roommate—is willing to accept one bag of popcorn for anything less than 2 loads of laundry.
TERMS OF TRADE: You are both willing to trade one popcorn for anything between ½ of a laundry and 2 laundry. The actual trade depends on bargaining strength. We'll assume
1 POPCORN TRADES FOR 1 LAUNDRY.

We can now use PPCs and CPCs to show that both parties are better off through specialization and trade.

*PPC: Production Possibilities Curve:* shows all of the combinations that can be produced without trade, or if a party is self-sufficient and only consumes what it produces on its own.

*CPC: Consumption Possibilities Curve:* shows all of the combinations that can be consumed through trade.

If the CPC lies above the PPC, then trade is beneficial. Each party to the trade can consume more through trade than without trade. Trade expands the possibilities for consumption.

We start with the PPCs. Assume that opportunity costs are constant. Figure 2-8 shows the PPCs and CPCs for both you and your roommate.

Without specialization, each of you can produce on your individual PPCs. With specialization, you would start at 8 bags of popcorn, and your roommate would start at 6 loads of laundry. If the terms of trade are 1 bag of popcorn for 1 load of laundry, then you would both be willing to trade 6 bags of popcorn for 6 loads of laundry.

With trade, you are both made better off. You now have 2 popcorn and 6 loads of laundry, which is more than the 2 bags of popcorn and 3 loads of laundry that you could produce on your own. Your roommate is also better off, because now she has 6 bags of popcorn and 0 loads of laundry, which is more than the 3 bags of popcorn and 0 loads of laundry that she could produce on her own.

This is the intuitively obvious case, since each of you were better at producing one of the goods. You had an absolute advantage in popcorn, while your roommate had an absolute advantage in laundry. We showed that you both could gain by specializing where you each had an absolute advantage. Since you were better at making popcorn, you should specialize in popcorn production, and since your roommate was better at doing laundry, then she should specialize in laundry. This all makes intuitive sense.

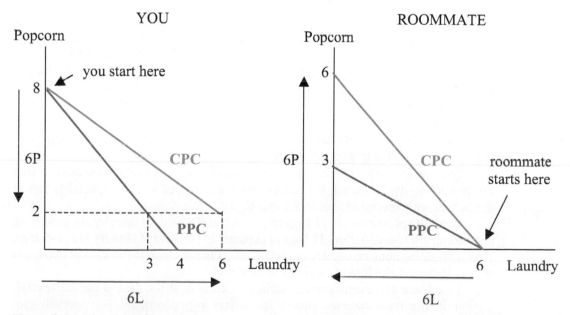

Figure 2-8   The Gains from Trade

What if you are better at both activities? Is there any reason to trade? We'll address this question in Example II.

Example II: New Roommate (comparative advantage)

Assume that you get a new roommate who is worse at both activities:

**Table 2-4**   A Case of Comparative Advantage

|  | You | Roommate |
|---|---|---|
| POPCORN / DAY | 8 | 6 |
| LAUNDRY / DAY | 4 | 2 |

Here, you are more efficient at both activities. You can produce both more popcorn and more laundry compared to your roommate. Is there any reason to specialize and trade? YES, as long as opportunity costs are different.

From the table note that you are more efficient at both activities, but you are relatively more efficient at laundry production. You can do twice as much laundry as your roommate, but only 4/3 as much popcorn as your roommate. You are better at both activities, but you are more better at laundry. So you have a comparative advantage in laundry.

Similarly, your roommate is worse at both activities, but she is relatively less worse at popcorn. Your roommate can produce ¾ the popcorn that you can produce, but only ½ of the amount of laundry. Since your roommate is less worse at making popcorn, she has a comparative advantage in popcorn production.

To determine opportunity costs:

You:

8P  = 4L
1P = ½L
1L  = 2P

Roommate:

6P = 2L
1P = ⅓L
1L = 3P

You are still the same person, so your opportunity costs are still the same. For you, the opportunity cost of one bag of popcorn is still ½ of a load of laundry, and the opportunity cost of one load of laundry is still two bags of popcorn. But now you have a new roommate. For her, the opportunity cost of a bag of popcorn is ⅓ of a load of laundry, and the opportunity cost of a load of laundry is three bags of popcorn.

Since you have a lower opportunity cost in laundry (2P v 3P), you should specialize in laundry production.

Since your roommate has a lower opportunity cost in popcorn (⅓L v ½L), then she should specialize in popcorn production.

To show that more goods can be produced with specialization, first assume that we have a two-day weekend. We can compare the output without specialization to the output with specialization, in Table 2-5.

Without specialization, 14 bags of popcorn and 6 loads of laundry are produced. With complete specialization, 12 bags of popcorn and 8 loads of laundry are produced. This is an ambiguous result. Are we better off? It is not clear. Is the gain of two loads of laundry worth the loss of two bags of popcorn?

To achieve an unambiguous result, we can look at the case of partial specialization. If your roommate completely specializes in popcorn, and you partially specialize in laundry (by moving a half-day from popcorn to laundry), then it is clear

**Table 2-5**  The Gains from Specialization II

| | Two-Day Weekend | | |
| | without specialization:<br><br>You – 1 day at each activity<br>Roommate – 1 day at each | with complete specialization:<br><br>You – 2 days at laundry<br>Roommate – 2 days at popcorn | with partial specialization:<br>You—1½ days at laundry<br>½ day at popcorn<br>RM – 2 days at popcorn |
|---|---|---|---|
| POPCORN | 8 + 6 = 14 | 2 × 6 = 12 | (½ × 8) + (2 × 6) = 16 |
| LAUNDRY | 4 + 2 = 6 | 2 × 4 = 8 | 1 ½ × 4 = 6 |

that the outcome is better with partial specialization. We have the same amount of laundry (6), but now we have 2 more bags of popcorn (16 instead of 14).

This result shows that more output can be produced through partial specialization, but we have not demonstrated that each of you would be better off through trade. To show that trade benefits both of you, we must return to the models of PPCs and CPCs. But first we must determine the terms of trade.

Here, you are specializing in laundry. On your own, you could give up the time it would take to do a load of laundry and produce two bags of popcorn. So you are only willing to trade a load of laundry if you receive more than two bags of popcorn in return. Similarly, your roommate is specializing in popcorn. On her own she would have to give up three bags of popcorn to have the time to do a load of laundry. So if she is able to sacrifice less than three bags of popcorn through trade for a load of laundry, then she will be made better off.

### Terms of Trade
You are willing to trade 1 load of laundry for anything greater than 2 bags of popcorn.

Your roommate is willing to accept 1 load of laundry for anything less than 3 bags of popcorn.

You are both willing to trade 1 laundry for anything between 2 and 3 popcorn.

Assume that you trade 1 laundry for 2 1/2 popcorn, or 2 laundry for 5 popcorn.

Graphically,

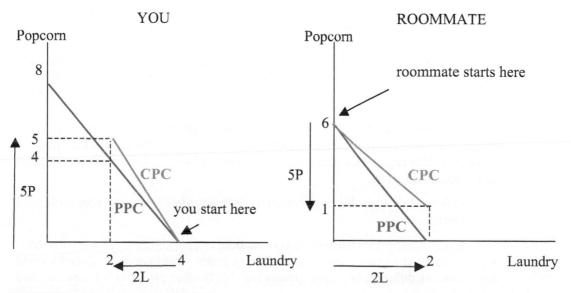

**Figure 2-9**  The Gains from Trade II

If you both trade 2 laundry for 5 popcorn, now you are both better off. You have 2 laundry and 5 popcorn, instead of the 2 laundry and 4 popcorn that you could produce on your own. Your roommate now has 2 laundry and 1 popcorn, which is more than the 2 laundry and 0 popcorn that she could produce on her own. Even if you are better at both activities, there are still benefits to specialization and trade.

## SUMMARY

In this chapter, we began to explore the ways in which economics uses models to study the world. After describing the concept of opportunity cost, we examined two models of economics, production possibilities curves and comparative advantage. PPCs can be used to model the choices that individuals or organizations face between two different activities. The law of increasing cost occurs because of the specialization of resources. Since resources are specialized, individuals, firms and governments have comparative advantages in some activities over others. As we will see in the next chapter, markets then guide these resources to seek their comparative advantage, where the resources will be put to their most valuable uses in the economy.

## FREE AND FAIR TRADE

The principle of comparative advantage is the primary argument that economists use to support free trade around the world. Economists believe that free trade increases standards of living around the world and that trade enables all countries involved to earn higher incomes and consume a greater quantity and quality of goods and services. Consumers benefit from lower prices and a greater variety of products. Free trade enables countries to learn about each other so that they can settle their differences peacefully. If the United States trades with other countries, those other countries earn the dollars necessary to purchase its exports.

*Free trade* is an absence of trade barriers such as tariffs or quotas. *Tariffs* are taxes on imports, while *quotas* are restrictions on the quantities of imports from a country.

Opponents of free trade, such as some environmental groups and labor unions, are opposed to the effects of free trade in many regions and in many ways. Some are opposed to the idea of a "race to the bottom," where countries around the world can lower their costs through such dangerous practices as poor workplace safety and health conditions, sweatshops, environmental degradation, and the use of child labor. Others worry about the loss of domestic jobs, the spreading of American culture around the world, or the loss of human rights in indigenous cultures through exploitation. The media is full of references to the evils of free trade and globalization. Economists tend to look instead toward the benefits of increased incomes around the world.

A compromise between the two viewpoints is often offered as the idea of fair trade. Fair trade recognizes the benefits of free trade in lifting incomes around the world, but also recognizes that trade can be abused to exploit the poor and to benefit corporate interests.

*Fair trade* is trade between countries with a goal of social and economic justice.

A major issue with fair trade is certification, or providing consumers with information about the quality and manufacturing processes of goods produced around the world. As different fair trade groups are able to offer products that are certified as fair trade, consumers can make the choice to change working conditions around the world. Some examples of fair-trade certificates are shown in Figure 2-10.

http://www.transfairusa.org/

http://www.fairtrade.net/producer_support.html

http://www.fairtradefederation.com

http://www.equalexchange.coop

http://www.tenthousandvillages.com/

http://www.globalexchangestore.org/

Figure 2-10    Some Fair Trade Certificates

# 3

# SUPPLY AND DEMAND ANALYSIS

The model of supply and demand is the most important in all of economics. It enables us to understand, analyze, and predict changes in markets. Why has the price of personal computers been falling? Why is the cost of health care increasing? Why does the United States grow so much corn? Supply and demand analysis helps to provide the answers to such questions. It provides a model of the ways in which consumers and producers interact in markets, and a theory of how price and quantity is determined in a market.

The demand side of a market shows how much consumers are willing and able to purchase at different prices. It is based on consumer preferences and income. The supply side of a market reflects how much producers are willing to supply at different prices. It is based on business expectations, technology, and costs.

## MARKETS

Since supply and demand analysis applies to markets, we should explore the idea of markets before we go further. First, a definition is necessary.

> A *market* is a collection of buyers and sellers where exchange takes place. Markets have three characteristics: they are defined over a geographic space, a product space, and a time period.

A market is where buyers and sellers meet to exchange goods or services. There are a wide variety of markets around the world, reflecting the diversity of the world's cultures. Markets can be small, such as a farmers' market in Ithaca, the red light district in Amsterdam, or an open-air market in Budapest. Markets can be large, such as the global market for petroleum, or the Chinese market for Western entertainment.

Markets are always defined over a particular geographic space—the market for Froot Loops in Binghamton, N.Y. or the market for soybeans around the world. More recently, the geographic base may be cyberspace, such as the markets found on E-bay or Amazon.com.

A market is also defined over a product space, or for a particularly defined type of product. When discussing a market, it is important to specify exactly what type of good or service you have in mind. A change in the product is a change in the market. For example, we can look at the market for 24-ounce bottles of Pepsi Cola, the market for Pepsi Cola, the market for cola products, the market for carbonated beverages, the market for soft drinks, and so on. As we change the product, we move to different markets. As the definition of the market expands, more and more types of goods are included in the market.

Finally, a market is defined for a given time period, even if implicitly. Demand and supply are flow variables. They measure the quantity consumed or the quantity produced per unit of time. So we must specify the time period over which the market exists. The more time available in a market the greater is the opportunity for consumers and producers to respond to price changes in that market. If no time period is specified, we generally assume that the time period is one year.

## RESOURCE ALLOCATION MECHANISMS

Before we examine supply and demand analysis in detail, we should step back for a moment to look at the bigger picture. Throughout history, societies have developed countless ways to determine how the economic pie is divided. Markets are only one mechanism available for resource allocation in society. There are many methods to determine who gets what, when and how.

Resource allocation mechanisms include:

1. Government edict—let the government determine the criteria for distribution.

2. Lottery—a random allocation mechanism could be used, such as pulling names from a hat or assigning random numbers.

3. First come, first served—the first on line gets the resource. In British English, this is known as "queuing."

4. Markets—resources are allocated to the highest bidder.

In order to illustrate the problem, let's examine a specific illustration. Suppose that due to our spirit of generosity around the world, the French government decides to reward the United States by sending us two million croissants. How should the government distribute these croissants? What is fair? What is practical? We will look at each mechanism in turn.

## Government Edict

One mechanism to distribute the croissants is to let the government decide based on some criterion. For example, the government may distribute the croissants to those who are members of their political party or who provide campaign contributions. Or the government could decide that those who are the hungriest should receive the croissants, and provide them to soup kitchens and food pantries. Or perhaps the government will allocate them based on egalitarianism, so that each citizen receives the same portion of croissants, no matter how small. There are many decision rules that can be employed here. The government can decide using merit-based criteria, such as income or achievement, or any arbitrary criteria, such as party affiliation or skin color, or a simple egalitarian rule.

## Lottery

A lottery would distribute the croissants based on chance, or a random allocation mechanism. The government could randomly choose zip codes or social security numbers to distribute the croissants. Or people could send in raffle tickets, and the government could anonymously choose the winners. With a lottery, each participant or ticket has an equal chance of obtaining the resource.

## First-come, First-served

In a first-come, first-served system, those on line first are the ones who get the goods or resources. The line could be a physical line, as in a queue for concert tickets or a spot on "American Idol." The line could also be in cyberspace, as when you register for courses. Those who register first get the classes that they want, while those at the end of the line often have to scramble for credits. With a queuing system, those with a low opportunity cost of time are the ones who can most afford to stand on line.

## Market

With a market allocation system, goods or resources go to the highest bidder. In this example, the government would auction off the croissants to the one willing to pay the most. The one willing to pay the most would then determine how the croissants are used. Since the one willing to pay the most will have the most valuable use for the croissants, markets are able to seek out the most valuable use for resources in ways that no other allocation mechanism can.

After considering the four types of allocation mechanisms, which do you think is the fairest? Think before you read the next sentence. Generally most people think that lotteries or egalitarianism are the fairest mechanisms, since everybody is treated equally. But there is no guarantee that a lottery will distribute resources to their most valuable uses.

Which do you think is most efficient? As described above, markets are the most efficient type of allocation mechanism, since only markets allocate resources to their most valuable uses. The government would require a lot of information to determine the best use of a resource. In a lottery, it is only by pure chance that a resource would go to its most valuable use. With a queuing system, the resource goes to its most valuable use only if the potential recipient has the time to stand in line. Only markets allow one use to outbid other uses to put the resource to its most valuable use. In this way, markets are efficient.

How would your answers change if the good in question was vaccines during a swine flu epidemic, rather than croissants? What would be the fairest way to allocate the vaccine? What would be the most efficient?

## THE DEMAND CURVE

The demand curve represents the preferences of consumers in the market. It shows the quantities of a particular good or service that consumers are willing and able to purchase at different prices. Demand is an inverse relationship between price and quantity. As any mathematical relationship, demand can be expressed through tables, graphs, or equations.

*Demand* is the relationship between the prices of a good or service and the quantity purchased in the market at those prices. It describes the quantity that consumers are willing and able to purchase at different prices. As the price of a good or service declines the quantity demanded will increase, *ceteris paribus.*

The *demand curve* is a model that shows the relationship between price and quantity demanded. It can be represented by a graph, table or equation. Since there is an inverse relationship between price and quantity demanded, the demand curve is downward-sloping.

*Quantity demanded* is a particular point on the demand curve. It shows the quantity that consumers are willing and able to purchase at a given price.

As the price of a good is increased, consumers are less able and willing to purchase the good, so less of the good is demanded. As the price of the good decreases, more consumers can afford and are willing to purchase the good, so more of the good is demanded. This means that the demand curve is downward-sloping. When the price falls, there is an increase in the quantity demanded. When the price rises, there is a decrease in the quantity demanded.

There are many variables that could affect the demand for a product. To simplify the world into a model, we assume that many other variables are being held constant, so we can look at the relationship between the two variables of price and quantity. The assumption that other variables are being held constant is known as *ceteris paribus,* a Latin phrase for everything else held constant.

To draw a demand curve, we put the price of the good (P) on the vertical axis and the quantity of the good (Q) on the horizontal axis. The demand curve slopes downward to the right, as shown in Figure 3-1:

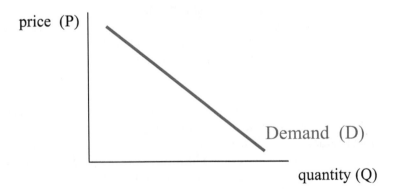

Figure 3-1   A Demand Curve

As the price of some good falls, the quantity demanded of that good will increase. Consumers want to purchase more of a good at low prices than they do at higher prices. As the price of a good falls, the opportunity cost of additional units of that good declines, so consumers want to purchase more. The demand curve shows the relationship between price and quantity demanded, holding many other variables constant. We now turn our attention to those other variables.

## THE DETERMINANTS OF DEMAND

What factors determine the demand for a product, or how much consumers want to purchase at different prices? To address this question, let us look at a specific example. Suppose that you and your friends go out for pizza on a Friday night. What are some of the factors that will influence how much pizza your group is willing and able to consume on that Friday night? What will affect your decision?

Let's allow the good in question, in this case pizza, to be called good X. Then your demand for pizza on a Friday night will depend on the following factors:

1. The price of the pizza ($P_X$)
2. The prices of substitutes and complements ($P_Y$)
3. Income (I)
4. Tastes and expectations (T)
5. Population (POP)

Your group's demand for pizza depends on the price of the pizza itself; the prices of substitutes, such as calzones or burgers; the prices of complements, such as soft drinks or beer; the amount of money the group has, or its income; your tastes for pizza, including if you had dinner that night or not; your expectations of future prices and income, which can also influence your tastes for pizza; and the number of friends you go out with that night, or the population of consumers.

Note that many different variables can affect the demand for a product. But we only have two dimensions on a graph. Mathematically, we can express these relationships in the following equation:

$$Q^D_X = F ( P_X, \overline{P_Y}, \overline{I}, \overline{T}, \overline{POP} )$$

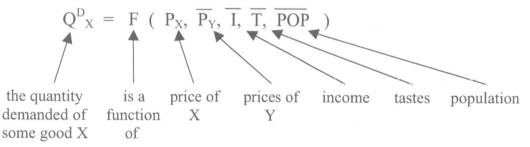

| the quantity demanded of some good X | is a function of | price of X | prices of Y | income | tastes | population |

The above equation lists all of the variables that may influence the demand for a product. Including the quantity demanded, there are six variables in this model. That is too many to graph, we do not have six dimensions. So we have to simplify the world through model-building. We use the *ceteris paribus* assumption to assume that the prices of substitutes and complements, income, tastes and population are being held constant, so that we can build a demand curve with just price and quantity. The bars above the variables mean that those are being held constant. Along a given demand curve, we hold all of these other variables constant. If any of these other variables change, the demand curve itself will shift. It is important to distinguish between movements along a demand curve versus shifts in the demand curve. Each has much different effects on the market.

*Demand* is the relationship between price and quantity. It is represented by the entire downward-sloping demand curve. So a change in demand is a shift of the entire demand curve. *Quantity demanded,* on the other hand, is just a point on the demand curve at a particular price. A change in quantity demanded is a movement along a given demand curve that results from a change in the price of the good.

## CHANGE IN QUANTITY DEMANDED

As mentioned above, a change in quantity demanded is shown as a movement along a given demand curve. The price of the good changes, but everything else besides the quantity of the good is held constant. A decrease in price, for example, will lead to an increase in the quantity demanded of the good. This is shown graphically in Figure 3-2.

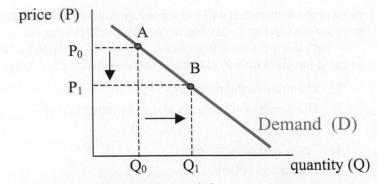

Figure 3-2    An Increase in Quantity Demanded

When the price of the good decreases from $P_0$ to $P_1$, consumers can now afford and are willing to purchase more of the good. The quantity demanded increases from $Q_0$ to $Q_1$. The demand curve itself stays the same, we just move to a different point on that demand curve. The market moves from point A to point B. The decrease in price leads to an increase in quantity as we move downward along the demand curve. As the price of the good falls, the quantity demanded of that good will increase.

## CHANGE IN DEMAND

A change in demand is represented by a shift of the entire demand curve. It occurs when there is a change in one of the variables that are being held constant along a given demand curve, such as the prices of substitutes and complements, income, tastes and population ($P_Y$, I, T, POP). If any of these variables change, there is a shift of the entire demand curve. An increase in demand, for example, is a rightward shift of the demand curve. Consumers are willing to purchase more of the good at any price. This is shown in Figure 3-3.

An increase in demand is a shift to the right of the entire demand curve. At any price, consumers are willing to purchase more than before.

What causes an increase in demand? Basically, an increase in demand is caused by certain changes in the factors that are held constant along a given demand curve. Specifically, we will examine each of these factors in turn.

When considering income changes, economists often distinguish between normal goods and inferior goods. For a normal good, an increase in income leads to an increase in demand. For an inferior good, an increase in income leads to a decrease in demand. Examples of inferior goods include boxed macaroni and cheese, Ramen noodles, Spam, second-hand clothes, public transportation (unfortunately), fast foods

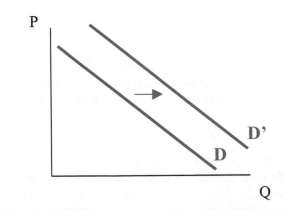

Figure 3-3    An Increase in Demand

(How many limousines do you ever see at McDonald's, except on prom night?), and any beer with the word "Milwaukee" in its name.

*An increase in demand may be caused by:*

1. *an increase in the price of a substitute.* If you and your friends go out for dinner at a pizzeria, a higher price of calzones may cause you to consume more pizza instead.

2. *a decrease in the price of a complement.* If the pizzeria is having a sale on pitchers of soda, you may buy more pizza. You have more money left over, and you have more soda to help wash down the pizza. Pizzeria delivery businesses near college towns often give away free sodas to increase the demand for their pizza.

3. *an increase in income if the good is normal.* If pizza is a normal good, then if you get funds from home that day, the increase in income will allow you to buy more pizza.

4. *a decrease in income if the good is inferior.* If pizza is an inferior good, then a decrease in income would cause you to buy more pizza and less fancy French dinners.

5. *an increase in tastes.* If you have not had dinner yet that evening, or if you really like the smell or ingredients of the pizza, then you will demand more pizza.

6. *an increase in expectations.* If you expect the price of pizza to rise next week, or if you expect higher income in the future, you may decide to purchase more pizza now.

7. *an increase in population.*

Any of these changes will cause an increase, or rightward shift, of the demand curve. Note that if the supply curve is upward-sloping, then an increase in demand leads to increases in both price and quantity. We now turn to an examination of the supply curve.

## THE SUPPLY CURVE

The supply curve represents the behavior of producers in the market. It shows the quantities of a good or service that firms are willing and able to produce at different prices. The supply curve depends on such factors as resource prices and technology. In general, the supply curve is upward-sloping to the right. As the price of a product is increased, more firms find it worthwhile to enter the market and supply the product, and existing producers find it profitable to supply more. Along a given supply curve, resource prices are held constant. As the price increases, the revenue per unit increases. If the revenue per unit increases while the cost per unit is constant, then the profit per unit will increase. With higher profit per unit, firms will produce more. As the price of a good increases, the quantity supplied of that good will also increase.

*Supply* is the relationship between the prices of a good or service and the quantity produced and offered for sale in the market at those prices. It describes the quantity that suppliers are willing and able to produce at different prices. As the price of a good or service increases the quantity supplied will increase, *ceteris paribus*.

The *supply curve* is a model that shows the relationship between price and quantity supplied. It can be represented by a graph, table or equation. Since there is a positive relationship between price and quantity supplied, the supply curve is upward-sloping.

*Quantity supplied* is a particular point on the supply curve. It shows the quantity that producers are willing and able to supply at a given price.

A supply curve is shown in Figure 3-4. Once again, price is on the vertical axis, while quantity is on the horizontal axis.

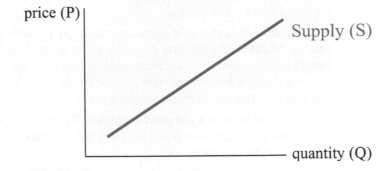

price (P)

Supply (S)

quantity (Q)

Figure 3-4   A Supply Curve

The supply curve is upward-sloping. As the price of a good is increased, producers are willing and able to supply more units of the good to the market. The higher the price of the good, then the greater is the firm's profit per unit, *ceteris paribus*. So an increase in price causes the quantity supplied to increase. Another way to explain the supply curve is to start with quantity. As the quantity of a good is increased, more resources are devoted to that good. Specialization means that we will eventually have to start using resources that are specialized in other uses as we increase the output of one good. As resources are bid away from increasingly more valuable uses, the opportunity costs of these resources will increase. As output is increased, the law of increasing cost suggests that the cost of producing each unit will increase. As costs increase, firms require higher prices to cover those higher costs. As the quantity supplied is increased in a market, the price must increase to cover the higher opportunity costs. The supply curve slopes upward.

## DETERMINANTS OF SUPPLY

As with demand, there are many factors that can influence the quantity of a good supplied in a market. In order to simplify the world to build a model of supply, we will assume that many factors are being held constant along a given supply curve showing the relationship between price and quantity. If any of these other factors change, the result is a shift in supply.

We return to our pizza example, but now let us look at the other side of the market. Suppose that a pizzeria owner, we will call him Luigi, is open for business on a Friday night. What are some of the variables that will affect how much pizza Luigi is willing and able to produce on a given Friday night? Again, let us assume that pizza is good X. Then Luigi's supply of pizza on a Friday night will depend on the following factors:

1. the price of the pizza ($P_X$)
2. the prices of resources used to produce pizza ($P_R$)
3. technology (TECH)
4. business expectations (EXP)
5. the number of firms in the market (N)
6. the prices of other goods that can be produced by the firm ($P_Z$).

Luigi's supply of pizza depends on many factors. If the price of pizza ($P_X$) increases, then Luigi's profit per unit increases, and Luigi will be willing to supply more pizza. Changes in the costs of ingredients ($P_R$) will change the supply curve for pizza. If the cost of mozzarella cheese declines, for example, then Luigi will be willing to supply more pizza. With an increase in technology (TECH), Luigi is able to supply more pizza then he could before. If it is homecoming weekend and Luigi expects big crowds (EXP), then he will be sure to order more ingredients and hire more help that Friday night to be able to increase his supply to meet the anticipated demand. Or if Luigi expects the price of pizza to be higher next week, he may try to sell less pizza this week. If a new pizzeria opens next door, the number of firms (N) will increase so more pizza will be supplied and Luigi will face more competition. Finally, if the price of calzones increases ($P_Z$), then Luigi may find it more profitable to use his pizza ovens for calzone production, and reduce his supply of pizza.

Mathematically, we can express the supply relationships in the following equation:

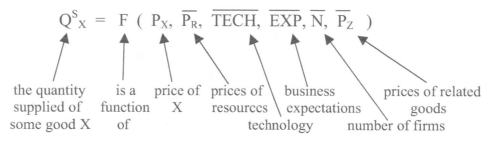

$$Q^S_X = F ( P_X, \overline{P_R}, \overline{TECH}, \overline{EXP}, \overline{N}, \overline{P_Z} )$$

| the quantity supplied of some good X | is a function of | price of X | prices of resources | business expectations technology | prices of related goods number of firms |

This is a model with seven variables, but we don't have seven dimensions with which to draw a graph. So again, we simplify the world by building a model. First, we use the ceteris paribus assumption to hold all of the other variables constant. These are represented by the bars above the variables being held constant. Then, along a given supply curve, we can examine the relationship between only two variables, price and quantity supplied. If any of the other variables change, such as resource prices, technology, business expectations, the number of firms, or the prices of related goods, then the entire supply curve itself will shift.

A change in the price of the good leads to a movement along the supply curve, or a change in quantity supplied. A change in any of the other variables that are being held fixed along a given supply curve will lead to a shift of the entire curve, or a change in supply.

## CHANGE IN QUANTITY SUPPLIED

A change in quantity supplied results from a change in the price of the good only. It is represented as a movement along a given supply curve. A decrease in price leads to a decrease in quantity supplied. If the price of the product increases, there will be an increase in quantity supplied. This is a movement along a given supply curve, as shown in Figure 3-5 on the next page.

When the price of the good increases (from $P_0$ to $P_1$), there is an increase in quantity supplied (from $Q_0$ to $Q_1$). This is represented by a movement upward along the supply curve, from point (a) to point (b).

## CHANGE IN SUPPLY

A change in supply is shown as a shift of the entire supply curve. A shift to the left of the supply curve is a decrease in supply. A shift to the right is an increase in supply.

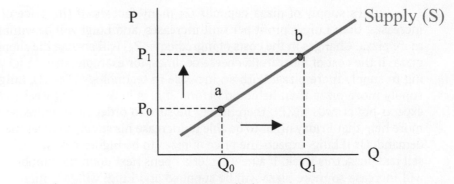

Figure 3-5    An Increase in Quantity Supplied

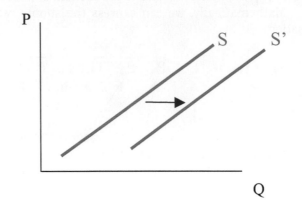

Figure 3-6    An Increase in Supply

A change in supply will occur when there is a change in any of the variables ($P_R$, TECH, EXP, N, $P_Z$) that are being held constant along a given supply curve. An increase in supply is shown in Figure 3-6.

An increase in supply is a rightward shift of the supply curve. At any price, producers are willing and able to supply more than they were before. A decrease in supply would shift the supply curve to the left. Note that changes in supply can be confusing, since an increase in supply looks like the supply curve is shifting down. It is important to look at supply changes horizontally, and not vertically, to avoid confusion.

What changes in these variables will lead to an increase in supply?

*An increase in supply may be caused by:*

1. *a decline in resource prices.* If the price of ingredients falls, then Luigi will be willing to supply any quantity of pizza at a lower price, or supply more at a given price.

2. *an increase in technology.* If Luigi buys bigger pizza ovens or a dough mixer, the increase in technology will allow him to supply more pizza.

3. *an increase in business expectations.* If Luigi expects the price to be lower in the future, or if he expects high demand, he will increase his supply of pizza.

4. *an increase in the number of firms.* If a new pizzeria opens up down the street from Luigi, then the supply of pizza in the market will increase.

5. *a decrease in the prices of related goods.* If calzone prices decline, then Luigi will use more of his pizza oven time to bake pizzas and less

time to bake calzones. If calzone prices are lower, the opportunity
cost of making pizza is lower, and Luigi will supply more pizza.

That's it for the supply curve. We now put together the supply and demand curves to show how markets work.

## MARKET EQUILIBRIUM

Equilibrium in the market occurs at the intersection of the supply and demand curves. Before we look at the graph, we should discuss the concept of equilibrium.

*Equilibrium* is a situation that will tend to persist over time.

In the natural sciences, equilibrium is associated with the idea of balance, or that an object is in equilibrium when all forces are in balance. When all forces are in balance, the situation will tend to persist until outside forces disrupt the balance.

Figure 3-7    A Ping Pong Ball

As a simple example, consider a ping pong ball resting on the edge of a bowl. If you gently nudge the ping pong ball into the bowl, what happens? It gently rolls back and forth until it comes to rest at the bottom of the bowl. It is now at equilibrium, where all forces are balanced. It will continue to stay at the bottom of the bowl as long as there are no outside forces acting on the ball or bowl. Market equilibrium is similar. Prices at first may be too high or too low, but eventually they will settle at equilibrium. Once they do, prices will tend to stay at equilibrium until demand or supply changes.

Figure 3-8 shows equilibrium in the market for pizza. At the equilibrium price, the quantity supplied is equal to the quantity demanded. There are no shortages or surpluses in the market. Firms are willing to produce just that quantity that demanders are willing to consume. We use "*" (star) to denote the equilibrium value of a variable.

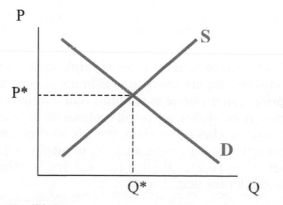

Figure 3-8    Market Equilibrium

To show that market forces will move the price toward equilibrium, let us see what happens if the price is above or below equilibrium. This is done in Figure 3-9.

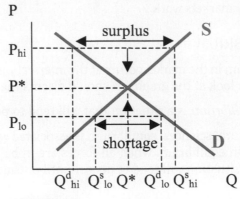

Figure 3-9  Shortage and Surplus

If the price is too high ($P_{hi}$), then a surplus exists in the market. The quantity demanded ($Q^d_{hi}$) is less than the quantity supplied ($Q^s_{hi}$). At the high price, consumers are unwilling to purchase all of the output that firms desire to supply. As firms produce unsold goods, inventories build up. As warehouses, store shelves, and new car dealer lots become overflowing, firms have an incentive to lower prices in order to sell more output. When the price is too high, market forces put downward pressure on the price.

Some common examples of surpluses include clearance sales after Christmas, manufacturer's rebates for new automobiles at the end of a model year, discount tables at book or CD stores, or the United States housing market between 2006 and 2009. In May of 2009, after record quarterly losses, the world's largest automobile manufacturer, Toyota, was even offering $1000 rebates on its hybrid Prius models. In each of these cases, a surplus in a market leads to a decline in the price of the good, bringing the price closer to equilibrium.

If the price is too low ($P_{lo}$), then a shortage in the market results. The quantity supplied ($Q^s_{lo}$) is less than the quantity demanded ($Q^d_{lo}$). At the low prices, firms are unwilling to supply all of the output that consumers would be willing to purchase. As consumers are unable to meet their demand for the product, some will have the incentive to raise their prices to bid the good away from other consumers. As prices rise, the market again approaches equilibrium.

Some common examples of markets where shortages may exist include tickets for concerts or sporting events, housing in urban areas, Wii videogame consoles, or Tickle-Me Elmo dolls. In each case, a shortage in the market causes the price to rise.

Note that in both the cases of surpluses and shortages, the market contains forces to bring the price back to equilibrium. As long as there is a surplus in the market, prices will continue to fall until equilibrium is reached. As long as there is a shortage in the market, prices will continue to rise until equilibrium is reached. Once the market reaches equilibrium, there is no reason for the price to change, unless there is a change in demand, a change in supply, or government intervention in the market. We will discuss the first two next, and save the issue of government controls in markets for the next chapter.

## CHANGES IN EQUILIBRIUM

A market will tend to stay at equilibrium unless there are changes in either demand, or supply, or both. If either the demand or supply curves shift, then new surpluses or shortages are created, and the market will eventually adjust to a new equilibrium.

For example, Figure 3-10 shows an increase in demand. The original equilibrium is at P* and Q*. Suppose that the Food and Drug Administration issues a report proving that pizza reduces the risk of cancer, so consumers want to purchase more pizza. Once demand increases, there is a shortage at the original price. The shortage ($Q^d$ – Q*) causes the price to increase, and as the price increases, the quantity demanded declines, while the quantity supplied increases, until the market reaches a new equilibrium. An increase in demand leads to an increase in price and quantity. The market moves from point (a) to point (b).

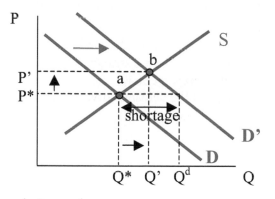

Figure 3-10   An Increase in Demand

Finally, Figure 3-11 shows an increase in supply. The original equilibrium is again at P* and Q*. Suppose that the price of mozzarella cheese falls, so the supply of pizza is increased. An increase in supply is a rightward shift of the supply curve. Once the supply curve is increased, there is a surplus at the original price. The surplus ($Q^s$ – Q*) causes the price to fall. As the price falls, the quantity demanded will increase and the quantity supplied will fall until a new equilibrium is reached at P' and Q'. An increase in supply leads to an increase in quantity and a decrease in price. The market moves from point (c) to point (d).

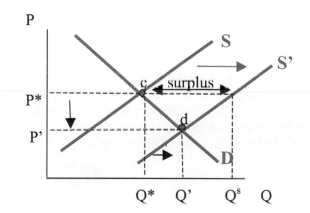

Figure 3-11   An Increase in Supply

Notice the power of supply and demand analysis. With two fairly simple curves, we are able to use the model to understand, analyze, and predict changes in markets. There is no model in all of social sciences that explains so much with so little.

To finish the chapter, we turn to an algebraic treatment of the supply and demand model. Enjoy!

## AN ALGEBRAIC MODEL OF SUPPLY AND DEMAND

Assume that the market for grape jelly can be given by the following equations:

$$\text{Demand:} \quad P = 120 - 3Q$$
$$\text{Supply:} \quad P = 30 + 2Q$$

**To graph demand:**

The vertical intercept is where $Q = 0$, so $P = 120$.
The horizontal intercept is where $P = 0$, so

$$0 = 120 - 3Q, \text{ so } Q = 40.$$

The demand curve is a straight line which goes from a vertical intercept of 120 to a horizontal intercept of 40.
The slope of the demand curve is $-3$, so

$$|\text{Slope}| = \text{vertical intercept/horizontal intercept}$$

or
$$\text{horizontal intercept} = |\text{vertical intercept/slope}|$$

Graphically,

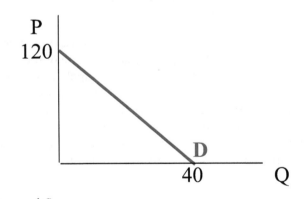

Figure 3-12   The Demand Curve

**To find the supply curve,** first note that the vertical intercept is 30 (when $Q = 0$).
For supply curves, the horizontal intercept is usually in the negative quadrant.
So for a second point, we can draw where the supply curve intersects the demand curve, or the equilibrium point.
To find equilibrium, set demand = supply

$$120 - 3Q = 30 + 2Q$$
$$90 = 5Q$$
$$\text{so} \quad Q^* = 18$$

To find price, plug in the equilibrium quantity into the demand and supply curves:

$$P^* = 120 - 3(18) = 66$$
$$P^* = 30 + 2(18) = 66 \text{ (check)}$$

Graphically,

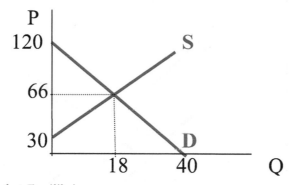

Figure 3-13    Market Equilibrium

**Effects of an increase in demand:**

Assume that the price of peanut butter declines (a complement), so that the demand for grape jelly increases. The new demand curve becomes:

$$\text{Demand}': \quad P = 150 - 3Q.$$

Since the intercept is now greater (150 > 120), then there has been an increase in demand.

With an increase in demand, at the old price there will be a shortage in the market. The quantity supplied remains at 18, but now the quantity demanded has increased due to the increase in demand. To find the quantity demanded at the old price, plug the old price of 66 into the new demand curve:

$$66 = 150 - 3Q$$
$$3Q = 84$$
$$Q_d = 28$$

Since $Q_s = 18$ but $Q_d = 28$, there is a shortage of 10 units at the old price. This shortage will cause prices to increase in the market until a new equilibrium is reached.

To find the new equilibrium, set the new demand curve equal to the old supply curve:

$$150 - 3Q = 30 + 2Q$$
$$120 = 5Q$$
$$Q' = 24$$

To find the equilibrium price, plug the quantity of 24 into the demand and supply curves:

$$P' = 150 - 3(24) = 78$$
$$P' = 30 + 2(24) = 78 \text{ (check)}$$

So an increase in the demand for grape jelly led to an increase in the quantity exchanged (from 18 to 24) and an increase in the price (from 66 to 78).

Graphically,

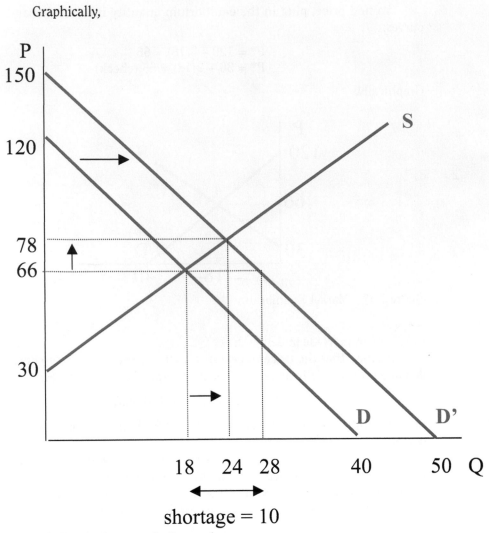

Figure 3-14   An Increase in Demand

The original equilibrium was at a price of 66 and a quantity of 18. With an increase in demand, there is a shortage of 10 units. The shortage causes the price to rise. Once the price increases, a new equilibrium is reached, at a price of 78 and a quantity of 24. The increase in demand led to an increase in price and quantity, as the model would predict.

That is the basic mechanics of supply and demand analysis. Next we turn to an analysis of how markets work and the relationships between markets and governments.

# 4

# MARKETS AND GOVERNMENT

In this chapter we explore the relationships between markets and governments, between economics and politics. When is it possible to rely on markets to allocate resources? When is it necessary for governments to intervene to improve market allocations? To solve the problems faced by society, should we rely on politics or economics? Is it better to have a political solution or an economic solution? We analyze these types of problems in the following pages.

For example, the provision of health care in our country has been an important social issue for decades. Some, especially economists, believe that it is better to rely on the market to provide incentives for the efficient production and consumption of health care. The competition between health care providers reduces the cost of health care and increases the quality of medical services. The high price paid by consumers discourages frivolous doctor visits. Others, especially health advocates, believe that health care is too important to leave to the market. The market mechanism tends to exclude those who lack the funds to pay for health care or those without health insurance. Insurance companies try to lower costs by excluding those with pre-existing conditions, so those who need medical insurance the most are often denied access. In this view, the market does a poor job of assuring a healthy population.

So who is right? Should we have a nationalized health care system or rely on market allocations? While this chapter will not answer the question directly, we will provide the tools to help you to come up with your own answers.

The chapter proceeds as follows. First, we will discuss how markets work to allocate resources, and examine the writings of Adam Smith, often known as the first economist, on the advantages of using markets compared to government intervention. If Adam Smith is correct in his praises of the market, then why is government necessary? Second, we examine the four fundamental economic questions that are faced by any society, and look at the different types of economic systems that have evolved over time to address these questions. Third, we will analyze the rationale for government intervention in the economy. On the one hand there are necessary conditions for markets to exist in the first place, and these conditions must be provided through government. On the other hand, markets may sometimes fail to allocate resources efficiently. In the first case, even if markets function efficiently, it is possible to justify government intervention to provide the necessary conditions for markets to exist and function effectively. In the second case, we can justify government intervention in those cases known as market failure. Under certain conditions, markets will fail to allocate resources efficiently. Finally, we conclude the chapter by recognizing that cases of government failure may also exist. It is not always clear whether or not governments can provide a more efficient allocation than markets.

## HOW MARKETS WORK

Markets respond to changes in consumer preferences. If consumers want to purchase more of a product, the demand for that product will increase. This increase in demand will lead to an increase in the price of the good, meaning that suppliers can now earn more revenue. This higher revenue acts as a signal to firms to increase output in order to increase profits. So in a market economy, firms respond to changes in consumer preferences by producing those items in demand by consumers.

As an example, let's examine the market for tuna fish. One important innovation in the tuna fish industry in the last twenty years has been the introduction of dolphin-safe tuna. In the 1950s, tuna fish producers discovered that dolphins liked to congregate above schools of tuna. Since dolphins were easier to spot than tuna, the tuna boats would encircle the dolphins with purse seine nets to catch the tuna below. With a purse-seine net, a small boat leads the net around in a circle from the larger boat, with weights attached so that the bottom of the net sinks. When a cord is pulled, the bottom of the net closes like a purse. The size of the holes in the net was too small to allow dolphins to escape. As a result of this practice, hundreds of thousands of dolphins were killed in the process of catching tuna, especially in the Eastern Tropical Pacific Ocean. By the late 1980s, many environmental groups, the tuna industry, and governments around the world began to recognize the problem, and many clamored for a solution. Since many countries were involved in the tuna industry, regulations from the United States alone would have little effect on the world market. But, as we will see, American consumers would have an important role to play in this saga.

In 1990 the Department of Commerce, in cooperation with the National Marine Fisheries Service, developed a dolphin-safe label for tuna fish cans. The inclusion of the label on a can of tuna fish meant that the tuna was caught with methods that did not harm dolphins. If the tuna was caught in the eastern Pacific using purse seine nets, then it must have not deliberately circled or netted any dolphins while catching the

tuna. An observer from the National Marine Fisheries Service (NMFS) on the boat at the time must verify the conditions under which the tuna was caught. If tuna is caught with different methods or in another area, then the tuna fish can can receive the label without any independent verification. As a result of the labeling requirements, the NMFS estimates that dolphin mortality has declined from 133,000 in 1986 to less than 2,000 per year since 1998. (*http://www.greenerchoices.org/ecolabels/label.cfm?LabelID=98& searchType=Product&searchValue=tuna &refpage=productSearch &refqstr=product%3Dtuna,* retrieved 5.11.09)

Before 1990, few American consumers were aware that their tuna fish consumption was harming dolphins. In the late 1980s and early 1990s, many environmental groups, such as the World Wildlife Fund and Greenpeace, began consumer education campaigns to inform tuna purchasers of the plight of dolphins around the world. The Dolphin Protection Consumer Information Act of 1990 prohibited the false labeling of tuna fish cans. If a can of tuna fish had a dolphin-safe label, then the capture of the tuna fish must not have resulted in harm to dolphins. The label enabled consumers to have information on the methods used to catch the tuna in their sandwiches. Armed with such information, consumers brought about significant reductions in dolphin deaths around the world. How do consumers have so much power?

Figure 4-1 shows the effects of these changes on the market for tuna fish. Assume that we can divide the market up into two sectors, the market for dolphin-safe tuna and the market for dolphin-killing tuna. We also assume that before 1990, consumers could not tell the difference between dolphin-safe and dolphin-killing tuna, and did not have enough information to care about the difference. We also assume that the costs of producing the two types of tuna are similar. You still have the same boats and crew, just different types of nets and techniques being used. Since consumers cannot tell the difference, and since production costs are similar, there would be no reason for price differentials between the two markets. If consumers cannot tell the difference anyway, then there is no reason for them to pay a higher price for one type of tuna over the other. So in 1990, the price of dolphin-safe tuna would be the same as that of dolphin-killing tuna.

Starting in 1990, the price of both types of tuna is P*. As consumers switch their tastes away from dolphin-killing tuna and toward dolphin-safe tuna, the demand for dolphin-safe tuna will increase, and the demand for dolphin-killing tuna will decline. In the dolphin-safe tuna market, the increase in demand leads to an increase in price and an increase in the quantity purchased. Profits will increase for those boats that catch dolphin-safe tuna. In the dolphin-killing tuna industry, the decrease

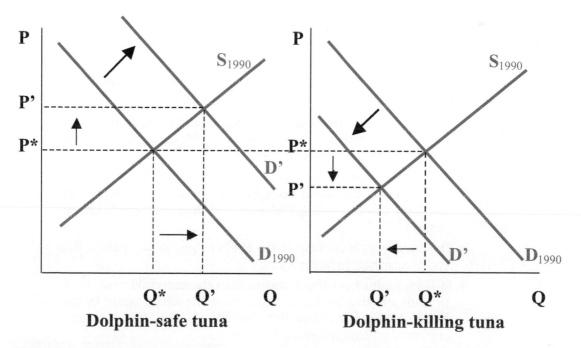

Figure 4-1  The Market for Tuna Fish

in demand leads to a decline in price and quantity. Profits will decline for those boats that continue to use the dolphin-killing purse seine nets.

If you were the captain of a tuna boat at the time, what would you have the incentive to do? Naturally, you would want to increase your profits by catching tuna in a manner that did not harm dolphins in the process. If consumers are willing to pay higher prices for dolphin-safe tuna, firms will increase their profits by switching resources into dolphin-safe tuna production. At the same time, as resources shift away from dolphin-killing production techniques, less dolphins are killed and consumers can feel better about their tuna fish sandwiches. In this way, markets respond to changes in consumer preferences.

There are two important economic concepts that were alluded to in the last few paragraphs. First is the idea of resource allocation, second is the principle of consumer sovereignty.

> *resource allocation:* In markets, prices and profits act as signals to firms to guide resources to their most valuable uses. Firms will produce more in markets where prices and profits are increasing, and less in markets where prices and profits are declining. Resources shift from markets where profits are declining to markets where profits are increasing.

> *consumer sovereignty:* Markets respond to changes in consumer preferences. Markets are relentless in giving consumers what they want.

Note that in the discussion above, the reduction in dolphin-killing tuna occurred without the need for much government intervention. As long as NMFS inspectors were on the ship to verify that dolphins were safe, consumers had all the information they needed to save the dolphins. It was not necessary for the U.S. government to adopt regulations about the types of nets or fishing procedures used in tuna capture, which would not be enforceable for other country's boats. The history of the tuna fish industry is replete with examples of failed or unenforceable international treaties. As long as consumers are receiving adequate information about the quality of their tuna, the power of the market provides enough incentive for tuna boats to protect dolphins. Government is necessary only to ensure that consumers are receiving true and verifiable information about dolphin safety. The market provides more effective incentives than does government regulation.

The power of consumers in markets is often underestimated. Indeed, social change seldom occurs without the exercise of consumer power. Think of how consumers have changed the world in the following examples:

- The Montgomery bus boycott in 1955 helped to bring about an end to racial segregation in the United States. *(http://www.watson.org/~lisa/blackhistory/civilrights-55-65/montbus.html)*
- The grape boycott led by Cesar Chavez in the late 1960s led to the recognition of the United Farm Workers union by farm owners in southern California. *(http://library.thinkquest.org/26504/History.html)*
- The divestment movement in the 1980s helped to bring about the end of Apartheid in South Africa.
- In 1996, Kathie Lee Gifford was forced to abandon child sweatshops in Honduras that produced her clothing line after a report by the National Labor Committee. *(http://66.244.199.219/CKUA_Archives/eng/archive/news_gifford.aspx)*
- Sales of the Toyota Prius, a hybrid vehicle with the designation as a "super ultra low emissions vehicle," reached 400,000 in the United

States by July 2007. *(http://www.iht.com/articles/2007/07/04/ business/hybrid.php)* (All downloaded 09.25.07)

In each of these examples, and many others, organized consumers collectively have had the power to effect important social change. How can markets be used to end global warming, sweatshops, or child labor? History provides us with many valuable examples.

## ADAM SMITH

Perhaps the first writer to recognize the power of markets was the man who is known as the father of economics, Adam Smith. Smith was born in 1723 in Kirkcaldy, Scotland to a widowed mother, and entered the University of Glasgow at the age of fourteen. After studying there and at Oxford, he became a chair of logic at the University of Glasgow in 1751, then chair of moral philosophy in 1752. Back then, academics were divided much differently than today. There were basic classes in logic and rhetoric, the classics (Greek and Latin), natural history, and moral philosophy. Moral philosophy is similar to what we would call ethics today, but also includes the rudiments of the social sciences.

In 1764, Smith left the university and became a tutor for the young Duke of Buccleuch. As a tutor he and the duke traveled in France, where they met French thinkers such as Voltaire and Rousseau. After his duties as a tutor were complete, Smith obtained a life pension, studied the industrial revolution just starting in England, and returned to Kirkcaldy. It took him ten years to write his monumental work, *An Inquiry into the Nature and Causes of the Wealth of Nations* (often called *The Wealth of Nations*), which was published in 1776. While the book is an extensive treatise with many important ideas in political economy, we will focus on three: rational self-interest, the invisible hand, and the division of labor.

As a professor of moral philosophy, Smith was interested in the struggle between altruism and self-interest. Is it better to have a society consisting of altruistic individuals who are constantly looking out for the welfare of others, or is it better to have self-interested individuals who look out for their own welfare? As an economist, Smith believed that a society would be more productive if individuals pursued their own

**Adam Smith**
*(http://www.library.hbs.edu/hc/collections/kress/kress_img/adam_smith2.htm,* retrieved 5.11.09)

self-interest, rather than constantly looking out for the welfare of others. We are our own best judge of our talents, skills, likes and dislikes. We can provide for ourselves better than others who may attempt to make us better off. For example, which would you rather receive, a $100 check from your mother, or a care package of $100 worth of items that your mother chose for you? No matter how much your mother loves you and looks out for your interests, most everybody would rather take the cash. You are a better judge of your interests than is your mother.

The importance of self-interest is related in the following passage:

> Man has almost constant occasion for the help of his brethren, and it is in vain for him to expect it from their benevolence only. . . . It is not from the benevolence of the butcher, the brewer, or the baker, that we can expect our dinner, but from their regard to their own interest.
> (*http://www.econlib.org/library/Enc/bios/Smith.html,* downloaded 09.25.07)

Smith believed that self-interest made the economy more productive because if people are free to choose their own occupations, they will naturally choose those where they can earn the greatest income and contribute the most to the economy. Smith had an idea of absolute advantage here. If people were free to pursue their own self-interest, they would choose those occupations where they were better than others, and this pursuit of absolute advantage would increase the wealth of the nation. It was left to David Ricardo in the early 1800s to develop the idea of comparative advantage.

Another important idea contained in the book is that of the "invisible hand" of the market system. Although Smith only mentions the term once in a five-volume tome, economists have used it as a shorthand to describe (and simplify) Smith's ideas. In order to understand the idea of the invisible hand, one must first understand the context of the counterpart, the visible hand of government intervention. In Smith's time, mercantilism was the dominant economic system for the countries of Western Europe. Mercantilism had three major features: bullionism, colonialism, and trade restrictions. Bullionism meant that international trade was meant to increase the amount of gold and silver, or bullion, in the King's treasury. Colonialism gave Europe the colonies where they could sell finished goods and extract natural resources. Trade restrictions were meant to increase exports and reduce imports. These included tariffs, quotas, and protecting monopolies, or charter companies such as the East India Tea Company, from domestic and foreign competition. Mercantilism was riddled with the problems of excessive government intervention.

Rather than the visible hand of government intervention that was evident in Europe at the time, Smith preferred the invisible hand of the market system. Individuals who had the economic freedom to pursue their own self-interest and trade with each other in free markets would produce more, and society would be wealthier, than where government restricted economic activity in the attempt to increase the king's gold.

The most famous passage in *The Wealth of Nations* is this:

> By directing that industry in such a manner as its produce may be of greatest value, he intends only his own gain, and he is in this, as in many other cases, led by an invisible hand to promote an end which was no part of his intention. Nor is it always the worse for society that it was no part of it. By pursuing his own interest he frequently promotes that of the society more effectually than when he intends to promote it.
> (*http://www.econlib.org/library/Enc/bios/Smith.html,* downloaded 09.25.07)

The concept of the invisible hand is often referred to as "laissez faire", French for "to leave to be." The idea of laissez faire is that government should leave the economy, markets, and individuals alone to increase the wealth of the nation.

A final idea that will be discussed here is specialization and division of labor. Smith believed that if production tasks were divided up, and if individuals were allowed to specialize in these tasks, then production would be greatly increased. In his travels, Smith visited a pin factory. He marveled at the effectiveness of the factory system in producing pins:

> To take an example, therefore, from a very trifling manufacture; but one in which the division of labour has been very often taken notice of, the trade of the pin-maker; a workman not educated to this business (which the division of labour has rendered a distinct trade), nor acquainted with the use of the machinery employed in it (to the invention of which the same division of labour has probably given occasion), could scarce, perhaps, with his utmost industry, make one pin in a day, and certainly could not make twenty. But in the way in which this business is now carried on, not only the whole work is a peculiar trade, but it is divided into a number of branches, of which the greater part are likewise peculiar trades. One man draws out the wire, another straights it, a third cuts it, a fourth points it, a fifth grinds it at the top for receiving the head; to make the head requires two or three distinct operations; to put it on, is a peculiar business, to whiten the pins is another; it is even a trade by itself to put them into the paper; and the important business of making a pin is, in this manner, divided into about eighteen distinct operations, which, in some manufactories, are all performed by distinct hands, though in others the same man will sometimes perform two or three of them. I have seen a small manufactory of this kind where ten men only were employed, and where some of them consequently performed two or three distinct operations. But though they were very poor, and therefore but indifferently accommodated with the necessary machinery, they could, when they exerted themselves, make among them about twelve pounds of pins in a day. There are in a pound upwards of four thousand pins of a middling size. Those ten persons, therefore, could make among them upwards of forty-eight thousand pins in a day. Each person, therefore, making a tenth part of forty-eight thousand pins, might be considered as making four thousand eight hundred pins in a day. But if they had all wrought separately and independently, and without any of them having been educated to this peculiar business, they certainly could not each of them have made twenty, perhaps not one pin in a day; that is, certainly, not the two hundred and fortieth, perhaps not the four thousand eight hundredth part of what they are at present capable of performing, in consequence of a proper division and combination of their different operations.
> *(http://www.econlib.org/LIBRARY/Smith/smWN.html,* downloaded 09.25.07)

While Smith recognized the importance of the specialization and division of labor in increasing the standard of living in society, he also realized that factory work may be exhausting and dehumanizing.

In sum, Smith believed that prosperity resulted from self-interested individuals in free markets with the ability to divide up their labor and specialize. The invisible hand of the market provides for a wealthier society than does the visible hand of a meddling government.

## ECONOMIC AND POLITICAL FREEDOMS

Adam Smith wrote *The Wealth of Nations* in 1776, the same year that the Declaration of Independence was written by Thomas Jefferson. While it is an historical coincidence that both documents were published in the same year, it is no accident that both were written in the same era. Both depended on the ideas of earlier philosophers such as John Locke and Thomas Hobbes, who spoke of concepts such as natural rights and social contracts. And both depended on each other. Jefferson spoke of political freedom, while Smith supported economic freedom. Each freedom depends on the other. Economic freedom is worthless without political freedom. You cannot start a business if you do not have the freedom of speech to advertise that business. You cannot find your best occupation if you do not have the freedom to choose where to live. You cannot start a factory if you do not have the freedom of assembly to gather workers at that factory. Economic freedom needs political freedom.

Similarly, political freedom requires economic freedom. It is little use to be able to choose your own leaders if you cannot support yourself or your family due to a lack of economic opportunity. Starving people seldom work on political campaigns or contribute to candidates. You must have the freedom to provide for yourself economically before you can enjoy your political freedoms.

The United States was fortunate in that we had both concepts of freedom developing at the same time in 1776. Similarly, the reforms in the Soviet Union under Gorbachev in the 1980s recognized the importance of both types of freedom. There was perestroika, or economic restructuring, and glasnost, or political opening. Gorbachev recognized that both types of freedom were necessary if reform was to be successful.

China has taken a different path. Although they have grown immensely through economic restructuring, Chinese citizens still lack most basic political freedoms. Tiananmen Square in 1989 was a sign of the struggle between political repression and economic freedom. Significant resources must be devoted to smothering the political desires of the citizenry. As seen first in Eastern Europe and the Soviet Union, when citizens lack basic political freedoms, they are unable to control the environmental degradation caused by rampant industrial production. Modern urban areas in China provide an unfortunate current example of this hypothesis.

## FOUR BASIC ECONOMIC QUESTIONS

No matter how much or how little government intervention exists in an economy, any economy must address four fundamental economic questions. Over time, different types of economic systems have evolved to handle these fundamental problems. Some systems have included large amounts of government intervention, while others provide for a greater role for markets.

As an example, let's assume that we all get stuck on campus during a blizzard. To make it biblical, we will assume that the meteorologists have predicted that we will get snow for the next forty days and forty nights. So for the next forty days, the campus will be completely isolated and cut off from the outside world. Given this situation, what kinds of decisions would we have to make as a campus?

First, we would have to decide on what to do with our time. How do we make use of the resources available on campus? What do we do with ourselves? We could continue to go to classes as if nothing changed, or we could try to entertain ourselves. Drama students could put on plays, music students could provide concerts, and athletes could play games for us to watch. Economists could draw graphs in the snow. Whatever we do, we would have to decide how to allocate our time and what to produce while we are on campus.

Second, we would have to decide on how we produce goods and services. Suppose that we decide to dig our way off of campus to go downtown. We could use hundreds of students with teaspoons from the cafeteria, who could go out to the main road and start digging. Or we could use a few physical plant workers with tractors. We have to decide on the optimal mix of capital and labor to produce digging services, whether it is a lot of students with teaspoons or a few workers with tractors.

Third, we would have to decide who gets the goods and services available on campus. Do we use meal plans to distribute the food, or would it be better to distribute food on the basis of seniority? If we use meal plans, then professors would lack access to food. If we used seniority, then freshman would be last in line for food, even though they paid for meal plans. How would we sleep? Would students with dorm rooms on campus get to keep them, or would they have to share with faculty? We might take turns sleeping so that there would be enough beds for everyone. We would also have to decide who gets heat, showers, television, etc. There probably would not be enough resources for everybody.

Finally, we would have to decide on our rate of consumption. Do we eat all of our food at once, or do we try to eat one-fortieth each day so that it would last for forty days? If we have tomatoes in the cafeteria, do we eat the seeds now, or try to plant the seeds in greenhouses so that we can have more tomatoes in the future? How long would beer and snacks last on campus? We would have to decide how much to consume now and how much to save for later.

In the same way that our campus would have to make these choices, any economy faces these similar choices. Whether large or small, or having an active government or not, any type of economic system must address these four fundamental economic questions:

1. *What and how much to produce?* Any economic system must choose a point on its production possibilities curve.

2. *How to produce?* Any economic system must determine the optimal mix of resources in production.

3. *For whom to produce?* Any economic system must determine the distribution of income, who gets what in the economy.

4. *When to consume?* Any economic system must determine the rate at which resources are used up.

Throughout history, different types of economic systems have evolved to address these issues in very different ways. Some have relied on massive government intervention in the economy, some have relied on custom, while others have depended on markets as the chief means of allocating resources. We will examine these types of economic systems, and how they answer these four fundamental economic questions, in the next section.

## TYPES OF ECONOMIC SYSTEMS

Generally, there are three broad types of economic systems that can be observed throughout history. These are:

1. traditional economies
2. command and control economies (central planning)
3. market economies

We will examine each of these in turn.

In traditional economies, economic decisions are based on custom or what was done in the past. The four fundamental economic questions are answered through age-old practices and production techniques. If your parents grew wheat, then you became a wheat farmer. If they used oxen and hoes, then you used oxen and hoes. The distribution of output was also determined through tradition. Traditional societies were marked by social stratification (chiefs, warriors, medicine men, laborers, etc.), and your place in society often determined the goods and services you received. Those who were higher up on the social ladder got more.

An obvious disadvantage of traditional economies is a lack of technological progress. If each generation follows the example of its parents, there will be very little

**Iroquois agriculture**
*http://www.nysm.nysed.gov/IroquoisVillage/images/growingfieldspanlg.jpg*

innovation and invention, so the standard of living will tend to be stagnant. There will not be the growing economic pie that comes from technological innovations and an increasing quantity of resources. Another disadvantage is that many individuals will not be able to put their own skills and talents to their best uses, if they are forced to take the same occupations as their parents. The comparative advantage of the children may be much different than that of the parents, yet with different skills and talents the children are required to undertake the same occupations as the parents.

An advantage of traditional economies is stability. Since society does not change much over time, it is possible for policy-makers to be very forward-looking. For example, the Iroquois nation occupied upstate New York before Europeans killed most of them. In Iroquois society, there was a policy that no social decision could be made without taking into account the effects on the next seven generations of Iroquois. For example, if a forest was to be cleared for farmland, the village would have to be sure that no harm would come to the next seven generations as a result. When society changes little, it is possible for the members of that society to be concerned about future generations. On the other hand, our society changes so much that we do not even know what life will be like at the end of our own lifetimes, much less what our lives will look like seven generations from now. Our society cannot be so forward-looking because we change so much.

The second type of economic system is command and control, or centrally planned, economies. In a command and control economy, economic decisions are made by government bureaucrats. The four fundamental economic questions are answered through planning agencies. The prototype of central planning was the former Soviet Union. There, the central planning agency, known as Gosplan, established five-year plans that established goals for production in different industries and agriculture. Each minister of a particular industry would be responsible for meeting the goals set for that industry. Every five years, results would be reviewed and a new five-year plan would be adopted by the Communist Party. What and how much to produce would be determined through the five-year plans. How to produce would be determined by government bureaucrats responsible for that particular industry. For whom to produce was largely determined by party affiliation. Those who were members of the Communist Party usually got more than those who were not. When to consume was determined by the five year plan. Political leaders often postpone current consumption in favor of devoting resources to capital formation.

Soviet agriculture
*(http://soviethistory.org/index.php?page=subject&show=images&SubjectID=1939tract or&Year=1939&Theme=436f756e74727973696465&navi=byTheme,* retrieved 5.11.09)

After the collapse of the Soviet Union and the fall of the Berlin Wall, many of the centrally-planned economies vanished. The three left today are Cuba, North Korea, and Albania.

An advantage of centrally planned economies is personal security. The planners make sure that everyone is provided for. Everyone gets a place to live, food to eat, and a job to earn income. The government can direct resources in the manner they deem best. For example, under Lenin and Stalin, the Soviet Union made a determined effort to shift resources into the military and industrial production, and away from consumer goods. This helped to develop the Soviet economy into the super-power status that it once enjoyed. When planners decide to take action on an issue, they have the power to shift resources in the manner desired, without having to worry about changing consumer preferences first. For example, October 4, 2007 marked the 50th anniversary of Sputnik (and my parents' marriage). At the beginnings of the space race, the Soviet Union was able to devote resources to space exploration more quickly than the capitalist economy of the United States.

Sputnik
*(http://www.google.com/search?hl=en&q=sputnik+images&aq=0&oq=sputnik+image,* retrieved 5.11.09)

An important disadvantage of centrally-planned economies is a lack of personal freedom. If the government is providing the necessities of life for you, you do not have the personal freedom to obtain those necessities in other ways. Another disadvantage of central planning is inefficiency. Central planners lack information about consumer preferences, resource costs, and production techniques. The amount of information necessary for efficient decision-making under central-planning is over-whelming. It may be impossible to gather enough information across the country to make efficient resource allocation choices. For example, to help families afford to eat, the price of bread was kept excessively low. In fact, the price of bread was actually lower than the price of grain, so farmers would feed their pigs bread instead of grain. This is obviously inefficient, since the pigs could just eat the grain without the additional cost of transforming the grain into bread. Also, central planners may not be aware of consumer preferences. For example, a female Soviet economist visiting Cornell in the 1980s reported that the Soviet Union lacked sanitary napkins. Why? The planners were men. Government bureaucrats may often lack the information necessary to meet the needs of consumers.

The third type of economic system is a market economy, or capitalism. Capitalism is a system where capital is privately owned rather than owned by the state or government. As we saw in the discussion of Adam Smith, market economies can lead to prosperity through the efficient allocation of resources, self-interest, economic freedom, specialization and division of labor. In a market economy, economic decisions are decentralized and based on price. The four fundamental economic questions are answered through the price mechanism. What and how much to produce is determined by the market price of goods. As in the dolphin-safe tuna fish market, firms produce more in those markets where prices are increasing. Producers only need the price as information concerning whether to produce or not. If the price is high enough, the firm decides to produce in that market. If the price is too low, the firm will seek other production opportunities. How to produce is determined by resource prices. If labor is cheap, production will be labor intensive. If capital is cheap, production will be capital intensive. For whom to produce is determined by resource prices and the endowment of resources among households. Each household owns resources, and their market value determines household income. Finally, when to consume is determined by interest rates, or the price of money. If interest rates are high, some households may decide to save more of their income to earn interest payments and increase their purchasing power in the future, rather than consuming their income today.

Advantages of market economies include efficiency and personal freedom. The market coordinates the personal choices of thousands of individuals to provide each of the goods and services we are able to enjoy each day. Overall, per capita GDP tends to be higher in market economies. But that does not imply that everyone gets what they need in a market economy. A major disadvantage of market economies may be

**American agriculture**
*(http://www.fotosearch.com/photos-images/combine-farm_2.html,* retrieved 5.12.09)

a lack of equity. There is no guarantee that everyone will have enough to eat, a place to live, or a job for support. Also, governments may find it difficult to direct resources to achieve policy goals. In comparing central planning and market economies, there is a tradeoff between equity and efficiency. Centrally planned economies can promote equity but are often inefficient. Capitalist economies can promote efficiency, but often at the expense of equity.

## WHY GOVERNMENT?

If Adam Smith was correct about the invisible hand of the market system, and if markets can allocate resources efficiently, then why do we need government? Why not avoid the costs of government and live in anarchy? There are several economic rationale for the intervention of government. First, there are some necessary conditions for the existence of markets in the first place. Without government to create these conditions, markets will not be able to function effectively. Second, there are situations where markets may fail to allocate resources efficiently for one reason or another. These cases are collectively known as market failure. At the same time, we must also realize that there may be many examples of government failure. Relying on government may be no better than using markets to solve our social problems.

## NECESSARY CONDITIONS FOR THE EXISTENCE OF MARKETS

There are three conditions without which markets would fail to exist. In the absence of these, markets do not have the ability to allocate resources efficiently, function effectively, or even exist. The three necessary conditions for the existence of markets are:

1. establishing property rights
2. maintaining law and order
3. enforcing contracts

Next, we will discuss each of these, and explain why they are necessary for the existence of markets.

## Establishing Property Rights

Markets cannot function without the ability to assign and transfer property rights. Property rights provide the incentives necessary to produce and consume. Without property rights, producers would not be able to sell the fruits of their labor for a profit. A property right allows a producer to sell the good to another, and the sale implies that the property right has been transferred from the seller to the buyer. If a producer cannot transfer a property right, then consumers have no reason to purchase the good, and the firm cannot earn revenue. Without a property right, the consumer cannot determine how the good is disposed of. If you cannot control the use of a good after purchase, you have no reason to purchase that good in the first place. Property rights provide incentives to produce and consume, since producers can earn revenue by selling property rights, and buyers can control the use of goods through their purchases. Without these rights to determine how a good is used, there is no reason for production and consumption to occur. Markets cannot function without property rights.

## Maintaining Law and Order

Law and order are also necessary for markets to exist. Producers and consumers must feel safe in making decisions and carrying out their activities. An entrepreneur is unlikely to open a storefront when it is likely that bricks will be thrown through windows or merchandise stolen. Consumers are unlikely to go shopping if they are afraid of getting mugged, robbed or beaten. One of the reasons why malls are popular in the United States is because malls can maintain law and order. They are private spaces with private security guards and video cameras to assure the stores' and shoppers' safety. In upstate New York, many downtown urban areas have deteriorated as more and more consumers head to the malls. As customers dry up stores close down, and urban areas become even more dangerous. Even more people go to the malls.

Law and order are also crucial from an international perspective. A nation must provide national defense to protect itself from foreign aggression. Markets cannot function if foreign armies are constantly disrupting them. Also, law and order tend to promote political stability. With a stable political system, a country is much more likely to attract international capital to foster economic growth. A corporation is not going to be willing to invest in a country that is politically unstable, since there is a threat of revolution that may nationalize factories and take away that country's profits. Markets cannot exist without law and order to allow producers and consumers to feel safe in making their decisions.

## Enforcing Contracts

Contracts help to increase certainty in markets, and they also allow for the process of lending and borrowing. If an automobile manufacturer has a contract with a steel producer to deliver steel on a certain date, then the automobile manufacturer knows that the steel will be available when needed, and can then schedule its workers accordingly. If the steel does not arrive on time, the steel producer can be sued for breach of contract. This provides an incentive for the steel producer to make deliveries on time, and increases certainty for the automobile manufacturer.

Any class exists because of contracts. By paying tuition, you have a contract with your university, college, or school to receive an education. Your professor also has a contract to teach your class. This increases certainty on both sides. Your professor is assured of earning an income, while the school knows that there will be someone to teach the class. Without a contract, you may have to make a separate tuition payment each day. Your school would have to find a new professor each day. Professors would have to look for new jobs each day. The existence of contracts increases certainty for all of us. Professors know that they will have students and get paid if they show up, and you know that you will have someone to teach the class each day, and the same teacher for the entire semester.

Contracts also allow borrowing and lending to occur. A lender can use a contract to spell out the terms of a loan, and to have a legal document to force payment should a default occur. The borrower is able to obtain a loan, and know the terms of repayment from the contract. Without contracts, lenders would not be able to force repayment from borrowers, and lending would not take place. Without lending so that borrowers can purchase new homes or autos, economic activity would quickly decline.

As we will see in the end of the chapter, contracts are an important feature of legal markets. The judicial system, from the Supreme Court to a Small Claims Court, exists to enforce contracts. When a good is illegal, the judicial system cannot be used to enforce contracts. Violence then becomes the means of contract enforcement.

These three conditions—property rights, law and order, and contracts, must be in place before markets can exist at all. They provide a minimal rationale for government intervention in the economy. Even the most conservative ideologues, such as Ronald Reagan or Milton Friedman, would agree that government intervention is necessary in these areas so that markets can function effectively. So a basic purpose of government is to provide these necessary conditions for markets to exist. Almost everyone agrees on these. A more controversial topic is the proper role of government when markets fail to allocate resources efficiently. These cases are known collectively as market failure, to which we now turn.

## MARKET FAILURE

Public finance is a field of economics that examines how economic principles can be applied to political decision-making. Within the field of public finance, there is a long history of literature on the topic of market failure. Market failure occurs when a market fails to allocate resources efficiently. When markets fail, government intervention may be justified. We will cover six types of market failure:

1. monopoly power
2. information asymmetries
3. externalities
4. public goods
5. equity
6. macroeconomic stability

In each of these cases, a private market will fail to provide an efficient allocation of resources without some type of collective action. The controversy arises over what type of collective action is necessary, whether by government or some other type of social institution. We now discuss each of these.

## Monopoly Power

A monopoly is a market that consists of only one firm. Monopoly power is when a firm has control over the market price. Monopolists are obviously able to exercise monopoly power, but so can other firms that produce in markets with only a few other firms. When a firm uses monopoly power to set the price in a market, the resulting quantity is inefficient. To maximize profits, a monopolist will charge higher prices than would exist in a competitive market. As the monopolist raises her price along a given demand curve, the quantity demanded will decline. The resulting output is inefficient since at the monopolist's output level, the price that consumers are willing to pay for an additional unit is greater than the cost of providing that additional unit. Net benefits to society as a whole would increase with more output, since consumers are willing to pay a price higher than the cost of production for the next unit. But since the monopolist is concerned with maximizing his own profit, rather than maximizing social welfare, the monopolist restricts her output to charge a higher price in the market. The resulting quantity is inefficiently low, since the monopolist is restricting output to charge higher prices.

For example, in Ithaca, New York, Time Warner Cable has a monopoly over the provision of cable television services. To raise its profits it charges higher prices than would exist in a competitive market. This is inefficient because at the higher prices, less households are able to afford cable television, if the cost of provision is less than what they are willing to pay. Suppose that it costs $30 per month to provide a home with cable television service. Also suppose that Mrs. Couch Potato is willing to pay $40 per month for cable television service. Economic efficiency requires that she be provided cable services, since her benefits of $40 are greater than the firm's cost of $30. The net benefit to society as a whole will increase by $10 when she is provided with cable television. But if Time Warner cable decides to charge $50 per month to maximize its profits, then Mrs. Potato decides not to purchase cable service. Thus society loses the net benefits that would come from the exchange. A monopolist's output is inefficiently low since it is charging high prices that restrict output in a market.

To control monopoly power in the United States, we have several laws and agencies that promote competition in domestic markets. The Sherman Anti-Trust Act of 1883, the Clayton Anti-Trust Act of 1914, and the Federal Trade Commission Act of 1914 all are attempts to control monopoly power in markets. To implement these laws, The United States has the Anti-Trust Division of the Justice Department, and the Federal Trade Commission, to encourage competition in markets and to prohibit deceptive advertising and price-fixing practices. A good example of anti-trust policy in action is the Microsoft case that was decided in 1996, where the Justice Department argued, and the courts agreed, that Microsoft's operating system provided monopoly power in other software markets (*http://www.usdoj.gov/atr/cases/f3800/msjudgex .htm*, retrieved 5.12.09).

## Information Asymmetries

In some markets, one party to a trade may have more relevant information than another party. For example, the seller of a used car has more information about its quality than does a buyer of a used car. Consumers lack information about the proper types and doses of medicine to take to cure an illness. Consumers do not know the ingredients and healthfulness of the foods they eat. Consumers do not know how their tuna fish was caught. In debt markets, borrowers may not know the full details of a loan, and lenders lack information about the likelihood of the loan being repaid. In each of these cases, a lack of information may prevent the market from reaching an efficient allocation. Government intervention to increase the amount of information available may help to increase efficiency in markets.

There are many examples of government regulations intended to increase the availability and accuracy of information in markets. We have already discussed the Dolphin Protection Consumer Information Act of 1990, which set standards for dolphin labels on cans of tuna fish. The Federal Trade Commission requires that advertising not be deceptive, and that gas stations must post octane ratings and insulation producers must disclose the R-value (insulating power) of insulation. The Food and Drug Administration requires that food packages clearly state the ingredients and nutritional quality of the food in the box. The Federal Aviation Administration requires that airlines publish their record of on-time flights in the last month. The Federal Deposit Insurance Corporation is responsible for truth-in-lending laws. In all of these cases, government regulations serve to increase the quantity and quality of information available in markets. Without adequate information, consumers are unable to make efficient choices.

Two of the most important types of information asymmetries are adverse selection and moral hazard. *Adverse selection* occurs before a transaction, when the costliest customers are those most likely to seek a good or service. The sickest people are those most likely to seek health insurance, or the riskiest borrowers are the ones most likely to seek loans. *Moral hazard* occurs after a transaction, when the costs of an action can be transferred to third parties so incentives are changed. People drive rental cars more recklessly than their own cars, or those with health insurance may visit doctors more often, since these parties can transfer the costs of their actions to others. A common complaint of the recent bailout bills (the Emergency Economic Stabilization Act of 2008) and the stimulus package (The American Recovery and Reinvestment Act of 2009) is that of moral hazard. Skeptics fear that these bailouts will only encourage risk taking and reckless behavior in the future, since those receiving the bailouts will not be punished for their past wrong decisions.

## Externalities

When we examined markets in Chapter Three, we implicitly assumed that all relevant costs and benefits were reflected in the market. The demand curve included all of the benefits going to consumers in a market, and the supply curve contained all of the costs of production. When all costs and benefits are not reflected in the market price, then the resulting quantity of output will be inefficient. This is the case of externalities.

> *Externalities:* Costs or benefits that accrue to individuals not directly involved in the transaction.

In the process of production and consumption, there may be some costs or benefits that are external to the market. Externalities can be negative, imposing costs on others external to the market, or positive, providing benefits to others not directly involved in the market transaction. Also, externalities can arise from production or consumption. We will examine two examples.

First, there may be negative externalities involved in the production of a good. For example, in the past Pittsburgh was a city with a great number of steel mills. In the process of producing steel, the mills also created a lot of air pollution which imposed costs on the residents of Pittsburgh, even if they were not directly involved in the steel industry. A household may not purchase any steel or work in the steel industry, yet it would still have costs imposed on it from the production of steel. Residents may have to wash their cars and clothes more often because of the soot. If clothes cannot be hung out to dry, there is the additional expense of using indoor clothes dryers. People may have additional medical expenses due to air pollution that causes bronchitis, emphysema, or lung cancer. City workers have to clean statues and buildings more often. The production of steel imposes costs on others that are not directly involved in the transaction. It involves negative externalities.

The problem with negative externalities is that the private market provides the wrong incentives. Since producers do not have to pay for the full costs of their actions

A Pittsburgh Steel Mill, 1890
(*http://explorepahistory.com/displayimage.php?imgId=1118,* retrieved 5.12.09)

including the external costs, then a private market will provide too much of the good compared to the socially optimal quantity. Since the price charged for the steel does not include all of the costs of producing steel, the price of steel is too low and consumers purchase too much steel. The economy as a whole would be better off if less steel was produced at a price high enough to cover the external costs. But since the firm does not have to pay these costs, it produces too much steel.

A graph may help to illuminate the situation of negative production externalities. Suppose that in the market for steel in Pittsburgh, the demand curve is as shown in the graph. We assume that the demand curve reflects all of the benefits of consumption. We can think of the demand curve as the marginal private benefit (MPB) curve. It shows how much consumers are willing to pay for the next unit of a good, based on how much they value, or the marginal benefit received, from the next unit of the good. If there are no external benefits received from the market, then the marginal private benefit is identical to the marginal social benefit (MSB).

For the supply curve, however, there is a difference between marginal private costs (MPC) and marginal social costs (MSC). The supply curve reflects the private costs of production not including the costs imposed on others. The supply curve shows that the firm must receive a price sufficient to cover its own opportunity costs of production. The marginal private cost curve is similar to the supply curve, and the marginal private benefit curve is the same as the demand curve. When externalities exist, the marginal social costs or benefits differ from the marginal private costs or benefits. This results in inefficiency.

In the presence of negative externalities, a private market will produce too much compared to the social optimum. This is shown in Figure 4-2. The social optimum is at Q*, where the marginal social benefits are equal to the marginal social costs. We have produced all of those units of output that add more to social benefits than they add to social costs. A private market, however, will produce where MPB = MPC. A firm is concerned only with its own costs and benefits, not with social costs and benefits. The private market will produce at $Q_{pvt}$, or where the private supply and demand curves intersect. The quantity produced is greater than the social optimum. The private market produces too much.

A private market will produce at $Q_{pvt}$ and charge a price of $P_{pvt}$, where the marginal private benefits are equal to the marginal private costs. The social optimum is

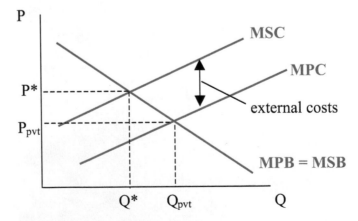

Figure 4-2   The Market for Steel in Pittsburgh
Key: MSC = marginal social cost
     MPC = marginal private cost
     MPB = marginal private benefit
     MSB = marginal social benefit

where marginal social benefits are equal to marginal social costs, at Q* and P*. Since the private market produces more than Q*, in the presence of negative externalities a private market will produce an inefficiently high quantity of the good. Since firms do not have to pay the full costs of their production, they can charge a lower price, and too much of the good is produced and consumed.

There are many potential governmental responses to negative externalities. A tax on steel equal to the external cost would raise the firms' supply curve until it was identical to the MSC curve. The firms would then have an incentive to produce at the social optimum. The government could place restrictions on the quantity of steel produced or on the techniques used to produce steel. As in the Clean Air Act of 1972, the government could require the best available technology be used for pollution control. Or the government might place a tax on the pollution created (an effluent fee), or create a market for the pollution and allow firms to buy and sell pollution credits. All of these approaches have been used to control negative externalities in markets.

Other examples of negative externalities include secondhand smoke, the carbon monoxide and other pollutants that are emitted when you drive your car, the noise from a loud party, the vibrations caused by road construction or large trucks in a neighborhood, or talking in class.

Another example of an externality would be a positive consumption externality, where one person's consumption of a good benefits others not directly involved in the transaction. For example, elementary education provides benefits not only to the child consuming the education but also to society as a whole, because education provides benefits to society as a whole in having a literate citizenry. It would be dangerous to live in a society where people could not read stop signs or instructions for power tools. Literacy helps a citizen contribute to civic life.

If left to its own devices, a private market would provide an inefficiently small quantity of education. If we had to rely on private schools for elementary education, the quantity of education consumed in our country would be woefully inadequate. Many poor people would not be able to afford a private education, and others may feel that the costs of an education outweigh the benefits. Society as a whole would be denied the benefits of an educated populace.

We can show this situation in Figure 4-3. We assume that the marginal private costs of education are similar to the marginal private benefits of education. The externality arises in that the marginal social benefits of education are greater than the marginal private benefits of education. There are positive externalities. Since individuals do not consider all of the benefits of education including the external benefits, a private market would provide too little education. This is shown in Figure 4-3 below.

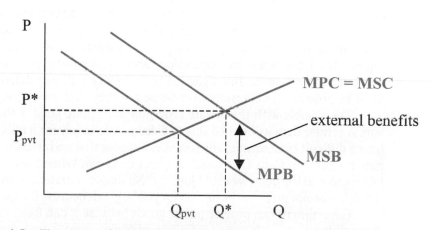

Figure 4-3   The Market for Elementary Education

An educational system composed of only private schools would provide a level of education at $Q_{pvt}$ and charge a price equal to $P_{pvt}$, where marginal private benefits are equal to marginal private costs. But society as a whole is willing to pay more for education due to the social benefits of receiving an education. When the external benefits are included, the optimum quantity of education is $Q^*$. In the presence of positive externalities, a private market provides an inefficiently low quantity of the good. Society as a whole would be better off if more of the good or service was produced.

An important government remedy for positive externalities is subsidies. The government requires compulsory public education up to the age of 16, and then subsidizes that education by providing it for free and paying for it with tax dollars. In this way, society gets more of the benefits of elementary education. Other methods of encouraging positive externalities include tax cuts for renewable energy systems or hybrid vehicles, widespread free distribution of immunization shots, or recognition awards for neighborhood beautification. In these ways, the government can use its powers to promote desirable behavior.

When externalities exist, whether positive or negative, the private market will not provide an efficient allocation of resources. For this reason, externalities provide a rationale for government intervention in markets.

## Public Goods

In the case of public goods, such as national defense, roads and bridges, public parks, police and fire protection, or lighthouses, a private firm will find it difficult or impossible to provide these goods since it cannot force people to pay for the goods. It cannot force people to pay because it is costly or impossible to exclude consumers once the good is provided. The consumer can enjoy the good without having to pay for it. She can be a free-rider. The provision of public goods requires collective action.

*Public good:* A good that is non-rival in consumption and non-excludable. It is non-rival in that I can consume the good and you can consume the good at the same time, and my consumption does not detract from your consumption. Non-excludable means that once the good is provided, it is provided to everyone and it is costly or impossible to exclude an individual from consuming that good.

*Free-rider problem:* Since public goods are non-excludable, individuals can consume a public good once it is provided without having to pay for that good.

The purest example of a public good is probably national defense. National defense is non-rival. I can consume national defense and you can consume national defense, and one person's consumption does not take away anything from the other person. National defense is also non-excludable. Once it is provided it is provided for everyone. Suppose that everyone has paid their taxes besides me. If an Iraqi jet is flying overhead, the rest of the population cannot just point at me and say "Bomb him, bomb him, because he didn't pay his taxes." Once national defense is provided, it must be provided for everyone whether or not they paid their taxes.

The trouble with the private provision of a public good is the free-rider problem. A private firm will not be able to force people to pay for a public good, so it will have a difficult time earning any revenue. Suppose that we hired Coca-Cola to provide national defense. Coca-Cola could not force us to pay. When the Coca-Cola representative came to the door, we could just say "No thanks, I prefer not to pay today." A private firm cannot profit in the market for public goods because it cannot force payment.

Government can provide public goods because it can force us to pay for them through taxation. In fact, one definition of government is that government is institutionalized coercion. Government is the only institution that we allow to have coercive powers over us. It can take our money through taxation. It can take our time through the draft or imprisonment. It can take our land through a process known as eminent domain. It can take our lives through wars or capital punishment. Government is the only institution to which we give these types of powers.

In order to enjoy public goods, we must have government provide them. Government is the only institution that can force us to pay for these goods through taxes. Any other institution would face the free-rider problem.

Politicians often ignore the importance of public goods and the free-rider problem. Conservatives sometimes complain of "tax and spend liberals" who are trying to increase government spending and taxes. To criticize government for its "tax and spend" policies misses the point. One of the most important functions of government is to tax and spend. Government taxes us to force payment for public goods, and then spends that tax revenue to provide those public goods.

## Equity

There is nothing to guarantee that a private market economy will provide an equitable distribution of income. Some may not have enough food to eat, clothes to wear, a place to live, or a job to support themselves. There are many ways that government helps to supplement incomes so that the poor can participate and survive in a market economy. Examples include unemployment insurance, Temporary Assistance to Needy Families (TANF), food stamps, section 8 housing assistance, or home heating assistance. These programs help to reduce poverty and create a slightly more equitable distribution of income.

## Macroeconomic Stability

A market economy may not lead to stable rates of growth with low rates of inflation and unemployment. As we will see for most of the rest of the course, the government can use its economic policy tools to help promote and sustain a stable macroeconomy.

In each of these cases, the market fails to allocate resources efficiently or fails in meeting some other social goal such as equity or stability. These cases of market failure provide an economic rationale for government intervention in a market or the economy. But we must recognize that in trying to solve our social problems, government may be no better of a solution than markets. There may be many examples of government failure also, when governments can interfere with the efficiency of markets. We now turn to these.

## GOVERNMENT FAILURE

As we saw in the last section, government is required to provide the necessary conditions for markets to exist, and to help to address situations of market failure. But we must recognize that government may be no better than markets in allocating resources efficiently. In this last section we will discuss five types of government failure:

1. political influence
2. price floors and price ceilings (price controls)
3. taxes
4. majority rule voting paradox
5. myopic viewpoint
6. illegal markets

## Political Influence

Political decisions are often made to benefit those with access to the political system. Since producers are more concentrated and have more gain from policy decisions than consumers, policy decisions tend to benefit producers. For example, politicians often favor protectionist policies for industries in their district. Congressmen from Michigan will seek to protect the automobile industry, and Senators from Washington State will seek to prevent foreign competition from harming the aerospace industry. Producers have more of an incentive to gain political access than do consumers. The benefits of protectionist policies go to a few producers with political access, while the costs of protectionism are spread out among millions of disorganized consumers who must now pay higher prices for these products. No single consumer has much of an incentive to lobby Congress for lower prices, since their own individual benefit will be small. However, the benefits to producers of protectionism are large, so they have more of an incentive to gain political access. Since they have political influence, policy decisions will often favor producers at the expense of consumers. Government may fail to allocate resources impartially or efficiently.

## Price Floors and Price Ceilings

Through the use of price controls the government prevents the market from rationing the available supply of the good among demanders in that market. With a price floor, the government sets a minimum price above the market price, causing a surplus in the market. Examples of price floors include minimum wage laws and agricultural price supports. Price ceilings occur when the government sets a maximum price below the equilibrium price, causing a shortage in the market. Examples include rent controls or gasoline price controls in the 1970s. In both cases, government mandates prevent the market price from reaching equilibrium and inefficiency results.

*Price floor:* A price floor occurs when the government sets a minimum price above the equilibrium price. A surplus results.

Figure 4-4 shows a price floor in the labor market, otherwise known as a minimum wage. In the labor market, firms are the demanders of labor and households are the suppliers of labor. The equilibrium wage rate would be at P* with a quantity of Q* labor hired. Assume that the minimum wage is set at P^. At this price, the quantity supplied of labor, $Q_s$, is greater than the quantity demanded of labor, $Q_d$. A

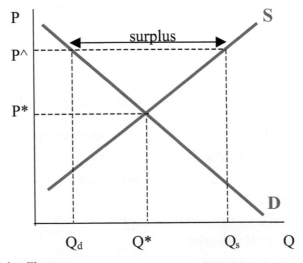

Figure 4-4   A Price Floor

surplus in the labor market, or unemployment, results. This is the basic economic argument against minimum wage laws.

The problem with the basic argument against minimum wages is that it is based on a static model of the labor market. But the minimum wage law may serve to increase the demand for labor. If workers are more productive due to better morale, firms will want to hire more of them. If higher incomes increase the demand for goods and services, then firms will need to hire more workers. If the demand for labor increases as a result of minimum wage laws, then the resulting surplus may be reduced or eliminated.

"On May 25, 2007, the Fair Labor Standards Act (FLSA) was amended to increase the federal minimum wage in three steps: to $5.85 per hour effective July 24, 2007; to $6.55 per hour effective July 24, 2008; and to $7.25 per hour effective July 24, 2009" (*http://www.dol.gov/compliance/guide/minwage.htm,* retrieved 5.12.09).

*Price ceiling:* A price ceiling occurs when the government sets a price below the equilibrium price. A shortage results.

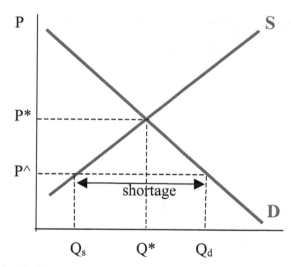

Figure 4-5   A Price Ceiling

Figure 4-5 shows the effects of a price ceiling, say rent control in New York City. Without rent control, the equilibrium price of an apartment would be P* and the quantity at Q*. If a price ceiling for rents is set at P^, the quantity demanded of apartments, $Q_d$, is greater than the quantity supplied, $Q_s$. A shortage results as shown above. At the rent-controlled rates, more people want to live in New York City then the number of apartments available. A shortage of housing results in homelessness.

In both cases, price floors and price ceilings, government regulation of the market price prevents the market from rationing the good or service efficiently.

## Taxes

When the government imposes a tax in a particular market, economic behavior may be changed. The tax places a wedge between the price paid by consumers and the price received by producers. For each unit of output sold, the difference between the price paid by consumers and the price received by producers is the tax revenue per unit. There are several ways that a government can impose sales taxes in a market. Taxes may be imposed on producers or consumers. Taxes may be excise taxes, a tax per unit of output, or ad valorem taxes, a tax based on the percentage of the price of the good. In all cases, a tax in the market reduces the quantity below the socially efficient amount.

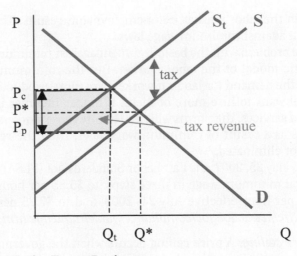

Figure 4-6    An Excise Tax on Producers

Figure 4-6 shows the case of an excise tax on producers of sunglasses. Since an excise tax is a tax per unit, the tax remains the same at different quantities even though the price of sunglasses may be higher. An excise tax on producers will lead to a leftward shift (decrease) of the supply curve in the market. The price paid by consumers increases while the price received by producers declines. The difference is the tax revenue the government receives for each pair of sunglasses sold. The quantity of sunglasses sold in the market declines. If the original market provided the socially optimal quantity of sunglasses, the tax forces the market to become inefficient by reducing the quantity of sunglasses exchanged.

An excise tax on producers will increase the vertical intercept of the supply curve by the amount of the tax. This leads to a parallel decrease (or upward shift) of the supply curve. Now for each quantity of output sold, firms require the original price shown by the first supply curve, plus the tax they must now pay. As a result, the quantity exchanged in the market declines from $Q^*$ to $Q_t$. The price paid by consumers increase from $P^*$ to $P_c$, while the price received by producers falls from $P^*$ to $P_p$. The difference between the two prices $(P_c - P_p)$ is the tax revenue received by the government for each unit of output. Total tax revenue in the market is $(P_c - P_p) \times Q_t$, shown by the green rectangle.

If the market was originally at a socially efficient equilibrium, then the tax will introduce inefficiencies in the market. At the quantity that results from the tax, $Q_t$, the marginal social benefit as given by the demand curve is greater than the marginal social cost as given by the original supply curve. Net social benefits would be increased if output in the market was increased from $Q_t$ to $Q^*$, since the marginal willingness to pay for consumers is greater than the marginal cost to producers. The tax introduces inefficiencies in the market.

If, on the other hand, the market originally contained negative production externalities as in Figure 4-2, then a tax in the market may actually increase efficiency by forcing producers to internalize the external costs of production. If the government is able to devise a tax equal to the external costs of production, the tax will result in an efficient market where marginal social benefits are equal to marginal social costs. This is the theoretical underpinning for the idea of a carbon tax to help reduce greenhouse gases.

## Majority Rule Voting Paradox

When majority rule is used to determine the outcome of public policy, often the results may be inconsistent. The policy that wins may depend on the order of the vote. It may not be clear what the will of the majority may actually be.

**Table 4-1**   The Voting Paradox

| A: nuke Iraq | hawks: 33 Senators |
| B: withdraw from Iraq | doves: 33 Senators |
| C: continue conventional war | moderates: 33 Senators |

|  | hawks | doves | moderates |
|---|---|---|---|
| first choice | A | B | C |
| second choice | B | C | A |
| third choice | C | A | B |

For example, suppose that there are 99 Senators voting on policy toward Iraq. The three options are to attack Iraq with nuclear weapons, withdraw from Iraq entirely, or continue the conventional war we have been fighting since 2003. Suppose that one-third of the Senators support each position. In particular, assume that the preferences of each group, hawks, doves, and moderates, are as given in Table 4-1.

Suppose that the vote is A versus B. In that case, A wins. Both the hawks and moderates prefer A over B. If the vote is B versus C, then B wins. Both the hawks and doves prefer B over C. Since A beats B and B beats C, transitivity would imply that A should beat C. But when A goes against C, both the doves and moderates prefer C and C wins. Any alternative can win depending on the order of the vote. When majority rule is used for public policy-making, the outcome may be inconsistent. Those who control the agenda can influence the outcome by manipulating the order of voting.

## Myopic Viewpoint

Politicians are often myopic, or short-sighted when making public policy. An important assumption of political economy is that politicians seek to maximize the likelihood of being re-elected. Many legislators, including those in the House of Representatives, have two-year terms. They are much more likely to support programs that will provide benefits to their constituents within two years, so that their chances of being re-elected are maximized. Long-term policies may be ignored by politicians who are trying to provide their constituents with immediate benefits.

## Illegal Markets

There are many markets, such as heroin, cocaine, marijuana, prostitution, or gambling, where the government prohibits production and consumption in an attempt to protect its citizens. In many ways, when the government makes a market illegal, it only serves to make that market more dangerous.

As pointed out in Miller, Benjamin, and North's chapter five, there are many effects both on the supply side and the demand side of the market when a good becomes illegal. On the supply side, the effects of making a good illegal are to decrease the supply of the good. Supply decreases because there are now increased costs of production, including the resources used to evade detection and the risks of getting caught and potential prison time. For most illegal markets, the decrease in supply leads to higher revenues and profits for those who supply the market. The more the government tries to penalize suppliers in the market, the higher are the rewards of entering the market, and more people are likely to enter the market as suppliers.

Another problem is that criminals have a comparative advantage in entering the market. Criminals already know how to evade police detection, police routes, whom to bribe, and the best areas to distribute their product. Someone with a prior record has a lower opportunity cost of a conviction than a student with a clean record who wants to go to law school. Also, since there are no avenues to enforce contracts legally, violence becomes the means of contract enforcement. The illegal drug trade and gun violence are connected in many areas of the United States.

Suppliers do not have the responsibility to maintain the quality of their product since they do not have to worry about their reputation, brand names, or repeat customers. During Prohibition many died from moonshine that was cut with diethylene glycol, an anti-freeze. Prostitutes in Nevada, who are legal, have virtually no transmission of HIV or other sexually transmitted diseases, while it is estimated that over 50% of prostitutes in Newark and Miami, who are illegal, have AIDS. Many people die from overdoses of heroin or cocaine that are either too strong or cut with dangerous additives such as arsenic or rat poison. In the 1970s, dealers sold marijuana that was sprayed with paraquat, a chemical that was sprayed by the United States government on Mexican marijuana crops.

Suppliers also have an incentive to sell more potent products to increase their value per volume. Since the goods are illegal they must be concealed. The smaller an item, and the more potent, the greater is the value per volume of what is being carried around. An ounce of marijuana may sell for $400, but an ounce of cocaine may sell for $4000. The potential profit per volume of cocaine is greater, so dealers have an incentive to supply cocaine rather than marijuana, ceteris paribus. For those who do supply marijuana, attempts to prohibit importation have led to increases in domestic production. As more is produced in the United States, genetic engineering has allowed the potency of marijuana to increase by perhaps twenty times. As potency increases, the supplier can charge more per ounce.

On the demand side, making a good illegal will cause a decline in demand for the good. Some will continue to consume the good, and others may begin to consume because the good is illegal. When a good becomes illegal, consumption becomes more intensive. Coca-Cola is so named because it used to contain cocaine before 1906 when cocaine became illegal. People consumed cocaine back then the way we consume caffeine today—extensively, or taking small amounts over long periods of time. Once a good becomes illegal, consumption becomes much more intensive. Now cocaine is consumed much more intensively, in large amounts over short periods of time. Now people inject or inhale large amounts of cocaine rather than sipping small amounts. The same principle can be seen in the fact that marijuana cigarettes do not have filters while tobacco cigarettes often do, or in the use of bongs to smoke marijuana, or in the problem of binge drinking among college students. In all of these cases, when a good becomes illegal, the consumption of that good becomes more intensive.

Consumers lack information concerning the quality of the good, since producers do not have brand names to convey signals about their quality. Consumers also have an incentive to consume more potent versions of the product in order to make it easier to hide. In all of these cases, when the government prohibits the production and consumption of a good to protect its citizens, it often ends up making the market more dangerous.

## SUMMARY

This concludes our journey through political economy. We have examined how markets work, the teachings of Adam Smith, the four fundamental economic questions and types of economic systems, the necessary conditions for the market to exist, and cases of market and government failure. Government intervention may be justified to help markets to function effectively or to alleviate situations of market failure and increase efficiency. But the government is an imperfect tool at best. In trying to find tools to solve our social problems, the presumption should be in favor of market solutions. Only when markets fail should political solutions replace economic solutions. And even in these cases, it may be better to try to establish property rights and create markets where none had existed before.

# 5

# MEASURING NATIONAL INCOME AND OUTPUT

In this chapter, we begin our exploration into the topics of macroeconomics. Remember from Chapter One that macroeconomics is the study of aggregate economic variables. Macroeconomists analyze concepts such as Gross Domestic Product, inflation, and unemployment, how these variables are measured, how they affect each other, and, ultimately, how they influence the standard of living in any economy. Macroeconomics is concerned with both short run fluctuations in the economy which contribute to business cycles, and to long run trends which can explain economic growth. It examines such questions as the causes of contractions and expansions in the economy, and why some countries are rich while others are poor.

In this chapter, we look at the concept of Gross Domestic Product, or GDP. GDP is a measure of the amount of output produced in the economy, or the amount of income generated in the production of that output. But before we dive into GDP, we will briefly provide an overview of macroeconomics, to preview what we will be doing for the rest of the course.

## AN OVERVIEW OF MACROECONOMICS

*Macroeconomics:* the study of the relationships between aggregate economic variables, and the choices made by policy makers to influence those variables.

Remember that economics is primarily about scarcity and choice. In macroeconomics, we study the choices that government policy makers face in trying to achieve certain macroeconomic goals. In order to determine if it is meeting its goals, the government must monitor the economy. In the United States, the primary agencies that derive economic statistics are the Bureau of Economic Analysis and the Bureau of Labor Statistics. These agencies help the government to find out if they are meeting their economic goals. The primary macroeconomic variables measure output, inflation, unemployment, the international economy, and the monetary system. In macroeconomics, we first will study how these variables are measured, why they are important, and problems with measuring these variables accurately. Next, we will build models that show how these variables are related to each other. Finally, we will use these models to show how the government can meet its macroeconomic goals using fiscal and monetary policy.

Let us start with an introduction to the basic macroeconomic variables.

## OUTPUT

The most important measure of output in the economy is Gross Domestic Product, or GDP. Changes in output determine whether the economy is in expansion or recession. The tendency for GDP to fluctuate around a trend is known as the *business cycle*. Sometimes GDP is expanding, sometimes GDP is contracting. The goal of policymakers is to minimize the times of contraction, also known as recession. Measures of output include *nominal GDP*, which measures output produced within a country using current prices, *real GDP*, which measures output produced within a country using constant (or base year) prices, and *Gross National Product*, which measures the output produced by a nation's resources around the world.

## INFLATION

*Inflation* is a sustained increase in the average level of prices in an economy over time. Another way of defining inflation is a decrease in the value (or purchasing power) of money. If the prices of goods and services are higher, then each unit of currency is able to purchase less of those goods and services. Inflation is an increase in the absolute level of prices, but relative prices need not change if all prices are increased proportionately. For instance, if all prices and wages are doubled, then economic behavior will remain unchanged. Your income can still buy the same amount of goods and services, just the absolute levels of prices and wages have changed.

In the United States economy, there are four primary measures of inflation. The Bureau of Economic Analysis (BEA) publishes the GDP Price Deflator, which measures the change in the prices of all goods and services included in GDP statistics. Within the GDP statistics the Personal Consumption Expenditures (PCE) Price Index measures the prices of goods and services included in consumption spending. The Bureau of Labor Statistics (BLS) provides two measures of inflation, the Consumer Price Index and the Producer Price Index. The Consumer Price Index (CPI) is the most widely reported of the inflation measures. It measures the retail prices paid for about 80,000 different goods and services purchased by typical urban households. The Producer Price Index (PPI), on the other hand, measures changes in the wholesale prices received by producers.

## UNEMPLOYMENT

*The unemployment rate* is a measure of the percentage of the labor force that is actively seeking but not finding work. It is measured as

$$\frac{\text{number actively seeking but not finding work}}{\text{number in labor force}} \times 100$$

The labor force consists of those who are over 16 years of age, who are not students, retired, in prisons or hospitals, or in the military, and who are either actively seeking work or working. For college students, you are counted as employed if you have a job, but you are not considered to be unemployed if you are without work, since you are a college student rather than a member of the labor force.

There are several reasons why the official unemployment rate as published by the Bureau of Labor Statistics may underestimate the actual incidence of unemployment in the economy. First, the unemployment rate is measured using a household Current Population Survey, part of which is conducted over the telephone. Since those without homes and telephones are more likely to be unemployed, the sample that is surveyed is biased toward those who are more likely to have jobs. Second, the unemployment rate ignores those who are underemployed. Someone who is working fewer hours than desired, or who is working well below their skill level, may be seeking a better job. But as long as they are working one hour a week, they will be counted as employed. Finally, the official unemployment rate ignores discouraged workers. If someone has given up looking for a job, she is not considered a member of the labor force, and she is not counted among the unemployed. So it is likely that the actual unemployment rate is greater than the official rate as reported by the Bureau of Labor Statistics.

## THE INTERNATIONAL ECONOMY

As globalization increases around the world, keeping track of the international economy becomes increasingly important. Net exports are included in GDP, so they are important in determining how quickly the economy is expanding or contracting. Foreign investors can affect the value of assets in the home country and the costs of borrowing money. Important measures of the international economy are the Balance of Payments, the Current Account, and exchange rates.

*The Balance of Payments* is the record of a country's flows of goods, services, income, gifts, capital, and financial assets with the rest of the world.

*The Current Account* is a subset of the Balance of Payments that is used to measure a country's trade deficit or surplus. It measures the flows of goods, services, gifts and income with the rest of the world. If the current account is positive, the country has a trade surplus. If the current account is negative, the country has a trade deficit.

*The Balance of Trade* is a country's position in the current account. The country has a trade deficit if its balance of trade is negative, so that imports and income payments are greater than exports and income receipts. On the other hand, if the balance of trade is positive, then the country is experiencing a trade surplus.

*Exchange rate* is the value of one country's currency in terms of another country's currency. Currency is traded in *currency markets* or *foreign exchange markets,* which exist in the largest banks in major cities around the world.

## THE MONETARY SYSTEM

There are many economic variables that measure the flows of financial capital in the monetary system of the economy. The Federal Reserve System (Fed), our central bank, uses several methods of measuring the money supply. It pays careful attention to the quantity of reserves in the banking system and the flows of funds into different financial markets such as mortgages or automobile loans. There are also many interest rates that are studied by the Fed, such as the discount rate, federal funds rate, prime rate, mortgage rates, consumer loan rates, etc. We will study each of these later in the course when we study monetary policy.

*Interest rate:* the price of money, or the cost of borrowing funds and the benefit of lending funds.

*Money supply:* the quantity of money in circulation at a given point of time. The rate of change in the money supply is an important determinant of several economic variables.

## MACROECONOMIC POLICY GOALS

Economic policy makers must be aware of these many variables to see if they are meeting their responsibilities in achieving certain macroeconomic policy goals. Since after World War II, the federal government in the United States has been given the obligation to assure that the economy is stable and growing. The legislation that requires the government to oversee the economy includes the Full Employment and Stabilization Act of 1946 and the Humphrey Hawkins Act of 1978. The three major macroeconomic policy goals laid out in these pieces of legislation are:

- a stable rate of GDP growth
- high employment (or low unemployment)
- a stable price level (or low inflation)

To achieve these goals the federal government possesses two important policy tools, fiscal policy and monetary policy.

## FISCAL AND MONETARY POLICY

In order to influence macroeconomic variables, the government can use fiscal or monetary policies.

*Fiscal policy* is a change in government spending or taxes to influence a macroeconomic variable such as GDP or inflation. Fiscal policy is a tool used by the administration. The president or Congress proposes a policy, Congress must pass legislation, and then the president must agree to sign the legislation. It will take time for the change in spending or taxes to have any effect on the economy. Fiscal policy can be used only with significant lags in its formulation and implementation. Despite this, fiscal policy is sometimes used, especially in attempts to fight recession. Examples of fiscal policy include Franklin D. Roosevelt's New Deal programs to increase employment known as the Civilian Conservation Corps and Works Project Administration, John F. Kennedy's tax cuts in 1963, and George W. Bush's tax cuts in 2001, 2003 and 2008, and President Obama's American Recovery and Reinvestment Act of 2009. In all of these cases, fiscal policy was used to increase disposable income and consumption spending in the economy.

*Monetary policy* is a change in the money supply or interest rates to influence a macroeconomic variable. Monetary policy is exercised by the Federal Reserve System (Fed). Congress has delegated its power over monetary policy to the Fed, and the Fed is kept insulated from political pressures so that monetary policy can be independent. The most frequent form of monetary policy is when the Federal Open Market Committee sets a target for the federal funds rate, which is the rate that banks charge each other for loans from their Federal Reserve accounts. Since the Fed can act independently there is less of a lag for monetary policy compared to fiscal policy, although it may still take some time for a change in interest rates to work its way through the economy.

In sum, the federal government can use its tools of fiscal and monetary policy to help maintain a stable macroeconomy. In order to know how it is doing it must measure many macroeconomic variables. This is the process that we will study for the rest of the semester. For the rest of the chapter, we now turn our attention to the first important macroeconomic variable, Gross Domestic Product.

## GROSS DOMESTIC PRODUCT

*Gross Domestic Product (or GDP):* the market value of all final goods and services produced within a country's borders in a year.

GDP is a measure of the value of output produced by an economy. As we will see, GDP can be measured in several ways, including as output, as income, or as expenditures. Also, economists distinguish between nominal GDP, which measures output using current prices, and real GDP, which measures output using constant, or base year, prices. We now turn to the issues inherent in the definition of GDP

## ISSUES IN CALCULATING GDP

### Market Value

GDP measures the market value of goods and services, or the value as expressed by market prices. To calculate GDP, economists do not just add up the quantities of goods and services; that would literally be adding up apples and oranges. In order to have a common measuring stick, we express all of the output in terms of its value in market prices.

For some goods, such as police services or the value of owner-occupied housing, there may not be market prices that exist to measure the value. If a policeman reports your stolen bicycle, you do not have to pay him a price for that service. For someone who owns a house, they receive services from that house each year without having to pay for those services. When no market price exists, the value of output is measured by the cost of providing the good or service. The value of a policeman's service is the cost of providing that service. The value of owner-occupied housing is imputed rent, or what the owner would have received if the house was rented at an average market price. In all cases, we are adding up dollar values of goods and services to measure GDP. Currently, the value of nominal GDP is just over $14 trillion in 2009 (*http://www.bea.gov/bea/dn/dpga.txt*).

### Final Goods and Services

GDP measures the value of *final* goods and services. It includes only those goods and services purchased by final consumers. It excludes intermediate goods, or those goods produced by one firm as inputs into other firms. Intermediate goods are excluded to avoid double-counting. For instance, tires sold to a car manufacturer are not counted in GDP, since these tires are intermediate goods that will be counted as part of the final automobile sold to the consumer. Tires sold directly to a consumer, on the other hand, are final goods that would be included in GDP. Flour sold to a baker would not be included in GDP, but flour sold to a final consumer would be included in GDP.

Adding up final goods and services can provide an accurate measure of the value of output produced in an economy, but a problem with using the final goods and services approach is that it does not provide a way of measuring the value of how much each sector has contributed to GDP. For example, by examining final goods and services, we do not account for the value of output produced by tire manufacturers or flour producers, since some of their output included intermediate goods. To rectify this situation, economists have developed an alternative means of measuring GDP, known as the value-added approach.

## Value-Added Approach

Instead of aggregating final goods and services, the value-added approach measures the amount of value that is added to GDP in each stage of the production process. Table 5-1 explores the process of production in the life of a loaf of bread.

**Table 5-1**   Producing a Loaf of Bread

| Activity | Value-Added |
|---|---|
| A farmer sells 20¢ of wheat to a miller | 20¢ |
| A miller sells 40¢ of flour to a baker | 20¢ |
| A baker sells 80¢ of bread to a grocer | 40¢ |
| A grocer sells $1.00 of bread to a final consumer | 20¢ |
| Total | $1.00 |

The loaf of bread starts as wheat grown by the farmer. Assuming that the farmer started with free seeds and then grew and sold 20¢ of wheat to a miller, then the farmer has added 20¢ to the value of the bread. When the miller takes the 20¢ of wheat and mills it into 40¢ of flour, the miller adds 20¢ (40¢ – 20¢) to the value of the bread. Once the baker takes the 40¢ of flour and produces 80¢ of bread, the baker adds 40¢ (80¢ – 40¢) to the value of bread. Finally, by putting the bread on a store shelf and providing light and a cashier, the grocer adds 20¢ ($1.00 – 80¢) to the value of the bread.

Given Table 5-1, there are two ways of measuring GDP. First, we can measure GDP as the value of final output, or $1.00 of bread sold to the final consumer. But that does not provide any information about the relative contributions of each sector. Second, we can sum up the value-added in each stage of the production process. What we cannot do is add up the value of all of the goods sold in the process of production. All of this is summarized in Table 5-2.

**Table 5-2**   Ways of Measuring Value of Loaf of Bread

**Correct ways of measuring value:**
  Value of Final Good = $1.00
  Sum of Value-Added = 20¢ + 20¢ + 40¢ + 20¢ = $1.00

**Incorrect way of measuring value:**
  Sum of Intermediate Goods = 20¢ + 40¢ + 80¢ + $1.00 = $2.40

Counting final goods and services provides the easiest way to calculate GDP. Using the value-added approach gives an indication of how much each sector has contributed to the economy. We cannot just sum up the value of all intermediate goods, since in this case, that would mean that we are quadruple-counting the wheat, triple-counting the flour, and double-counting the loaf of bread. There was $1.00 of output produced, not $2.40. The first two methods provide accurate ways of measuring an economy's output.

## Produced Within a Country's Borders

Gross *Domestic* Product measures all of the final output produced on a country's soil, or domestically, regardless of which country actually owns the resources used in production. U.S. GDP, for example, includes the output produced by foreign resources on American soil. As we will see, Gross *National* Product measures the value of output produced by a nation's resources around the world.

## In a Year

GDP is a flow variable, so it is measured over a certain period of time. It looks at how much is produced over a certain interval of time. Generally, we measure the annual value of final output when calculating GDP. Even though the GDP statistics are published quarterly, they measure the amount of output that would be produced in a year if the economy operated at that quarterly rate.

## Non-Market Transactions Are Excluded

Some transactions are excluded from GDP statistics, even though they provide value to the economy. For instance, the value of domestic labor, or work done inside the household by household members, is excluded from GDP. When your mother watches your younger siblings, or when you do the dishes at home or paint your house, these activities are not included in GDP statistics. Since the transactions do not take place through a market, but rather inside the home, these are not considered to be market transactions, so they are not included in GDP.

Such a methodology imposes several anomalies in the measurement of GDP. For instance, if I clean my house and my sister cleans her house, the activities would not be included in GDP. However, if I paid my sister to clean my house, and she paid me to clean her house, and we both reported the income, then the activities would be included in GDP. Also, those countries where more activities are performed in the home, rather than exchanged in markets, will have lower per capita GDP, everything else being equal. Since there are no market prices and few records are kept, including the value of domestic goods and services in GDP would be difficult.

A second type of non-market transaction that is excluded from GDP calculations is illegal markets. Since the government has prohibited the production, distribution, sale, and consumption of many items, the official GDP statistics pretend that these markets do not exist. Services such as gambling and prostitution, and goods such as marijuana, cocaine, LSD and heroin are not included in the calculation of GDP. This has several implications for GDP statistics. First, if any of these goods or services became legal GDP would increase, even if economic activity remained unchanged. Second, in comparing similar countries, those with more legal activities will have higher per capita GDP, everything else being equal. Third, in some areas, ignoring these markets vastly underestimates the actual amount of economic activity in that area.

## Non-Productive Transactions Are Excluded

Since GDP is a measure of the value of final output produced, exchanges that do not increase production are not included in GDP. Government transfer payments, such as unemployment insurance, Social Security, food stamps, or Temporary Assistance to Needy Families (TANF) payments, are not included in GDP. Government transfer payments represent a redistribution of wealth from taxpayers to recipients, but not any production in the economy. For similar reasons, the sale and purchase of securities (stocks and bonds) are also excluded from GDP calculations. If I buy a stock, there is only a transfer of assets, but no production takes place. Finally, private gifts are excluded, since they do not represent any increase in current output.

## Second-Hand Goods Are Excluded

For obvious reasons, second-hand goods, such as used cars, bicycles, or clothing, are not counted in the current year's GDP. If they were included, then the goods would be counted more than once, first in the year they were produced and second in the years when they were resold. To avoid such double- or triple-counting, the sale and purchase of second hand goods is omitted from GDP numbers. The profit earned by a used car dealer may be included in GDP as income, but the used car itself would not be included.

## Goods Produced but Not Sold

How does GDP treat those goods that are produced in the current year but not sold in that year? If a good is produced but not sold, it is included in GDP as a part of inventory changes, a component of investment. Consider a bicycle produced by Huffy in the United States in 2007. If that bicycle is sold to a U.S. consumer, it is counted as consumption spending. If it is sold to a foreign customer, it is treated as export spending. If it is sold to the federal government for use by National Park Service employees, it is included in government spending. But if the bicycle remains unsold in 2007, it is treated as an increase in inventories for Huffy, as a part of investment spending. Increases in inventories are treated as increases in the company's investment spending.

As described above, the calculation of GDP is a complex process, and as we will see, there are several methods that can be used to measure GDP.

## METHODS OF CALCULATING GDP

Any transaction can be looked at from two sides; we can focus on the good or service being exchanged, or the payment for that good or service. Similarly, GDP can be approached from two perspectives. We can look at GDP as the value of final output produced, or we can measure GDP as the income earned in the production of that output. GDP can be measured as expenditure or as income. In particular, there are four methods that can be used to calculate GDP.

GDP can be measured as

1. the value of final goods and services produced.
2. the value of expenditures on that output.
3. the sources of income earned in the production of that output.
4. the uses of income earned in the production of that output.

We will examine each method in turn.

## GDP as the Value of Final Output

GDP can be measured as the value of final output, or the sum of the market value of final goods and services sold. Mathematically, GDP is the summation of the prices of each good times the quantity produced of each good:

$$GDP = \sum (P_i \times Q_i)$$

## GDP as Expenditures

GDP can be measured as expenditures, or as the sum of consumption spending by households (C), investment spending by firms (I), government spending (G), and net export spending by the foreign sector (X – M), which is the difference between exports (X) and imports (M). Mathematically,

$$GDP = C + I + G + (X - M)$$

## GDP as the Sources of Income

GDP can also be measured as the sources of income. Labor earns wage income (W) in the process of production. Capital owners earn interest (i), land owners earn rent (R), and entrepreneurs (business owners) earn profit. Also, foreign resources must be paid to be used in domestic production, and U.S. resources earn income abroad. This is reflected in the term Net Factor Income from Abroad (NFIA), which is the difference between the income earned by U.S. resources abroad and the income paid to foreign resources in the United States. Finally, depreciation costs, or the Capital Consumption Allowance (CCA) and a statistical discrepancy (SD) must be taken into account. This gives

$$GDP = W + i + R + profit - NFIA + CCA + SD$$

It can be shown that measuring GDP as expenditures is equivalent to measuring GDP as the sources of income.

For any firm,

$$profit = sales - costs$$

For all firms producing final goods and services in the economy,

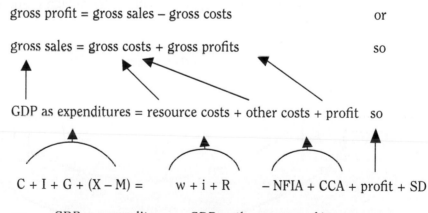

gross profit = gross sales – gross costs    or

gross sales = gross costs + gross profits    so

GDP as expenditures = resource costs + other costs + profit  so

C + I + G + (X – M) =    w + i + R    – NFIA + CCA + profit + SD

so    GDP as expenditures = GDP as the sources of income.

As shown above, measuring GDP as expenditures is equivalent to measuring GDP as the sources of income. The first looks at the spending on goods and services, while the second focuses on the income earned in the production of goods and services. As long as all costs and the statistical discrepancy (a fudge factor) are taken into account, the two approaches are measuring two sides of the same coin. The statistical discrepancy term is added (or subtracted) to assure that both sides of the equation are equal.

There are several reasons why the statistical discrepancy term is necessary. There may be mistakes or omissions in entering data. People may not report income but stores will report their spending. Foreigners may earn income from illegal markets that are not included in GDP and then spend their gains purchasing our imports which are included in GDP. For these reasons and others, the statistical discrepancy term is necessary for expenditures and income to be equal.

## GDP as the Uses of Income

Finally, GDP can be measured as the uses of income. Once households earn income from the resources they supply, there are several options for disposing of the income. These include consumption spending (C), saving (S), taxes (T), and import spending (M). Specifically,

$$GDP = C + S + T + M$$

## THE CIRCULAR FLOW MODEL

One tool that can be used to illustrate the ways of measuring GDP is the circular flow model. The simple circular flow model shows the interactions between households and firms in two markets, product markets and resource markets. In the product markets, firms supply goods and services to households, who then in turn provide revenue to the firm in the form of payments for these goods and services. In the resource markets, households supply resources such as labor and capital in return for the income payments from firms. In the simple circular flow model shown in Figure 5-1, GDP can be measured either as flows of output in the upper loop or as flows of income in the lower loop.

In the simple circular flow model, households and firms interact in both product and resource markets. GDP can be measured either as the value of expenditures in product markets or the value of income earned in resource markets.

The extended circular flow model is shown in Figure 5-2 on the next page. Here the model is extended in several ways. First, along with households and firms, two more sectors of the economy, government and the foreign sector, are added. These are

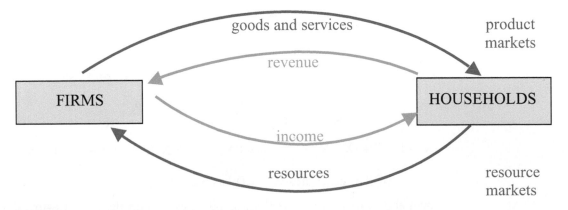

Figure 5-1    The Simple Circular Flow Model

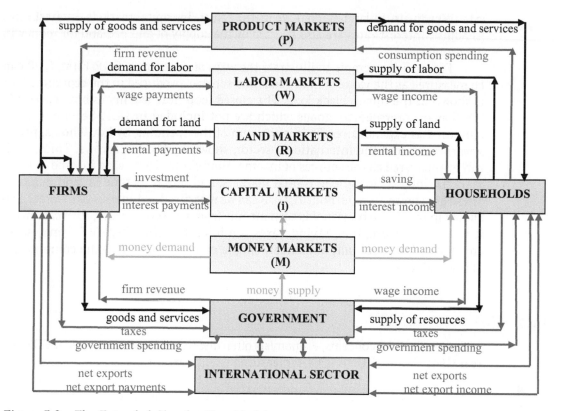

Figure 5-2   The Extended Circular Flow Model

key: &#8596;   tangible goods and services in product, land and labor markets

&#8596;   aggregate expenditures or uses of income

&#8596;   sources of income

&#8596;   money flows

GDP can be defined in the following ways:

1. value of output: GDP = PQ (black)

2. aggregate expenditures: GDP = C + I + G + (X – M) (red)

3. sources of income: GDP = W + i + R + profits – NFIA + CCA + SD

4. uses of income: GDP = C + S + T + M

shown by the blue boxes. Government interacts with households and firms through taxation and the provision of public goods and services. Some households provide resources to the government, and some firms may provide their products to the government. Households, firms, and the government interact with the foreign sector by purchasing imports from, selling exports to, and exchanging resources with those in other countries. Three resource markets, labor, land and capital, are included in the figure (yellow boxes). Households supply these resources and firms demand these resources. The resource payments by firms become income for households. The government also influences the money supply, which has an effect on interest rates in the economy.

In each market, there is a price that adjusts to bring equilibrium to that market. In the product market, the price level (P) adjusts. In the labor market, the wage rate (W) adjusts. In land markets, rents (R) adjust. In capital markets, interest rates (i) adjust. Interest rates are also affected by the supply of and demand for money in the economy.

Figure 5-2 attempts to illustrate the ways of measuring GDP. First, GDP can be measured as the value of final goods and services produced in the economy. This is shown in the upper, black loop. The closed loop near the firm's box represents the flow of intermediate goods which are not included in GDP. Second, GDP is measured as expenditures. This is the sum of the spending by households, firms, government, and the international sector, shown by the red arrows. Third, GDP can be measured as the sources of income. Households earn wage income in labor markets, interest income in capital markets, and rental income in land markets. These are shown in blue. Fourth, GDP can be measured as the uses of income, also shown in red. Once households earn income from various sources, they can divide it between consumption, saving, taxes and imports. While Figure 5-2 may seem complicated, it is actually a relatively simple model compared to the complexities of the real world.

## REAL AND NOMINAL GDP

In discussing GDP concepts, economists often distinguish between nominal GDP and real GDP. Nominal GDP is GDP measured using current prices. As nominal GDP increases over time, the change could be due to an increase in output, but it could also be due to an increase in the price level. In order to isolate and understand changes in output in the economy, economists use real GDP. By keeping prices constant, changes in real GDP show changes in output over time.

For example, consider the following economy. Suppose that Simpleland produces three goods, beer, wine, and bread, in two years, year 1 and year 2. Beer and wine are substitutes for each other. We will assume that year 1 is the base year.

The prices and quantities for years one and two are as follows:

**Table 5-3**   The Economy of Simpleland

| | Year 1 | | | Year 2 | | |
|---|---|---|---|---|---|---|
| | $P_1$ | $Q_1$ | $P_1 \times Q_1$ | $P_2$ | $Q_2$ | $P_2 \times Q_2$ |
| BEER | 4 | 100 | 400 | 5 | 200 | 1000 |
| WINE | 3 | 200 | 600 | 6 | 200 | 1200 |
| BREAD | 2 | 500 | 1000 | 3 | 600 | 1800 |
| | | | $\Sigma(P_1 \times Q_1) = 2000$ | | | $\Sigma(P_2 \times Q_2) = 4000$ |

According to our calculations, nominal GDP for year 1 is $2000, while nominal GDP for year 2 is $4000. To measure the percent change (%Δ) in some macroeconomic variable X, we can use the following formula:

$$\%\Delta X = [(X_2 - X_1) / X_1] \times 100.$$

So nominal GDP grew by

$$\%\Delta \text{ nominal GDP} = \frac{4000 - 2000}{2000} \times 100 = 100\% \text{ increase}$$

Even though nominal GDP doubled (100% increase) we cannot say that output has doubled. Some of the increase in nominal GDP may be due to higher prices. In order to determine how much output increased, we need to look at real GDP, which keeps prices constant. Since year 1 is the base year, the same set of prices will be used to measure both nominal and real GDP in year 1. Nominal GDP uses current year prices. Real GDP uses base year prices. In the base year, both are the same. So in year 1,

$$\text{nominal GDP}_1 = \text{real GDP}_1 = \Sigma(P_1 \times Q_1) = \$2000$$

For real GDP in year 2, we must calculate the value of output in year 2 valued at year 1 prices:

**Table 5-4**   Calculating Real GDP

| | | Year 2 | |
| --- | --- | --- | --- |
| | $P_1$ | $Q_2$ | $P_1 \times Q_2$ |
| BEER | 4 | 200 | 800 |
| WINE | 3 | 200 | 600 |
| BREAD | 2 | 600 | 1200 |
| | | $\Sigma(P_1 \times Q_2) = 2600$ | |

Real GDP in year 2 is $2600.

The percent change in real GDP, which measures the percent change in output, is

$$\%\Delta \text{ real GDP} = \frac{2600 - 2000}{2000} \times 100 = 30\% \text{ increase.}$$

While nominal GDP increased by 100%, real GDP increased by only 30%. So output, measured in year 1 prices, increased by 30%. We can measure price changes by using the GDP Price Deflator:

$$\text{GDP Price Deflator}_t = (\text{Nominal GDP}_t/\text{Real GDP}_t) \times 100 \text{ so}$$
$$\text{GDP Price Deflator}_1 = 2000/2000 \times 100 = 100$$

(A price index is always equal to 100 in the base year. The subscript t signifies the year.)

$$\text{GDP Price Deflator}_2 = 4000/2600 \times 100 = 153.85$$

So prices increased by 53.85% using the simple base year approach.

Up until 1995, this is how the BEA calculated real GDP. As time went on, it became increasingly evident to staff at the BEA that there were problems with using a simple base year approach to GDP. Every 5 years a new base year was chosen, so the whole series would have to be recalculated every five years. Another problem using the simple base year approach was that as the base year got farther and farther away, a bias was introduced which overestimated real GDP growth. The simple base year approach puts too much weight on those goods and services whose prices have increased the least, so it underestimates inflation and overestimates real GDP growth.

For example, here beer and wine are substitutes. The price of wine doubled (from $3 to $6), while the price of beer only increased by 25% (from $4 to $5). Since beer is now relatively cheaper, beer consumption increased (from 100 to 200), while wine consumption stayed the same (at 200). This is a simple substitution effect from a price change. The problem is that the simple base year approach puts too much weight on beer, whose prices have increased the least. Notice that in measuring nominal GDP, wine gets more weight (600 v 400 and 1200 v 1000). But in measuring real GDP using year 1 as the base year, now beer gets more weight (800 v 600). So this method puts the most weight on those goods and services (beer) whose prices have increased the least. This approach will underestimate inflation and overestimate real GDP growth.

An alternative approach would be to use year 2 as the base year. But this would have the opposite problem, that too much weight would be put on those goods and services (such as wine) whose prices have increased the most.

As a compromise, the BEA developed the measure of chain-type real GDP, which uses information about prices in both years, which is why it is called a chain. The rate of growth of chain-type real GDP is just the geometric mean of the rate of growth using year 1 prices and the rate of growth using year 2 prices.

To find the chain-type growth rate (g):

$$g = \sqrt{\frac{\Sigma(P_1 \times Q_2)}{\Sigma(P_1 \times Q_1)} \times \frac{\Sigma(P_2 \times Q_2)}{\Sigma(P_2 \times Q_1)}}$$

The first term gives the rate of growth using year 1 prices, while the second term gives the rate of growth using year 2 prices.

The only term we haven't calculated is $\Sigma(P_2 \times Q_1)$. To find this, we must calculate the value of year 1 output measured in year 2 prices:

**Table 5-5**   Real GDP Using Year 2 Prices

| | Year 1 | | |
|---|---|---|---|
| | **$P_2$** | **$Q_1$** | **$P_2 \times Q_1$** |
| BEER | 5 | 100 | 500 |
| WINE | 6 | 200 | 1200 |
| BREAD | 3 | 500 | 1500 |
| | | $\Sigma(P_2 \times Q_1) = 3200$ | |

Notice that in this formulation, wine receives more weight (1200) than beer (500). To find g:

$$g = \sqrt{\frac{2600}{2000} \times \frac{4000}{3200}} = \sqrt{1.3 \times 1.25} = \sqrt{1.625}$$
$$= 1.275.$$

So chain-type real GDP increased by 27.5 % [(1.275 – 1) × 100]

Notice that by using year 1 prices, the rate of growth was 30%, but using year 2 prices, the rate of growth was only 25%. The chain-type rate of growth is the average (geometric mean) of these two growth rates, at 27.5%.

From g, we can calculate the level of chain-type real GDP and the chain-type GDP Price Deflator:

Chain-type real GDP$_2$ = g × real GDP$_1$ = 1.275 × 2000 = \$2550.

So the chain-type measure of real GDP (\$2550) provides a lower estimate of real GDP then the simple base year approach (\$2600).

$$\text{Chain-type GDP Price Deflator}_t = \frac{\text{nominal GDP}_t}{\text{chain-type real GDP}_t} \times 100$$

$$\text{Chain-type GDP Price Deflator}_1 = (2000/2000) \times 100 = 100$$
$$\text{Chain-type GDP Price Deflator}_2 = (4000/2550) \times 100 = 156.86$$

Notice that the chain-type GDP Price Deflator provides a higher estimate of the rate of inflation (56.86%) than the simple base-year approach (53.85%).

## Summary

The chain-type measure of real GDP provides a lower estimate of real GDP and a higher estimate of the rate of inflation compared to the simple base year approach, as long as prices have increased during the time period in question.

## NATIONAL INCOME AND PRODUCT ACCOUNTS

The National Income and Product Accounts of the Bureau of Economic Analysis contain the country's GDP statistics. As well as Gross Domestic Product, other measures of economic activity are provided, such as Gross National Product (GNP), Net National Product (NNP), National Income (NI), and Personal Income (PI). The relationships between these measures are shown in Table 5-6.

The methodology of calculating GNP was developed by a Department of Commerce economist named Simon Kuznets. In 1934, Kuznets published the first study using GNP data to measure the effects of the Great Depression on the American economy. He found that between 1929 and 1933, real GNP had declined by 25%. Kuznets was awarded the Nobel Prize in Economics in 1971 for his role as the father of national income accounting.

Table 5-6 uses the expenditure approach in measuring national income. GDP is the sum of each sector's spending, C + I + G + (X – M). In going from GDP to GNP, the factor income earned by Americans abroad is added in, and the factor income earned by foreigners in the United States is subtracted out. The term "Net Factor Income from Abroad" is the difference between the factor income earned by Americans abroad and the factor income earned by foreigners in the United States. "Factor" is just another name for a resource.

Net National Product measures the amount of output produced after depreciation of capital is taken into account. It is equal to GNP less the capital consumption

**Table 5-6**   National Income and Product Accounts

---

GDP = C + I + G + (X – M)

GNP = GDP + NFIA

NNP = GNP – CCA

NI = NNP – SD

PI = NI + Income received but not earned (dividends, government transfer payments, personal interest income)

    – Income earned but not received (corporate profits, social insurance contributions, net interest, indirect business taxes)

DPI = PI – Personal taxes

(NFIA = receipts of factor income from the rest of the world – payments of factor income to the rest of the world.)

---

allowance (CCA). National Income measures the amount of income earned by producers in the economy. It is equal to NNP minus a statistical discrepancy. The statistical discrepancy is necessary because not all of the billions of transactions in the economy each year will be accurately recorded.

National Income, from the expenditure approach, is equal to

$$NI = GDP + NFIA - CCA - SD$$

From the income approach, national income is the sum of factor payments:

$$NI = W + i + R + \text{profits}$$

The statistical discrepancy is the number, or fudge factor, that is necessary to ensure that the two approaches provide the same measure of National Income and GDP.

$$SD = (GDP + NFIA - CCA) - (W + i + R + \text{profits}) = NNP - NI$$

Next, Personal Income is a measure of the income received by households. To go from National Income to Personal Income, some factors have to be added while others are subtracted as shown in Table 5-6. Finally, Disposable Personal Income measures the amount of income available to households after taxes are paid.

## TRENDS IN GROSS DOMESTIC PRODUCT IN THE UNITED STATES

The following graphs show trends in nominal and real GDP in the United States since 1947, after the end of World War II. The effects of the 2008–2009 recession are evident in the graphs. Figure 5-3 shows nominal and real GDP from 1947 to the first quarter of 2009. The shaded areas represent periods of recession, which is commonly defined as two consecutive quarters of declining real GDP. In the United States it is a bit more complicated. A recession is defined by the National Bureau of Economic Research, a private group. As of this writing, the economy continues to be in the recession that was declared to have begun in December of 2007. Note that in recessions, real GDP declines but not necessarily nominal GDP since nominal GDP also includes price changes in the economy. Output may be declining but if inflation is high enough, then nominal GDP will still be increasing. This is particularly evident during the recession of 1974–1975. where real GDP is declining but nominal GDP continues to increase

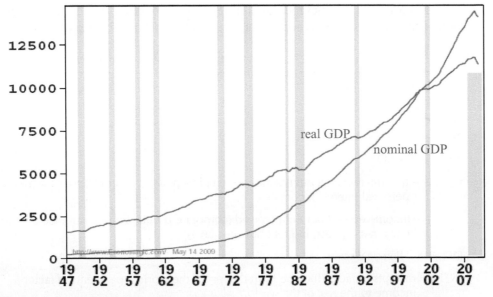

Figure 5-3    Nominal and Real GDP 1947–2009

because of high rates of inflation. Note also that the most recent decline seems to be particularly severe compared to the experience of the last sixty years.

Another feature of Figure 5-3 is that real GDP and nominal GDP intersect each other in the year 2000, or the base year. In the base year, the set of prices measuring real GDP is the same as that measuring nominal GDP. As shown in this chapter, in the base year nominal GDP and real GDP must be equal to each other.

Figure 5-4 shows the percent change in real GDP for the same time period. Since this graph is displaying percent changes the graph looks more erratic. In most time periods real GDP is increasing (the rate of change is greater than zero), but occasionally real GDP growth is negative. As shown, these are the periods of recession for the economy.

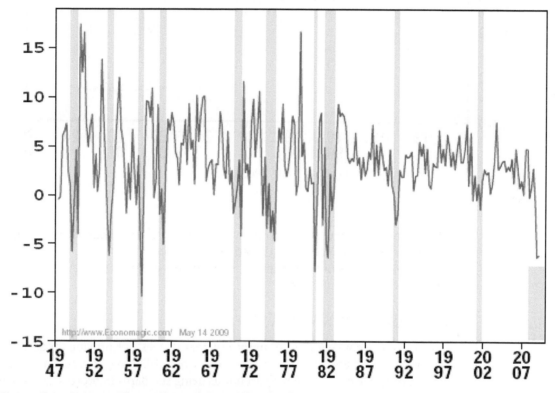

Figure 5-4    Percent Change in Real GDP 1947–2009

Since World War II, the United States economy has experienced eleven recessions. These occurred in 1948, 1953, 1958, 1961, 1969, 1974–75, 1979, 1981–82, 1991, 2001, and 2008–09. As evident in the graph, before 1982 the U.S. economy suffered from recessions roughly every five years, but since 1982 the economy has had recessions roughly every ten years. As shown above, the recent recession is the worst since the late 1970s.

Finally, Figure 5-5 shows the components of real GDP, consumption, investment, government spending, and net exports, and how they have been changing since 1990. Note that in most recessions, the real culprit is investment spending. Investment spending tends to be volatile and fluctuates more than the other sources of spending. During recessions investment spending falls more than consumption or government spending. Government spending is relatively stable over time. Consumption spending increases gradually, and in the 1991 and 2001 recessions consumption spending barely declined. The recession of 2008–09 is an exception, where consumption spending has been declining more drastically due to decreases in household wealth and rising unemployment rates. Net exports are negative, reflecting the

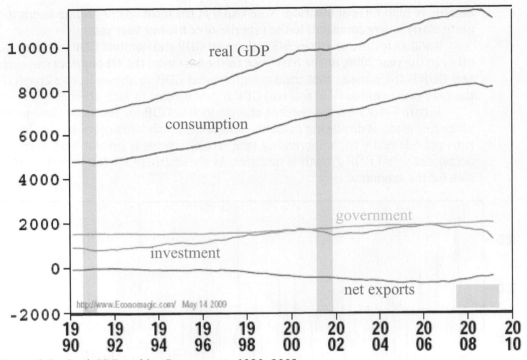

Figure 5-5   Real GDP and its Components 1990–2009

trade deficits of the United States economy. The global recession has actually helped to improve the trade balance of the United States in recent quarters.

Real GDP consists of consumption, investment, government, and net export spending.

## IS GDP A GOOD MEASURE OF SOCIAL WELFARE?

Many critics of the concept of GDP point out that it does not provide an accurate measure of social welfare. There are many cases where GDP may increase as people are being made worse off, or GDP may decline as living standards improve. GDP is only a rough measure of social welfare, and ignores many of the important amenities that may improve the quality of life. On the other hand, many economists and international researchers use GDP as a method to gauge and compare the quality of life in different countries. So who is right? Does GDP provide an accurate measure of economic welfare?

On the positive side, there is a strong correlation between per capita GDP and many indicators of socioeconomic progress. Those countries with higher per capita GDPs tend to score higher on social variables such as infant mortality rates, life expectancy, literacy rates, and percentage of homes with running water. There is a great deal of statistical evidence to support the claim that countries with higher per capita GDP also have higher standards of living. Those with more to spend can do better for themselves. Higher incomes enable a society to provide more for its citizens.

A limitation with this approach, however, is that there are many situations where an increase in real GDP may imply a decline in the standard of living. On the negative side of the argument, increases in GDP are not always associated with increases in social welfare. Because of the methods used to calculate GDP that we discussed early in this chapter, there are many anomalies in using GDP as a measure of human happiness. Increases in GDP may not always lead to increases in our standard of living. It is also problematic to use GDP to compare economic welfare between countries. A higher per capita GDP does not always mean that a country necessarily has a more improved standard of living. Money doesn't always buy happiness.

Here are some examples where GDP may not be an accurate indicator of social welfare.

## Defensive Expenditures

There are several examples where GDP increases because people spend to protect themselves from perceived threats to their health or safety. These are known as *defensive expenditures*. When individuals spend money to defend themselves from crime, disease, or environmental pollution, GDP will increase while these individuals are being made worse off. If people are afraid of swine flu and spend more money on medicines and doctor visits, GDP will increase but those involved would be better off if they did not have to be concerned about swine flu to begin with. Conversely, if everyone quit smoking cigarettes then public health would improve, but GDP would decrease with declines in cigarette production. When a population becomes healthier, GDP may decline.

If everyone had to purchase gas masks because the air was excessively polluted, then GDP would increase, but people are worse off. We would be better off if we never had to spend this money to begin with and had cleaner air. We purchase bottled water because we can no longer trust tap water. Bottled water sales increase GDP, but we would be better off if we could just drink our tap water instead. When the Exxon Valdez oil spill occurred in Prince William Sound in Alaska in 1989 we lost about a million dollars worth of oil, but we spent over $1 billion on clean-up costs. The clean-up effort increased GDP in 1989 and 1990, but we would be better off if the spill had never occurred in the first place. When defensive expenditures are made to control the negative effects of pollution, GDP increases but we would be better off if we never had to spend the money in the first place.

Defensive expenditures may also be devoted to protecting individuals from perceived threats to their safety through crime. Money spent on alarm systems, security guards, or guard dogs increases GDP because people do not originally feel safe. We would be better off if this money did not have to be spent to begin with. In the past several decades many wealthy couples have moved to gated communities in the south, especially in Florida and in Arizona. Billions have been spent to create walls around neighborhoods, and continue to be spent on security guards at the entrances, to allow wealthy people to feel safe in their communities. All of this spending increases GDP, while isolating the wealthy from the rest of society. The more isolated the wealthy become, the more they distrust others, and the more they want to spend to protect themselves. If different classes were able to interact more, they would become familiar with each other, and develop a greater sense of trust and mutual respect. Instead, the wealthy wall themselves off to achieve a false sense of security. GDP increases as people become more fearful of each other.

With defensive expenditures on such items as health care, the environment, or crime, GDP increases as we devote resources to protecting ourselves from perceived threats. But we would clearly be better off if we did not have to spend this money to begin with.

## Value of Leisure

Another problem with using GDP as a measure of social welfare is that it does not include the value of leisure. Leisure time may increase human happiness, but because workers are not producing anything while consuming leisure time, then the value of leisure time is not included in GDP statistics. If half of the labor force in the United States decided to take a month off to meditate on mountaintops, then GDP would decline but people would probably be happier. Increases in leisure will reduce GDP.

In Mexico, the rise of *maquiladoras* (US factories) along the Texas border has increased GDP in Mexico. The problem is that the workers must tend to the machines while they are running all day, so they no longer have time for siestas. An important piece of Mexican culture is the *siesta,* or nap, in the middle of the day when the sun is hottest. Those working in *maquiladoras* are not able to take their *siestas* because the factory machinery must be kept in operation. The increase in GDP leads to less leisure time. Mexico now has a higher GDP, but Mexican culture suffers as a result.

As shown in Table 5-7, labor in the United States tends to work longer hours, at 42.8 hours per week, than in most other countries. In the table, only South Korea, Mexico, and Columbia have higher hours of work per week than in the United States. One cost of our high level of GDP is less time for friends, family, and hobbies as American workers put in longer hours than most of their counterparts around the world. U.S. workers trade their leisure time for higher levels of GDP. We have more output but less time for ourselves. On the other hand, as leisure increases in an economy, ceteris paribus, people are made happier even though GDP declines.

**Table 5-7**  Hours Worked Per Week in Selected Countries, 2006

| | |
|---|---|
| Australia | 34.7 |
| Austria | 34.2 |
| Belarus | 31.8 |
| Canada | 31.6 |
| Colombia | 46.8 |
| Finland | 35.9 |
| Germany | 38.4 |
| Greece | 40.3 |
| Ireland | 36.5 |
| Israel | 36.3 |
| Italy | 34.8 |
| Japan | 41.7 |
| Korea (South) | 43.4 |
| Mexico | 44.7 |
| Norway | 34.5 |
| Poland | 40 |
| Russia | 35.4 |
| Sweden | 36.4 |
| United Kingdom | 39.5 |
| United States | 42.8 |

Source: International Labor Organization *http://laborsta.ilo.org*

## Population Differences

In trying to compare countries using GDP statistics, one has to be careful about population differences between countries. For example, India, at $4.164 trillion, has roughly twice the GDP as the United Kingdom, at $1.928 trillion *(https://www.cia.gov/library/publications/the-world-factbook/fields/2001.html)*. If India has twice the GDP, does that mean that Indians are twice as better off as Britons? Of course not, since population differences must be taken into account. Even though India has twice the GDP as the United Kingdom, it has over 18 times the population.

So the per capita GDP for India is much smaller than that for the United Kingdom, at \$3,800 in 2006 compared to \$31,800 for Britain *(https://www.cia.gov/library/ publications/the-world-factbook/fields/2004.html).* To control for population differences, per capita GDP must be compared across countries.

*Per capita GDP* is equal to the GDP of an economy divided by its population. It measures how much GDP is available on average for each person in the economy. It is given by

$$\text{per capita GDP} = \text{GDP} / \text{population}.$$

Per capita GDP provides a much more meaningful comparison between countries than does overall GDP since it controls for population differences between countries. But even per capita GDP does not provide an accurate measure of economic welfare in an economy, since it ignores the distribution of income.

## The Distribution of Income

Economic welfare in a country will depend in part on the distribution of income in an economy. The more evenly distributed is the income of an economy, then the greater the share of goods and services that can be enjoyed by the average person. High per capita GDP may disguise great inequalities in income in an economy. For example, both Greece and Kuwait have roughly the same per capita GDP, at about \$24,000 per person *(https://www.cia.gov/library/publications/the-world-factbook/fields/ 2004.html).* But this does not mean that consumers in both countries enjoy the same standard of living. In Kuwait, much of the country's wealth is concentrated within the royal family. In Greece, there is a much more egalitarian distribution of income. So an average Greek citizen is better off than an average Kuwaiti, since she would be able to enjoy a greater share of the per capita GDP. Per capita GDP statistics tell us nothing about the distribution of income in an economy, which is an important factor in determining the quality of life. If increases in per capita GDP occur from increases in the wealth of the richest, then the average person in the economy is made no better off.

## Cultural Differences

Because of the way that GDP is calculated, differences in cultures between countries can make comparisons based on per capita GDP difficult. Since GDP does not include domestic goods that are produced inside the home for consumption inside the home, those countries where more goods are produced inside the home will have lower per capita GDP, ceteris paribus. Yet domestically-produced goods may provide more human satisfaction than store-bought goods. A sweater knit by your grandmother is more enjoyable than one purchased from Walmart. Children are probably better off being raised by relatives than in daycare centers. Food that is grown at home is healthier and more satisfying than a McDonald's hamburger. GDP does not provide a good measure of economic welfare since those countries that produce more goods inside the home will have lower GDP but probably provide more happiness than market-dominated economies.

Another cultural difference is that countries have different laws concerning what exchanges are legal and illegal. Those countries with more legal goods and services will have higher GDP compared to those countries where more activities are illegal. In Amsterdam, local GDP is higher because marijuana is legal. In Nevada, state GDP is greater because prostitution is legal in most counties. Differences in morals and beliefs can contribute to differences in per capita GDP across countries.

Also, cultures differ in how they value leisure. As alluded to earlier, those countries which value leisure more highly will have lower per capita GDP, everything else held constant.

Finally, cultures may differ in the acceptability of divorce and divorce rates. When a couple gets divorced, goods and services that were provided in the home may now have to be purchased in markets instead. For example, if a man is married to a tax accountant, then the wife can do the taxes within the home for free. This service is domestic production that is not included in GDP. But if the couple gets divorced, then the man will have to hire a tax accountant as a market exchange, and GDP will increase. When a couple gets divorced, more goods and services must be purchased outside the home, and twice as many households must be established. For these reasons increases in the divorce rate increase GDP, although high divorce rates are a sign of social dissatisfaction. Countries with higher divorce rates will have higher per capita GDP, ceteris paribus.

## Prices and Exchange Rates

Changes in prices or exchange rates can affect the relative positions of countries that are being compared using per capita GDP statistics. If a country experiences inflation, nominal GDP will increase even if output is stagnant. As the price level in an economy increases, its exchange rate will fall. Exchange rates affect the value of one country's currency in terms of dollars. When comparing the per capita GDP in different countries, the domestic currencies must be converted to dollars. The exchange rate of the domestic currency in dollars will affect the level of that country's per capita GDP in dollars. For example, as the value of the US dollar falls, the per capita GDP of other countries measured in dollars increases even though economic activity may remain unchanged. As the value of the dollar falls, domestic currencies around the world increase in value, making their economies appear richer even if nothing else changes.

## Quality Changes

GDP statistics do not always capture quality changes in the products included. Increases in the quality of products will make us happier, but GDP may not always increase as a result. For example, laptop computers have increased in memory, applications, and processing speed as the price of them has fallen. A purchase of a laptop provides more satisfaction as quality increases, but GDP still only includes one laptop, and the contribution of that laptop to nominal GDP will be falling as prices decline. The Bureau of Economic Analysis provides "hedonic adjustments" for large purchases such as automobiles or home appliances, but it is still difficult to quantify quality changes that affect our happiness. On the other side, the quality of airline travel has declined in recent years, yet the airline industry's contribution to GDP has generally increased over time. Quality changes influence our happiness but they are not always accurately reflected in GDP statistics.

## Wars and Natural Disasters

Finally, wars and natural disasters may change GDP in ways that do not reflect changes in happiness. The War on Iraq has increased GDP in the United States, but we are not happier for having fought the war. Natural disasters such as Hurricane Katrina will increase GDP in subsequent years as money is spent on clean-up and rebuilding. Rebuilding the World Trade Center will increase GDP in those years of construction, but we would be better off if the World Trade Center was never attacked in the first place. Wars and natural disasters can increase GDP and social misery at the same time.

In sum, GDP is at best an imperfect measure of happiness, but in comparing the standards of living across countries it is the best that we have. But we must be careful in using per capita GDP to compare economic welfare across countries, since there are many cases where GDP may increase as human happiness declines, or countries where lower GDP implies a more satisfying lifestyle. GDP is not a great measure but it is the best we have got.

## ALTERNATIVE MEASURES OF ECONOMIC WELFARE

Due to the problems with using GDP as a measure of economic welfare discussed above, there have been many attempts to provide alternative measures of economic welfare. A few of these are described in the following paragraphs.

### The Index of Sustainable Economic Welfare (ISEW)

Originally developed by Herman Daly and John Cobb in 1989, the Index of Sustainable Economic Welfare attempts to make adjustments to GDP to provide a more accurate measure of social welfare. The index is now compiled and publicized by the Friends of the Earth, a British environmental organization. The Friends of the Earth does not feel that GDP is a good measure of economic welfare. GDP is a brute measure of progress which does not take into account how the side-effects of economic growth can make us worse off.

> GDP takes no account of increasing inequality, pollution or damage to people's health and the environment. It treats crime, divorce, and other elements of social progress as economic gains. *(http://www.foe.co.uk/campaigns/sustainable_ development/progress)*

The Index of Sustainable Economic Welfare attempts to adjust GDP to include better indicators of the quality of life. It tries to measure increases in the quality of life, not just increases in output. Overall, there are nineteen adjustments which the ISEW makes to GDP calculations. The Index is calculated by the Centre for Environmental Strategy and the New Economics Foundation, in collaboration with the Friends of the Earth and other groups, mostly British. It has been calculated for eight countries.

The ISEW adjusts GDP in several ways. It includes calculations for such indicators as income inequality, domestic labor, health, education, services from consumer durables, air pollution, climate change and ozone depletion, and other factors such as the costs of commuting, car accidents, the costs of noise and water pollution, and loss of habitat and farmlands. In this way, ISEW provides a better measure of the quality of life in an economy.

### The Measure of Economic Welfare (MEW)

The Measure of Economic Welfare (MEW) was originally developed by Samuel Nordhaus and James Tobin in 1972, and is now calculated by the United Nations Statistics Division. The MEW adjusts national output to include only the consumption and investment activities that contribute directly to economic well-being. For example, it adds the value of leisure and contributions of the underground economy, and subtracts negative externalities such as environmental damage.

Both statistics show that economic welfare has not grown as much as GDP for the countries that were studied.

## The Global (Ecological) Footprint

All of the indicators that we have discussed so far have used dollars to measure the extent of economic activity. Instead, the global footprint measures the amount of land that is used up in economic activity. The act of consumption requires land for production, distribution, and disposal of wastes. The global footprint measures how much land is used up in different types of economic activities so that individuals can measure their own global footprints. It helps to highlight the limits that the earth places on economic activities.

Given the quantity of usable land, each year the world population uses up 1.2 planets. Each year we take more from the planet than can be reproduced. What is consumed of the earth's resources in one year would take 1.2 years to replace. This is known as an ecological deficit. On average Americans use up 90 acres per person per year. If everyone around the planet lived like American consumers, we would require 4.5 planets just to have enough land to support this economic activity. There are limits to what the planet can produce. The more resources that we use up, the less will be available for the rest of the world. It is important to find ways to reduce our global footprint over time *(http://www.myfootprint.org/en/your_carbon_footprint)*.

That's it for GDP!

# 6

# Measuring International Transactions

In order to measure GDP, we must have a method to account for international transactions, the flows of goods, services, incomes, and financial assets between countries. Remember that from the expenditure approach, Gross Domestic Product is equal to

$$GDP = C + I + G + (X - M)$$

where X is exports and M is imports, and (X – M) is net exports. In order to accurately measure GDP, we must have a way of accounting for imports and exports.

Any market will have both a quantity and price. In international markets, the quantity of transactions is recorded in the balance of payments accounts. The price is affected by exchange rates, or the value of one country's currency. Since most countries have different currencies, for those countries to trade they must have a means of exchanging currencies. The balance of payments and exchange rates are the topics of this chapter.

## THE BALANCE OF PAYMENTS ACCOUNTS

The flows of goods, services, income and financial assets between countries is documented in the balance of payments accounts for each country. The balance of payments consists of two separate accounts, the current account and the capital and financial accounts. The balance of payments accounts uses a technique known as double-entry bookkeeping, where each transaction is recorded as both a credit and a debit. Because of this, the overall balance of payments is always equal to zero.

We will begin with some definitions:

*Exports (X):* Goods and services produced domestically that are purchased by foreigners.

*Imports (M):* Goods and services produced in foreign countries that are purchased domestically.

*Net exports (X – M):* The difference between exports and imports, or the difference between what a country sells abroad and what it purchases from other countries.

*Balance of payments accounts:* A record of one country's trade in goods, services, income, and financial assets with the rest of the world. The balance of payments consists of the current account and the capital and financial accounts.

*Current account:* An account of the balance of payments that measures the flows of goods, services, income, and unilateral transfers (gifts).

*Capital and financial accounts:* Accounts of the balance of payments that measure the flows of financial assets, such as stocks, bonds, bank deposits, bank loans, real estate, and firm assets.

*Double-entry bookkeeping:* An accounting technique where each transaction is recorded as both a credit and a debit. A credit is a positive entry, while a debit is a negative entry.

An export, which brings revenue into the country, is treated as a credit. The payment for that export is treated as a debit in the balance of payments. An import, which represents revenue leaving the country, is treated as a debit. The payment for that import is recorded as a credit.

The implications of double-entry bookkeeping are important for the balance of payments accounts. To appreciate this idea, here is an example of how one transaction would be recorded in the balance of payments accounts.

## Double-Entry Bookkeeping

Suppose that a French winery needs a tractor to help on the farm. It decides to import a tractor from John Deere, a tractor manufacturer in the United States. The tractor sells for $75,000. The balance of payments accounts in the United States would record the transaction in the following way:

| Activity | Credit | Debit |
|---|---|---|
| John Deere exports a tractor and receives a payment of $75,000 from French winery | + $75,000 | |
| French winery imports a tractor and withdraws $75,000 from a U.S. bank account to pay John Deere | | – $75,000 |
| | + $75,000 | – $75,000 |

Notice that the overall effect of this transaction on the balance of payments is 0. The credits balance out the debits. This is why it is called the balance of payments. The credits and debits are in balance, so the overall balance of payments is zero.

Since the overall balance of payments is equal to zero, any deficit in one account must be made up with a surplus in the other account. For example, since 1992 the United States has had a deficit in its current account. We import more from the rest of the world than we export to the rest of the world. Since we are not earning the foreign currency to purchase exports by selling the rest of the world our imports, we must finance the export spending by selling off our financial assets to the rest of the world.

This leads to a surplus in the capital and financial account. So the United States finances its current account deficit through a surplus in its capital and financial accounts. This is shown below in Table 6-1, which shows the preliminary United States balance of payments accounts for 2008.

**Table 6-1**   U.S. Balance of Payments, 2008
(millions of dollars, preliminary data)

|  | Credits | Debits | Net |
|---|---|---|---|
| *Current Account* | | | |
| goods | 1,291,371 | –2,112,196 | –820,825 |
| services | 544,414 | –404,719 | 139,695 |
| income | 755,468 | –627,891 | 127,577 |
| subtotal | 2,591,253 | –3,144,806 | –553,553 |
| net transfers | | | –119,713 |
| *balance on current account* | | | –673,266 |
| *Capital Account, net* | | | –2,600 |
| *Financial Account* | | | |
| U.S.-owned assets abroad | | –52,459 | |
| foreign-owned assets in U.S. | 599,049 | | |
| financial derivatives, net | | | 0 |
| *balance on capital and financial accounts* | | | 543,990 |
| statistical discrepancy | | | 129,276 |
| *overall balance of payments* | | | 0 |

Source: Bureau of Economic Analysis

In Table 6-1, the credits include those items that bring revenue into the United States, such as exports and income earned by Americans abroad, while the debits represent those items where revenue is leaving the country, such as imports and income earned by foreigners in the United States. The top portion of the table shows the current account, while the bottom shows the capital and financial accounts. The current account includes goods, services, income, and net transfers. The financial account includes foreign assets purchased by Americans, U.S. assets purchased by foreigners, and financial derivatives such as stock and commodity options and futures. The statistical discrepancy is the adjustment that must be made to account for missing and incorrect data. Once the statistical discrepancy is included, notice that the overall balance of payments equals zero. The credits and debits balance each other out.

In 2008, the United States exported more than 1.2 trillion dollars worth of goods or merchandise. It also imported more than 2.1 trillion dollars worth of goods, so it has a goods deficit of $820 billion. In 2008 the United States purchased $820 billion more worth of goods from the rest of the world than it sold to the rest of the world. How did the United States obtain the additional currency to purchase all of these exports? Since over $820 billion was not earned by selling exports, the currency must be obtained by selling off the country's financial assets. This is the surplus in the capital and financial accounts.

As shown in the table, the United States usually has a services surplus. In 2008, the United States sold over $544 billion worth of services to the rest of the world and purchased almost $404 billion worth of services, for a services surplus of almost $140 billion. For many type of services, such as military, financial, education, tourism, and entertainment, the United States tends to sell more of these services to the rest

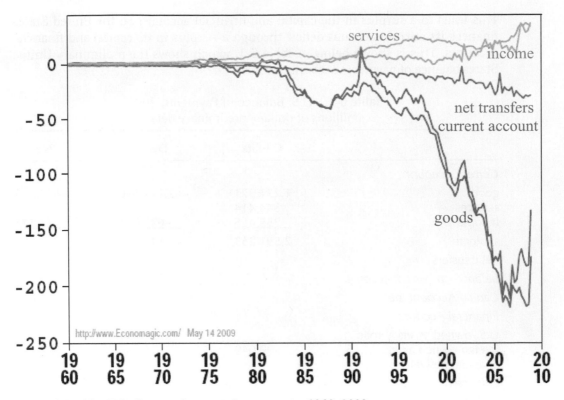

Figure 6-1    The U.S. Current Account Components, 1960–2009

of the world than it purchases from the rest of the world. This results in a surplus in the services category.

When we combine the balances on goods, services, income, and net unilateral transfers, the balance on the current account for 2008 comes to –$673 billion. This is the number that is most widely quoted in the media as the "trade deficit," or "trade balance," the balance on the current account. This means that in 2008, the United States purchased $673 billion more worth of goods and services from the rest of the world than it sold to the rest of the world. As mentioned earlier, it finances this trade deficit through a surplus in its capital and financial accounts. In 2008, investors in the United States purchased $52 billion worth of foreign financial assets, while foreigners purchased $599 billion worth of assets in the United States, so the balance on the capital and financial accounts is a surplus of $543 billion. So U.S. consumers financed roughly $600 billion of import spending in 2008 by selling off roughly $600 billion of financial assets.

Figure 6-1 shows the U.S. current account position (balance of trade) from 1960–2009. The components of the current account, goods, services, income, and transfers, are also shown. Note that there is a surplus on services, the green line is above 0. Income and net transfers just about cancel each other out. The large deficit in the current account is caused by the large deficit in the goods (or merchandise) category of the current account.

From 1960 to 1975, the U.S. trade position was relatively balanced, as all of these variables were close to 0. After 1975, the Arab Oil Embargo and rising price of foreign oil began to create a trade deficit in the United States. After 1980, the trade deficit increased as the value of the dollar increased. (See Figure 6-2.) When Ronald Reagan started to run large budget deficits in 1982, the increase in the demand for bonds to finance the deficits raised the yield on U.S. Treasury bonds, so more foreigners wanted to purchase these bonds. As the global demand for U.S. treasury bonds increased, the value of the dollar increased and our trade position began to deterio-rate. This created the *twin deficits* of the period, when the economy had both budget deficits and trade deficits. After a brief return to trade balance in 1992, the U.S. econ-omy has been on a large spending binge since then. Our large deficit in goods has cre-ated large deficits in the current account in general. It is only recently that the global recession has led to a slight improvement in the U.S. trade position.

The trade situation of the United States can be compared to your own household. An analogy to the current position would be if your family was spending more than it was earning each year. Since all of your bills are not paid through the income being earned annually, your family must find other ways of coming up with the rest of the money. To pay the remainder of your bills, suppose that your family sells off a room in your house each year to fund the balance of expenditures not covered by income. This may be a viable solution for a few years, especially if you have a big house in a desirable location. But eventually you will run out of rooms to sell, or the rooms become less desirable as more and more people are living in your house. To attract new buyers of rooms in your house to fund your excess spending, you will have to start to lower the price of those rooms. This story is very similar to what we have been doing as an economy as a whole.

As discussed above, the United States is funding its trade deficit of $600 billion by selling off $600 billion of financial assets. In 2006, for comparison, the trade deficit was roughly $800 billion, so we had to sell off $800 billion of financial assets that year. The longer the country is on this spending binge, the more we have to lower the price of these assets to the rest of the world to finance this binge. The price of U.S. assets to the rest of the world is reflected through exchange rates, or the values of one country's currency in terms of other countries' currencies. From the recession of 2002 until 2008, the value of the dollar had been generally falling against most other currencies. As the value of the dollar fell, the cost of U.S. financial assets to the rest of the world also declined. As the value of the dollar fell, U.S. exports became less expensive to foreigners, so exports increased. Foreign imports became more expen-sive for U.S. consumers, so imports declined. As exports rose and imports fell, net exports increased, and the current account deficit improved. In recent quarters, the global recession has also led to a slight improvement in the U.S. trade position. As other countries economies have contracted more severely than the U.S. economy, the value of the dollar has begun to increase again. Trends in the value of the dollar compared to a broad index of major currencies are shown in Figure 6-2.

Figure 6-2   The Value of the Dollar, Broad Index, 1973–2009

The value of the dollar in general increased from 1973 to 2001 as the global demand for U.S. products and financial assets increased. After 2001, the value of the dollar fell as we had to lower the price of our financial assets to encourage continued global investments in U.S. financial assets. Since the global recession commenced at the end of 2007, the value of the dollar has increased again.

Since changes in exchange rates play an important role in changes in the flows of imports and exports around the world, they are an important variable in international markets. The remainder of the chapter explores exchange rates and how they affect international trade.

## EXCHANGE RATES

Since different countries use different currencies, there must be a means of exchanging currencies for countries to be able to trade goods and services. Large banks in major cities around the world provide these currency exchange services for a fee in what are known as currency or foreign exchange markets. The price of one currency in terms of another in these markets is known as the exchange rate. Exchange rates will fluctuate in response to supply and demand conditions in these markets.

Here are some definitions:

*Exchange rate:* The value of one country's currency in terms of another.

*Currency (foreign exchange) markets:* Markets where currency is exchanged, usually large banks in major cities around the world.

*Appreciation:* An increase in the value of a currency in terms of another.

*Depreciation:* A decrease in the value of a currency in terms of another.

Exchange rates are reciprocals, or inverses, of each other. For example, if a British pound is worth 2 dollars, than a dollar is worth ½ of a British pound. Common notations for currencies include:

$ = U.S. dollar
€ = Euro
¥ = Japanese yen
£ = British pound

As an example, we will examine the exchange rates for eight major currencies on October 23, 2007 as provided by Bloomberg.com, shown in Table 6-2. The table shows the exchange rates for each of the countries' currencies in terms of the other seven currencies. For example, the value of one dollar on October 23 was equal to 7.7513 Hong Kong dollars or 1.173 Swiss Francs. A Euro was worth 1.5782 Australian dollars or 0.6957 of a British pound. For any currency, you can read down the column to find the value of that currency in terms of the other major currencies shown in the table.

Using our notation above, some exchange rates listed are:

| | | |
|---|---|---|
| $1 = €0.7013 | so | €1 = $(1 / 0.7013) = $1.4259 |
| $1 = ¥114.68 | so | ¥1 = $0.0087 |
| ¥1 = €0.0061 | so | €1 = ¥163.5188 |

**Table 6-2**   Benchmark Currency Rates
October 23, 2007

|      | USD    | EUR      | JPY    | GBP      | CHF     | CAD      | AUD      | HKD     |
|------|--------|----------|--------|----------|---------|----------|----------|---------|
| HKD  | 7.7513 | 11.0523  | 0.0676 | 15.8867  | 6.6081  | 8.0245   | 7.0031   |         |
| AUD  | 1.1068 | 1.5782   | 0.0097 | 2.2685   | 0.9436  | 1.1458   |          | 0.1428  |
| CAD  | 0.966  | 1.3773   | 0.0084 | 1.9798   | 0.8235  |          | 0.8727   | 0.1246  |
| CHF  | 1.173  | 1.6725   | 0.0102 | 2.4041   |         | 1.2143   | 1.0598   | 0.1513  |
| GBP  | 0.4879 | 0.6957   | 0.0043 |          | 0.416   | 0.5051   | 0.4408   | 0.0629  |
| JPY  | 114.68 | 163.5188 |        | 235.0424 | 97.7664 | 118.7225 | 103.6111 | 14.7949 |
| EUR  | 0.7013 |          | 0.0061 | 1.4374   | 0.5979  | 0.726    | 0.6336   | 0.0905  |
| USD  |        | 1.4259   | 0.0087 | 2.0496   | 0.8525  | 1.0353   | 0.9035   | 0.129   |

The chart is designed to display the cross rates of eight major world currencies. Scan across the chart to find the rate of exchange between any two of these currencies.

Currency Key

| USD: | U.S. Dollar       | CAD: | Canadian Dollar   |
|------|-------------------|------|-------------------|
| GBP: | British Pound     | EUR: | Euro              |
| CHF: | Swiss Franc       | AUD: | Australian Dollar |
| HKD: | Hong Kong Dollar  | JPY: | Japanese Yen      |

Source: *http://www.bloomberg.com/markets/currencies/fxc.html*

Given the exchange rates listed above, is it possible to find any opportunities for profit? Is there anyway to get rich by exchanging currency at any given point in time? Suppose that we start with $1.00. We could then trade $1.00 for ¥114.68. From this, we could trade the ¥114.68 for $114.68 \times 0.0061 = €0.699548$. We could then trade €0.699548 for $0.699548 \times 1.4259 = \$0.997485$. If we start with a dollar, we end up with a sum very close to a dollar. The only reason we do not have a dollar is due to rounding error. Since most banks charge a 1% transaction fee for currency exchanges, the costs of swapping currencies would outweigh any potential profits.

Or we could start with €1.00. If we trade €1.00 for ¥163.5188, then trade ¥163.5188 for $163.5188 \times 0.0087 = \$1.4226$, and finally trade $1.4226 for $1.4226 \times 0.7013 = €0.9976$. Once again, we start with one Euro and end up with an amount very close to one Euro. There is no potential for profit opportunities here.

The idea that we cannot benefit through differences in currency values is known as purchasing power parity. Purchasing power parity states that currencies should have the same purchasing power in different countries. One currency should buy no more of another currency in one country compared to another country. For example, the dollar price of yen in the U.S. is that ¥1 = $0.0087, and the dollar price of yen in Europe is ¥1 = $€0.0061 \times 1.4259 = \$0.0087$. So in both the United States and Europe the price of yen is the same. It is impossible to profit by buying yen in one country and selling it in the other country.

If it is not possible to profit through exchanging currencies at a given point in time, how do currency speculators profit? They do so by betting on changes in the value of currency over periods of time. For example, if you believe that the euro will appreciate in the future, you can profit (if you are correct) by purchasing euros or euro-denominated securities. To correctly predict changes in exchange rates, it is useful to have a model of how exchange rates are determined. Two such models of exchange rate determination are purchasing power parity theory and supply and demand analysis.

## MODELS OF EXCHANGE RATE DETERMINATION

The two models of exchange rate determination covered here are purchasing power parity (PPP) theory and supply and demand analysis. PPP theory is more useful in explaining long run trends in exchange rates. Exchange rates will adjust to bring purchasing power parity to different countries. PPP was a common theory in earlier times when exchange rates were often fixed by the respective governments. Supply and demand analysis is more useful in explaining minute-by-minute changes in exchange rates in response to ever-changing conditions in world markets. Since most governments now allow their exchange rates to fluctuate (floating exchange rates), supply and demand provides a strong tool for analysis in these markets.

### Purchasing Power Parity (PPP) Theory

Purchasing Power Parity theory states that the price of a bundle of goods and services should be the same in different countries given exchange rates. To say the same thing, currencies should have the same purchasing power in different countries. The equilibrium exchange rate between two countries is the rate that brings purchasing power parity to the prices of goods and services produced in those countries.

*Purchasing Power Parity (PPP) theory:* currencies should have the same purchasing power in different countries.

PPP theory is given by the following equation:

$$P = P^f \times E$$

where
P = domestic price
$P^f$ = foreign price
E = exchange rate, expressed as units of home currency per unit of foreign currency.

This equation both provides a means to calculate foreign prices and a theory of exchange rate movements. First, it can be used to figure how much domestic currency is necessary to make a foreign purchase, for example, how many dollars does it take to purchase a hotel room in France that sells for 100 euros? Second, the equation provides a theory of exchange rate movements. If purchasing power parity does not hold, then international arbitrage will result, bringing prices and exchange rates closer to parity.

*International arbitrage:* the process of profiting through price differentials by buying a good in a low-priced country and selling that good in a high-priced country.

For example, suppose that exchange rates between the United States and Japan are that one dollar trades for 100 yen, and a yen trades for a penny. In October 2007 the dollar was trading for 118 yen, so the assumption is not too far from reality and simplifies the math. Also suppose that a ton of wheat has a price of $50 in the United States. The PPP equation above provides a means to figure out the yen price of wheat in the United States, or how many yen a Japanese consumer would need to purchase the $50 in U.S. currency necessary for the wheat.

So

$$\$1 = \yen100 \text{ and } \yen1 = \$0.01$$
$$P = P^f \times E \text{ and } P = \$50, \, E = 0.01$$
$$50 = P^f \times .01 \text{ so } P^f = 50/0.01 = \yen5,000$$

If a ton of wheat costs $50 in the United States, then it has a yen price of ¥5,000. A Japanese consumer would need ¥5,000 to have enough yen to purchase the dollars necessary to purchase a ton of wheat. So the PPP equation provides a way of determining foreign prices.

The PPP equation also provides a theory of exchange rate movements over time. If prices in different countries do not exhibit purchasing power parity, then international arbitrage will bring prices closer to parity in both countries as prices and exchange rates adjust. If goods are cheaper in one country compared to others, the demand for that country's currency will rise, and the value of its currency will increase. International arbitrage will lead to increases in supply of goods in high-priced countries and declines in the supply of goods in low-priced countries, so that prices will become closer to parity.

For instance, suppose that in the example above, the price of wheat in the United States remains at $50, but the price of wheat in Japan rises to ¥10,000. Also assume that it costs $10 to ship one ton of wheat from one country to the other. If exchange rates remain the same, then purchasing power parity does not hold. In this situation, profit opportunities exist. To see this, please examine Table 6-3.

As shown in the table, it is possible to profit from the price differential between the countries. One can profit by shipping wheat from the United States to Japan, originally by $40 for each ton. As wheat is shipped from the United States to Japan, the supply of wheat in the United States will decline and the supply of wheat in Japan will increase. The decrease in the supply of wheat will cause an increase in the price of wheat in the United States. The increase in the supply of wheat will cause a decrease in the price of wheat in Japan. The price of wheat increases in the low-priced country and it declines in the high-priced country, bringing prices closer to parity. Eventually, the only differences in prices between the countries should reflect the shipping costs. In this example, once the price differential is $10 or less, it is no longer profitable to ship wheat from one country to the other. But the process of international arbitrage will bring prices close to parity between countries until the only difference between prices reflects shipping costs.

**Table 6-3**  Profiting from International Arbitrage

| Activity | Result |
| --- | --- |
| purchase one ton of wheat in U.S. | – $50 |
| ship one ton of wheat to Japan | – $10 |
| sell one ton of wheat in Japan for ¥10,000, exchange ¥10,000 for $100 | +$100 |
| net change | + $40 |

So far, we have examined price changes as the means of achieving purchasing power parity. But PPP theory is a model of exchange rate determination. If prices are fixed or sluggish in an economy due to price controls or other market imperfections, then exchange rates will play a greater role in bringing about purchasing power parity. If wheat is cheaper in the United States, then wheat consumers around the world will increase their demand for U.S. wheat. The increase in the demand for wheat will lead to an increase in the demand for dollars, pushing up the value of the dollar relative to other currencies.

For the example above, suppose that the price of wheat remains at $50 in the United States and at ¥10,000 in Japan, and that both prices are fixed by price controls. Then exchange rates must adjust to achieve PPP. This is shown by using the PPP equation:

$$P = P^f \times E \text{ so } \$50 = ¥10,000 \times E \text{ or } E = 50/10,000 = .005.$$

The exchange rate E has declined from E = 0.01 to E = 0.005. Since E is the units of home currency per unit of foreign currency, it is the value of the yen. So the value of the yen has declined from ¥1 = $0.01 to ¥1 = $0.005. The yen depreciates from being equal to one penny to being equal to only one-half of a penny. Since the yen depreciates the dollar appreciates, from $1 = ¥100 to $1 = ¥200. Since the United States had the lower priced wheat, the increase in the demand for the dollar led to an increase in the value of the dollar.

## The Big Mac Index

One popular indicator of the purchasing power parity of currencies around the world is known as the Big Mac Index. The Big Mac Index was developed by the Economist magazine in 1986 as a tongue-in-cheek guide to purchasing power parity theory. The Index uses the prices of Big Macs, which are produced locally in over 120 countries, as a test of whether exchange rates are at their "correct level" as compared to the implied PPP given by Big Mac prices.

As a simplified example, assume that a Big Mac costs $3.00 in the United States and ¥150 in Japan. If the current exchange rate is E = .01 (so that ¥1 = $.01 and $1 = ¥100), then the dollar price of Big Macs in Japan would be 150 × .01 = $1.50. So purchasing power parity does not hold, since the dollar price of a Big Mac in Japan ($1.50) is less than the dollar price of a Big Mac in the United States ($3.00).

Purchasing power parity suggests that, in the long run, exchange rates should adjust so that the price of a basket of goods and services in different countries is similar. Here the basket of goods and services is the Big Mac. If the price of Big Macs holds in both countries, then the Big Mac index implies that the exchange rate that would result in purchasing power parity would be given by the following equation:

$$P = P^f \times E$$

or   E = $3/¥150 = .02, so that the implied PPP exchange rate is ¥1 = $.02
or $1 = ¥50.

This means that the Big Mac Index shows that the yen is currently undervalued. The current exchange rate is ¥1 = $.01, but the implied PPP exchange rate is ¥1 = $.02. So purchasing power parity suggests that the yen should be increasing in value from one cent per yen to two cents per yen, in order to equalize Big Mac prices in both countries. When current exchange rates show that the Big Mac costs less in other countries compared to the American price, then those countries have currencies that are undervalued relative to the dollar.

The Big Mac Index can be found at *www.economist.com/markets/bigmac*.

## Supply and Demand Analysis

A second model of exchange rate determination is supply and demand analysis. While PPP theory is useful in explaining long-term changes in exchange rates over time, supply and demand analysis provides a better model in explaining minute-by-minute changes in currency markets that are seen in the real world. With supply and demand analysis in currency markets, we can examine two interrelated markets, the market for a foreign currency at home and the market for domestic currency abroad. The supply and demand curves in these markets are interdependent. An increase in the demand for a currency in one country leads to an increase in the supply of the other currency in another country, as consumers in one country exchange their domestic currency for foreign currency.

As an example, we return to the currency market between the United States and Japan. Assume that we still have the same exchange rates, so that $1 = ¥100$ and $¥1 = $0.01$. In the currency market, we can look at two sides of the market. First, there is the market for yen in the United States. American consumers must trade their dollars for yen to be able to purchase Japanese products. Second, there is the market for dollars in Japan. Japanese consumers demand dollars to purchase American products. These markets are interrelated. The demand for yen in the United States is similar to the supply of dollars in Japan. As Americans trade their dollars for yen, a supply of dollars is created in Japan. An increase in the demand for yen in the United States will lead to an increase in the supply of dollars in Japan. Similarly, the demand for dollars in Japan is equivalent to the supply of yen in the United States. As Japanese consumers exchange their yen for dollars, a supply of yen in the United States is created. An increase in the demand for dollars in Japan leads to an increase in the supply of yen in the United States. The two markets are interdependent.

In the market for yen in the United States, the relevant price is the price of yen in dollars, or $/¥, or what we called "E" in the PPP equation. Remember that "E" is the exchange rate expressed as units of home currency per unit of foreign currency. So "E" tells us the price of yen in dollars. The quantity in the market is the quantity of yen that are exchanged for dollars. So the vertical axis has the price of yen, and the horizontal axis has the quantity of yen. In the market for dollars in Japan, the relevant price is the price of dollars in yen, or ¥/$, or 1/E. The vertical axis shows the price of dollars, and the horizontal axis shows the quantity of dollars.

The supply and demand graphs for these markets are shown in Figure 6-3. The market for yen in the United States is originally in equilibrium at $¥1 = $0.01$ and at a quantity of yen equal to $Q_¥$*. The market for dollars in Japan is originally in equilibrium at $1 = ¥100$ and at a quantity of dollars equal to $Q_$$*. From these original equilibrium positions, suppose that there is an increase in the U.S. demand for Japanese MP3 players. This will cause an increase in the demand for yen in the U.S, and an increase in the supply of dollars in Japan.

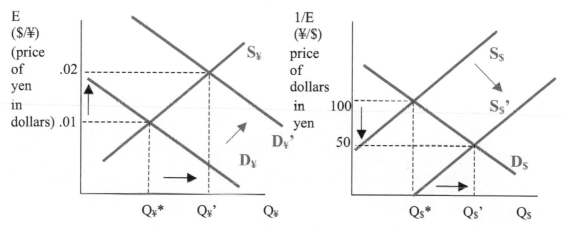

**Market for yen in the U.S.**   **Market for dollars in Japan**

Figure 6-3    Currency Markets in the U.S. and Japan

An increase in the U.S. demand for Japanese products will lead to an increase in the demand for yen in the United States. U.S. consumers will need yen to purchase Japanese products. As American consumers trade their dollars for yen, the supply of dollars will increase. The quantity of yen increases, as does the quantity of dollars exchanged. The yen appreciates as its value increases from $0.01 to $0.02. The dollar depreciates as its value declines from ¥100 to ¥50. As shown above, when the demand for a country's goods, services, or financial assets increases, the increase in the demand for that country's currency will cause the currency to appreciate. When the demand for Japanese products rises, the value of the yen will increase relative to other currencies.

## SUMMARY

In this section we have examined two models of exchange rate theory. The Purchasing Power Parity model helps to explain long-run movements in exchange rates over time. Exchange rates will adjust to bring parity to the prices of goods and services in different countries. Supply and demand analysis helps to explain minute-by-minute changes in exchange rates. As shown in media reports, exchange rates change momentarily in response to changes in supply and demand conditions in currency markets. Supply and demand analysis helps us to understand these frequent movements in the values of currencies.

# 7

# UNEMPLOYMENT AND INFLATION

Recall that the three macroeconomic goals for the federal government include maintaining a stable rate of output growth, high employment, and stable prices. Real GDP provides information about how well the government is meeting its goal of stable output growth. To determine how well the government is meeting its other two goals, we need different variables. The unemployment rate helps to measure if the government is meeting its employment goal, while the inflation rate provides information about the stability of prices in the economy. To monitor the economy properly, policy makers must have information about inflation and unemployment.

In this chapter, we will first examine unemployment. We explore how the unemployment rate is measured, problems with its measurement, the types of unemployment, and the costs of unemployment. Next, we turn to an examination of inflation. We discuss the characteristics of inflation, measuring inflation, types of inflation, the costs of inflation, and causes of inflation. When we finish this chapter, we will have covered the important economic variables except those related to monetary policy. We can then start to build models of the economy to show how these variables are related to each other, and how macroeconomic policy goals may be achieved through fiscal and monetary policies.

## UNEMPLOYMENT

In its most fundamental sense, unemployment is a lack of work. When people are unemployed, they are unable to obtain a job to earn the incomes to support themselves. Poverty, homelessness, and hunger result. There are high economic and social costs associated with high levels of unemployment, so there are important social, economic and political reasons to minimize the rate of unemployment. We start again with some definitions:

Labor markets: Markets where labor services are exchanged. Households supply labor services to earn incomes and firms demand labor services as a resource used in production.

Wage rate: The return to labor resources. The wage rate is the total compensation to labor, including wages, salaries, and fringe benefits. The *nominal wage rate* is the wage expressed in monetary units, such as the number of dollars paid per hour. The *real wage rate* is the nominal wage rate divided by the price level. It measures the purchasing power of a given wage rate, or how many goods and services can be purchased with a given wage.

wage = nominal wage rate
P = price level
W = real wage rate

where W = wage/P.

Real wages tell us the purchasing power of a given nominal wage. Real wages can be increasing because nominal wages are rising, or because the price level is falling. With inflation and constant nominal wages, real wages will fall.

## Measuring Unemployment

*The unemployment rate* is the percentage of those in the labor force who are actively seeking but not finding work. The unemployment rate is measured as:

$$\text{Unemployment rate} = \frac{\text{number of unemployed}}{\text{number in labor force}} \times 100$$

To accurately measure the rate of unemployment, we must have accurate counts of the number of unemployed and the number in the labor force. This is how each of these terms are defined:

Number of unemployed: Those in the labor force who are actively seeking but not finding jobs.

Number in labor force: Those in the population who are either employed or unemployed.

To be part of the labor force, an individual must be:

- over 16 years of age
- not a student or retiree
- not a household worker
- not institutionalized
- not in the military
- actively seeking employment or employed

The unemployment rate is measured as the percentage of all of those who meet these qualifications who are actively seeking work but that do not have a job. Discouraged workers, those who have given up looking for work, are not included as part of the labor force or among the unemployed. They are part of the population who are not considered as employed or unemployed.

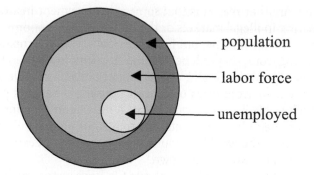

Figure 7-1   Measuring Unemployment

*Discouraged workers* are those in the population who have given up looking for work. Discouraged workers are not considered as part of the labor force, so discouraged workers are not counted as unemployed, even though they do not have jobs.

A schematic diagram of unemployment is shown in Figure 7-1. Out of the entire population, those who are younger than 16, retired, students, institutionalized, domestic workers, or in the military, or not actively seeking work, are the segment of the population not in the civilian labor force. Of the rest, the labor force is divided between the employed and the unemployed. The unemployment rate is the percentage of those in the labor force (not the entire population) who are actively seeking but not finding work.

## Is The Official Unemployment Rate an Accurate Measure of Actual Unemployment?

There are many reasons why the unemployment rate as measured by the Bureau of Labor Statistics may provide an inaccurate measure of the true rate of unemployment in the economy. First, there are several reasons why the official unemployment rate may underestimate the actual rate of unemployment. Discouraged workers are not included in the unemployment statistics even though they are without a job. Those who are underemployed, such as part-time workers or those working below their skill level, may be seeking a better job or more hours per week but are counted as employed as long as they have any hours of work that week. In April 2009, the official unemployment rate was 8.9%, the highest since 1983. If discouraged workers, marginal workers and part-time workers are included, the unemployment rate would have been 15.8% *(http://www.bls.gov/news.release/empsit.t12.htm)*. Also, a telephone survey is used to measure unemployment. The Current Population Survey of the Bureau of the Census chooses households to survey about unemployment and other characteristics for a six-month period. In the first month a survey researcher visits the household. In the next five months, a telephone survey is used. Those who are more likely to be unemployed, such as those without homes or telephones, are excluded from the survey sample. The sample is biased in that it excludes those most likely to be unemployed, and surveys those most likely to have jobs.

On the other hand, there are some reasons why the official unemployment rate may overestimate the actual rate of unemployment. People may cheat the system for their own advantage. There may be reported employment seeking. In most states, to collect unemployment a recipient must be actively seeking employment and prove it by filling a form listing the employers that were contacted for work. One can fill in the form fairly easily with friends and acquaintances without actually seeking work. If one is not actively seeking work, then by definition they are not unemployed, even though they may be collecting unemployment insurance and be counted as unemployed. Another reason is that some unemployment insurance recipients may be participating in illegal markets or the underground economy. They may have illegal jobs that provide income, but if they are collecting unemployment insurance or actively seeking work, they will be counted as unemployed even though they have an illegal source of income. Finally, workers may have an incentive to hide income from the government to avoid taxes or protect household benefits provided by the government such as Medicaid or food stamps. A union construction worker may be laid off and collect unemployment benefits through her union while performing odd jobs at the same time. She would be counted as unemployed even though she is able to find under-the-table work on her own.

So is the official unemployment rate too large or too small? While it is possible to make a case on either side, it is more likely that the official unemployment rate underestimates the actual rate of unemployment, or joblessness, in the economy. Since unemployment benefits are usually only available for twenty-six weeks, there is only a limited time where an individual can benefit from falsely claiming to be unemployed. So the effects that overestimate unemployment are likely to be short-lived. On the other hand, the effects that underestimate unemployment are much more permanent. People may be discouraged workers, underemployed, or homeless or phone-less for very long periods of time. It is likely that the unemployment numbers provided by the government are too small compared to actual joblessness in the economy.

## Types of Unemployment

Why do workers become separated from their jobs? What are the reasons for unemployment? Economists recognize four types of unemployment: frictional, structural, seasonal, and cyclical. The first three are due to natural changes in labor markets, technology, or climate, and are unavoidable and in some cases even desirable. The last type of unemployment, cyclical unemployment, is what economic policymakers try to minimize through fiscal and monetary policies.

*Frictional unemployment* occurs when workers are between jobs or are temporarily unemployed to have the time to find a better job. A college student may not take the first job offer she receives. It might be worthwhile to wait a few months to see if she can obtain a job that is a better match for her preferences. Someone might get sick of working for his boss and quit to find a more satisfying job or to start his own business. A waitress may obtain a nursing degree through night school and quit their waitress job to launch a nursing career. These are all examples of frictional unemployment. Note that frictional unemployment, in many instances, is actually desirable in that it means that the labor market is able to find a more efficient allocation, and workers end up with more satisfying and more productive jobs. Without frictional unemployment all workers would be stuck with their first jobs unless they could find different employment the next day, no matter how miserable those first jobs happened to be. Frictional unemployment, in the end, allows workers to be happier than they otherwise would be.

*Structural unemployment* is unemployment that results from technological change as some jobs become obsolete. As technology increases, old products are replaced with new products. Those who produce the old products lose their jobs. Until they can learn new skills or find a similar employer with a need for their old skills, they remain unemployed. For example, my grandfather was a telegraph operator (telegrapher) for the railroad. As telephones replaced telegraphs and as automobiles replaced passenger trains, he lost his job. Years later, I was hired by AT&T to train telephone operators who were losing their jobs to computers. They were being trained to take tests for other positions within the company.

With structural change, the job loss is permanent. The workers who lose their jobs to structural unemployment do not have the same jobs to go back to when the economy recovers. The factory disappears, or the skills that were once in demand become obsolete. Since globalization has resulted from technological change, especially the internet, then job losses due to outsourcing are a form of structural unemployment. But unless we want to live in a world without laptops and i-phones, then technological change, and the structural unemployment that goes with it, is inevitable.

*Seasonal unemployment* occurs due to changes in seasons throughout the year. In the northern climes of the United States, most ice cream stores close down for the winter or ski slopes are closed in the summer. Employees lose their jobs when their products or services are no longer needed for the season. Department stores only need Santa Clauses in the Christmas season or Easter Bunnies during Easter. In other times of the year these workers may go unemployed. Seasonal unemployment results from the natural change in seasons in many climates, and in this way it is unavoidable.

*Cyclical unemployment* is unemployment that results from the business cycle. The unemployment rate is countercyclical; it increases during recessions and declines during expansions of the economy. A factory or distributor may face a lack of orders due to a slowdown in economic conditions and be forced to lay off workers until business improves. The workers often receive "pink slips" which allow them to collect unemployment insurance benefits for the next two weeks. If the employer has more work, the workers are rehired. If not, the employer issues more pink slips and the workers continue to receive unemployment insurance benefits. Cyclical unemployment is temporary; the factories and shops still remain, and workers can return to their same jobs once economic conditions improve.

Note that of all the types of unemployment, the first three, frictional, structural, and seasonal, are unavoidable if not desirable. Our lives improve when we can seek better jobs, have technological change, or have changes in seasons. It is the last type of unemployment, cyclical, that policy makers try to minimize through fiscal and monetary policies. Cyclical unemployment is wasteful. The factories and stores are still

Unemployment Line in South Dakota, 2009
*http://www.southdakota.com/blog/wp-content/uploads/2009/02/ unemployment_line-2009.jpg*

there, but a lack of labor demand prevents these employees from being hired. By stabilizing the fluctuations of the business cycle, the government helps to minimize cyclical unemployment.

## Patterns of Unemployment in the United States

Figure 7-2 shows unemployment rates in the United States from 1948–2009. In April 2009, the unemployment rate was 8.9%. Unemployment rates have risen sharply in 2009 as a result of the growing recession. Unemployment rates tend to fluctuate with a regular pattern. During times of recession unemployment rates rise fairly dramatically. In times of economic expansion unemployment rates decline slowly. Each peak in the unemployment rate represents a recessionary period in U.S. economic history. Since 1948, the U.S. has suffered recessions in 1949, 1953, 1958, 1961, 1972, 1975, 1979, 1981–82, 1991, 2001, and 2008–09. Recessions were more frequent before 1982 than they have been since then.

Figure 7-3 shows patterns of unemployment in the United States according to race and ethnicity. African-Americans have the highest unemployment rates, followed by Hispanics, Whites, and recently, Asians. Since the U.S. Census Bureau began to classify Asians separately, that group has had some of the lowest unemployment rates. In 2006, the latest date on the chart, the rate for whites was 4% while the rate for African-Americans was almost 9%. African-Americans have over twice the unemployment rate of whites, and this has been consistent throughout time. Figure 7-3 implies that there is still significant discrimination in labor markets in the United States, although the gap has been narrowing slowly over time. This is reinforced in Table 7-1, which shows the unemployment rates for different demographic groups in April 2009.

As shown in Table 7-1, blacks continue to have about twice the rates of unemployment than whites. Recently, unemployment among men in general has been higher than that for women. Teens have higher rates of unemployment, with black teens having the highest rates of unemployment in the current recession at 34.7%.

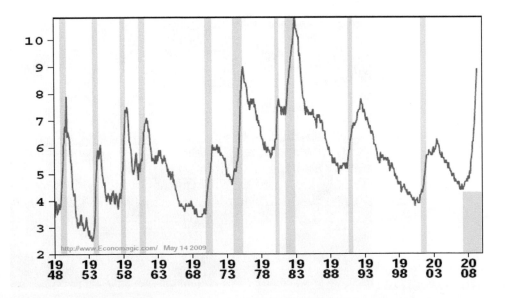

**Figure 7-2**  Unemployment Rates in the United States 1948–2009

Source: Bureau of Labor Statistics

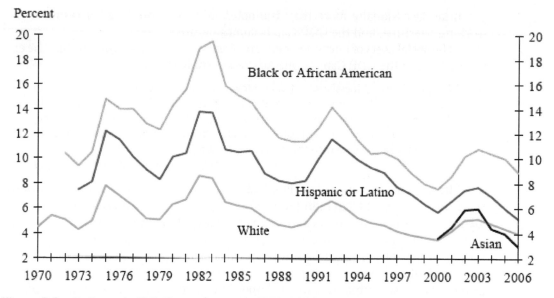

Percent

**Figure 7-3**  Patterns in U.S. Unemployment, 1970–2006

NOTE: Persons whose ethnicity is identified as Hispanic or Latino may be of any race. Data for Asians only available since 2000.

Source: Bureau of Labor Statistics

**Table 7-1**  Selected Unemployment Rates April 2009
(seasonally adjusted)

| | |
|---|---|
| White men | 8.5% |
| White women | 6.4% |
| White teens | 19.7% |
| Black men | 17.2% |
| Black women | 11.5% |
| Black teens | 34.7% |

Source: Bureau of Labor Statistics

## The Costs of Unemployment

The costs of unemployment can be divided into two broad categories, the economic costs and the social costs. The economic costs of unemployment result from the lost output that is not produced due to the idleness of workers. The social costs result from the loss of social identity and self-esteem that come from the loss of employment. If these costs were insignificant, there would be no reason for economic policy to concern itself with high rates of unemployment.

The economic costs of unemployment can be measured through a concept known as the GDP gap. The *GDP Gap* is the difference between potential real GDP and actual real GDP. It is the output lost as a result of cyclical unemployment in the economy.

GDP GAP = Potential Real GDP − Actual Real GDP

*Potential Real GDP (or Full Employment Real GDP)* is the quantity of output produced in the absence of cyclical unemployment, or the amount of real GDP produced when resources are fully employed and the economy is operating on the long-run Production Possibilities Curve. Usually the economy produces below or near its potential. Occasionally more than the potential can be produced if resources are working overtime, and the GDP Gap becomes negative.

The social costs of unemployment are often more damaging overall than the economic costs of the GDP Gap. As one Australian study states,

> The personal and social costs of unemployment include severe financial hardship and poverty, debt, homelessness and housing stress, family tensions and break-down, boredom, alienation, shame and stigma, increased social isolation, crime, erosion of confidence and self-esteem, the atrophying of work skills and ill-health. Most of these increase with the duration of unemployment.
>
> *http://www.bsl.org.au/pdfs/social.pdf*

In the United States, one should add drug and alcohol abuse to the list of the social ills that result from high levels of unemployment. In American society, one's identity is very often determined through occupation. When we describe a person, one of the first items we mention is what that person does for a living. When a person loses his job he also loses the social identity provided by that job. Without a social identity an individual's self-esteem may plummet. As a result, the individual may turn to drug or alcohol abuse, crime, suicide or domestic violence. Without a job a person has more time to use drugs or alcohol, and he does not have to worry about being hung over for work the next day. There is more time for criminal activities, and a person may be forced to resort to theft to support herself and her family. For various similar reasons, divorces and the break-up of families will increase. There are many social evils that result from high rates of unemployment. The government serves its citizens well by using its economic policy powers to establish and maintain low rates of unemployment through time.

In sum, there are two costs of unemployment, economic costs and social costs. While both are harmful, the social costs are probably more damaging to the country as a whole. While we can always produce more output in the future, it may be impossible to put back together a family that has fallen apart. Remember Humpty Dumpty:

> Humpty Dumpty sat on a wall,
> Humpty Dumpty had a great fall.
> All the King's horses, And all the King's men
> Couldn't put Humpty together again!

Once social stability is destroyed through high rates of unemployment, poverty, hunger, and homelessness, it may be difficult to reconstruct the social fabric that is lost.

The unemployment rate continues to be the most important economic variable in the U.S. political landscape. The recent increase in the rate of unemployment to 8.9% has been a topic in the media and a subject of Obama's press conferences. Politicians pay close attention to employment and unemployment, and like to take credit when unemployment rates are low. Another variable that politicians like to boast about is the inflation rate, especially when it is stable and low.

## BUSINESS CYCLES

As shown in Figure 7-2, unemployment rates tend to exhibit a regular pattern. Unemployment rates decline when the economy is expanding and increase when the economy is contracting. Unemployment rates are countercyclical—they move in the opposite direction of the business cycle.

*The business cycle* is the tendency of capitalist economies to exhibit regular patterns of expansion and contraction over time. During times of expansion, confi-

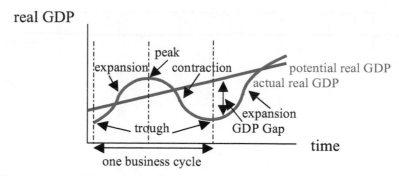

Figure 7-4   A Typical Business Cycle

dence about the future of the economy and growing incomes lead to increases in consumption and investment spending, which then lead to increases in real GDP. Eventually this confidence leads to increases in production beyond the capacity of spenders to purchase that output, and rising inventories cause output to decline. This is a typical cause of the booms and busts of the business cycle, including the current downturn in the economy which was largely caused by overproduction in housing markets.

Figure 7-4 shows a typical business cycle. Starting at a trough, increasing confidence and incomes lead to an increase in real GDP and an expansion of the economy. Eventually the economy reaches a peak, after which the economy experiences a contraction. After a point new economic opportunities may present themselves, especially due to changes in technology, and the cycle starts over again. As shown, actual real GDP tends to fluctuate around a trend level, or the potential or full employment GDP. During a recession or contraction of the economy, the GDP Gap is shown by the difference between actual real GDP and potential real GDP.

Starting at a trough, Figure 7-4 displays a typical business cycle. At first the economy expands, then reaches a peak, and then begins to contract again until it reaches the next trough. The time between one trough and the next (or one peak and the next) is one business cycle. In a recession actual GDP falls below potential GDP. The difference between potential and actual GDP is the GDP Gap.

Data for the U.S. economy from 1947–2009 is shown in Figure 7-5. Note that the actual GDP line tends to fluctuate around the trend of potential GDP as estimated by the Congressional Budget Office. In times of recession the GDP Gap grows.

## Predicting Business Cycles

As you may imagine, it would be lucrative to have the ability to predict changes in the business cycle, particularly being able to time the peaks and troughs of the business cycle. If you knew when the values of assets would be falling you could sell them before they lost their value. If you knew when the values of assets were rising you could purchase them and realize capital gains. For these reasons, a whole industry has evolved over forecasting changes in the business cycle. Three common tools for predicting business cycles include the Index of Leading Economic Indicators, consumer confidence, and unemployment rates.

The Index of Leading Economic Indicators is published by the Conference Board, a private economic research group. It consists of ten variables, such as building permits, durable goods orders and stock prices, that are thought to move ahead of

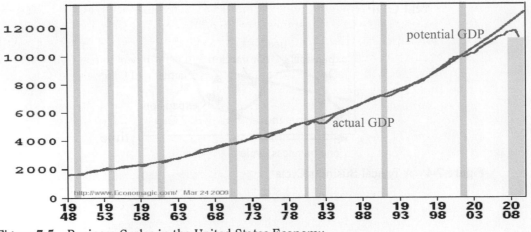

**Figure 7-5** Business Cycles in the United States Economy

Source: Economagic.com, Bureau of Economic Analysis, Congressional Budget Office

changes in the business cycle. The index works well in that it declines about six months before a recession begins. The problem is that it sometimes declines without a recession in the near future. A common quip is that the index has "predicted twelve of the last seven recessions." The index declines before a recession, but occasionally it declines without a recession.

Consumer Confidence Indices are also used to predict future movements in GDP. Since consumption spending makes up about two-thirds of GDP, changes in consumer expectations can have an effect on real GDP growth in the future. These indices are actually fairly accurate in predicting changes in GDP growth. The two most common indices of consumer confidence are published by the Conference Board and the University of Michigan.

Finally, as was shown earlier in the chapter, unemployment rates are counter-cyclical, as they move in the opposite direction of the business cycle. While unemployment rates are often thought to be a lagging variable, in times of contraction unemployment rates may be falling before a recession is officially declared. For example in 2008 unemployment rates were increasing, and non-farm payroll employment falling, throughout the year signaling that the economy was in recession, but the NBER did not officially declare the recession until December 2008 *(http://www .nber.org/cycles/dec2008.html)*. The declining labor market conditions throughout the year made it evident that the economy was in a recession long before the NBER made it official. The problem with using unemployment rates as a predictor of business cycles is that they often lag behind when the economy is expanding. Often GDP will be increasing before the economy sees significant declines in the unemployment rate. For example, Erica Groshen, an economist at the New York Fed, wrote and spoke of a "jobless recovery" after the 2001 recession where labor markets lagged behind the pace of expansion for the economy in general *(http://www.ny.frb.org/research/ current_issues/ci9-8/ci9-8.html)*. Unemployment rates are a better predictor of contractions than of expansions in the economy.

## INFLATION

The final economic variable we will examine for now is inflation. First, we will explore the characteristics of inflation. Second, we will look at the costs of inflation, both anticipated and unanticipated. Third, we look at the four primary ways that inflation is measured in the United States economy, the Consumer Price Index, the Producer Price Index, the Personal Consumption Expenditure Price Index, and the GDP Price Deflator. Finally, we examine the different types of inflation, and then introduce aggregate demand and aggregate supply analysis to explain the causes of inflation.

*Inflation* is a sustained increase in the average level of prices over time. Inflation occurs when the average level of prices are rising, but not necessarily all prices. We have had inflation throughout the 2000s even though the prices of laptop computers and clothing have been falling. Also, a rise in the price of a single item is not necessarily inflation. Inflation is a rise in the average of all prices over time, or aggregate prices, not just a single price.

If the price level is increasing, then the value of currency is falling. With an increase in the price level, each piece of currency can purchase less real goods or services than it could before. So another definition of inflation is as follows:

*Inflation* is a sustained decrease in the domestic value (or purchasing power) of currency over time. When prices rise, money is worth less. So inflation can be defined as either an increase in the price level, or a decrease in the value of money. They are two sides of the same coin.

For example, the most common measure of inflation is the Consumer Price Index, or CPI. Any price index uses a base year value of 100. For the CPI, the base year is 1982–1984, or actually right around July–August 1983. This is where the index is equal to 100. Some other values include:

CPI (Sept 1913) = 10
CPI (August 1983) = 100
CPI (March 2006) = 200
CPI (March 2009) = 212

What do these numbers mean? The CPI measures the average level of prices in the economy, using 1983 as the base year. In 1913 the CPI was 10, while in 2006 the CPI was 200. This means that prices increased by twenty times from 1913 to 2006. Put another way, the value of money fell by twenty times. What a nickel could purchase in 1913 would take a dollar to purchase in 2006. When prices increase by twenty times, the value of currency falls by twenty times.

*The inflation rate* is the percent increase in a price index from one period to another. For example, the current (March 2009) Consumer Price Index stands at 212. This means that prices have increased by 112% since the base year of 1983. Since a price index uses a base year value of 100, it is relatively easy to calculate percent changes from the base year. Remember that a percent change is given by the formula

$$\%\Delta CPI = \frac{CPI_1 - CPI_0}{CPI_0} \times 100 = \frac{CPI_1 - 100}{100} \times 100 = CPI_1 - 100$$

So for 2009, the percent change in the price level (or the inflation rate) from 1983 to 2009 is 212 − 100 = 112%. Prices have increased by 112% from the base year of 1983 to the most recent value of March 2009.

Inflation is an increase in the absolute level of prices in the economy, but not necessarily any change in relative prices. If all prices and wages increase by the same proportion, then relative prices and real wages will remain unchanged, so economic behavior may be little affected from inflation, especially if that inflation is anticipated. If workers know that prices will increase by 5% per year, they can make sure that nominal wages are increasing by 5% per year. In such a situation, real wages would remain unchanged from the beginning to the end of the year.

For a silly example, suppose that you go to bed one night and overnight an inflation fairy waves her magic wand and doubles all wages and prices. At first you earn

$20 an hour, apples cost $2 each and bananas cost $4 each. When you wake up the next day, you earn $40 an hour, apples cost $4 each, and bananas cost $8 each. Assuming apples and bananas are the only two goods, notice that nothing has really changed. Your real wage before is 20/2 = 10 apples or 20/4 = 5 bananas, and the relative price of apples is 2/4 = ½ of a banana. The next morning your real wage is 40/4 = 10 apples or 40/8 = 5 bananas, and the relative price of apples is still 4/8 = ½ of a banana. Real wages and relative prices have not changed, so there is no reason for economic behavior to change. You will work the same number of hours, and continue to purchase the same quantities of apples and bananas. Real variables have not changed. The only difference is you will have to carry twice the amount of currency to purchase the same quantities of apples and bananas.

Suppose instead that the inflation fairy still doubles prices and wages, but the doubling of prices is invisible to you. You recognize that nominal wages have doubled from $20 to $40, but the fairy is able to hide the doubling of prices from you. Suppose, for instance, that someone else in your family does the shopping, so you are not immediately aware of the price increase. In this situation, economic behavior may change. You are basing your decisions on nominal, or monetary, variables. Since you now believe you are earning more dollars per hour, you may decide to work more hours. Since you now believe that you have a higher nominal income, you may decide to purchase more apples and bananas before you learn about the price increases. In this case, you would be suffering from what is known as money illusion.

*Money illusion* occurs when economic decisions are based on nominal variables, not real variables. If labor supply decisions are based on monetary wages or purchases increase when nominal wages increase, then money illusion exists. If all decisions are based on real variables, then no money illusion exists. Decision makers would be aware of price level changes in the economy.

*Nominal variables* are measured in monetary units such as dollars or euros. In the example above, the nominal wage is $20 and the nominal price of apples is $2 each. These nominal wages and prices are expressed in dollars.

*Real variables* are measured in quantities of other goods or services. In the example above, the real wage is 10 apples and the real price of apples is ½ banana each. These wages and prices are expressed in quantities of other goods.

Overall, inflation does not have many economic effects as long as people are able to anticipate price increases in the economy. When inflation is unanticipated, however, it becomes much more costly to the economy. We will turn to an examination of the costs of these different types of inflation later in the chapter.

## Measuring Inflation

There are four primary ways of measuring inflation for the United States economy, the GDP Price Deflator, the Personal Consumption Expenditures (PCE) Price Index, the Consumer Price Index, and the Producer Price Index.

*The GDP Price Deflator (GDPPD)* is a price index that measures the prices of all goods and services included in Gross Domestic Product. It is calculated by the formula

$$\text{GDP Price Deflator}_t = (\text{Nominal GDP}_t \,/\, \text{Real GDP}_t) \times 100,$$

where t is the time of the year in question. The GDP Price Deflator (GDPPD) is a comprehensive price index, in that it includes the prices of all goods and services included in GDP. It is a flexible weight price index, since the weights attached to the categories of goods will fluctuate as consumption patterns in the economy change. Since GDP statistics will reflect changes in the composition of expenditures over time, the GDP Price Deflator will do the same. The quantities of goods and services included in the GDPPD fluctuate as consumer expenditures change. The GDPPD is issued by the Bureau of Economic Analysis, so it is a quarterly statistic.

*The Personal Consumption Expenditures (PCE) Price Index* is also measured by the Bureau of Economic Analysis. It measures the changes in the prices of personal consumption expenditures, the largest category of spending in GDP. Since the GPDPD is a flexible weight price index, so is the PCE Price Index. Since the PCE Price Index does not suffer from the substitution bias inherent in the Consumer Price Index (see below), it provides a more accurate measure of the changes in prices facing American consumers. For this reason, the PCE Price Index is the one most commonly used by the Federal Reserve to measure price changes in the economy.

*The Consumer Price Index (CPI)* measures the prices of a select bundle of 80,000 goods and services purchased by a typical urban household in the United States. The CPI is probably the most widely cited inflation statistic in the American media. It is a selective price index, in that it only measures goods or services purchased by urban households. It is a fixed weight price index, in that it measures the prices of the same bundle (or market basket) of goods or services over time. It will not adjust when consumers change their expenditure patterns. One way of thinking of the CPI is to imagine a shopping cart. The shopping cart consists of a select bundle of goods and services, and the CPI measures how the cost of this shopping cart changes over time. The problem is that the goods and services in the shopping cart stay the same over time, even though in the real world consumption patterns may change as relative prices change.

The CPI is like a shopping cart of goods and services.

Since the CPI does not adjust the bundle of goods and services included over time, it suffers from what is known as a *substitution bias*. It does not accurately reflect changes in consumption patterns when consumers switch away from products with increasing prices. For example, if the price of potatoes increases, consumers may purchase more rice. The Consumer Price Index will continue to attach the same weight to potatoes, even though consumers are now consuming fewer potatoes than before. In this way, the Consumer Price Index will overestimate the effects of inflation on consumer purchasing power. When the prices of some goods rise, consumers will consume less of those goods to mitigate the effects of inflation. Because it measures the prices of a fixed shopping cart of goods and services, the CPI will not reflect the changes in purchasing patterns the way that the GDP Price Deflator would. Since the CPI suffers from a substitution bias, it generally provides a higher estimate of inflation than the GDP Price Deflator. This is shown in Figure 7-4.

The CPI consists of eight categories, including food and beverages, housing, apparel, transportation, medical care, recreation, education and communication, and other (such as tobacco, haircuts and funerals). Each month, several hundred price checkers (Economic Assistants) visit various retail establishments, hospitals, and other institutions to report on prices charged for some of the 80,000 goods and services included in the CPI. The numbers are sent to Washington D.C. where statisticians collect the data from around the country. For each category, the weight assigned to price changes in that category depends on the percentage that that item made up in the consumer's budget based on a 2006 Consumer Expenditure Survey. For example, since food and beverages made up 15.7% of a consumer's budget in 2006, then changes in food and beverage prices are weighted as 15.7% of the CPI (*www.bls.gov*).

*The Producer Price Index* measures the prices received by producers in the economy for the goods and services for the economy as a whole and different commodities and industries. It is similar to the CPI except that it measures wholesale prices rather than retail prices. The PPI is measuring the first transaction involved for goods and many services produced in the economy. Since the PPI is measuring wholesale prices, it may often change ahead of CPI changes. If wholesale prices are rising, that is a good indication that retail prices will be rising in the near future. There are many types of Producer Price Indices that are measured for different commodities and industries in the United States economy. There are PPIs for commodities, such as finished goods, intermediate goods, passenger cars, and gasoline, and industries such as freight trucking, warehousing, electricity, groceries, and medical care. These separate indices help to measure price changes for particular sectors of the economy.

Both the PPI and CPI use a base year that is becoming dated. For the CPI, the base year is the average set of prices that existed between 1982 to1984. Actually, the CPI is equal to 100 right around July and August of 1983. For the PPI, the base year is 1982. Since the base year is so far away, the CPI has by now achieved a value greater than 200.

In general, a price index is given by the following formula:

$$\text{Price index} = \frac{\text{Cost of the market basket in the current year}}{\text{Cost of the market basket in the base year}} \times 100$$

In this way, a price index compares the prices over time for a fixed quantity of goods and services consumed. It shows how the cost of the shopping cart is changing over time. The inflation rate is just the percent change in the CPI from one period to another. In the base year, the price index is always equal to 100. As discussed earlier, this makes it easier to calculate percent changes from the base year. For example, the CPI for March 2009 is at 212. This means that prices have increased by 112% (212 – 100) from 1983 to March 2009.

Figure 7-6 shows the inflation rates in the U.S. economy from 1970–2009 as measured by both the GDP Price Deflator and Consumer Price Index. Generally, the two indices move together over time. The highest rates of inflation occurred in 1974–75 and 1979–80. These spikes were the results of the OPEC (Organization of Petroleum Exporting Countries) oil embargoes, when oil producers restricted supply to raise the price of oil. Since the mid 1980s, policy makers have done a much better job of stabilizing the inflation rate. The swings in the price level are much more subdued after 1992 compared to before that time, except for the most recent data shown where deflation is occurring for the first time since the Great Depression. Also note that for most periods, the CPI provides a higher estimate of inflation than the GDP Price Deflator. This is due to the substitution bias of the CPI.

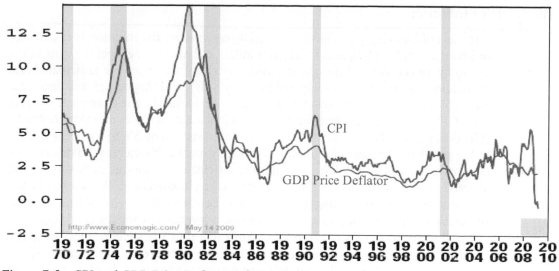

**Figure 7-6**    CPI and GDP Price Deflator Inflation Rates

Source: Economagic.com, Bureau of Labor Statistics, Bureau of Economic Analysis

## The Types of Inflation

Economists recognize four types of inflation or, more accurately, types of price changes in the economy. An economy may experience creeping inflation, hyperinflation, deflation, or disinflation.

*Creeping inflation* is a slow, steady increase in the price level over time. If inflation rates are slow and steady over time, then economic decision-makers can do a decent job in accurately predicting changes in the inflation rate over time. As shown above, most of the inflation in the United States since 1992 has been of this type.

*Hyperinflation* is an extremely large and dramatic increase in the price level that can occur over time. Currency rapidly loses its value as prices spiral out of control. With hyperinflation, the economy is disrupted as many economic resources are devoted to just keeping ahead of price changes in the economy. There are many famous examples of hyperinflation in the twentieth century, including Germany in the 1920s, Hungary in the 1940s, Chile and Zaire in the 1970s, Bolivia, Nicaragua and Argentina in the 1980s, Brazil and Yugoslavia in the 1990s, or Zimbabwe in the 2000s. Hyperinflations occur when governments recklessly print large amounts of money to fight wars or to pay their bills. The German experience with hyperinflation in 1923 is described in more detail below.

*Deflation* is the opposite of inflation. Deflation is a sustained decrease in the average level of prices over time. With deflation, the value or purchasing power of money is increasing. As described at the end of the chapter, deflation tends to be more socially and economically disruptive than inflations. The United States has not had any significant deflationary periods since the Great Depression, although the U.S. economy experienced a touch of deflation in the end of 2008.

*Disinflation* is a declining inflation rate. With disinflation, prices are still increasing, but they are increasing at a decreasing rate. The rate of inflation is slowing down. As shown in Figure 7-6, from 1980 to 1983 the rate of inflation declined from 14% to 2.5%, signifying a period of disinflation for the United States.

## The Costs of Inflation

The costs of inflation are different depending on whether the inflation is anticipated or unanticipated. Anticipated inflation is inflation that people expect to occur in the economy, so economic decisions are made taking into account the anticipated rate of inflation. Suppose that anticipated inflation is 5%, and that actual inflation actually is 5%, then not much has changed, as shown earlier in the chapter. If workers expect 5% inflation, they can demand 5% nominal wage increases in union contracts. If lenders expect 5% inflation, they can raise interest rates by 5% to cover the decline in the purchasing power of money. If landlords expect a 5% increase in prices, they can increase rents by 5%. When inflation is anticipated, economic decisions are not affected as long as the correct inflation rate is taken into account. Workers will work the same hours since real wages are the same. Lenders will provide the same quantity of loans when they can raise interest rates to compensate for the declining value of the loan payments they receive. Landlords will rent the same number of apartments if the purchasing power of their rental payments remains the same. When inflation can be anticipated accurately, the increase in the price level does not pose significant costs on the economy.

If inflation is unanticipated, on the other hand, it is much more costly to the economy. Economic decisions would have been made assuming a different rate of inflation. If the price increase is higher than expected, then workers, lenders and landlords will not earn as much as they anticipated, and may decide to supply less of their products or services.

*The costs of anticipated inflation* include menu costs, shoe leather costs, and increased uncertainty about future relative prices.

1. *Menu costs* are the costs of having to physically change prices as a result of inflation. Restaurants will have to print menus more often to reflect the higher prices of their meals. Gas stations will have to change their signs more often to inform their customers of the higher prices. Supermarkets will have to change their price signs and prices in the checkout scanners more often. In the late 1970s, when inflation rates were over 14% and price tags were still used to inform consumers and cashiers of the price of merchandise, there would often be a pile of five or six price tags on each can on the supermarket shelves. As prices rose, store clerks would have to put new price tags on the same cans over and over again. Menu costs also occur with deflations.

2. *Shoe leather costs* are the costs of resources devoted to keeping ahead of price changes in the economy. If consumers know that prices are rising rapidly, they will make efforts to go shopping more frequently so that they can make their purchases before prices are even higher. Drivers may go to the gas station once every week instead of every two weeks to get their gasoline before it costs more. Households may decide to keep more of their money in interest-bearing accounts at banks and then have to visit the banks or ATMs more often to access their cash for transaction purposes. When people have to go shopping or to the bank more often to keep ahead of price changes, they will wear out their shoes more quickly, hence the name of "shoe leather" costs.

3. *Increased uncertainty:* Even if households and firms know the rate of increase in the average level of prices, they will not necessarily

know the rate of change of relative prices. For consumers, food or housing prices may be rising more quickly than other prices in the economy. Even if real wages are constant, it may become more difficult to purchase the necessities of life if these prices are rising more quickly than average. For firms, it may be difficult to predict future profits even if the inflation rate is known. If the firm's product prices are rising more quickly than its resource prices, then revenues will be increasing more quickly than costs and profits will be rising. On the other hand, if the firm's revenue from its products is growing less quickly than its costs of production, then profits will be declining. With inflation, it becomes more difficult to determine if profits will be rising or falling.

One extreme example of shoe leather costs occurred in Germany in 1923 after World War I. As part of the settlement of the Treaty of Versailles ending the war, the German government was required to make war reparation payments to Britain and France for the bridges, roads, homes and factories that were destroyed by German attacks. In order to make these payments, the German government just printed more currency, marks, rather than trying to earn the currency through foreign exchange, issuing bonds or raising taxes. As a result, the German economy suffered from a severe hyperinflation. By the summer of 1923, prices in Germany were increasing at a rate of over 1000% per month. Prices were doubling every 49 hours. As shown below in Figure 7-7, the value of the dollar rose from 64 marks per dollar in 1919 to 4.2 trillion marks per dollar in 1923.

*The Economist* magazine describes the costs that were imposed by the hyperinflation.

> "For these ten marks I sold my virtue," were the words a Berliner noticed written on a banknote in 1923. He was buying a box of matches, all the note was worth by then. That was in the early days. By November 5th, a loaf of bread cost 140 billion marks. Workers were paid twice a day, and given half-hour breaks to rush to the shops with their satchels, suitcases or wheelbarrow, to buy something,

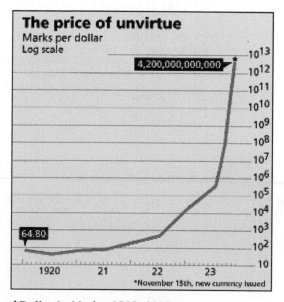

Figure 7-7   Value of Dollar in Marks, 1919–1923

Source: *http://www.economist.com/diversions/millennium/displayStory.cfm?Story_ID=347363*

anything, before their paper money halved in value yet again. By mid-November, when a new currency was issued, prices had added twelve noughts [zeros] since the first world war began in 1914. Currencies have collapsed, and inflation turned hyper- in other places: in Shanghai awaiting Maoist takeover in 1949, in Argentina in 1989, when, in July alone, prices rose 197%. But Germany's was the most spectacular bout of inflation ever to hit an advanced economy; and none has had more awful results. It was not the main reason for Hitler's rise, but it was as the leader of a failed mini-coup during the crisis that most Germans first heard of him. And the anger of those who had lost their all fed Nazism's growth.

*(http://www.economist.com/diversions/millennium/displayStory.cfm?
Story_ID=347363)*

German postage stamps, 1921–1923. Each stamp is worth ten times the value of the stamp to its left.

Source: *http://ingrimayne.com/econ/EconomicCatastrophe/HyperInflation.html*

Fifty million mark banknote, Germany, September 1923

Source: *http://www.missouriwestern.edu/orgs/germanclub/inflation2.html*

Zimbabwe 100 trillion dollar note, 2008

German children using marks as building blocks, 1923

German woman burning marks as fuel. It was cheaper to burn marks than to use them to buy firewood.

Source: *http://www.schoolhistory.co.uk/studentforum/lofiversion/index.php/t2139.html*

As German consumers would go shopping two or three times a day to keep ahead of price changes before their currency became even more worthless, the shoe leather costs involved were extreme. People would literally wear out the bottom of their shoes more quickly. Even though the dramatic price increases were widely anticipated after a few months of hyperinflation, the resources devoted to surviving amid such chaos led to significant disruptions in social, economic, and civic life.

*The costs of unanticipated inflation:* Compared to price rises that people expect to occur, the costs of unanticipated inflation can be much more severe. Recall that inflation can also be viewed as a decline in the domestic purchasing power of currency. With unanticipated inflation, fixed payments received from debt or rental contracts will be declining in purchasing power over time. For this reason, unanticipated inflation harms disproportionately those who receive fixed payments from an asset, such as savers, lenders, pension or trust beneficiaries, and landlords. Conversely, it helps spenders, borrowers, those who own assets whose prices are rising most rapidly, and tenants. We will explore why below.

Unanticipated inflation harms savers because the purchasing power of both their savings, and the interest earned on those savings, will be declining. Savers will end up with less purchasing power than they originally expected. For similar reasons, lenders are harmed by unanticipated inflation. They are being paid back in currency that is worth decreasingly less than the currency that they lent out. In order to take these effects into consideration, economists often distinguish between nominal interest rates and real interest rates. Real interest rates take into account the effects of inflation, and nominal interest rates, which are the interest rates stated by banks in their windows and on loan contracts, do not.

*Nominal interest rates (i):* the interest rates posted in bank windows; the named or stated interest rate charged for a loan. The effects of inflation in reducing purchasing power are not taken into account in nominal interest rates.

*Real interest rates (r):* interest rates that take into account the effects of inflation in reducing the amount actually earned.

*Inflation rate (Π):* the percentage increase in the average price level

The relationship between nominal and real interest rates can be given by a simple approximation, known as the Fisher formula, named for a famous American economist Irving Fisher. The Fisher equation is:

$$i = r + \Pi, \quad \text{or} \quad r = i - \Pi.$$

The nominal interest rate is equal to the real interest rate plus the rate of inflation. Given a nominal interest rate, as the rate of actual inflation increases, the real interest earned will decrease. If a lender ends up with inflation that is higher than expected, then the real interest earned on a loan will be less than expected. In this way, unanticipated inflation harms lenders.

For example, suppose that you lend $100 for one year at a 10% (0.10) interest rate. The amount you will receive in one year is equal to

$$\text{LOAN} \times (1 + i) = 100 \times (1 + 0.1) = \$110.$$

If there is no inflation, then the real interest earned on the loan is 10%. The money you receive next year has a purchasing power that is 10% greater than the money you lent out. But if there is inflation, the real interest earned on the loan will be reduced. At an extreme, assume that the rate of inflation is greater than the nominal interest rate. Then real interest rates would be negative, and you as the lender are actually worse off from having made the loan. From the Fisher equation,

$$r = i - \Pi = 10\% - 15\% = -5\%.$$

The loan would provide you a real interest rate of –5%, so you're losing money from the loan.

More accurately, the inflation will reduce the purchasing power of the $110 payment you receive next year. To calculate the purchasing power (or present value) today of the loan payment received in one year, we must discount the future payment received by the rate of inflation that is reducing the purchasing power of money in that year. For example, with an inflation rate of 0%, the present value today of the loan payment received in one year would be $110. If prices doubled (a 100% inflation rate), then the purchasing power of money in one year would only be half of that today, so the present value today of the $110 payment next year would be only $55. The dollars received next year would be worth only half of the dollars this year. If the inflation rate was 50%, then the $110 payment next year would be worth $73.33. In each case, the value today of the payment received in one year is

If Π = 0%, then the loan is worth $110/(1 + 0) = $110 today.
If Π = 100%, then the loan is worth $110/(1 + 1) = $55 today.
If Π = 50%, then the loan is worth $110/(1 + .5) = $73.33 today.

In general, the present value today of a loan payment received in one year is equal to

$$\text{PV} = \text{LOAN} \times (1 + i) / (1 + \Pi).$$

So in the example above, the value today of the $110 payment next year, if the inflation rate is 15%, would be

$$\text{PV} = \$100 \times (1 + 0.1) / (1 + 0.15) = \$95.65.$$

So again, you are worse off for having made this loan. You lend out an amount of money with a purchasing power of $100, but next year you receive a payment that is only worth $95.65 of today's goods and services. Unanticipated inflation reduces the value of wealth for lenders and savers.

As implied above, the Fisher equation is actually only an approximation. The real interest rate you earned was –5%, but the purchasing power of your money was $95.65, a little more than the –5% in real interest. The actual formula is a bit more involved.

Let's say you lend $X for one year. In terms of real interest, you will have X(1 + r) in purchasing power next year. In terms of nominal interest rates, you will earn $X(1 + i), but that amount will be reduced by inflation because nominal interest rates do not take into account the effects of inflation. The value in nominal terms is $X(1 + i)/(1 + \Pi)$.

So

$$\$X(1 + i)/(1 + \Pi) = \$X(1 + r)$$
$$(1 + i)/(1 + \Pi) = (1 + r)$$
$$1 + i = (1 + r)(1 + \Pi) = 1 + r + \Pi + r\Pi$$

so

$$i = r + \Pi + r\Pi \approx r + \Pi$$

since $r\Pi$ is the product of two decimals and is usually a small number.

Note that if inflation is greater than nominal interest rates, then real interest rates may actually be negative. Increases in inflation cause declines in real interest for any given nominal interest rate. Unanticipated inflation harms savers and lenders.

Two other groups that are harmed by unanticipated inflation are those who receive fixed incomes, and those who receive payments from fixed-price contracts (payees) such as landlords. If one receives fixed payments, the purchasing power of those payments will be declining over time. Elderly widows may be living off of a fixed pension or a young socialite may be living off of his uncle's trust fund. If the payments they receive are fixed, inflation means that they will see their constant nominal incomes able to buy less and less real goods and services.

For equivalent reasons, the opposite groups will benefit from unanticipated inflation. Spenders will not have any savings to have falling in value, and they will have spent their money at a time when they could take advantage of lower prices. Borrowers will gain since the real value of their loan payments will be declining, and represent less and less of a sacrifice of real goods and services. Those who own assets that are increasing in value more rapidly than other goods will also benefit. If the price of gold, art or real estate is growing more rapidly than the average rate of inflation, those who own these assets will benefit. Finally, tenants will benefit since the purchasing power of their fixed rental payments will be declining over time.

## The Causes of Inflation

From a macroeconomic perspective, there are two reasons why inflation may occur in the economy. First, inflation may occur because spending in the economy is increasing more quickly than output. This is known as demand-pull inflation. Demand-pull inflation results from increases in aggregate demand in the economy. Second, inflation may occur because of an increase in resource prices in the economy, which are passed on in the form of higher prices. This leads to a decrease in aggregate supply in the economy. To examine the causes of inflation, we must first take a detour through a brief introduction to aggregate demand and aggregate supply analysis.

*Demand-pull inflation* is inflation caused by an increase in aggregate demand.

*Cost-push inflation* is inflation caused by a decrease in aggregate supply.

*Aggregate Demand* is a model that shows the quantities of real GDP that spenders in the economy are willing and able to purchase at different price levels. The aggregate demand curve shows the amount of desired spending at different price levels. The aggregate demand curve is downward-sloping, since desired spending will increase as the price level declines.

*Aggregate Supply* is a model that shows the quantities of real GDP that firms and workers are willing and able to produce at different price levels. It shows desired output at different price levels. The ordinary aggregate supply curve is upward-sloping, since firms and workers will be willing and able to produce more as the price level increases.

In the aggregate demand/aggregate supply model, the equilibrium for the economy occurs at the intersection of the aggregate demand and aggregate supply curves. The model is similar, though not identical to, the supply and demand analysis we used for markets earlier in Chapters 3 and 4.

The different types of inflation can be depicted in Figure 7-8:

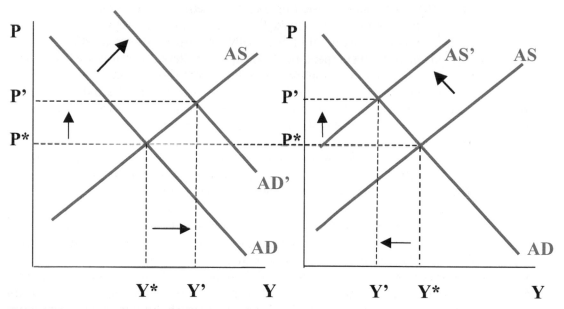

Figure 7-8   Demand-Pull Inflation and Cost-Push Inflation

where Y = real GDP and P = Price Level. With demand-pull inflation, the increase in aggregate demand causes an increase in the price level. With cost-push inflation, the decrease in aggregate supply causes an increase in the price level. In either case, the increase in the price level means that inflation exists in the economy. Much more will be said about aggregate demand and aggregate supply in Chapter 10.

## The Special Problem of Deflation

Deflation is a sustained decrease in the average level of prices over time. With deflation, the purchasing power of money increases. Those with money will find that the value of their wealth is increasing. Those with debts or other fixed payments to make will find the value of those payments increasing over time. Debts and bills become more and more difficult to pay. The situation of deflation is the opposite of inflation. Savers, lenders, those who receive fixed incomes, and payees of fixed-price contracts will benefit from unanticipated deflation. The purchasing power of the payments received will be increasing over time. Those who are spenders, borrowers, who own resources whose prices are declining the most, or are payers of fixed-price contracts, will see the value of their payments increasing over time. Greater and greater sacrifices will be made to make these fixed payments. In general, deflationary periods have been much more socially disruptive than times of inflation.

There are several reasons why deflations tend to wreak havoc from a social perspective. The prices of goods and services represent income to those who are producing those goods and services. The price of corn is income to a corn farmer, the price of babysitting services is income to babysitters. When prices fall, incomes fall. Those who have to rely on these incomes to pay their bills will find it more and more difficult to make these payments. They will have to sell more and more goods and services to receive the same nominal income to pay their bills. Life becomes more and more difficult for those who were already struggling to get by.

A second reason that deflation is harmful to the poor is that the purchasing power of the fixed payments they have to make will be increasing. Bills for mortgages, rent, car loans, or taxes will become more and more difficult to pay as the value of the payments increase. Borrowers and tenants have to sacrifice more and more real goods and services to make their fixed nominal bill payments.

A third reason that deflation is socially disruptive is due to its effects on consumption and investment spending. If consumers believe that prices are falling, they may postpone current consumption to wait for prices to be lower in the future. As consumption spending is delayed, firms will suffer a reduction in sales and may begin to lay off workers as inventories in the economy increase. The increase in layoffs will increase the unemployment rate, and the reduction in income will cause a reduction in the demand for products and further price declines throughout the economy. This series of events occurred in the United States during the Great Depression and in Japan from 1999–2005 *(http://www.stat.go.jp/english/data/cpi/zuhyou/1581h6.xls)*. Deflations can exacerbate the effects of an otherwise mild recession.

Notice that in general, unanticipated inflation tends to harm those with wealth or the upper-income households in the economy. If inflation reduces the purchasing power of money, those with money are the ones who are harmed the most. Savers, lenders, and landlords tend to be those with wealth in the economy. They are harmed when prices rise more than anticipated. Deflation, on the other hand, harms those without wealth, those who spend all their money, are borrowers, or tenants. If the value of money is increasing, it becomes harder to pay bills for those without money. When the Federal Reserve uses monetary policy to fight inflation, it is essentially protecting the interests of the wealthy in the U.S. economy.

*Shay's Rebellion:* An important event in the development of the U.S. Constitution. Daniel Shay was a farmer in Western Massachusetts during the 1780s. A significant period of deflation occurred in the newly formed United States during the period after the Revolutionary War from 1783–1786. (See, for example, Woody Holton, *Unruly Americans,* Hill and Wang, 2007.)

As the Loyalists, or "Tories," of the American Revolution left the United States to return to England after their side had lost the Revolution, they took much of the country's gold supply with them. Since Massachusetts lacked paper currency at the time, the decline in the gold supply led to lower prices as there was not enough money in circulation. As the supply of money fell, there was less spending that could occur and prices fell due to the lack of consumer demand. As prices fell, the incomes of farmers in Western Massachusetts declined. Most farmers in the area grew corn and then distilled the corn into whiskey. As the prices of corn and whiskey declined, farmers had harder times meeting their debt and tax obligations. By August 1786 foreclosures on farms in the area had become rampant, and farmers formed a militia

**Shay's Rebellion, January 1787**
Source: *www.constitutioncenter.org*

to disrupt the court proceedings so that their farms could be saved. Throughout the rest of 1786 and into 1787 the rebellion continued, and by early 1787 the Continental Congress decided to send troops to put down the rebellion. The rebellion was on the minds of many delegates to the Constitutional Convention in Philadelphia that summer, and buttressed the arguments for the need for a strong central government provided by the U.S. Constitution.

In fact, several of the provisions of the Constitution indirectly refer to the problems posed by Shay's Rebellion. In the Preamble there is the phrase "to insure domestic tranquility," which makes it sound like the Constitution will provide a world where the sun is streaming through the trees and the birds are chirping. But what the phrase really means is the ability to put down riots and rebellions. Article I, Section 4 includes the "Full Faith and Credit" clause:

> *Full Faith and Credit* shall be given in each State to the public Acts, Records, and judicial Proceedings of every other State. And the Congress may by general Laws prescribe the Manner in which such Acts, Records and Proceedings shall be proved, and the Effect thereof.

In part, these words mean that a debtor cannot escape his debts by moving from one state to another. The courts of one state are obligated to honor the debt contracts made in another state.

The development of our Constitution was greatly influenced by Shay's Rebellion, which was a result of high rates of deflation in the U.S. economy after the Revolutionary War. The rise of Hitler in Germany was at least partially caused by the hyperinflation in the German economy after World War I. These examples show that price changes are not innocuous; they can have profound effects on the history of a society. Everything from the development of the U.S. Constitution to the rise of Hitler can be at least partially attributed to price changes in those economies.

# 8

## THE CLASSICAL MODEL

In the next three chapters, we explore the various models of macroeconomics. These models are attempts to explain the ways in which macroeconomic variables are related to each other. In the last few chapters, we learned about GDP, the balance of payments, exchange rates, unemployment, business cycles, and inflation. Now we turn our attention to the ways that these variables influence each other and ultimately determine our standard of living.

### MACROECONOMIC MODELS

We will focus on three major macroeconomic models:

1. The classical model
2. The fixed-price Keynesian model
3. The aggregate demand/aggregate supply model.

*The classical model* is a model based on the writings of classical economists from Adam Smith to the Great Depression. It provides a model of a self-adjusting economy with markets that are flexible enough to keep the economy at full employment. Since the economy can solve its own problems, there is little role for government to play in the economy. Generally, classical economists believed that government intervention would only make the situation worse.

*The Keynesian model* is based on the writings of a British economist, John Maynard Keynes, especially his monumental work *The General Theory* in 1936. The book criticized the ability of the classical model to explain or cure the Great Depression, and offered in its place a model where markets may be unable to reach equilibrium for significant periods of time. One model we will examine is known as the fixed-price Keynesian model, which assumes that prices, wages, and interest rates are fixed, so that markets will not always "clear" or reach equilibrium. Keynes believed that government should play a more active role in assuring a stable and productive economy.

*The aggregate demand/aggregate supply model* is a model where the price level adjusts until desired spending is equal to desired output. The aggregate demand curve shows the amount of desired spending in the economy at different price levels. The aggregate supply curve shows the quantity of output that firms and workers are willing and able to produce at different price levels. The aggregate demand/aggregate supply model is a more modern model in macroeconomics, and it has many variants. We will study two different types of aggregate demand curves, one classical, one Keynesian. We will also explore five different types of aggregate supply curves.

The assumptions and results of these models differ in many ways. First, they differ in terms of the flexibility of prices, wages, and interest rates. Classical economists believed that wages, prices, and interest rates are fully flexible, so that markets are always in equilibrium. In the Keynesian model, prices, wages or interest rates may be rigid so that markets may not always be in equilibrium. The models also differ in terms of their time frame. The classical model is better at explaining long-run growth, while the Keynesian model is more appropriate for understanding short-run fluctuations in the economy. We will also analyze several models of aggregate demand and aggregate supply, which represent more modern treatments of modeling the behavior of the macroeconomy, somewhere in between the extremes of the classical and Keynesian models.

## COMPARING THE CLASSICAL AND KEYNESIAN MODELS: LABOR MARKETS

In the classical model it is assumed that markets always clear. In the labor market, real wages are flexible enough so that the market is always in equilibrium. If the quantity of labor demanded is always equal to the quantity of labor supplied, then there is no involuntary unemployment. In this model, anyone looking for a job is able to find one.

Keynes, on the other hand, recognized that wages may be sticky, so that involuntary unemployment may result. If wages cannot fall to their equilibrium, a surplus in the labor market, or involuntary unemployment, may result. In the classical model, an increase in labor supply will not result in unemployment. Wages will fall to bring the market back to equilibrium. In the Keynesian model, an increase in labor supply may increase unemployment if wages are inflexible. Figure 8-1 shows these differences graphically.

## THE CLASSICAL MODEL

As mentioned earlier, the classical model is an amalgamation of the writings of many different economists who wrote and spoke before the Great Depression. The graphical tools that we have used throughout this text were not available to most of the economists, so what is covered here is a more modern graphical treatment of the writings of several prominent economic thinkers throughout the two centuries before the 1930s. A version of this model also saw a resurgence in the 1980s in the form of Reaganomics or supply-side economics. The common themes throughout have been the efficacy of free markets and the harm of government intervention in the economy. The classical model relies on the methods and theories of microeconomics. In fact, before Keynes there was no distinction between microeconomics and macroeconomics. It was believed that the models of microeconomics were equally appropriate

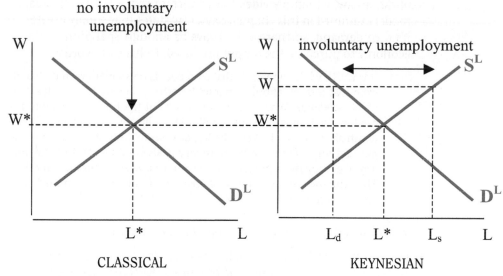

Figure 8-1   Classical and Keynesian Labor Markets

to the economy as a whole. Before the 1880s, there were few separations between political science and economics. Most colleges and universities had departments of moral science or moral philosophy, and then political economy. With specialization in society in general there was also specialization in academia. First political economy separated into distinct departments of political science and economics, and later economics separated into macroeconomics and microeconomics. During the time of classical economists there were no such distinctions.

## CLASSICAL ECONOMISTS

Some of the most famous and influential classical economists include:

- Adam Smith (1723–1790, Scotland)—is known as the founder of economics. He is best known for his work *The Wealth of Nations* (1776). As discussed in Chapter Four, Smith is famous for his ideas of self-interest, the invisible hand of the market system, specialization and the division of labor. He developed the idea of absolute advantage in his example of the butcher, brewer and baker.

- Thomas Malthus (1766–1834, England)—In his *An Essay on the Principle of Population,* published in 1798, Malthus argued that the global population would grow more quickly than the food supply, so the plight of the masses could not be improved and the world would face increasing famine and disease if population growth was unchecked. Obviously, Malthus underestimated the ability of technology to increase the food supply.

- Jean-Baptiste Say (1767–1832, France)—Jean-Baptiste Say was a French historian and economist who was a precursor to the ideas of supply and demand analysis. While Ricardo believed that value was created through production, Say believed that the demand side of the market would also influence the value of a good. He was one of the first to include entrepreneurship as a fourth factor of production. In his *Treatise on Political Economy* (1803) he introduced the idea of Say's Law, which provides the underpinnings for the classical model examined in this chapter. Say's Law states that supply creates its own demand, so there will always be enough spending in the economy to purchase the output produced. In his own words:

> It is worth while to remark, that a product is no sooner created, than it, from that instant, affords a market for other products to the full extent of its own value. When the producer has put the finishing hand to his product, he is most anxious to sell it immediately, lest its value should diminish in his hands. Nor is he less anxious to dispose of the money he may get for it; for the value of money is also perishable. But the only way of getting rid of money is in the purchase of some product or other. Thus the mere circumstance of creation of one product immediately opens a vent for other products. (J. B. Say, 1803: p. 138–9)

We will spend more time discussing Say's Law later in the chapter.

- David Ricardo (1772–1823, England)—Ricardo's landmark text *Principles of Political Economy and Taxation* (1817) provides much of the basis for classical economics. Here he discusses such concepts as the labor theory of value, the law of diminishing returns, and comparative advantage, expanding on Smith's idea of absolute advantage. Ricardo is also known for the concept of Ricardian equivalence, that financing government spending either through taxation or bonds will have the same effects on the economy.

- Karl Marx (1818–1883, Germany)—is probably one of the most influential philosophers of the last three centuries. Social scientists do not discuss Smithian ideology or Ricardian ideology in the way they mention Marxist ideology. A whole political and economic system in the 20th century known as Communism sprang from the writings of this one man. Though Marx reached much different results than other classical economists, he started with basically the same assumptions as others such as the labor theory of value. Indeed, Marx believed that all of world history was a product of human labor effort. In his famous two-volume work *Das Kapital* (1867, 1871), Marx argued that capitalism consisted of the bourgeoisie, or the owners of capital, and the proletariat, or the workers who supplied their labor effort to that capital. Capital has a vested interest in keeping wages low, and controls the state so that it can keep wages at a subsistence level. The "reserve army of the unemployed" will provide an easy supply of surplus labor to help keep wages low. The idea that wages are flexible is important to the model developed in this chapter. Unlike other classical economists, Marx believed that capitalism contained the seeds of its own destruction. Eventually the proletariat will rebel against its abject poverty and overthrow the bourgeoisie to control the means of production, and the communist system that resulted would, over time, eliminate private property and the state itself.

- John Stuart Mill (1806–1873, England)—was the son of another famous philosopher, the utilitarian James Mill. James Mill was a supporter of Jeremy Bentham, who believed that the purpose of government was utilitarianism, or to provide "the greatest happiness for the greatest number." James Mill was also a contemporary of David Ricardo. John Stuart Mill was raised by a strict father to be an outstanding intellectual, learning Greek at age three and Latin by age eight. At first he was under the tutelage of Bentham but later broke with his utilitarian ideas. John Stuart Mill is best known for his works *Principles of Political Economy* (1848), where he refines Ricardo's theory of value into the rudiments of modern price theory, and expanded on his ideas of comparative advantage and international trade, and *On Liberty* (1859) where he argued that government should maximize individual liberty rather than maximizing utility. His *Principles of Political Economy* remained a standard textbook in Britain until it was replaced by Alfred Marshall's *Principles of Economics* in 1890.

*http://www.iep.utm.edu/m/milljs.htm#SH2g*

- Leon Walras (1834–1910, France)—was one of the leaders of the Marginalist Revolution and the founder of general equilibrium theory. Marginalism is the idea that economic decisions must be examined in terms of the margin, or the additional costs and benefits rather than the total costs and benefits. This focus on the margin became known as the neoclassical school of economics, and provided the foundation for modern economics and supply and demand analysis. In his *Elements of Pure Economics* (1874), Walras was the first to introduce a mathematical, multi-market model of general equilibrium theory. He also explored ideas of subjective value theory and imperfect competition and monopoly.

- Francis Edgeworth (1845–1926, Ireland)—pioneered the use of mathematic models in economics to show that exchange improves welfare. He introduced the concepts of utility and indifference curve analysis in *Mathematical Physics* (1881).

- Vilfredo Pareto (1848–1923, Italy)—was the successor to Walras at the University of Lausanne. He extended the ideas of general equilibrium theory and was a supporter of free trade in the debates of his day. In his *Manual of Political Economy* (1906), he presented the models of economics in mathematical form and extended the ideas of indifference curves to what is now known as the Edgeworth Box. He is immortalized in the concept of Pareto optimality, a situation where one individual or group cannot be made better off without making someone else worse off. If a policy change or trade can improve one person's situation without harming others, then it is a Pareto-improving change or trade and should be carried out.

- Alfred Marshall (1842–1924, England)—was the leader of British economics in the early twentieth century and the founder of the Cambridge school of economic thought. His *Principles of Economics* (1890) was the dominant economics textbook throughout his lifetime and beyond. In the text, Marshall advanced the mathematics of marginal analysis and introduced the model of supply and demand analysis. Two of his more famous students were A. C. Pigou and John Maynard Keynes.

- Arthur Cecil Pigou (1877–1959, England) – inherited the Cambridge tradition from Alfred Marshall, which had by then become known as the "Cambridge neoclassicals." In his *Wealth and Welfare* (1912), he pioneered the inclusion of social welfare concepts into economic analysis and introduced the idea of market failure, or that social costs may differ from private costs of production or consumption. He believed that in the presence of negative externalities such as pollution, government taxation may be an appropriate public remedy.

*http://www.economyprofessor.com/theorists*

This is necessarily an incomplete list of influential economists during this period from 1776–1912, but the list provides a glimpse into the thinking of these pioneers in economics. The model called the "classical model" here is a synthesis of these verbal and mathematical models, even though many of these economists lacked graphs to illustrate their arguments. Some of the later models were also known as neoclassical economics at the time. We will examine a more modern graphical treatment of the combined thinking of these early classical economic theorists.

We will start by describing the assumptions of the classical model, and then we will show the graphs that can be derived from those assumptions. The classical model is divided into three markets, the labor market, the product market, and the capital market, and a production function for the economy as a whole. Next, we will show the effects of changes in labor markets or capital markets and how they influence the production function and product markets. Finally, we discuss the results of the model and the implications for monetary and fiscal policy.

## ASSUMPTIONS OF THE CLASSICAL MODEL

There are four primary assumptions of the classical model. These include:

1. *Rational self-interest:* Since Adam Smith's explorations into moral philosophy, economists have supported the value of self-interest in increasing the prosperity of the economy. Rational self-interest means that economic decisions are made with a purpose and not arbitrarily. Economic decision makers are able to gather the necessary information and make choices on the basis of marginal costs and benefits. Households make purchases to maximize their happiness (or utility) and supply resources to provide the best balance between income and leisure. Firms hire resources and choose an output level to maximize profits. Governments make decisions to maximize social welfare and politicians their chances of re-election.

2. *Market clearing:* The classical model assumes that wages, prices and interest rates are flexible enough so that markets always clear. "Market clearing" just means that markets are always in equilibrium. As we showed earlier in the chapter, the classical model believes that wages are flexible enough so that the labor market is always in equilibrium. The price level is flexible enough so that the product market always clears, or aggregate demand is equal to aggregate supply. Interest rates are flexible enough so that the capital (or loanable funds) market always clears, or saving is equal to investment in the economy. Market clearing means that there is fundamental flexibility so that the economy can be self-adjusting. If there is not enough spending to purchase the output produced in the economy, prices will fall and spending will increase. If there is not enough hiring to employ all those seeking work, wages will fall to encourage employers to hire more workers. If there is not enough investment to match saving in the economy, interest rates will fall so that investment increases.

Remember from our circular flow model in Figure 5-2 that three of the markets shown are the product market, labor market, and capital market. The classical model assumes that prices, wages, and interest rates are flexible enough so that these markets always clear.

3. *No money illusion:* Recall from Chapter Seven that money illusion occurs when economic agents are unaware of price changes in the economy so that economic decisions are based on nominal variables instead of real variables. If no money illusion exists, then economic decisions are based on real variables, not nominal variables. Workers make labor supply decisions on the basis of the purchasing power of their wages, not on the money wages they are earning. Lenders and borrowers are aware of and make their financial decisions based on real interest rates, not nominal interest rates. Consumers make their purchasing decisions on the information provided by relative prices, not on the absolute value of prices. No money illusion means that economic decision makers are aware of price changes and make their decisions utilizing this information.

4. *Diminishing marginal returns:* The classical model assumes that there are diminishing marginal returns to resources in the economy. As labor resources are increased in the economy, the additions to GDP will successively decline. The first million workers in the economy will add more to GDP than the last million workers add to GDP. The marginal product, or additional GDP produced, will decline as the quantity of labor increases in the economy. The law of diminishing returns means that the production function for the economy will be increasing at a decreasing rate.

Given these four assumptions, we can now build the pieces of the classical model. We start with a production function, and show how the labor demand can be derived from the production function. Together with labor supply, labor demand will determine the real wage rate and quantity of labor hired in the economy. From the production function, the quantity of labor will determine the amount of real GDP produced in the economy. The classical model assumes that the level of real GDP that firms and workers are willing and able to produce (aggregate supply) is independent of the price level. The price level is determined by aggregate demand, which depends on the money supply in the economy. The price level adjusts so that aggregate demand is equal to aggregate supply. Finally, in the loanable funds market real interest rates adjust so that saving is equal to investment.

## THE PRODUCTION FUNCTION

*The production function* is a model that shows the relationship between the quantity of labor employed in the economy and the amount of real GDP produced. As labor increases, real GDP increases. But because of the Law of Diminishing Returns, real GDP increases at a decreasing rate. Along a given production function we assume that capital and technology are held constant. A change in capital or technology will lead to shifts of the production function. We must now introduce some notation.

L = quantity of labor, measured as the number of workers or quantity of labor hours per year

K = quantity of capital, measured in units of tools, machines or factories per year

Y = real GDP, annual output measured in base year prices

P = price level, measured as the CPI or GDP Price Deflator
wage = nominal wage rate, earnings per hour measured in current dollars
W = real wage rate, or the purchasing power of the nominal wage rate

The real wage rate is measured in the quantity of goods and services that can be purchased with a nominal wage rate. We have

$$W = wage/P.$$

The real wage rate is equal to the nominal wage rate divided by the price level. The nominal wage is money earned for an hour of work, and the real wage shows the purchasing power, or the quantity of goods and services that can be purchased with the nominal wage for that hour of work.

For a given production function, we assume that the level of technology and quantity of capital are held constant. Real GDP then depends on the quantity of labor employed in the economy. The equation for the production function is

$$Y = F(\bar{K}, L)$$

where K is assumed to be fixed. The *short run* is a period of time where capital is fixed, while the *long run* is a period of time where capital is variable. The production function states the idea that real GDP is a function of a fixed amount of capital and a variable amount of labor. As labor is added to the fixed quantity of capital in the economy, GDP increases at a decreasing rate. The law of diminishing returns means that the production function will have the shape as shown in Figure 8-2.

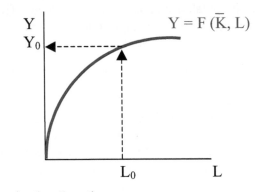

Figure 8-2   The Production Function

Along the production function, an increase in the quantity of labor leads to an increase in real GDP. For any given quantity of labor, such as $L_0$, the production function shows the quantity of real GDP that can be produced, $Y_0$. The law of diminishing returns implies that the production function is concave, or increases at a decreasing rate.

Note that the classical model has already determined the amount of real GDP in the economy without any consideration of the price level or nominal spending. As we will see, the idea that real variables can be separated from nominal variables in this way is known as the *classical dichotomy*.

## THE LABOR MARKET

The second piece of the classical puzzle is the labor market, which like any other market consists of demand and supply. Labor demand is the quantity of labor that firms in the economy want to hire at different wage rates in order to maximize their profits. Labor supply is the quantity of labor that households in the economy want to provide to firms to maximize their happiness. The classical model assumes that the labor market always clears, so that real wages are flexible enough to bring the labor market to equilibrium. Since the model assumes no money illusion, real wages are the relevant variable for labor demand and supply decisions.

## Labor Demand

The labor demand curve shows the quantities of labor that firms want to hire at different prices. Firms will seek to employ the quantity of labor that maximizes profits for the firm. Suppose that a firm needs to decide whether to hire one more worker. It must compare the additional benefits of hiring one more worker with the additional costs. In the classical model these costs and benefits are measured in real terms. The additional benefit of one more worker is the marginal product, or the additional output produced by one more unit of labor. The additional cost of one more worker is the real wage rate, or the output sacrificed to hire one more worker. As long as the marginal product of a worker is greater than the real wage rate, then the firm can increase its profits by hiring that worker since it will be adding more to its revenue than to its costs. So the firm will maximize profits when its hires labor up to the point where the real wage is equal to the marginal product of labor.

*Marginal product (MP)* is the additional output provided by one more unit of an input. For example, the marginal product of labor is the additional output produced by hiring one more unit of labor. The marginal product of labor is found by:

$$MP_L = \Delta Y / \Delta L$$

The marginal product of labor is the addition to GDP that is provided by hiring one more unit of labor in the economy. Since the marginal product is the increase in real GDP that results from an increase in labor, it is identical to the slope of the production function of Figure 8-2. Since the production function becomes flatter as labor increases, the slope or marginal product of labor will be declining as the quantity of labor increases. This is shown in Figure 8-3.

In Figure 8-3, suppose that the quantity of labor is measured in millions of workers, and output (Y) is measured in billions of dollars of real GDP. According to the production function, when the quantity of labor increases from 1 to 2 million, then real GDP increases by $3 billion. So the marginal product of labor between 1 and 2 million workers is

$$MP_L = \Delta Y / \Delta L = \$3 \text{ billion} / 1 \text{ million} = \$3000.$$

Similarly, the marginal product between 4 and 5 million workers is $2000, and the marginal product between 7 and 8 million workers is $1000. (For these numbers to make sense, assume that we define one unit of labor as a month of a worker's time.) Because of the law of diminishing returns, as the quantity of labor in the economy increases, the marginal product of labor falls. As shown in Figure 8-3, the marginal product of labor curve is downward-sloping. As the quantity of labor increases, each additional worker adds successively less to GDP. When the production function becomes flat its slope is zero, so the marginal product of labor is equal to zero.

As Figure 8-3 shows, the marginal product of labor is the slope of the production function, and since the production function becomes flatter as labor is increased, then the marginal product of labor curve is downward-sloping; the marginal product of labor declines as the quantity of labor increases, holding the quantities of other resources constant.

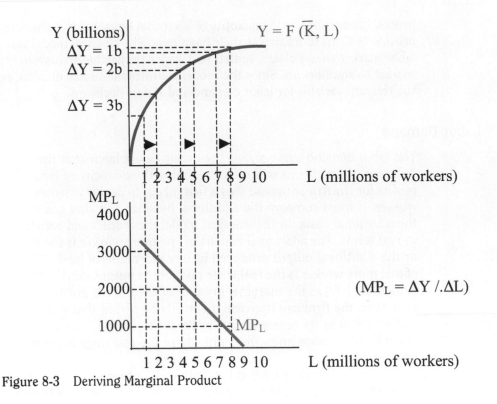

Figure 8-3   Deriving Marginal Product

## Profit Maximization

In general, firms will continue to hire a resource as long as it adds more to revenue than it adds to cost. In real terms, the additional revenue from another unit of a resource is its marginal product. For labor resources, the additional output is the marginal product of labor, what another unit of labor adds to output. The additional cost of the unit of labor is the real wage rate.

To take an example from the microeconomics of an individual firm, suppose that Fred Cornfarmer can hire workers by the hour to help him pick corn. The labor costs $20 per hour and the price of corn is $2 per bushel. If Joe Hornblower can pick 15 bushels of corn per hour, should Fred hire him?

If you answered yes, then perhaps you have a future in corn farming. Since the cost of labor is $20 per hour and the price of corn is $2 per bushel, than the real wage is $20/$2 = 10 bushels of corn per hour. Fred has to sacrifice 10 bushels of corn per hour to hire Joe. Since Joe can pick 15 bushels per hour, farm profits will increase if Joe is hired. For each hour of Joe's labor, Fred will gain 5 more bushels of corn than it costs to hire Joe. So Joe should be hired.

In fact, Fred Cornfarmer should hire farmhands as long as they can pick at least 10 bushels of corn per hour, or as long as the marginal product of labor is greater than the real wage rate. When Fred has hired all of those workers who can pick 10 bushels of corn or more per hour, then he has maximized profit. He does not want to hire workers who can only pick 9 bushels per hour, for example, since they would not be worth their cost.

Fred's situation is shown graphically in Figure 8-4. If the real wage rate is 10 bushels of corn, Fred will hire 8 workers, up to the point where the marginal product of the last worker is 10 bushels. As the real wage rate increases, Fred will hire less workers, since there will be fewer farmhands with a marginal product higher than the real wage. At a wage rate of $15, Fred will only hire 4 workers. Since the marginal product of labor curve is displaying the number of workers that Fred is willing to

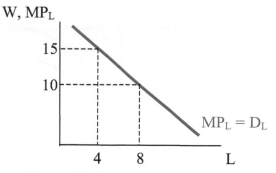

**Figure 8-4**   Fred Cornfarmer's Demand for Labor

hire at different wage rates, the marginal product of labor curve is the same as the demand curve for labor.

As the real wage increases, Fred will hire fewer workers. Since the marginal product of labor curve is showing the quantity of labor that Fred is willing to hire at different wage rates, the marginal product of labor curve is identical to Fred's demand curve for labor.

The analysis for Fred can be extended to the economy as a whole. The slope of the economy's production function is the marginal product of labor, which is downward-sloping due to the law of diminishing marginal returns. Since producers in the economy will hire labor until the real wage is equal to the marginal product of labor, then *the marginal product of labor curve is the same as the labor demand curve for the economy. Any change in the labor demand curve will also cause a shift in the production function, and any shift in the production function will lead to a change in labor demand.*

For example, throughout the 1990s increases in computer technology increased the productivity of workers. This led to increases in marginal product, so the demand for labor increased. Since each quantity of labor could now produce more than before, the production function for the economy shifted up. These changes are shown in Figure 8-5.

An increase in labor productivity will lead to an increase in the marginal product of labor and the demand for labor. Since workers are more productive, the production function shifts up. Any change in labor demand also causes a shift in the production function.

## Labor Supply

The classical model assumes that the labor supply function is upward-sloping. As the real wage rises, households will be willing to supply more labor in the economy. Households try to find the optimal mix between income and leisure. The opportunity cost of leisure is the real wage rate. If one consumes an hour of leisure by not working, the opportunity cost is the wage that could have been earned in that time instead. As the real wage rises the opportunity cost of leisure will increase, so households will decide to consume less leisure and supply more labor. Since as the real wage rises households decide to offer more labor, then the labor supply curve for the economy is upward sloping. This is shown in Figure 8-6.

The labor supply can increase in several ways. First, immigration can increase the supply of labor in a country. Second, increases in human capital through education and training can make more people eligible for the labor force. Third, changes in household preferences or daycare availability, so that more members of the household enter the workforce, can also lead to increases in labor supply.

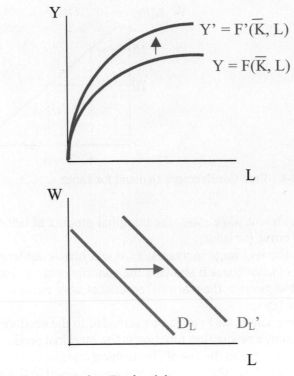

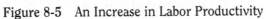

**Figure 8-5    An Increase in Labor Productivity**

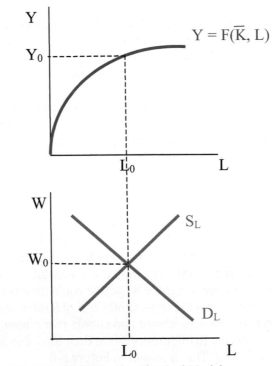

**Figure 8-6    Determining Real GDP in the Classical Model**

Figure 8-6 shows the labor market in the lower graph. Since the classical model assumes that wages are flexible, real wages are able to adjust so that the labor market is always in equilibrium where the labor supply and labor demand curves intersect. In the classical model, the labor market determines real wages and the quantity of labor. As shown in the upper graph, the quantity of labor then determines the level of real GDP through the production function.

In the labor market (lower graph), the classical model assumes that wages are flexible enough so that the labor market always clears. The market will reach and maintain the equilibrium real wage rate $W_0$, where the quantity demanded of labor equals the quantity supplied of labor and there is no involuntary unemployment in the economy. The quantity of labor exchanged in the labor market, $L_0$, then determines the quantity of real GDP produced given the production function. Note again that real GDP has been determined in this model without any consideration of prices or other nominal variables. This is the classical dichotomy. The classical model is a supply-side model in that real GDP is determined through the supply side of the economy. Prices are determined through the intersection of the aggregate demand and aggregate supply curves, as shown in the next section.

## THE PRODUCT MARKET: AGGREGATE DEMAND AND AGGREGATE SUPPLY

The third piece of the classical model consists of the product market where the price level adjusts so that desired spending is equal to desired output in the economy, or so that aggregate demand is equal to aggregate supply. We will first derive the aggregate supply curve, and then take a short detour through monetary policy to show how the aggregate demand curve is derived. In the classical model aggregate supply determines the level of real GDP, and aggregate demand determines the price level.

### Deriving Aggregate Supply

*The aggregate supply curve* is a model that shows the quantity of output that firms and workers are willing and able to produce at different price levels. In the classical model, the aggregate supply curve depends on labor market conditions and the production function. To derive the aggregate supply curve, we rely heavily on the assumptions of market clearing and no money illusion. We begin by showing the effects of a price increase on labor markets in Figure 8-7.

In Figure 8-7, the price level doubles from $P_0$ to $P_1$ so that $P_1 = 2P_0$. If the price level doubles, then real wages are cut in half, from $W_0$ to $W_1$. The decrease in the real wage results in a temporary shortage in the labor market. Since markets always clear, the shortage will lead to a doubling of nominal wages until the new real wage of $W_2$ is just equal to the original equilibrium wage of $W_0$. The quantity of labor $L_0$ remains the same so $Y_0$ does not change. Since an increase in the price level did not affect the quantity of real GDP produced, the aggregate supply curve is vertical.

To derive the aggregate supply curve, suppose that the price level doubles, say from a price index of 100 ($P_0$) to a price index of 200 ($P_1$). If the price level doubles, then real wages are cut in half. Any nominal wage can only buy half as many goods and services as it could before. Remember that real wages are equal to:

$$W = \text{real wage} = \text{nominal wage} / \text{price level} = \text{wage} / P$$

So a doubling of the price level will cut real wages in half.

Since there is no money illusion, the decline in real wages (from $W_0$ to $W_1$) will be known to workers and firms, and labor market decisions will be adjusted accordingly. With the decline in real wages, households would reduce the quantity supplied of labor while firms will increase the quantity demanded of labor, resulting in a

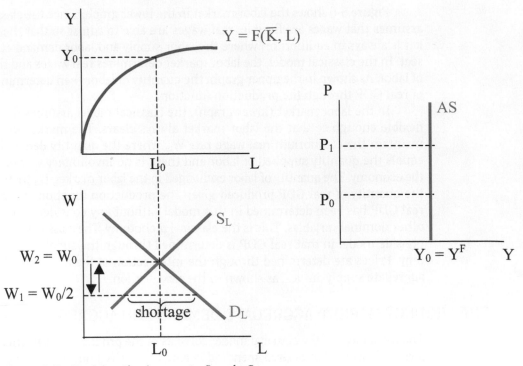

Figure 8-7   Deriving the Aggregate Supply Curve

shortage of labor. But since the classical model assumes that markets always clear, the shortage of labor will not last. Nominal wages will increase, in fact double, until the labor market returns to equilibrium. The real wage quickly returns to its equilibrium wage (where $W_2 = W_0$) the quantity of labor remains the same, so the amount of real GDP produced on the production function stays the same. Since an increase in the price level has not affected the level of real GDP, the aggregate supply curve is vertical. Since the labor market is always in equilibrium, the aggregate supply curve is vertical at the level of full employment ($Y^F$).

## Deriving Aggregate Demand

In the classical model, the aggregate demand curve depends on the money supply. In order to understand the concept of desired spending in this model, we must first take a short detour through monetary theory.

Classical economists based their theories of money on a simple formula that relates the amount of spending with the amount of production. Money in the economy has to circulate enough times to purchase all of the goods and services produced in nominal GDP. This is given by a formula known as the *equation of exchange:*

$$M \times V = P \times Y$$

where M = money supply, the quantity of money in circulation
   V = velocity, the turnover rate of money
   P = the price level
   Y = real GDP
   P × Y = nominal GDP

The equation of exchange states that money has to turn over enough times in a year to purchase the quantity of nominal GDP produced in that year. For example, the United States has a money supply of roughly $2 trillion and nominal GDP of about $14 trillion, so the velocity must be close to 7. If $2 trillion in money can purchase $14 trillion worth of goods and services, then each unit of currency must have been spent an average of 7 times that year. The equation of exchange is a tautology, or truism. It has to be true for there to be enough spending to purchase the nominal GDP produced.

The classical model revises the equation of exchange by assuming that velocity and real GDP are constant. Velocity is constant because it is assumed that households always hold the same percentage of their income in money. For example, if households hold one-half of their income in money, then velocity must be two: Each dollar must be spent twice to purchase the nominal GDP produced and income earned. If the percentage of income held in money is constant, then velocity is constant. As shown above, real GDP is constant because the aggregate supply curve is vertical

If velocity and real GDP are constant, we have the *quantity theory of money:*

$$M \times \overline{V} = P \times \overline{Y}$$

Here, any change in the money supply will lead to a proportionate change in the price level. If the price level doubles, the money supply will double. If the money supply is cut by a third, the price level will be cut by a third. In the classical model, inflation is a monetary phenomenon.

From the quantity theory, we can derive a theory of desired spending. The amount of purchases that spenders are willing and able to make will depend on the quantity of money in circulation. The equation above can be arranged to:

$$P = M \times \overline{V} / Y$$

This formula provides a relationship between the price level and the amount of real GDP that spenders want to purchase. The equation is the aggregate demand curve for the classical model. As shown, the aggregate demand in the classical model depends on the quantity of money in circulation. If the money supply increases, the aggregate demand curve will increase. The aggregate demand curve as shown in Figure 8-8 is a rectangular hyperbola. The rectangles underneath the demand curve always have the same area, or PY = MV (= 800 in this case). If the money supply increases the rectangles will get larger, and the aggregate demand curve will shift to the right.

The aggregate demand curve shows that as the price level falls, the amount of desired spending in the economy increases.

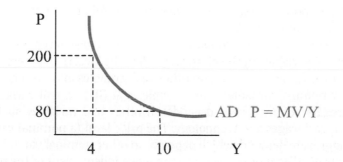

Figure 8-8   The Classical Aggregate Demand Curve

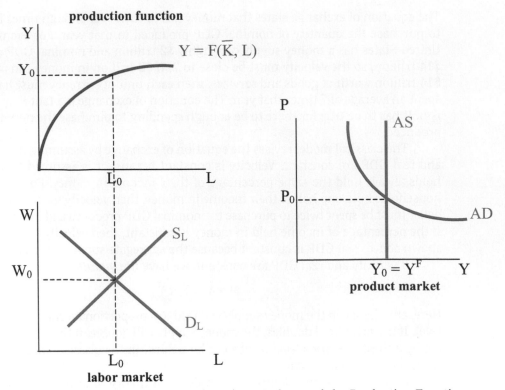

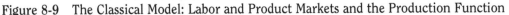

Figure 8-9    The Classical Model: Labor and Product Markets and the Production Function

## PUTTING THE PIECES TOGETHER

We can now bring together the different pieces of the classical model described in the last few sections. This is done in Figure 8-9.

In the classical model, the labor market determines the real wage rate and the quantity of labor. Through the production function, the quantity of labor determines the amount of real GDP produced. Since wages are flexible and there is no money illusion, the aggregate supply curve is vertical at the level of full employment. The aggregate demand curve, which depends on the money supply, determines the price level in this model. Any changes in labor demand or labor supply will lead to changes in W, L, Y and P.

## THREE IMPORTANT RESULTS

Three important results of the classical model are the classical dichotomy, money neutrality, and Say's Law.

*The classical dichotomy* is the idea that real variables can be separated from nominal variables in the classical model. The factors that determine each are different. Real variables depend on other real variables and nominal variables depend on other nominal variables. For example, real GDP (a real variable) is determined by aggregate supply, which depends on other real variables such as the quantity of labor, real wages and technology. The price level (a nominal variable) is determined by aggregate demand, which depends on other nominal variables such as the money supply. Real economic decisions are made independent of the price level in the classical model. The price level depends on the quantity of money in circulation, but it has no effect on the quantity of real GDP produced. A variant of the classical dichotomy is the idea of money neutrality.

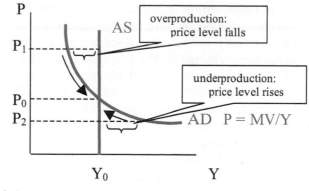

Figure 8-10    Say's Law

*Money neutrality* means that a change in the money supply has no effect on real variables, only nominal variables. Changes in aggregate demand, which are caused by changes in the money supply, only affect the price level but have no effect on real GDP since the aggregate supply curve is vertical. Money neutrality is explored further at the end of the chapter.

*Say's Law* states that supply creates its own demand. In the process of production, enough income is generated to purchase the output produced. If not, prices will adjust. As quoted in the introduction, the process of production creates sales which generate income for the producer. Say believed that overproduction was impossible since production would create income to purchase that output.

For example, suppose that the economy is at a price level above equilibrium, $P_1$ in Figure 8-10. Here, the quantity of output that spenders want to purchase is less than the quantity of output that firms and workers are willing and able to produce. Overproduction would result, but Say believed that prices would fall instead. As prices fall, the quantity of desired spending will decrease until there is enough spending to purchase the output produced.

On the other hand, if prices were at $P_2$ below equilibrium, then underproduction would result. Since spenders cannot purchase all of the output desired, prices will be bid up and spending will increase until the economy returns to equilibrium at $P_0$. In the classical model, prices are assumed to be flexible enough so that the economy is always at equilibrium with enough spending to purchase the output produced.

As shown in Figure 8-10, according to Say's Law prices are flexible enough so that the economy will have enough spending to purchase the quantity of output that firms and workers are willing and able to produce. *In the classical model, spending adjusts to output in the economy.*

Another important result of the classical model is the idea of complete crowding out, that any increase in government spending is exactly offset by declines in private spending. But this must wait for an examination of the loanable funds market in the classical model. First, we turn our attention to the effects of changes in the labor market and the determinants of economic growth in the classical model.

## CHANGES IN LABOR MARKET CONDITIONS

Basically there are two ways that the labor market can change, either labor demand can change or labor supply can change. As shown earlier, any change in labor demand will also change the production function, since the demand for labor is the marginal product of labor, which is the slope of the production function. When the labor demand shifts the production function shifts accordingly. Since the labor supply curve is based on household decisions, a change in labor supply does not on its own lead to any other changes to the curves in the model.

If either labor demand or supply changes, real wages and the quantity of labor will change. The change in the quantity of labor will lead to changes in real GDP along the production function, which itself may shift if the demand for labor changes. The change in real GDP will shift the aggregate supply curve. The price level will then adjust according to Say's Law so that there is a change in spending in the economy to match the change in output. The labor and product markets will quickly return to equilibrium since wages and prices are flexible in the classical model.

## An Increase in Labor Supply

An increase in labor supply may be caused by many factors, such as immigration, demographics, or changes in household preferences. In countries such as the United States or Israel, immigration has consistently added new workers to the labor force and led to increases in labor supply. Increases in those of working age in the population, perhaps as a result of a baby boom, will create an increase in the supply of labor. Finally, if more women or elderly from households decide to enter the workforce, as happened in the United States for women in the 1970s or elderly in the 2000s, then the labor supply will increase. An increase in labor supply is represented by a rightward shift of the labor supply curve.

Recall that the classical model consists of three graphs: the labor market, the production function, and aggregate supply/aggregate demand graphs. An increase in the supply of labor shifts the labor supply curve to the right, and this will cause an increase in the quantity of labor and a decline in the real wage rate. The increase in the quantity of labor causes an increase in real GDP along the production function. This increase in real GDP causes the aggregate supply curve to shift to the right, so, according to Say's law, the price level must fall so that spenders are willing to purchase the increase in output. The effects of an increase in the labor supply are shown in Figure 8-11.

Since the increase in the labor supply has lead to an increase in real GDP, economic growth has occurred. As we will discuss later in the chapter, economic growth can be modeled as rightward increases in the economy's aggregate supply curve over time.

In Figure 8-11, we begin by assuming that the economy is originally in equilibrium at a real wage rate of W*, quantity of labor L*, real GDP Y*, and at a price level of P*, as shown in the respective graphs.

An increase in labor supply causes a rightward shift of the labor supply curve so that real wages fall and the quantity of labor increases. The increase in the quantity of labor will lead to an increase in real GDP in the production function graph. The increase in real GDP causes the aggregate supply curve to shift to the right. For the product market to clear, the price level must fall so that there is an increase in spending to match the increase in output. In the classical model, economic growth may be accompanied by deflation.

A decrease in labor supply would have the opposite effects on the economy. The labor supply curve would shift to the left, and real wages would increase, the quantity of labor would decline, real GDP would fall, the aggregate supply curve would shift to the left, and the price level would rise. As an exercise, draw the graphs and see for yourself.

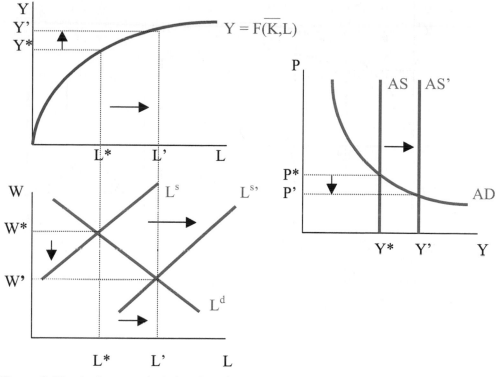

Figure 8-11   An Increase in Labor Supply

## An Increase in Labor Demand

Another way that the labor market may change is through shifts in the demand for labor. Since the demand for labor is the same as the marginal product of labor, any factor that changes the productivity of labor will also change the demand for labor. For example, increases in human capital through education or training can increase the marginal product of labor. If labor has more resources to work with, through increases in capital, land, or technology, then the increase in labor productivity will lead to an increase in labor demand. Any increase in labor demand will also lead to an increase in the production function since the marginal product of labor has increased.

Figure 8-12 shows the effects of an increase in labor demand. Once again, we begin by assuming equilibrium at L*, W*, Y* and P*. An increase in the demand for labor shifts the demand curve for labor to the right. This will cause an increase in the quantity of labor and an increase in the real wage rate. As the marginal product of labor (the labor demand curve) increases, the production function shifts up. The increase in the quantity of labor causes an increase in real GDP along the production function. This causes the AS curve to shift to the right, so, according to Say's law, the price level must fall so that spenders are willing to purchase the increase in output. Once again, wages and prices adjust so that the labor and product markets remain in equilibrium.

As you can imagine, a decrease in labor demand would have the opposite effect. The labor demand curve would shift to the left, and the production function would decline (shift down) as a result of the decline in the marginal product of labor. Real wages would fall and the quantity of labor would decrease, causing a decline in real GDP along the now lower production function. As a result of the decline in real GDP the aggregate supply curve would shift to the left, and prices would rise to reduce

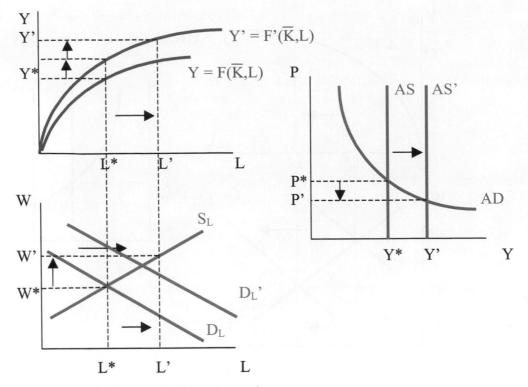

Figure 8-12   An Increase in Labor Demand

the amount of desired spending in the economy so that spending would again be equal to output. For practice, try it and see.

Notice that in the last two examples increases in the quantity of labor led to increases in real GDP, which caused rightward shifts of the aggregate supply curve. In the classical model, economic growth occurs when the aggregate supply curve shifts to the right over time like this. Increases in the quantity or productivity of labor are two factors that may contribute to economic growth over time.

## ECONOMIC GROWTH IN THE CLASSICAL MODEL

Traditionally, economists define economic growth in the following way.

*Economic growth* is an increase in per capita real GDP over time. If the amount of output that an economy is producing per person is increasing, then an economy is experiencing growth.

As discussed above, in the classical model economic growth occurs when the aggregate supply curve shifts to the right over time. Since the aggregate supply curve is vertical, changes in aggregate demand will have no effect on real GDP, only the price level. This is the result of the classical dichotomy. The only way for economic growth to occur is to increase the aggregate supply curve to the right through changes in real variables. In this way, the classical model is essentially a supply-side model of the economy. The only way to change real GDP is through changes in aggregate supply.

The aggregate supply curve may increase through improvements in labor market conditions, such as increases in labor demand or supply, or through increases in the production function, which may occur through increases in capital, the productivity of capital, or technology. These types of changes will lead to rightward shifts in the aggregate supply curve over time.

*The determinants of economic growth in the classical model are:*

1. the quantity of labor
2. the marginal product of labor
3. the quantity of capital
4. the marginal product of capital
5. technology

Increases in any of these will lead to increases in per capita real GDP over time.

1. Increases in the quantity of labor can be achieved through increases in the supply of labor. As discussed above, labor supply depends on household preferences between income and leisure and the number of households in the economy. Historically, institutions such as slavery and indentured servitude have been used to increase the supply of labor in an economy. More recently, immigration has been the major cause of increases in the labor supply for many countries. Labor supply will also increase if household preferences for labor increase. Technological changes, such as household appliances, may reduce the amount of time necessary for production in the home and free up more time to supply labor outside of the home. Socioeconomic trends, such as a decline in birth rates, improvements in day care services, or a general desire for higher incomes, may allow or force more women or elderly to enter the work force over time. Changes in participation rates will lead to changes in the labor supply for an economy. As shown in Figure 8-11, an increase in labor supply will lead to an increase in real GDP and a rightward shift of the aggregate supply curve.

2. Increases in the marginal product of labor are achieved through increases in labor productivity. One of the most important ways of bringing about an increase in the marginal product of labor is through education and training. Unskilled workers cannot add much to the economy. As individuals gain skills through schooling and experience, they are able to offer more to the economy and increase the output produced. Public health can also influence the productivity of labor. A healthy and strong workforce will produce more output than a sick and weak one. Increases in worker morale may also cause workers to be more productive. As shown in Figure 8-12, an increase in labor productivity leads to an increase in the demand for labor and an upward shift of the production function. Both of these changes have the effects of increasing real GDP and the aggregate supply curve. The basic process of economic growth in the classical model is reproduced in Figure 8-13.

   In the classical model, economic growth occurs through rightward shifts of the aggregate supply curve. As the aggregate supply curve shifts to the right, real GDP increases. Without an increase in the money supply to increase aggregate demand, the classical model predicts that economic growth will be accompanied by deflation.

3. Increases in the quantity of capital are another means of creating economic growth. With increases in capital, each unit of labor has more to work with and the marginal product of labor increases. For example, when a new factory is built, workers can now produce more.

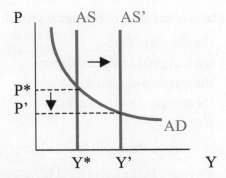

Figure 8-13   Economic Growth in the Classical Model

If a firm buys more computers, its workers can become more efficient. Often, increases in capital in the developing world are achieved through international investment. Many countries in Asia and South America have witnessed remarkable rates of economic growth through infusions of capital by multinational corporations. The standards of living and levels of poverty in these countries have drastically improved as a result.

An increase in the quantity of capital has an effect on the economy similar to that shown in Figure 8-12. Since capital is held constant along a given production function, an increase in capital will lead to an increase in the production function. Since the slope of the production function increases, any increase in the quantity of labor will now add more to real GDP, and the marginal product of labor increases. The increase in the marginal product of labor leads to an increase in the demand for labor. The overall result is an increase in real GDP and a decline in the price level, as shown in Figures 8-12 and 8-13.

4.  Increases in the marginal product of capital occur when capital becomes more productive, or when an increase in capital by one unit provides a larger increase in real GDP. As computers have more and more memory capacity and processing speeds, they can contribute more to output. An increase in computers by one unit adds more to real GDP than it did before. As automobile factories become more computerized and as robots replace humans in production, these increases in the marginal product of capital mean that a new automobile factory will now produce more real GDP than it would before. Improvements in tools, such as battery-powered saws and pneumatic nail guns, have enabled construction workers to become more productive. In all of these cases, improvements in capital lead to increases in the marginal product of capital. As the marginal product of capital increases, the production function shifts up and the demand for labor increases. Economic growth results in a manner similar to that shown in Figures 8-12 and 8-13.

5.  Increases in technology occur when new products or production techniques are introduced that revolutionize previous patterns of production, distribution, and consumption in the economy. Important examples include such inventions as the steam engine, railroads, the automobile, television, and personal computers. These increases in technology increased real GDP in several ways. First, the produc-

tion of the new technology itself, such as cars or TVs, and the capital necessary for the new technology increases output in the economy. Second, the new technology may enable existing resources to become more productive. Third, the new technology may allow for changes in the social relations between buyers and sellers that lead to increases in real GDP. In all of these cases, the increase in technology will lead to the same types of changes as those shown in Figures 8-12 or 8-13.

In sum, note that in all five of these cases either an increase in labor supply or labor demand leads to an increase in the quantity of labor and real GDP. The resulting rightward shift in the aggregate supply curve represents economic growth in the classical model. The economy is able to achieve full employment with a higher level of real GDP being produced. Economic growth is an important goal because it allows the pie to grow and for the economy to provide a higher standard of living for the average household. While money does not buy happiness, economic growth is an important engine for the reduction of poverty around the world.

## REAL INTEREST RATES IN THE CLASSICAL MODEL

The last piece of the classical model puzzle is to examine the role of real interest rates. Recall from Chapter Seven that real interest rates take into account the effects of inflation on the future purchasing power of money. Since we assume that there is no money illusion in the classical model, the real interest rate is the relevant variable for lending and borrowing decisions. The real interest rate (r) is the difference between the nominal interest rate (i) and the rate of inflation ($\Pi$):

$$r = i - \Pi$$

In the classical model, it is also assumed that the real interest rate is flexible. In the classical model, real interest rates adjust so that saving is equal to investment in the loanable funds market. The loanable funds market connects lenders and borrowers. Lenders can earn interest payments on excess funds by lending them to borrowers with more productive uses for those funds. Borrowers are willing to pay interest to use these funds for investment or consumption expenditures. Ideally, both lenders and borrowers benefit from such exchanges in the loanable funds market.

To simplify the model, we assume that the supply of loanable funds comes from household saving. When households consume less than their disposable income, a supply of excess funds is created which can be lent to banks in the form of saving. The saving function is upward-sloping. An increase in real interest rates will lead to an increase in household saving. As real interest rates rise, the opportunity cost of consumption spending increases, so households will save more and consume less. The saving function is shown in Figure 8-14.

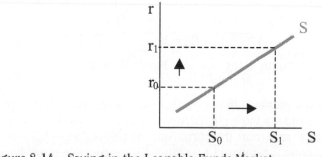

Figure 8-14   Saving in the Loanable Funds Market

Here, S = saving and r = real interest rates. An increase in real interest rates leads to an increase in household saving. As real interest rates rise, the opportunity cost of consumption spending increases, and households save more and consume less.

We also assume that the demand for loanable funds is for investment expenditures. When firms need funds for purchases of capital, they can either use their own funds or they can borrow funds from others. In either case, they are relying on the supply of loanable funds to finance their investment spending. There is an inverse relationship between real interest rates and investment spending, so the investment function is downward-sloping. An increase in real interest rates increases the real cost of borrowing, so investment expenditures decline as real interest rates increase. The classical investment function is shown in Figure 8-15.

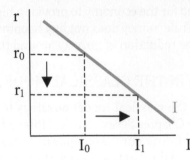

Figure 8-15    Investment in the Loanable Funds Market

Here, I = investment and r = real interest rates. The investment function slopes downward. A decrease in real interest rates leads to an increase in investment spending as the real cost of borrowing falls.

As you may imagine by now, the equilibrium in the loanable funds market occurs where saving is equal to investment. Real interest rates adjust so that the supply of loanable funds is equal to the demand for loanable funds, at the intersection of the saving and investment curves. Equilibrium occurs when there is an interest rate such that the quantity of funds that households want to save is just equal to the quantity of funds that firms want to borrow, or where saving is equal to investment. Equilibrium in the loanable funds market is shown in Figure 8-16.

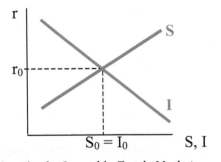

Figure 8-16    Equilibrium in the Loanable Funds Market

Equilibrium in the loanable funds market occurs where saving is equal to investment. If interest rates are too high, there would be a surplus of loanable funds. Households would want to save more than firms want to invest. As savings pile up in financial institutions, interest rates would be reduced to encourage more borrowing of the loanable funds. If interest rates are too low a shortage of loanable funds would result.

Those with more productive uses of those funds would be willing to pay higher interest rates to bid the funds away from other borrowers. Interest rates would increase to eliminate the shortage of funds. When real interest rates are above equilibrium, there is pressure in the market for interest rates to fall as banks seek to make more loans. When real interest rates are below equilibrium, there is upward pressure on interest rates as some borrowers outbid others. In this way, real interest rates adjust in the loanable funds market so that saving is equal to investment. Because interest rates are flexible, changes in either saving or investment lead to changes in real interest rates that create counteracting changes to spending in the economy, so that overall spending remains unchanged. This means that changes in spending in the classical model do not affect aggregate demand, as explained in the next section.

## CHANGES IN SPENDING IN THE CLASSICAL MODEL

As discussed above, changes in spending do not affect aggregate demand in the classical model. A change in one variable leads to opposite changes in another variable, so that overall spending, and aggregate demand, remains unchanged. Remember that in the classical model, aggregate demand is a function of the money supply. Since changes in spending do not affect the money supply in circulation, they do not affect the aggregate demand curve. The only way to increase aggregate demand in the classical model is to increase the money supply. Other changes cancel each other out.

### A Change in Investment Spending

A change in the investment function may be caused by changes in variables other than the real interest rate. Changes in the real interest rate will lead to movements along a given investment function. Changes in other variables, such as business confidence, capacity utilization, or the cost of capital, will lead to shifts in the investment function. For example, if businesses become more optimistic about the future of the economy, they are more likely to increase their purchases of capital in the present, and investment spending will increase. An increase in investment will lead to a rightward shift of the investment function, as shown in Figure 8-17.

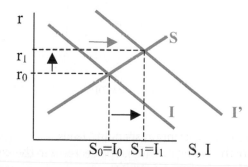

Figure 8-17   An Increase in Investment Spending

In the loanable funds market, an increase in investment spending leads to a rightward shift of the investment function. Interest rates increase to bring the market back to equilibrium. As interest rates increase, saving in the economy increases to match the increase in investment spending. As investment increases from $I_0$ to $I_1$ saving increases from $S_0$ to $S_1$. Since the real interest rate in the classical model always adjusts so that saving is equal to investment, any increase investment is matched by an increase in saving. Since real income is assumed to be fixed in the classical model (since real GDP is fixed), an increase in saving can only be achieved through an equal reduction in consumption spending. If households increase saving by $100 million, than they must be reducing consumption spending by that same $100 million. So the increase in investment spending has led to an equal increase in saving, which is the same as a decrease in consumption spending. So the increase in investment spending leads to an equal decrease in consumption spending, so overall spending in the economy, and aggregate demand, remain unchanged. The increase in investment spending has no effect on aggregate demand in the classical model because interest rates are assumed to be flexible and real GDP is fixed.

> *In the classical model, an increase in investment spending leads to an equal decrease in consumption spending, so overall spending in the economy remains unchanged.*

A decrease in investment spending would have the opposite effect. There would be a leftward shift of the investment function and real interest rates would fall. There would be a decline in saving due to the fall in interest rates to match the decrease in investment spending. The decline in saving means an increase in consumption spending equal to the decline in investment spending, so again overall spending would remain unchanged.

## A Change in Consumption Spending

In the loanable funds model, a change in consumption spending can be represented by an opposite change in saving. Since real income is fixed, if consumption spending increases then saving will decrease by an equal amount. If consumption spending declines, then saving will increase by an equal amount. An increase in consumption spending would be shown graphically as a decline in saving, as seen in Figure 8-18.

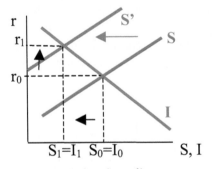

**Figure 8-18**   An Increase in Consumption Spending

An increase in consumption spending leads to an equal decrease in saving and a leftward shift of the saving function. The decrease in the saving function causes an increase in the real interest rate (from $r_0$ to $r_1$) and a decrease in saving (from $S_0$ to $S_1$). Since real interest rates increase, investment spending also declines to match the decrease in saving (from $I_0$ to $I_1$). Here, the increase in consumption spending has led to an equal decline in saving. Real interest rates increase as a result and investment spending falls by the same amount as the decline in saving. So overall, the increase in consumption spending is matched by an equal decrease in investment spending. Once again, overall spending and aggregate demand in the economy remain unchanged.

> *In the classical model, an increase in consumption spending leads to an equal decrease in investment spending, so overall spending in the economy remains unchanged.*

A decrease in consumption spending would have the opposite effect. The decline in consumption means an increase in saving, so the saving function would shift to the right and the real interest rate would fall. The decline in interest rates would cause an increase in investment spending identical to the decrease in consumption spending, so again overall spending and aggregate demand would remain unchanged.

Increases in saving are generally seen as desirable in the classical model. As described in the last paragraph, an increase in saving leads to a lower real interest rate and an increase in investment spending. While overall spending remains constant, the composition of spending has changed. The increase in saving means there is less consumption spending and more investment spending. With more investment, there is more capital being created so there is a greater potential for economic growth in the future. Recall from Chapter Two that as an economy devotes more resources to capital rather than consumption goods, then the movements along the present Production Possibilities Curve toward more capital goods will enable the economy to grow more in the future. In a nutshell, in the classical model saving is desirable because it provides a pool of funds for capital purchases which enable the economy to grow more in the future.

While increases in saving do not affect aggregate demand in the short run, strangely enough increases in saving will affect aggregate supply in the long run because they allow increases in the stock of capital.

Note that in the last two sections, changes in investment or consumption spending did not affect the amount of overall spending or aggregate demand in the economy, just the composition of that spending between consumption and investment. An increase in one type of spending led to an offsetting decline in the other type of spending. Since real GDP is fixed by the supply side of the economy, spending adjusts in the classical model so that spending is equal to output, according to Say's Law. So a change in one component of spending does not affect overall spending, since overall spending must be equal to output. A change in investment or consumption spending by itself has no effect on aggregate demand or real GDP. This is also true for changes in government spending, as described in the next section.

## FISCAL POLICY IN THE CLASSICAL MODEL

Remember that fiscal policy represents changes in government spending or taxes to influence some macroeconomic variable. For example, the government may increase spending to try to reduce unemployment. Or it may raise taxes in an attempt to control inflation. In the classical model, since it is believed that the economy is self-adjusting, fiscal policy has no effect on real GDP or the price level in the short run. There is a limited role for government to play in this model.

Before we go any further, we should introduce some definitions. Let

> B = government budget position
> G = government spending
> T = tax revenue
> Def = deficit

Then

$$B = T - G$$

If B > 0, so that T > G, then the budget has a surplus.
If B < 0, so that G > T, then the budget has a deficit.

If the deficit is treated as a positive number, then

$$Def = G - T.$$

If government spending exceeds tax revenue, then the government budget has a deficit.

> *Budget position* is the difference between tax revenue and government spending.
>
> *Budget surplus* occurs when tax revenue is greater than government spending.
>
> *Budget deficit* occurs when government spending is greater than tax revenue.

Given these definitions, we can now examine the effects of fiscal policy in the classical model.

Let us assume that the government desires to use expansionary fiscal policy to stimulate the economy. Expansionary fiscal policy would include either increases in government spending or tax cuts. President Obama's American Recovery and Reinvestment Act of 2009 contained provisions for both. The effects of changes in government spending or taxes are similar to the effects of changes in consumption or investment spending in the classical model, that they have no effect on overall spending or on aggregate demand. Changes in government spending or taxes have no effect in the short run in the classical model. We will examine several cases.

## Case I: An Increase in Government Spending with No Change in Taxes

Assume that in an attempt to stimulate the economy, the government increases its spending with no changes in taxes. In such a situation, the government's budget deficit would increase. If the government is raising more in tax revenue than it is spending, it would have a budget surplus. If the government is spending more than it raises in tax revenue, it would have a budget deficit. The government's budget position depends on its revenues compared to its spending. If the government increases spending with no increases in taxes, then the budget deficit will increase. To finance this deficit, the Treasury Department will issue securities such as Treasury bonds to borrow the money from investors. When the government borrows money to finance deficit spending, the demand for loanable funds will increase. Besides the private investment demand for loanable funds, there will now be a public demand for loanable funds. If I (investment) is the private demand for loanable funds, then I + Def (investment plus deficit) would be the total demand for loanable funds, including both the private demand and the public demand. The increase in the demand for loanable funds is shown in Figure 8-19.

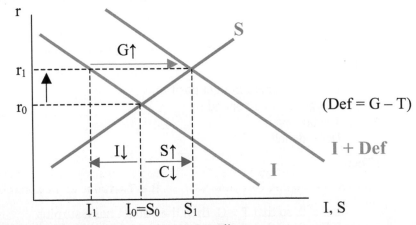

Figure 8-19   An Increase in Government Spending

In Figure 8-19, assume that the loanable funds market begins in equilibrium at a real interest rate of $r_0$, a level of investment of $I_0$, and a level of saving of $S_0$, where saving is equal to investment. If the government borrows money by issuing bonds to finance a deficit, the demand for loanable funds will increase by the amount of the deficit. The increase in the demand for loanable funds leads to an increase in real interest rates. As real interest rates increase, the amount of investment spending declines and the quantity of saving increases. Investment falls from $I_0$ to $I_1$, while saving increases from $S_0$ to $S_1$. The increase in saving leads to an equal decrease in consumption spending.

Note that the overall effect on spending here is zero. The increase in government spending, $G\uparrow$ as shown by the orange arrow, is just equal to the declines in private spending, $I\downarrow + C\downarrow$, as shown by the blue arrows. In the classical model, any increase in government spending is exactly offset by declines in private spending, so that the overall change in spending is zero. This is known as complete crowding out. Fiscal policy has no effect on the aggregate demand curve in the classical model. Changes in government spending are negated by equal opposite changes in private spending.

*Crowding out effect:* An increase in government spending will lead to an increase in real interest rates, causing investment and consumption spending to decline.

*Complete crowding out* occurs when an increase in government spending is exactly offset by declines in private spending, so that the aggregate demand curve remains unchanged.

In the short run, fiscal policy has no effect on aggregate demand so prices and real GDP remain unchanged. In the long run, however, the government deficit causes real interest rates to increase, so that investment spending declines. The decrease in investment spending means that less capital is being created. With a lower rate of capital formation, the economy will suffer lower rates of economic growth in the future. This is shown in Figure 8-20.

Figure 8-20 shows the classical product market model and the production possibilities curve for the economy as a whole. The PPC is drawn with capital goods (K) on the vertical axis and consumption goods (C) on the horizontal axis. The economy

| **Product market** | **Production Possibilities Curve** |
|---|---|
| 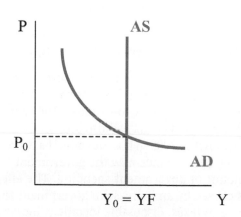 | 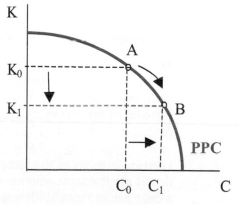 |

Due to complete crowding out, an increase in government spending has no immediate effect on AD, prices or real GDP . . .

But in the long term, higher real interest rates reduce investment and capital formation, so the potential for economic growth is less.

Figure 8-20   The Effects of an Increase in Government Spending

begins at the allocation of capital and consumption spending shown by point A with $K_0$ units of capital goods and $C_0$ units of consumption goods. In the product market, the level of real GDP is $Y_0$ and the price level is $P_0$. Due to complete crowding out, an increase in government spending has no effect on aggregate demand, so an increase in government spending has no effect on real GDP or the price level. But that is not the end of the story. The higher real interest rates reduce the volume of investment spending in the economy, which reduces the capital stock. As investment declines, less resources are devoted to capital formation, so the economy moves along its PPC from Point A to B. With less capital being produced, the potential for economic growth will be reduced.

In sum, a deficit that results from an increase in government spending on its own has no immediate effect in the classical model. Complete crowding out means that any increase in government spending is exactly offset by declines in private spending, so overall spending and aggregate demand remain unchanged. If aggregate demand is unchanged and since fiscal policy has no effect on aggregate supply, then an increase in government spending has no effect on real GDP or the price level. So expansionary fiscal policy, or trying to expand the economy through increases in government spending, is ineffective in the classical model. Fiscal policy cannot be used to bring the economy out of a recession here.

Even though the budget deficit has no immediate effects on prices and real GDP, it does cause higher real interest rates which reduce the amount of investment spending. The decline in investment spending leads to less capital formation, which reduces the potential for economic growth in the future. So the economic costs of budget deficits are higher real interest rates and a lower potential for economic growth in the future. With less economic growth, our children and grandchildren will inherit a world with a lower real GDP than would have occurred with higher rates of growth. By reducing future GDP, budget deficits impose a cost on future generations.

There is also a social cost to high budget deficits. With high budget deficits, we postpone taxation today so the present generation may have a higher standard of living. But in the process, we are imposing greater tax burdens on future generations. There are moral implications to high budget deficits. By avoiding taxes and providing a higher standard of living for today's generation, we are imposing tax payments and a lower standard of living for future generations. We are forcing our children and grandchildren to pay for the spending binges of the current generation. We live better today so that our children can pay our bills.

## Case II: A Decrease in Taxes with No Change in Government Spending

Another way that the government can create a deficit besides increasing spending is to cut taxes without changing government spending. Tax cuts have been the primary fiscal policy tool of the Bush II presidency. In order to stimulate the economy, Bush introduced tax cuts in 2001, 2003 and 2008. Obama has also proposed tax cuts in the American Recovery and Reinvestment Act of 2009. A tax cut without a decrease in government spending will also lead to a deficit, since now the government has less tax revenue to support the same amount of government spending. The effects of the deficit are the same whether it is caused by an increase in government spending or a decrease in taxes. With a decrease in taxes, disposable income is increased by the amount of the tax cut. If the government cuts your taxes by $100, your disposable income will increase by $100. Out of this increase in income, part will be spent on consumption and the rest will be put into saving. Since saving is always equal to investment in the classical model, the increase in saving leads to lower interest rates that lead to an equal increase in investment spending. So the tax cut leads to an increase in income which is split between consumption and investment spending. A $600 decrease in taxes will lead to a $600 increase in consumption and investment spending.

In order to finance the cut in taxes which cause a deficit, the government will need to issue bonds and increase the demand for loanable funds. The effects are the same as those shown in Figure 8-20. The deficit causes an increase in the demand for loanable funds, which causes an increase in real interest rates. The rise in interest rates leads to declines in investment and consumption spending equal to the original tax cut. So the tax cut leads to both an equal increase in consumption and investment spending and an equal decrease in consumption and investment spending. Everything cancels out, and the net increase in spending is zero. Once again, we have complete crowding out. The tax cut causes an increase in spending that is offset by equal declines in spending. The effects of a tax cut on the loanable funds market is shown in Figure 8-21.

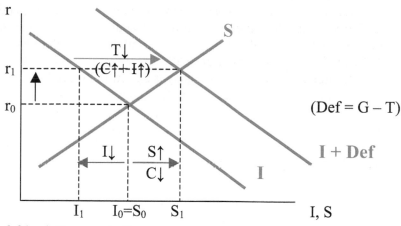

Figure 8-21   A Decrease in Taxes

The decrease in taxes leads to a deficit that increases the demand for loanable funds from $I$ to $I + Def$. The tax cut causes an increase in consumption and investment spending ($C\uparrow + I\uparrow$) that is just matched by the decline in investment and consumption spending ($I\downarrow + C\downarrow$). Once again, complete crowding out means that the increase in spending spurred by the tax cut is exactly offset by declines in spending, so the overall effect on spending and aggregate demand is zero. The effects are the same as in the case of a government spending increase. There is complete crowding out in the short run. The long run effects are that the higher interest rates cause lower rates of investment, capital formation, and economic growth in the future. We impose costs on future generations by postponing the payment of deficits today.

## Case III: An Increase in Government Spending with an Equal Increase in Taxes

Suppose that the government tries to stimulate the economy by increasing spending, but pays for that spending with an equal increase in taxes. This is known as a balanced budget change. In this situation, the increase in spending from the government will be matched by the decreases in consumption and investment spending that result from the tax increase. Again, the fiscal policy change will have no effect on aggregate demand, the price level or real GDP.

*Balanced budget change* is when any change in government spending is matched by an equal and opposite change in taxes, so that the government budget position remains unchanged.

In all three cases we have examined, fiscal policy is ineffective in the classical model. A change in government spending or taxes has no impact on aggregate demand, prices, and real GDP in the short run when capital is fixed. In the long run when capital is variable, the fiscal policy change will influence real interest rates, capital formation, and the potential for economic growth in the future.

## MONETARY POLICY IN THE CLASSICAL MODEL

Recall from our discussion of the classical aggregate demand curve that aggregate demand depends on the quantity of money in circulation. The equation for aggregate demand is given by $P = MV / Y$. If V is being held constant as in the quantity theory of money, then an increase in money supply will lead to an increase in aggregate demand. Note from our previous discussions that an increase in the money supply is the only way to increase aggregate demand. Increases in consumption, investment, or government spending will have no effect on aggregate demand. Changes in one type of spending just lead to opposite changes in another type of spending. Changes in real interest rates affect the composition of spending between consumption and investment but not the overall quantity of spending. It is only changes in the money supply that will cause changes in the aggregate demand curve in the classical model.

An increase in the money supply is shown in Figure 8-22. The increase in the money supply leads to an increase in the aggregate demand curve, which leads to an increase in the price level. Since the aggregate supply curve is vertical, there is no change in real GDP that results from the increase in the money supply. In the classical model, inflation is a monetary phenomenon. Inflation occurs from an increase in the money supply in the classical model.

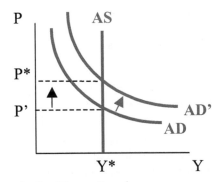

Figure 8-22    An Increase in the Money Supply

An increase in the money supply causes an increase in aggregate demand, which leads to an increase in the price level and no change in real GDP. Increases in the money supply cause inflation in the classical model.

Figure 8-22 illustrates the idea of *money neutrality* discussed earlier in the chapter. Changes in the money supply only affect nominal variables, but not real variables. Here, the increase in the money supply leads to an increase in aggregate demand, which causes an increase in the price level, a nominal variable. But since the aggregate supply curve is vertical, the increase in the aggregate demand curve has no effect on real GDP or other real variables. So a change in the money supply only affects nominal variables but not real variables in the classical model.

Echoes of the classical model are heard in the halls of Congress today during the current debates over the stimulus package and the government's response to the recession of 2008–2009. Republicans and other opponents of Obama's policies believe that it is better to allow the banks and automobile companies to fail rather than receiving large government bail outs. The markets should police themselves by punishing those who made risky decisions or produced goods that consumers did not want. By letting banks, other financial institutions, or the automobile companies suffer the consequences of their poor decisions and fail, the companies that arise from the ashes will be stronger, more resilient, and more efficient as a result. Many fear that the current expansionary monetary policies followed by the Fed will cause inflation in a year or two down the road. Those who still follow the tenets of the classical model believe that we are better off in the long run if we just allow the economy to run its course rather than having expansionary monetary and fiscal policies that will only cause inflation and reduce economic growth in the long run.

That's it for the classical model. Next we turn our attention to the Keynesian model and Keynes' critique of the classical model.

# 9

## THE FIXED-PRICE KEYNESIAN MODEL

In the last chapter, we examined the classical model of the economy that was dominant before the Great Depression. In the classical model, the economy can correct its own problems because wages, prices and interest rates are flexible enough so that markets always clear. After the stock market crash of 1929, the economy entered a prolonged contraction known as the Great Depression, where unemployment rates increased to 25% and the economy lost a quarter of its output from 1929 to 1932. Herbert Hoover was president at the time. His economic advisors, being classical economists, argued for a limited role for government and that the economy could take care of its own problems. Rather than increasing government spending or cutting taxes to stimulate the economy, Hoover provided for a tax increase so that the government would not have a deficit. Rather than reducing trade barriers to increase exports, Hoover signed the Smoot-Hawley tariffs which led to a decline in world trade as other countries retaliated against our trade restrictions. Hoover believed that these measures would resolve the Great Depression, but from 1929, to 1930, to 1931 and 1932, the economy continued to suffer. According to the classical model, wages should have fallen to reduce unemployment, the price level should have declined to increase spending, and interest rates should have fallen to increase investment spending. As the Great Depression wore on, many economists became disenchanted with the ability of the classical model to provide understanding of the factors causing the Great Depression and to offer a successful remedy. One of these critics of the classical approach was a British economist by the name of John Maynard Keynes.

John Maynard Keynes was born in Cambridge, England in 1883. He was the son of another famous British economist, John Neville Keynes. He attended King's College in Cambridge, earning a degree in Mathematics in 1905. After graduating, he remained at Cambridge to study monetary theory under Alfred Marshall and

A.C. Pigou, two prominent classical economists. After college he went to work for the British Civil Service, and returned to Cambridge as a lecturer in 1908. He then went to work for the British Treasury. In 1919 he was the British Treasury's representative to the Peace Conference at Versailles, where he argued against war reparations payments by Germany and Austria urged by the British and the French because he felt that such harsh treatment would create economic instability in these countries. His opposition was so strong that he resigned from the commission. His prophesies turned out to be correct as hyperinflation in Germany during the 1920s led to the rise of Hitler and the need to fight another world war.

After writing *The Economic Consequences of the Peace* which laid out his arguments against the Treaty of Versailles, Keynes became well known as an economic analyst and pundit. In the 1920s he returned to Cambridge and began to write about monetary theory. His two-volume book *A Treatise on Money,* which expanded on the quantity theory developed by Alfred Marshall, furthered his reputation as an economic philosopher. These early works were still in the tradition of the classical model, but his thinking was soon to change as the Great Depression gripped England. As unemployment rates reached 20% in Britain, Keynes began to study the problems of unemployment and began to develop a radical new way of looking at the economy. His research culminated in the publishing in 1936 of *The General Theory of Employment, Interest, and Money (The General Theory),* the work for which Keynes is best known and the work that revolutionized the way in which economists study the world.

While Keynes laid out the bare elements of a new model of macroeconomics, much of what is now called "Keynesian Economics" arose from the work of his intellectual successors. Some of the more famous Keynesian economists include John Hicks of Cambridge, James Tobin of Yale, Paul Samuelson of Harvard and MIT, Alan Blinder of Princeton, Robert Solow of MIT, William Nordhaus of Yale, Walter Heller from Minnesota, Arthur Okun from Yale, and Paul Krugman from Princeton. Both Heller and Okun were on Presidents Kennedy's and Johnson's Council of Economic Advisors in the 1960s, which were the height of Keynesian economics in the United States. From a global perspective, Keynesian economics is probably the one area where American economists have had the greatest influence. *(http://www.econlib .org/library/Enc/bios/Keynes.html)*

The model that Keynes developed in the *General Theory* represented a radical departure from the orthodox economics of the day. Keynes believed that governments should be active in trying to stimulate the economy rather than letting the economy correct itself through flexible markets. Keynes highlighted the importance of deficit spending in relieving economic contractions. If the economy was below full employment, as it was during the Great Depression, Keynes believed that increases in government spending or tax cuts that would increase the government's budget deficit could help to stimulate the economy. After Roosevelt became president in 1933, he put these Keynesian ideas into practice in the United States through the New Deal programs such as the Civilian Conservation Corps and the Work Projects Administration. These are government agencies that created public works programs for the unemployed in the United States to increase employment and income in the country during the Great Depression. The New Deal, and similar programs in other countries at the time, represented the first times that Keynesian economics had been put into practice. The economics profession has not been the same since.

## THE KEYNESIAN CRITIQUE OF THE CLASSICAL MODEL

In the *General Theory,* Keynes first provided a critique of the classical model in its inability to explain the causes or offer a remedy for the Great Depression, and then offered an alternative model in its place. Keynes believed that the assumptions of the

John Maynard Keynes appeared on the cover of *Time* magazine in 1965.
Source: *http://www.malaspina.com/jpg/keynes.jpg,* retrieved 05.15.09

classical model were misguided, and the practice of classical economics was only
making the Great Depression worse. Rather than letting the economy correct itself,
Keynes believed that the government should have taken a more active role in solving the problems of the Great Depression. Here are his criticisms of the classical
model:

1. Wages, prices and interest rates may be "sticky," or inflexible, so that
   markets may not always clear. The classical model assumed that wages
   were flexible enough so that labor markets always cleared; the price
   level was flexible enough so the product market always cleared; and
   real interest rates were flexible enough so that saving is always equal
   to investment so that the loanable funds market cleared. Keynes
   rejected these assumptions, believing instead that these markets may
   not always be in equilibrium. Wages may be rigid downward due to
   minimum wage laws, union contracts, or implicit contracts between
   workers and firms to improve worker morale. This means that labor
   markets may not always be in equilibrium. Prices may not be flexible, so that overproduction in the product market may persist. It may
   be possible for the economy to produce more than spenders want to
   purchase. If there is a lack of business confidence, investment may not
   increase to equal saving no matter how low interest rates become. If
   markets are rigid in this way, then equilibrium is not guaranteed.

   A comparison of the classical and Keynesian views of the labor market is provided in Chapter Eight. (See Figure 8-1.) The classical model
   believed that wages are flexible, so that there is never any involuntary
   unemployment. Keynes, on the other hand, believed that involuntary
   unemployment may exist if wages fail to fall to their equilibrium level.

2. Money illusion may exist. In the classical model it is assumed that
   there is no money illusion, so all economic decisions are based on real
   variables, not nominal. Keynes recognized that workers may not have
   information about price changes in the economy, so that they may not
   know the actual real wage being paid. In this situation, economic

decisions may be based on nominal variables rather than real variables. When economic decisions are based on nominal variables, then money illusion is said to exist.

3.  Short run fluctuations matter. Keynes believed that small changes in spending could lead to much larger changes in GDP in the economy. In the classical model, the aggregate supply curve is vertical, so that the economy should always be at full employment. Given the level of output, classical economists were then concerned over how income was divided between capital and labor or how expenditures were split between consumption and investment. But if the level of output is assumed to be fixed, then the model cannot explain short-run fluctuations in the economy as occurred during the Great Depression. In place of the classical model, Keynes developed what he believed to be a more general theory that could explain output and employment when the economy was not at full employment.

4.  Expectations matter. Keynes believed that the expectations of consumers and producers are important in determining the overall level of economic activity. Consumption spending depends, in part, on consumer expectations about the future of the economy. If consumers lack confidence in the future of the economy and their own earning potential, they may decide to hoard their money and not spend it no matter how low prices become. Price declines will not automatically increase aggregate expenditures in the economy if consumers lack confidence about the future of the economy. This situation is known as a "liquidity trap," where consumers want liquidity rather than spending their income on goods and services. In a liquidity trap, consumption spending does not increase regardless of how low the price level becomes. Households hoard their money because of fear of the future.

    Similarly, investment spending depends on business confidence. If businesses lack confidence in the future of the economy, then investment may be insufficient to keep the economy at full employment. If businesses do not expect to sell any output in the future, there is no reason to increase investment expenditures in the present. With a lack of business confidence, investment spending may not increase no matter how low interest rates become.

5.  Expenditures matter. Keynes believed that, unlike the classical model, expenditures were the determinant of real GDP in the economy. It is often said that Keynes turned Say's Law on its head. While Say's Law stated that supply creates its own demand, so that spending adjusts to output, Keynes believed in the opposite, that demand creates its own supply or output adjusts to spending. The differences between Say's Law and the Keynesian approach are illustrated in Figure 9-1.

As shown in Figure 9-1, the production of aggregate output (GDP) requires resource payments to land, labor, capital, and entrepreneurs that generate a certain level of national income (NI). This national income provides the source of funds for aggregate expenditures (spending) in the economy. Once we have a certain level of aggregate expenditures, the question becomes, is there enough spending to purchase the output produced? If not, which will adjust, output or spending? This question lies at the heart of the difference between the classical and Keynesian models. In the classical model, Say's Law suggests that prices are flexible enough so that aggregate

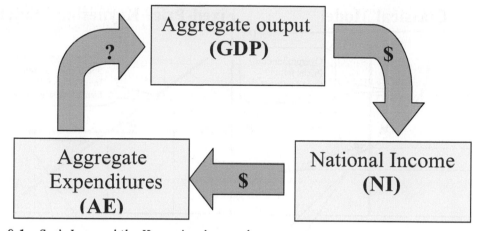

Figure 9-1    Say's Law and the Keynesian Approach

expenditures can change to equal the amount of output produced. In the classical model, spending adjusts to output. Keynes, on the other hand, believed that prices may be rigid so that spending may not be able to adjust to output. In this case, Keynes believed that firms will reduce their output rather than lowering prices to increase spending in the economy. In the Keynesian model, output adjusts to spending.

Classical model (Say's Law) → Spending adjusts to output
Fixed-price Keynesian model → Output adjusts to spending

The difference between the two models is also illustrated in Figure 9-2, which compares the two models from the product market or aggregate demand and aggregate supply perspective. As we saw in Chapter Eight, the aggregate supply curve in the classical model is vertical. The level of real GDP produced is independent of the price level. Prices adjust so that spending changes along the aggregate demand curve until the amount of spending is just enough to purchase the amount of output being produced. Remember that Say's Law is often stated as "supply creates its own demand." Given the output shown by the aggregate supply curve, the spending along the aggregate demand curve will adjust as the price level changes until the amount of spending in the economy is just sufficient to purchase the amount of output produced.

Keynes believed instead that prices may not be so flexible as to always keep spending equal to output. In the extreme case, Keynes believed that prices may be fixed in the short run. In this case the aggregate supply curve would be a horizontal line at the current price level. The equilibrium level of GDP is determined by the aggregate demand curve in this model. If the economy is not in equilibrium where aggregate demand is equal to aggregate supply, then output will adjust until it is just equal to spending. We will discuss the differences between the aggregate demand curves in the classical and fixed-price Keynesian models in the next chapter.

In the classical model the aggregate supply curve is vertical, so the level of real GDP (Y) is determined through the supply-side of the economy. Given the amount of output that firms and workers are willing and able to produce, then according to Say's Law prices will adjust so that spending changes until the amount of desired spending is just sufficient to purchase the quantity of output produced. Spending adjusts to output in the classical model.

In the fixed-price Keynesian model the opposite situation occurs. Since the price level is fixed, the aggregate supply curve is horizontal at the current price level in the economy. Firms in the economy are willing to produce as much as is demanded at the going price level. The quantity of real GDP, $Y^*$, is determined by the amount

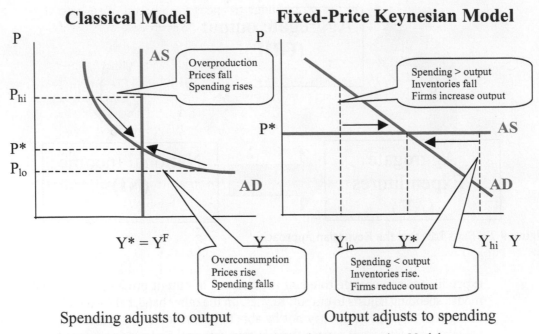

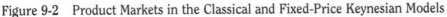

Figure 9-2   Product Markets in the Classical and Fixed-Price Keynesian Models

of spending in the economy, or the aggregate demand curve. If the level of output is below $Y^*$, such as at $Y_{lo}$, then spending is greater than output since the AD curve lies above the AS curve. If the amount of spending is greater than the amount of output produced, then inventories in the economy will be falling. As inventories fall, firms have the incentive to increase their levels of output. On the other hand, if the level of output is greater than equilibrium, such as at $Y_{hi}$, then the aggregate supply curve lies above the aggregate demand curve and output is greater than spending. If firms produce more than is being purchased in the economy inventories will rise. As inventories rise firms have the incentive to reduce their output.

When real GDP is less than equilibrium, spending is greater than output so inventories fall. As inventories fall, firms increase output. When real GDP is greater than equilibrium, the output is greater than spending and inventories increase. As inventories increase, firms will reduce their output. In this way, output adjusts to spending in the fixed-price Keynesian model.

Now that we have examined the Keynesian critique of the classical model, let us see the model that Keynes offered in its place. As with any model, first we will start with the assumptions of the model. Next we explore the idea of equilibrium in the fixed-price Keynesian model. Finally, we will examine some of the results of the model.

## THE ASSUMPTIONS OF THE FIXED-PRICE KEYNESIAN MODEL

To build the fixed-price Keynesian model of the economy, we start with the assumptions necessary to the model. These include:

1.  Rational self-interest: As in the classical model, we assume that economic decisions are made with a purpose. If economic decisions were arbitrary, it would be impossible to build a model of those decisions.

2.  The price level is fixed: In the short run, there is not enough time for prices to adjust in the economy. In this model we assume that prices

are fixed, so they cannot change to affect the amount of aggregate demand in the economy. Spending depends on other factors besides the price level in the economy.

3. Interest rates are fixed: There is not enough time for interest rates to adjust in the economy. Here we assume that interest rates are held constant, so we assume away the crowding out effect in the fixed-price Keynesian model. If the price level is fixed, then there is no reason to distinguish between nominal and real interest rates.

4. GDP is equivalent to National Income: We assume that Net Factor Income from Abroad is equal to zero, and that the Capital Consumption Allowance is equal to zero, so that Gross Domestic Product (output) is the same as National Income (income).

5. Consumption spending depends on income: We assume that consumption spending in the economy depends on the level of disposable income in the economy, or that consumption spending depends on other variables in the model. When a variable is determined inside the model in this way, it is said to be "induced" or "endogenous." So we assume that consumption is endogenous, or determined inside the model.

6. Investment, government spending, and exports are fixed: We assume that the levels of spending by firms, governments, and foreigners are fixed or determined outside of the model. If a variable is fixed and not dependent on other variables in the model, then the variable is said to "autonomous" or "exogenous," or determined outside of the model. So in this model, investment, government spending and exports are just given as fixed and do not depend on other variables in the model.

7. Imports are autonomous: For now, we assume that imports are fixed or exogenous or determined outside of the model.

8. Taxes are equal to zero: For simplicity, we assume that taxes are equal to zero, so that National Income is the same as disposable income.

We will relax the last two assumptions after we build the simple fixed-price Keynesian model. So for now, we will assume that imports are fixed and taxes are equal to zero. Later, we will examine a model where imports are endogenous and taxes are greater than zero.

Now that we have examined the assumptions, we can begin to build the details of the fixed-price Keynesian model. The model starts with the idea of a consumption function.

## THE CONSUMPTION AND SAVING FUNCTIONS

Consumption spending in the United States economy represents about 2/3 of the nation's Gross Domestic Product. Since Keynes was interested in the role of spending in the economy, it was natural to start by examining the relationship between consumption spending and disposable income by developing the idea of a consumption function. In the same way that the classical model started with the labor market and production function since it is a supply-side model, Keynes starts with the consumption function since it is a demand-side model. The consumption function shows the relationship between consumption spending and disposable income in the economy.

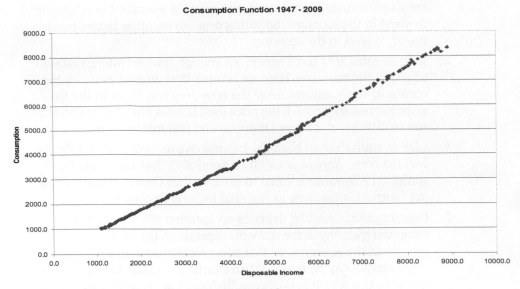

**Figure 9-3** U.S. Consumption Function 1947–2009
Source: Bureau of Economic Analysis

A *Consumption function* is a model that shows the relationship between consumption spending and disposable income in the economy. It can be represented as an equation, graph or table.

A consumption function for the U.S. economy is shown in Figure 9-3 for the time period 1947–2009. Note how close the relationship is between consumption spending on the vertical axis and disposable income on the horizontal axis. In all of the social sciences there are few relationships with this strong of a correlation. As disposable increases, consumption spending increases in a predictable manner. Note that the last two points are slightly below trend, representing the recession of 2008–2009 when consumption spending declined relative to income.

To build a consumption function, we begin by introducing some notation for the model:

$C$ = consumption spending
$Y$ = GDP, measured as either output or income
$C_0$ = autonomous consumption spending, the level of subsistence consumption spending when income = 0
$b$ = the marginal propensity to consume, or MPC
$T$ = taxes
$Y_d$ = disposable income, where $Y_d = Y - T$

Given this notation, the consumption function becomes

$$C = C_0 + bY_d.$$

According to the consumption function, consumption spending consists of two components. First is autonomous consumption spending $C_0$. This amount of consumption spending is independent of income, and is the amount of consumption spending when disposable income is equal to zero. Next, there is a part of consumption spending that increases with disposable income. This is the $bY_d$ term. When disposable income increases by one dollar, consumption spending increases by b, or the marginal propensity to consume. The consumption function is just an equation for a straight line, where $C_0$ is the vertical intercept and b is the slope of the consumption function.

The marginal propensity to consume, or the b term, deserves a little discussion. As shown in the equation above, the MPC is the slope of the consumption function. It tells us the change in consumption that results from a $1.00 change in disposable income. Since the MPC is positive, it means that the consumption function slopes upward. An increase in income causes an increase in consumption spending. Also, as we will see later, the MPC has to be less than one in this model for the economy to have equilibrium. When income increases by a dollar, some of that dollar is spent and some of it is saved. The portion that is consumed is the MPC. (My daughter's initials are MPC.)

From the discussion above, we have

$$b = MPC = \Delta C / \Delta Y_d, \qquad 0 < b < 1$$

The consumption function is vital to the fixed-price Keynesian model. The entire model is built around it. From the consumption function we can also derive a saving function.

A saving function describes the relationship between saving and disposable income in the economy. Saving is the part of income that is not consumed. Out of a given dollar increase in income, the portion that is not consumed is saved. Disposable income is equal to consumption plus saving:

$$Y_d = C + S$$

so

$$S = Y_d - C$$

Saving is the difference between disposable income and consumption. If we plug the consumption function into the saving formula above, we get

$$S = Y_d - C = Y_d - (C_0 + bY_d) = Y_d - C_0 - bY_d$$

so

$$S = - C_0 + (1 - b)Y_d$$

Saving in the economy is equal to a fixed amount of autonomous dissaving, $-C_0$, plus a variable amount of saving that increases with income, $(1 - b)Y_d$. The term $(1 - b)$ is the slope of the saving function, and it is also known as the marginal propensity to save, or MPS. The marginal propensity to save tells us how much saving increases when disposable income increases by a dollar. The sum of the MPC plus the MPS must be equal to 1. Whatever is not consumed out of a dollar increase in income will be saved. Mathematically,

$$(1 - b) = MPS = \Delta S / \Delta Y_d \qquad 0 < MPS < 1$$
$$MPC + MPS = 1$$

The marginal propensity to save is the change in saving divided by the change in disposable income. The MPS must be between 0 and 1. The sum of the MPC plus the MPS must be equal to 1. Any increase in income will be either consumed or saved.

A *Saving function* is a model that shows the relationship between saving and disposable income in the economy. It is found by subtracting the consumption function from disposable income. Saving is the difference between disposable income and consumption spending.

Besides modeling the consumption and saving functions through equations, we can also use graphs or tables to illustrate these relationships. The graphs of the

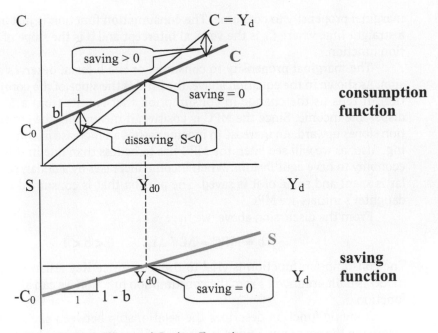

Figure 9-4   Consumption and Saving Functions

consumption and saving functions are shown in Figure 9-4. The upper graph shows the consumption function. The vertical axis measures consumption spending, while the horizontal axis measures disposable income. We will often use the geometric trick of a 45-degree line, which shows all of the points where the two variables are equal to each other, as long as the two axes are using the same scale of measurement. Here, the 45-degree line shows all of the combinations of C and $Y_d$ where C is equal to $Y_d$ or where saving is equal to zero. When the consumption function intersects the 45-degree line, at $Y_{d0}$, then consumption spending is equal to disposable income and saving is equal to zero. At levels of income below $Y_{d0}$, consumption is greater than disposable income so saving is less than zero (dissaving). At levels of income above $Y_{d0}$, consumption spending is less than disposable income so that saving is greater than zero (saving). The saving function is shown below the consumption function so that the levels of disposable income are the same in both graphs. When the consumption function crosses the 45-degree line, the saving function crosses the horizontal axis since at that level of income saving is zero.

The consumption function shows a positive relationship between consumption spending and disposable income. When disposable income rises, consumption spending increases. The vertical intercept of the consumption function is $C_0$ and the slope is b or the MPC. When the consumption function crosses the 45-degree line saving is equal to zero. The saving function also slopes upward, with a vertical intercept of $-C_0$ and a slope of $1-b$, or the MPS. There needs to be a negative quadrant in the saving graph since there are ranges of disposable income where saving is negative.

We will use these models of consumption and saving when looking at aggregate expenditures for the economy. First, we will look at a simple example.

## An Example

Suppose that the level of autonomous consumption in Mudville is 100, and that the MPC is 0.9. The consumption function is given by:

$$C = 100 + 0.9Y_d$$

The saving function is

$$S = -100 + 0.1Y_d.$$

The level of income where saving is equal to zero can be found in two ways. First, if saving is equal to zero, then $C = Y_d$. If we plug that into the consumption function, we get

$$Y_d = 100 + 0.9Y_d$$
$$0.1Y_d = 100$$
$$Y_d = 1000$$

Or we could set saving = 0 in the saving function:

$$0 = -100 + 0.1Y_d$$
$$-0.1Y_d = -100$$
$$Y_d = 1000$$

Graphically, the model looks like this:

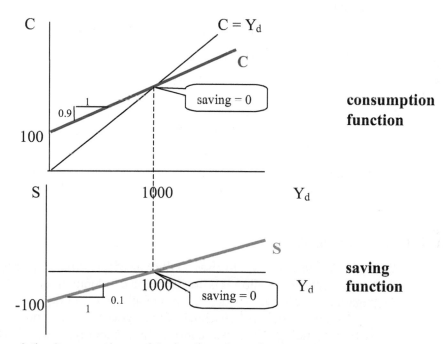

Figure 9-5   Consumption and Saving Functions: An Example

In this example, the consumption function has a vertical intercept of 100 and a slope equal to the MPC of 0.9. The saving function has a vertical intercept of –100 and a slope equal to the MPS of 0.1. Saving is equal to zero when disposable income is equal to 1000.

The consumption and saving functions can also be shown through a table as in Table 9-1. Suppose that disposable income increases by 1000 for each row in the table. The levels of consumption and saving can be found by plugging in $Y_d$ into the consumption and saving functions. We can derive the following table:

**Table 9-1**   Consumption and Saving Functions

| Disposable Income | Consumption | Saving |
|---|---|---|
| 0 | 100 | −100 |
| 1000 | 1000 | 0 |
| 2000 | 1900 | 100 |
| 3000 | 2800 | 200 |
| 4000 | 3700 | 300 |
| 5000 | 4600 | 400 |

As disposable income increases, both consumption and saving also increase. When disposable income is zero, then consumption is equal to $100 and saving is equal to −$100. These are the intercepts of the consumption and saving functions. When disposable income is equal to $1000, then consumption spending is also equal to $1000 and saving is equal to zero. At income levels below $1000 saving is negative. At income levels above $1000 saving is greater than zero. When disposable income increases by 1000, consumption spending increases by 900. So the marginal propensity to consume is

$$MPC = \Delta C / \Delta Y_d = 900 / 1000 = 0.9$$

And the marginal propensity to save is

$$MPS = \Delta S / \Delta Y_d = 100 / 1000 = 0.1$$

and

$$MPC + MPS = 0.9 + 0.1 = 1.$$

Now that we have explored the consumption and saving functions in the fixed-price Keynesian model, we now turn our attention to the concepts of aggregate expenditure and equilibrium in the fixed-price Keynesian model.

## AGGREGATE EXPENDITURE

Since the Keynesian model focuses on the role of spending in the economy, the concept of aggregate expenditures is crucial to the development of the model as a whole. Aggregate expenditures are just the sum of all the spending in the economy by the different sectors, such as households, firms, governments, and the foreign sector. Household spending is known as consumption spending, as we saw above. Spending by firms is known as investment spending. Government spending is just that, and spending by the foreign sector is net export spending, or exports minus imports. So overall, aggregate expenditures are the sum of consumption, investment, government, and net export spending, or

$$AE = C + I + G + (X - M)$$

where
AE = aggregate expenditures
C  = consumption
I  = investment
G  = government spending
X  = exports
M  = imports

*Aggregate expenditures* are equal to the sum of consumption, investment, government, and net export spending in an economy. The aggregate expenditure function shows the amount of total spending in the economy at different levels of income.

For now we will introduce the assumption mentioned earlier that taxes are equal to zero. If this is the case, then disposable income, $Y_d$, is the same as national income, or Y. Since

$$Y_d = Y - T,$$
if T = 0 then $Y_d$ = Y.

We will relax this assumption later on with a more complicated model, but for now we will assume that taxes are equal to zero and that imports are fixed. We will sometimes call this the "simple fixed-price Keynesian model," although it may not always seem so simple.

To derive the aggregate expenditure function, we start with two equations, the consumption function and the aggregate expenditure identity: (Remember that T = 0.)

$$C = C_0 + bY$$
$$AE = C + I + G + (X - M)$$

Combining these, we get

$$AE = C_0 + bY + I + G + (X - M)$$

Since every term but bY is just a fixed number, we can combine these autonomous terms into a single notation, $AE_0$, or autonomous aggregate expenditures.

*Autonomous aggregate expenditures ($AE_0$)* are the sum of fixed, or autonomous, spending in the economy,

$$AE_0 = C_0 + I + G + (X - M)$$

From the equation above

$$AE = C_0 + bY + I + G + (X - M)$$
$$AE = [C_0 + I + G + (X - M)] + bY$$
$$AE = [AE_0] + bY$$

So $$AE = AE_0 + bY$$

The aggregate expenditure function is an upward-sloping straight line with a vertical intercept of $AE_0$, autonomous aggregate expenditures, and a slope of b, the marginal propensity to consume. Since the only part of aggregate expenditures that changes is consumption spending, changes in aggregate expenditures will only occur with changes in consumption. This is shown more clearly in Figure 9-6.

As shown in Figure 9-6, consumption spending is upward-sloping, while the other forms of spending, investment, government, and net export spending, are all held fixed and thus horizontal lines. When these are added together we get the aggregate expenditure function. Since everything else is horizontal, the slope of the aggregate expenditure function is the same as the slope of the consumption function, the marginal propensity to consume. The aggregate expenditure function is shown again in Figure 9-7.

The aggregate expenditure function is upward-sloping with a vertical intercept of $AE_0$ and a slope of b.

## EQUILIBRIUM IN THE FIXED-PRICE KEYNESIAN MODEL

In the fixed-price Keynesian model, output adjusts until it is equal to spending in the economy. In equilibrium, output or real GDP (Y) must be equal to the amount of

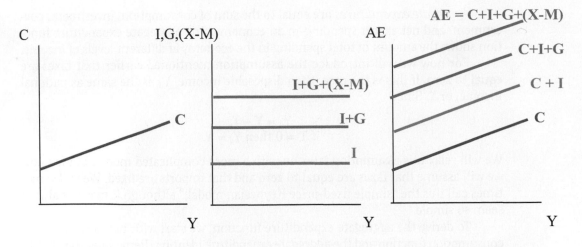

**Consumption Function     I, G, and (X – M) are fixed.     Their sum is aggregate expenditures.**

Figure 9-6    Deriving the Aggregate Expenditure Function

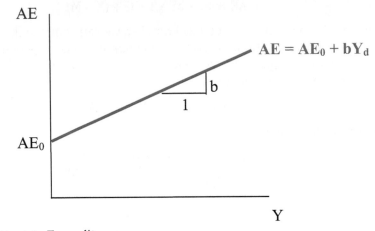

Figure 9-7    Aggregate Expenditures

spending in the economy (AE). If not, inventories will change, causing firms to adjust their output. This output adjustment process is explained in the paragraphs below.

*Keynesian equilibrium* occurs where output in the economy is equal to spending, or where real GDP is equal to aggregate expenditures.

Keynesian equilibrium is where

$$Y = AE$$

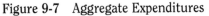

output = spending.

To find the equilibrium level of real GDP or Y, we can use the formula above, plug in the aggregate expenditure function, and solve the expression for Y. The resulting equation provides the formula for the equilibrium value of Y in this model.

$$Y = AE$$
$$Y = AE_0 + bY$$
$$Y - bY = AE_0$$
$$Y(1 - b) = AE_0$$

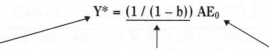

$$Y^* = (1 / (1 - b)) \, AE_0$$

**Equilibrium GDP = spending multiplier · autonomous aggregate expenditures**

The equilibrium level of real GDP ($Y^*$) is equal to a first term, $1/(1 - b)$ that is known as the spending multiplier, times autonomous aggregate expenditures, or $AE_0$. From this we can derive the spending multiplier formula, or

$$\Delta Y = (1 / (1 - b)) \, AE_0.$$

Equilibrium in the fixed-price Keynesian model is shown graphically in Figure 9-8. This graph is commonly known as the "Keynesian cross" diagram.

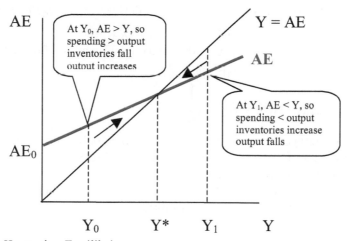

**Figure 9-8**   Keynesian Equilibrium

The equilibrium level of real GDP occurs at $Y^*$, where $Y = AE$ and the aggregate expenditure function crosses the 45-degree line. Here, the 45-degree line shows all of the combinations of real GDP and aggregate expenditures where $Y = AE$ and the economy is in equilibrium. Where the aggregate expenditure function crosses the 45-degree line that is the one point on the AE function where the economy is in equilibrium. At levels of output below equilibrium, such as $Y_0$, the AE function lies above the 45-degree line, so spending is greater than output. If spending is greater than output, then the extra spending must be coming from output that was produced in previous periods, or inventories. When spending is greater than output, inventories in the economy will be falling. As inventories fall, firms have the incentive to increase their output. This process will continue until equilibrium is reached where output is just equal to spending.

If output is above equilibrium, such as at $Y_1$, then the AE function lies below the 45-degree line and spending is less than output. If spending is less than output, then firms are producing more than spenders in the economy are purchasing, and inventories will increase. As inventories rise, firms have the incentive to reduce their output until output declines enough so that it is again equal to spending. In the Keynesian model, if the economy is not in equilibrium then inventories will change, and the change in inventories provides firms with the incentive to alter their output. In this way, output adjusts to spending in the fixed-price Keynesian model.

## EQUILIBRIUM IN THE FIXED-PRICE KEYNESIAN MODEL: AN EXAMPLE

We will now explore an example of Keynesian equilibrium starting with the consumption function described earlier. Suppose that we have the following information for the economy of Macroland:

$$C = 100 + 0.9Y_d \qquad X = 150$$
$$I = 100 \qquad\qquad M = 100$$
$$G = 50 \qquad\qquad T = 0$$

Here we have a model where consumption is induced, or depends on income through the consumption function. If taxes are equal to zero, then $Y_d = Y$ so the term Y can be used in the consumption function. The model also shows that investment, government spending, exports and imports are fixed or autonomous. The levels of these variables do not depend on other variables in the model.

Given this information, we can derive the aggregate expenditure function:

$$AE = C + I + G + (X - M)$$
$$AE = 100 + 0.9Y + 100 + 50 + (150 - 100)$$

$$AE = 300 + 0.9Y$$

$$\uparrow \qquad \uparrow$$
$$AE_0 \qquad b$$

The aggregate expenditure function is an equation for a straight line with a vertical intercept of autonomous aggregate expenditures, $AE_0$, and a slope of the marginal propensity to consume, or b.

In equilibrium in the fixed price Keynesian model, output (or Y) must be equal to spending (or AE). So, in equilibrium,

$$Y = AE$$
$$Y = 300 + 0.9Y$$
$$Y - 0.9Y = 300$$
$$Y(1 - 0.9) = 300$$
$$Y^* = [1/(1 - 0.9)] \times 300 = 10 \times 300 = 3{,}000$$

$$\uparrow \qquad\qquad \uparrow \qquad\qquad\qquad \uparrow$$

Spending multiplier $\times$ $AE_0$ = equilibrium GDP

In this example, the equilibrium level of GDP is equal to $3,000, where Y = AE.

The idea of Keynesian equilibrium can also be illustrated through a table. Table 9-2 shows the different components of spending at different levels of GDP. The first column measures GDP or national income. The second column shows consumption spending, which is found by plugging in those values of income into the consumption function shown in Table 9-1. The next three columns show investment, government, and net export spending. Note that I, G and (X – M) are autonomous here. They are just fixed columns of numbers that do not change with increases in income. Consumption spending, on the other hand, is induced or endogenous, since it increases with increases in income. The MPC is equal to 0.9, since a $1000 increase in income leads to a $900 increase in consumption spending, so $\Delta C / \Delta Y_d = 900/1000 = 0.9$.

The AE column shows the sum of spending, $C + I + G + (X - M)$. The column labeled Y – AE shows the unplanned change in inventories. If output is greater than spending inventories will rise. If output is less than spending inventories will fall. When output is equal to spending there is no change in inventories so firms have no incentive to change their output. The last column shows how firms in the economy will respond to the change in inventories. When inventories are increasing firms will reduce their output, but when inventories are falling firms will increase their output.

**Table 9-2** Equilibrium in the Fixed-Price Keynesian Model: An Example

| GDP (Y) | C | I | G | X – M | AE | Y – AE | Δoutput |
|---|---|---|---|---|---|---|---|
| 0 | 100 | 100 | 50 | 50 | 300 | –300 | Increase |
| 1000 | 1000 | 100 | 50 | 50 | 1200 | –200 | Increase |
| 2000 | 1900 | 100 | 50 | 50 | 2100 | –100 | Increase |
| 3000 | 2800 | 100 | 50 | 50 | 3000 | 0 | No change |
| 4000 | 3700 | 100 | 50 | 50 | 3900 | 100 | Decrease |
| 5000 | 4600 | 100 | 50 | 50 | 4800 | 200 | Decrease |

Table 9-2 shows that equilibrium occurs when GDP is equal to $3000, since this is the only level of GDP where spending is equal to output. When GDP is less than equilibrium, say at Y = $1000, then the amount of spending, $1200, is greater than the amount of GDP produced, $1000. When output is less than spending, then inventories will decline (by $200), and firms have the incentive to increase their output. When GDP is greater than equilibrium, say at GDP – $4000, then output of $4000 is greater than spending of $3900 and inventories will increase by $100. If inventories are increasing, firms have the incentive to reduce their output until equilibrium is reached. The only time that firms do not have the incentive to change their output is when the economy is in equilibrium so that output is equal to spending and there is no change in inventories, or at the equilibrium level of GDP of $3000.

This is the essence of the idea of Keynesian equilibrium. When firms are producing below equilibrium, inventories fall so firms have the incentive to increase output. When firms are producing above equilibrium, inventories rise and firms have the incentive to reduce their output. Output adjusts to spending in this way until output is equal to spending, or firms are producing just the amount of output that spenders in the economy desire to purchase at that level of income. If the economy is not in equilibrium, inventory changes provide the incentive for firms to adjust their output until output is equal to spending in the economy.

The equilibrium shown in Table 9-2 can also be shown graphically as in Figure 9-9. The aggregate expenditure function crosses the 45-degree line when the economy is in equilibrium at Y = 3000. At levels of output less than $3000, say at Y = 2000, then spending is greater than output and the decline in inventories will cause firms to increase their output. At output levels greater than $3000, say at Y = 4000, then spending is less than output and firms will reduce their output as inventories increase. It is only at equilibrium GDP of $3000 where spending is equal to output, and since inventories are not changing there is no incentive for firms to change their level of output.

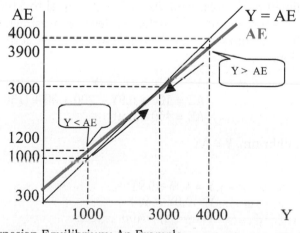

Figure 9-9 Keynesian Equilibrium: An Example

## AN INCREASE IN INVESTMENT SPENDING

Continuing with our example, let us suppose that there is an increase in autonomous aggregate expenditures. For instance, assume that investment spending increases by $100. How does the increase in investment spending affect the equilibrium level of real GDP?

Mathematically, we can solve for the new equilibrium GDP in two ways. First, we can use the spending multiplier formula. Second, we could plug the new level of investment into the original aggregate expenditure curve and find the new equilibrium. Here we will use both approaches to show that they are equivalent.

### The Spending Multiplier Formula

First, we can use the multiplier formula to find the change in Y. The multiplier formula is given by the equation

$$\Delta Y = (1 / (1 - b)) \Delta AE_0.$$

In this example, the change in autonomous aggregate expenditures ($\Delta AE_0$) is the increase in investment spending of $100. The MPC (or b) is equal to 0.9, so the spending multiplier is equal to

$$1/(1 - b) = 1/(1 - 0.9) = 1 / 0.1 = 10.$$

So the change in GDP is equal to

$$\Delta Y = (1 / (1 - b)) \Delta AE_0 = 1/(1 - 0.9) \times 100 = 10 \times 100 = 1,000.$$

According to the multiplier formula, an increase in investment spending of $100 will lead to an increase in GDP of $1000. The new equilibrium level of GDP, $Y^{**}$, is equal to

$$Y^{**} = Y^* + \Delta Y$$

So $Y^{**} = 3000 + 1000 = 4000$. When investment spending increases by $100 in this example the equilibrium level of GDP increases from $3000 to $4000.

### Plugging in to the Original Formula

We can also find the new equilibrium level of GDP by plugging in the new level of investment spending into the original aggregate expenditure formula and solving for equilibrium. If investment was originally equal to $100, then with an increase in investment spending of $100 the new level of investment spending would be $200. If we plug this into the original formula we can arrive at the new aggregate expenditure function.

$$AE = C + I + G + (X - M)$$
$$AE = 100 + 0.9Y + 200 + 50 + (150 - 100)$$
$$AE = 400 + 0.9Y$$

In equilibrium, Y = AE, so

$$Y = AE$$
$$Y = 400 + 0.9Y$$
$$Y - 0.9Y = 400$$
$$Y(1 - 0.9) = 400$$

$$Y^{**} = [1 /(1 - 0.9)] \times 400 = 10 \times 400 = 4,000$$

**Table 9-3**  An Increase in Investment Spending

| Y (GDP) | C | AE (I = 100) | AE (I = 200) |
|---|---|---|---|
| 0 | 100 | 300 | 400 |
| 1000 | 1000 | 1200 | 1300 |
| 2000 | 1900 | 2100 | 2200 |
| 3000 | 2800 | 3000 | 3100 |
| 4000 | 3700 | 3900 | 4000 |
| 5000 | 4600 | 4800 | 4900 |

With either approach, we find that the new equilibrium level of real GDP is $4000. A $100 increase in investment spending led to a $1000 increase in equilibrium GDP.

We can also show the effects of an increase in investment spending through a table. Table 9-3 shows the levels of aggregate expenditure for Macroland when investment is equal to $100 and when investment is equal to $200. Note that, as shown earlier, when investment spending is $100 the equilibrium level of GDP where output is equal to spending is at Y = 3000. When investment spending increases to $200, the new equilibrium where Y = AE occurs at a level of GDP equal to $4000. The increase in investment of $100 increases equilibrium GDP by $1000.

When investment spending is equal to $100, the equilibrium GDP occurs where Y = AE at a level of GDP of $3000. When investment spending is equal to $200, the equilibrium level of GDP occurs where Y = AE at a level of GDP equal to $4000. The increase in investment spending of $100 led to a $1000 increase in real GDP.

Finally, we can display the effects of an increase in investment spending graphically. Figure 9-10 shows the effects of an increase in investment spending in the Keynesian cross diagram. The effect of the increase in investment spending of $100 is to increase the vertical intercept of the aggregate expenditure function by $100, from 300 to 400. When the aggregate expenditure function increases by $100, the equilibrium level of GDP increases by $1000 from $3000 to $4000.

The idea of the Keynesian spending multiplier is implicit in Figure 9-10. We originally start at equilibrium where GDP = $3000 and output is equal to spending of $3000. When investment spending increases by $100, the economy is no longer in equilibrium at Y = 3000, since now output is $3000 but spending is now $3100. Since

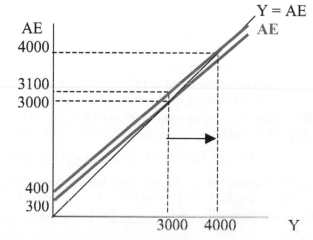

Figure 9-10   An Increase in Investment Spending

spending is now greater than output, inventories will fall and firms will want to increase their output. So output increases by $100 so that it is equal to spending. But when output is increased by $100, income increases by $100 as resources receive income from production. Since the MPC is equal to 0.9, the $100 increase in income will generate $100 \times 0.9 = \$90$ in additional spending. Since spending increases by $90, firms will increase their output by $90 and create another $90 worth of income. This $90 increase in income will then lead to $90 \times 0.9 = \$81$ in additional spending. As spending increases firms increase their output, generating even more income and spending. As this process continues, the changes in income and spending become smaller and smaller until eventually a new equilibrium level of GDP at $4000 is reached. This spending multiplier process in the fixed-price Keynesian model is explained in excruciating detail in the next section.

## THE SPENDING MULTIPLIER

The spending multiplier occurs because of a simple fact: one person's spending becomes another person's income. When someone receives income, they will save a certain portion, given by the MPS, and spend the rest. That spending becomes someone else's income, which generates even more spending in the economy. As we will see, an infinite series of spending and income changes in the economy can result from some initial change in spending in the economy.

As an example, suppose that the MPC in Multiplierville is equal to 0.5, so that for any increase in income, half of that increase will be spent and the other half will be saved. Let us assume that we have an increase in investment spending of $100. Bob the Builder needs to buy a new power saw for $100, an investment expenditure on capital in the economy. Bob buys the saw from Carla the Carpenter, who owns a hardware store and then spends half of her income on dinner ($50) and saves the other half ($50). The money spent on dinner goes to David's Diner. David will spend half ($25) on a new shirt at Edna's Emporium and save the other half ($25). Edna will then receive $25 in income, and spend half ($12.50) on lunch at Fred's Franks and save the other half ($12.50). Fred will receive $12.50 in income, and spend half ($6.25) and save the other half. This process continues until the original increase in spending of $100 is eventually saved throughout the economy. Notice that the initial change in spending leads to a whole series of increases in income and spending. This is the basics of the multiplier process.

The first purchase of the $100 saw led to a whole series of increases in spending and income in the economy equal to:

$$\$100 + 50 + 25 + 12.50 + 6.25 + 3.125 + . . .$$

Table 9-4 shows the change in spending and saving that results from ten rounds of the multiplier process.

After ten rounds of this process, the total change in spending is $199.80 and the total change in saving is equal to $99.80. After ten rounds, all but $0.20 of the original increase in spending has been saved. The increase in spending, or income and real GDP, is only $0.20 away from $200, which is the amount predicted by the spending multiplier formula:

$$\Delta Y = (1 / (1 - b)) \Delta AE_0 = 1/(1 - 0.5) \times 100 = 2 \times 100 = 200$$

After ten rounds, the economy is only twenty cents away from the equilibrium value of an increase in $200. The rest of the series of changes in spending and saving throughout the economy will continue until the other twenty cents is spent and saved.

**Table 9-4**  The Keynesian Multiplier Process
(Assumptions: Δ investment = 100, MPC = 0.5)

| Round | Δ spending (AE) | Δ saving (S) | Δ income (GDP) |
|---|---|---|---|
| 1 | $100 | $ 0 | $100 |
| 2 | 50 | 50 | $100 + .5(100) |
| 3 | 25 | 25 | $100 + .5(100) + .5(.5(100)) |
| 4 | 12.50 | 12.50 | $100 + .5(100) + .5(.5(100)) + .5(.5(.5(100))) |
| 5 | 6.25 | 6.25 | Et cetera |
| 6 | 3.125 | 3.125 | |
| 7 | 1.5625 | 1.5625 | |
| 8 | 0.78125 | 0.78125 | |
| 9 | 0.390625 | 0.390625 | |
| 10 | 0.1953125 | 0.1953125 | |
| Total change | 199.80465 | 99.80465 | |

## The Algebra of the Multiplier

The fourth column of Table 9-4 shows the total increase in GDP that results from the original $100 increase in spending. First spending increases by $100, then half of $100, then half of that, and half of that, etc. Since the increase in spending will equal the increase in income, the total increase in income will be equal to:

$$\Delta Y = \$100 + .5(100) + .5(.5(100)) + .5(.5(.5(100))) + .5(.5(.5(.5(100)))) + \ldots$$
$$\Delta Y = \$100 + .5(100) + .5^2(100) + .5^3(100) + .5^4(100) + \ldots$$

If we substitute this equation for its algebraic equivalent, we can let $\Delta I = 100$ and the MPC = b = 0.5. The equation becomes

$$\Delta Y = \Delta I + b\Delta I + b^2 \Delta I + b^3 \Delta I + \ldots$$

Since each term on the right hand side of the equation has a $\Delta I$ in it, we can factor out the $\Delta I$ and obtain:

$$\Delta Y = \Delta I (1 + b + b^2 + b^3 + \ldots)$$
If we let $Z = (1 + b + b^2 + b^3 + \ldots)$, then $\Delta Y = Z \times \Delta I$ and
$$Z = 1 + b (1 + b + b^2 + b^3 + \ldots) = 1 + bZ$$

If $Z = 1 + bZ$ then $Z - bZ = 1$ and
$$Z(1 - b) = 1 \text{ so}$$
$$Z = 1/(1 - b)$$

and

$$\Delta Y = [1 / (1 - b)] \Delta I$$

The spending multiplier, $1/ 1 - b$, is just the formula that solves the infinite series of expenditure increases in the economy, $1 + b + b^2 + b^3 + \ldots$. As long as the MPC (b) is less than one, the economy will converge to a new equilibrium. In each round of the multiplier process, as long as some of the increase in income is saved, there will be less income created in the next round and the economy will converge to a new equilibrium. If the MPC is equal to 1, on the other hand, then the increase in income will be perpetually spent and the economy will never reach a new equilibrium. If the MPC is greater than one, then each stage of spending will create even more income, so the economy blows up even faster. As long as the MPC is less than one the economy will have a new equilibrium.

## EXTENDING THE MODEL: IMPORTS AND TAXES

In this section, we extend the simple fixed-price Keynesian model by introducing an import function and taxes. We now assume that imports are induced or endogenous, that they depend on disposable income in the economy through an import function. We also assume that taxes are greater than zero, so that we now need to include the disposable income term in the model. Once we describe how the model has been changed, we will examine the new aggregate expenditure function and formula for equilibrium. As we will see, introducing an import function also changes the spending multiplier in this model, and with taxes we can examine the concept of the tax multiplier.

The import function is similar to the consumption function. It consists of two terms, one of which is fixed and the other that varies with income. We will let $M_0$ represent autonomous import spending, or the amount of import spending when disposable income is equal to zero. We also define d as the marginal propensity to import (MPIM), or the change in import spending resulting from a one dollar increase in income in the economy. Similar to the MPC, the MPIM must be less than one for the economy to have equilibrium.

If taxes are greater than zero, then disposable income is the difference between national income and taxes in the economy. Let us define the following variables:

T = taxes (lump-sum taxes that do not depend on income)
$Y_d = Y - T$ (disposable income)
d = MPIM (marginal propensity to import)
$MPIM = \Delta M / \Delta Y_d$

## Aggregate Expenditures

With this notation, we can build the following model:

$$C = C_0 + bY_d$$
$$M = M_0 + dY_d$$

The import function is similar to the consumption function. The term $M_0$ is autonomous import spending, or the quantity of import spending when disposable income is equal to zero. The term d is the MPIM, or the marginal propensity to import. $Y_d$ is disposable income. When disposable income increases by one dollar, import spending increases by d or the marginal propensity to import.

With both consumption and import functions, the aggregate expenditure function becomes

$$AE = C + I + G + (X - M)$$
$$AE = C_0 + bY_d + I + G + (X - (M_0 + dY_d))$$
$$AE = [C_0 + I + G + X - M_0] + bY_d - dY_d$$

Since everything in the brackets is just fixed spending, we can combine these fixed terms and again call it autonomous aggregate expenditures or $AE_0$. Combining the $Y_d$ terms we obtain

$$AE = [AE_0] + (b - d)Y_d$$

Since $Y_d = Y - T$, we can plug in disposable income and get

$$AE = AE_0 + (b - d)(Y - T)$$
$$AE = AE_0 + (b - d)Y - (b - d)T.$$

Combining fixed terms, we get

$$AE = \underbrace{AE_0 - (b - d)T}_{\text{Vertical intercept}} + \underbrace{(b - d)Y}_{\text{slope}}$$

In this extended model the aggregate expenditure function is still a straight line, with a vertical intercept of $AE_0 - (b - d)T$ and a slope of $(b - d)$. When Y increases by \$1.00, aggregate expenditures increase by $(b - d)$. Note that if taxes are equal to zero, and if imports are fixed so that $d = 0$, then we end up with the original aggregate expenditure function, $AE = AE_0 + bY$.

## Equilibrium

Remember that in Keynesian equilibrium, output must be equal to spending or

$$Y = AE.$$

If we set Y equal to the aggregate expenditure formula above, we can derive an expression for equilibrium in this extended model, and also find the spending and tax multipliers for this model.

In equilibrium, $Y = AE$

So $$Y = AE_0 - (b - d)T + (b - d)Y$$

Solving for Y, we get

$$Y - (b - d)Y = AE_0 - (b - d)T$$
$$Y(1 - b + d) = AE_0 - (b - d)T$$

$$Y^* = [1 / (1 - b + d)] \, AE_0 + [(-b + d) / (1 - b + d)] \, T$$

The expression above is the equilibrium level of GDP in the extended model. There are two terms, one attached to $AE_0$ and the other attached to T. These terms provide the formulas for the spending and tax multipliers in the model. The multiplier formula in this model is

$$\Delta Y = [1 / (1 - b + d)] \, \Delta AE_0 + [(-b + d) / (1 - b + d)] \, \Delta T$$

If aggregate expenditures increase by \$1.00, then real GDP (Y) will increase by \$1 / $(1 - b + d)$. This is the spending multiplier in the model. If taxes increase by \$1.00, then real GDP will change by \$$(-b + d) / (1 - b + d)$. Note that the tax multiplier is negative. An increase in taxes will reduce real GDP, while a tax cut will increase real GDP. The rationale for tax cuts is that they increase disposable income, which increases consumption spending, which leads to multiplied increases in real GDP in the economy.

From the formula above, we can derive the multiplier formulas.

$$\text{Spending multiplier} = \frac{1}{(1 - b + d)} = \frac{1}{(1 - MPC + MPIM)}$$

So $$\Delta Y = [1/(1 - b + d)] \, \Delta AE_0$$

An increase in autonomous aggregate expenditures leads to a multiplied increase in real GDP. Note that the multiplier here is smaller than in the simple model where imports are fixed. With induced imports, the multiplier is smaller because some income will be spent on imports in each stage of the multiplier process, so there is less income spent on domestic consumption to become income in the next round.

When imports are fixed, $d = 0$ and the multiplier is the same as in the simple model, $1/(1 - b)$.

The tax multiplier is also contained in the multiplier formula.

$$\text{Tax multiplier} = \frac{-b + d}{1 - b + d} = \frac{-MPC + MPIM}{1 - MPC + MPIM}$$

So $\qquad\qquad\qquad \Delta Y = [(-b + d) / (1 - b + d)] \Delta T$

The tax multiplier is less than zero as long as $b > d$, or the MPC is greater than the MPIM. As long as households consume more domestic goods than foreign goods out of an increase in income, the tax multiplier will be negative. An increase in taxes will lead to a multiplied decline in GDP, and a decrease in taxes will lead to a multiplied increase in real GDP. The economic rationale behind George Bush's tax cuts of 2001, 2003 and 2008 lay in this idea of the tax multiplier. Perhaps the greatest stimulus package in American history, Obama's American Recovery and Reinvestment Act of 2009 relies on both of these multipliers in its attempts to revive the U.S. economy.

We will further utilize these spending and tax multipliers in Chapter 11 on fiscal policy. For now, we turn to a graph of equilibrium in the extended model and then an examination of an alternative notion of equilibrium to finish this chapter on the fixed-price Keynesian model.

Figure 9-11 shows the graph of equilibrium in the extended model. The intercept is less than that of the simple model, since the existence of taxes reduces autonomous consumption when income is zero. The slope is also less, since the existence of induced imports means that an increase in income leads to less of an increase in consumption spending in the economy since some of that income is spent on imports instead.

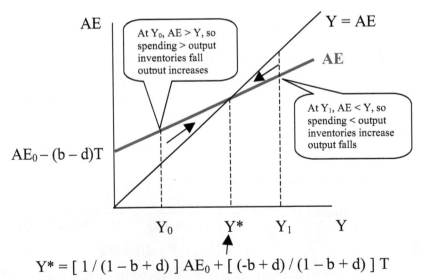

$$Y^* = [\, 1 / (1 - b + d) \,] AE_0 + [\, (-b + d) / (1 - b + d) \,] T$$

Figure 9-11    Keynesian Equilibrium in the Extended Model

## LEAKAGES AND INJECTIONS

There is an alternative method to determine equilibrium in the fixed-price Keynesian model besides finding where output is equal to spending in the economy. Another notion of equilibrium is that leakages have to equal injections. Leakages consist of income that households have received but not spent on current domestic output. Injections are sources of spending by other sectors of the economy, such as firms, the government, and the foreign sector. Whatever income is not spent by households on current domestic output must be spent by other sectors if the total amount of spending will be enough to purchase the output that generated that income.

Leakages consist of saving, taxes, and imports. These are the other uses of household income besides consumption spending on current domestic output. Injections consist of investment, government, and net export spending. These are sources of domestic spending in the economy other than household consumption spending. Whatever households do not spend must be spent by other sectors if there is going to be equilibrium in the economy. The basic ideas are summarized below.

Equilibrium occurs where

| Leakages | = | Injections |
|---|---|---|
| $S + T + M$ | = | $I + G + X$ |

| income received by households not spent on current domestic output | = | spending by other sectors of the economy besides households |
|---|---|---|

In Figure 9-12 we reproduce the simple circular flow model from Chapter Five, except now we include "other sectors," such as financial institutions, governments, and the foreign sector, as a third component of the economy besides firms and households. Whatever is leaking out of the economy in the form of income not spent by households must be returned to the economy in the form of spending by other sectors if there is to be enough spending to purchase the quantity of output produced.

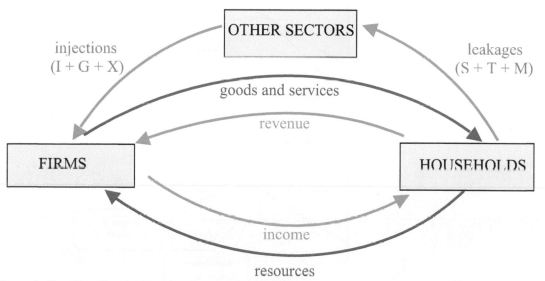

Figure 9-12   The Simple Circular Flow Model Revisited

Whatever is leaking out of the economy must be replaced by injections if the volume of output and spending is to be consistent in the circular flow model.

Think of a bathtub. If the volume of water flowing into the tub (injections) is greater than the volume of water flowing out (leakages), then the volume of water in the tub will be increasing. If more is flowing out than is flowing in, then leakages are greater than injections and the volume of water in the tub will be falling. The tub will be in equilibrium, or the volume of water will stay the same, when leakages are equal to injections. In the same way, when the spending entering the economy is equal to the spending leaving the economy, the volume of spending and income will be constant and the economy will be in equilibrium.

The graphical version of this notion of equilibrium is shown in Figure 9-13. The top graph shows the typical Keynesian cross diagram where equilibrium occurs at the level of GDP where Y = AE. The lower graph shows leakages and injections. Since saving and imports increase with income, the leakages function slopes upward. Since saving may be negative, part of the leakages function lies below the horizontal axis. Since investment, government, and export spending are fixed, the injections function is just a horizontal line. When leakages are equal to injections, the economy is in equilibrium.

As shown in Figure 9-13, equilibrium occurs where leakages are equal to injections, or where S + T + M = I + G + X. When real GDP is below equilibrium, as at $Y_0$, then injections are greater than leakages and income will be increasing. When GDP is above equilibrium, as at $Y_1$, then leakages are greater than injections and income will be falling in the economy. It is only at Y* where leakages are equal to injections, so the income being added to the economy is just equal to the income leaking out of the economy so income remains constant and the economy is in equilibrium.

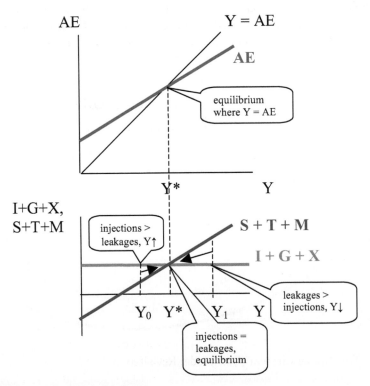

Figure 9-13    Leakages and Injections

## An Example

We can borrow the example from Table 9-2 to show that leakages are equal to injections in equilibrium. Remember in that example the equilibrium level of GDP was at Y = $3000. This is also where leakages are equal to injections, as shown in Table 9-5.

**Table 9-5**  Leakages and Injections

| GDP (Y) | AE | C | S | T | M | S + T + M | I | G | X | I + G + X |
|---|---|---|---|---|---|---|---|---|---|---|
| 0 | 300 | 100 | −100 | 0 | 100 | 0 | 100 | 50 | 150 | 300 |
| 1000 | 1200 | 1000 | 0 | 0 | 100 | 100 | 100 | 50 | 150 | 300 |
| 2000 | 2100 | 1900 | 100 | 0 | 100 | 200 | 100 | 50 | 150 | 300 |
| 3000 | 3000 | 2800 | 200 | 0 | 100 | 300 | 100 | 50 | 150 | 300 |
| 4000 | 3900 | 3700 | 300 | 0 | 100 | 400 | 100 | 50 | 150 | 300 |
| 5000 | 4800 | 4600 | 400 | 0 | 100 | 500 | 100 | 50 | 150 | 300 |

As shown in Table 9-5, in this example equilibrium occurs at $Y^* = 3000$ where GDP is equal to aggregate expenditures. This is also the level of output where injections of $300 are equal to leakages of $300. By inspection of the leakages (S+T+M) and injections (I+G+X) columns, you can tell that at Y = 3000 is the only level of GDP where leakages are equal to injections. So equilibrium in the Keynesian model can be found where either Y = AE or where S + T + M = I + G + X. Both conditions imply that there is enough spending to purchase the amount of output produced.

## THE PARADOX OF THRIFT

A final topic to be discussed in this chapter on the fixed-price Keynesian model is the paradox of thrift. In this model, an increase in saving will reduce GDP since an increase in saving means a reduction in consumption spending. With a reduction in consumption spending the economy will see a multiplied decline in real GDP.

The paradox of thrift can be shown in both the Keynesian cross diagram and the leakages/injections diagram. These are shown in Figure 9-14. In the upper graph, an increase in saving means a decrease in consumption spending, so the aggregate expenditure function shifts downward. The increase in saving leads to a decline in real GDP. In the lower graph, the increase in saving from $S_0$ to $S_1$ causes the leakages function to shift upward. At the old equilibrium leakages are greater than injections, so income falls until a new equilibrium is reached. Again, the increase in saving has led to a decline in real GDP in the fixed-price Keynesian model.

As shown in Figure 9-14, an increase in saving leads to a decrease in real GDP in the fixed-price Keynesian model. In the lower graph, the increase in saving causes the leakages function to shift upward. At $Y^*$ now leakages are greater than injections so income falls until the economy is again in equilibrium, where leakages are equal to injections at $Y'$. In the upper graph, the increase in saving leads to a decline in consumption spending, so aggregate expenditures fall and real GDP declines.

Note that this result is much different than the effects of an increase in saving in the classical model. In the classical model, an increase in saving in the loanable funds market means that real interest rates decline and investment spending increases. With greater investment, more capital is formed and the economy has the potential for greater rates of growth in the future. In the fixed-price Keynesian model, on the other hand, the increase in saving leads to a decrease in GDP.

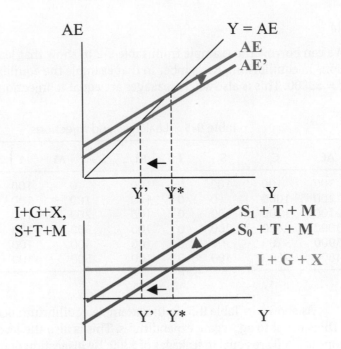

Figure 9-14   The Paradox of Thrift

How do we reconcile these models? Remember that the classical model is better at explaining long run trends, while the Keynesian model is more focused on short run fluctuations in the economy. In the long run saving is beneficial because it provides a pool of funds for investment and capital formation which will make the economy more productive in the future. However, in the short run saving may be harmful because it implies a lack of consumption spending to purchase the goods produced with all of this capital. So saving can be both beneficial in the long run and harmful in the short run.

That's it for the fixed-price Keynesian model. Next we relax the assumption that prices are fixed and derive the aggregate demand/aggregate supply model.

# 10

# AGGREGATE DEMAND AND AGGREGATE SUPPLY

In the last two chapters we examined models of the macroeconomy where at least one important variable was being held fixed. In the classical model, the quantity of real GDP is held constant since the aggregate supply curve is vertical. In the fixed-price Keynesian model, the price level is held constant since the aggregate supply curve is assumed to be horizontal. In the real world, both real GDP and prices may fluctuate at the same time. So the classical and Keynesian models face limitations in their abilities to explain changes in the economy. In this chapter, we will allow both the quantity of real GDP and the price level to vary at the same time through the model of aggregate demand and aggregate supply.

In the classical model of the economy, the shapes of the aggregate demand and aggregate supply curves depended on the assumptions of the model. The aggregate demand curve was derived from the equation of exchange and quantity theory of money. Changes in aggregate demand resulted only from changes in the money supply. In the classical model, changes in spending had no effect on aggregate demand since an increase in one area of spending led to equal decreases in other areas of spending, so that overall spending remained the same. Here we examine a different model of aggregate demand where changes in spending do have an effect on the aggregate demand curve. From now on, we will refer to the classical model's version of aggregate demand as classical aggregate demand, and this chapter's version of aggregate demand as the Keynesian aggregate demand curve or simply as aggregate demand.

For the aggregate supply curve, the classical model assumed it was vertical due to the assumptions of flexible wages and no money illusion. Wages could always adjust to bring equilibrium in the labor market, and economic decisions were based on real variables so that workers were always aware of price changes in the economy. Here we relax these assumptions and examine a model where nominal wages are fixed and money illusion may exist, so that economic decisions are based on nominal variables and it takes time to learn about price changes in the economy. As we will see, the shape of the aggregate supply curve depends on the assumptions made about the flexibility of wages and the existence of money illusion. In total we will identify five different types of aggregate supply curves depending on the assumptions made about the economy.

Before we go on, let us provide some basic definitions:

*Aggregate demand* is a model that shows the amount of desired spending that consumers, investors, governments, and the foreign sector are willing and able to purchase at different price levels in the economy. The aggregate demand curve is downward-sloping; a decrease in the price level will lead to an increase in desired spending as purchasers in the economy can afford to buy more goods and services.

*Aggregate supply* is a model that shows the amount of desired output that firms and workers in the economy are willing and able to produce at different price levels. The shape of the aggregate supply curve depends on the assumptions made about the flexibility of wages and the existence of money illusion in the economy.

## DERIVING THE AGGREGATE DEMAND CURVE

The aggregate demand curve can be derived from the Keynesian-cross diagram of the fixed-price Keynesian model. This is shown in Figure 10-1. We now relax the assumption that prices are fixed. Instead, assume that the price level is variable and declines from $P_0$ to $P_1$ to $P_2$. Suppose that the when the price level is $P_0$ aggregate expenditures are given by $AE(P_0)$ and the original equilibrium level of real GDP is at $Y_0$. This is shown by the intersection of the aggregate expenditure function and the 45-degree line. As the price level declines, from $P_0$ to $P_1$ to $P_2$, the aggregate expenditure function increases as spenders in the economy can afford to purchase more. As the aggregate expenditure function increases, the equilibrium level of GDP increases. If we plot out the equilibrium levels of desired spending at different price levels, we can derive the aggregate demand curve shown in the lower graph of Figure 10-1.

There are several reasons why the aggregate demand curve is downward-sloping as in Figure 10-1. A decrease in the price level leads to increases in consumption, investment, and export spending. We will examine each of these below.

## REASONS WHY THE AGGREGATE DEMAND CURVE IS DOWNWARD-SLOPING

There are three reasons why the aggregate demand curve is downward-sloping, or why there is an inverse relationship between the price level and the amount of real GDP that spenders want to purchase in the economy. These reasons are known as the real income (or wealth) effect, the interest rate effect, and the international trade (or net export) effect.

The Real Income Effect

$$P \downarrow \rightarrow \text{real income} \uparrow \rightarrow C \uparrow \rightarrow AE \uparrow \rightarrow Y \uparrow$$

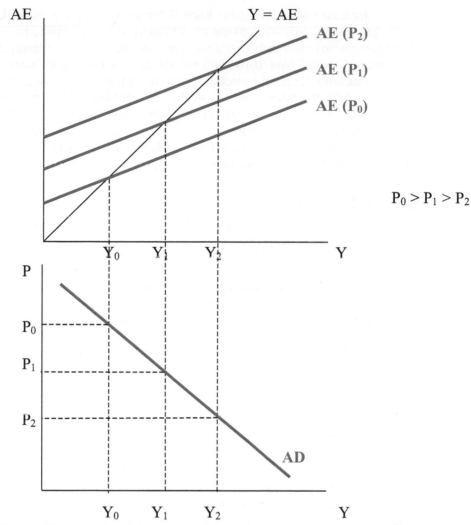

**Figure 10-1**  Deriving the Aggregate Demand Curve. As the price level declines from $P_0$ to $P_1$ to $P_2$, aggregate expenditures increase and the equilibrium level of GDP rises. If we plot the equilibrium levels of GDP at different price levels, we can derive the aggregate demand curve in the lower graph. The aggregate demand curve shows the equilibrium levels of GDP, or amounts of desired spending, in the economy at different price levels. If we allow the price level to vary in this way in the "fixed-price" Keynesian model, we can thus derive the aggregate demand curve. The aggregate demand curve shows that as the price level declines, the quantity of desired spending in the economy increases. The aggregate demand curve is downward-sloping.

A decrease in the price level increases the purchasing power of any given amount of nominal income, so real income (or real wealth) increases. With higher real income, households increase their consumption spending. The increase in consumption spending leads to an increase in aggregate expenditures and a multiplied increase in the equilibrium level of real GDP. As the price level falls, consumption spending increases.

The Interest Rate Effect

$$P \downarrow \rightarrow \text{money demand} \downarrow \rightarrow i \downarrow \rightarrow I \uparrow \rightarrow AE \uparrow \rightarrow Y \uparrow$$

A decrease in the price level leads to a decrease in the demand for money. If prices are lower, consumers do not need to carry as much cash to make purchases. If consumers carry less cash, then more funds can be deposited into savings at banks. With more funds to lend, banks will reduce interest rates to encourage more borrowing. Interest rates are the price of money. As with any other market, if the demand for money falls, the price of money or the interest rate will decline. The decline in interest rates leads to an increase in investment spending as the cost of borrowing declines. The increase in investment spending leads to an increase in aggregate expenditures and a multiplied increase in the equilibrium level of real GDP. As the price level falls, investment spending increases.

## The International Trade Effect

$$P \downarrow \rightarrow \text{domestic prices} \downarrow \rightarrow X \uparrow \rightarrow AE \uparrow \rightarrow Y \uparrow$$

A decline in the price level means that American products become relatively cheaper compared to foreign products. The decline in domestic prices leads to an increase in exports as foreigners purchase more American products. The increase in export spending leads to an increase in aggregate expenditures and a multiplied increase in the equilibrium level of real GDP. As the price level falls, export spending increases.

Combined, the three effects mean that a decrease in the price level leads to increases in consumption, investment, and export spending in the economy. A decrease in the price level leads to an increase in desired spending in the economy. Conversely, an increase in the price level will cause a decline in desired spending. The aggregate demand curve is downward-sloping.

Note from the discussion above that the aggregate demand curve is a much different animal than the market demand curve we discussed in Chapters Three and Four. For the market demand curve, the vertical axis measures the price and the horizontal axis measures the quantity of a particular good. For the aggregate demand curve, the vertical axis measures the price level and the horizontal axis measures the amount of real GDP for the economy as a whole. The market demand curve is downward-sloping due to opportunity costs. As the price of a good is declining, the opportunity cost of that good decreases and consumers can afford to purchase more of that good. With an aggregate demand curve the entire price level is changing, so opportunity costs may or may not be changing. Instead, the aggregate demand curve is downward-sloping due to the three reasons described above.

Another difference between the market demand curve and the aggregate demand curve lies in the *ceteris paribus* assumptions, or the variables being held constant along a given demand curve. For the market demand curve, we held constant the prices of substitutes and complements, consumer income, tastes and population. For the aggregate demand curve there are many more variables being held constant, as we will explore in the next section.

## THE DETERMINANTS OF AGGREGATE DEMAND

The aggregate demand curve shows the relationship between the price level and the quantity of real GDP demanded. If the price level changes, we have a change in the quantity of aggregate demand, or a movement along a given aggregate demand curve. This is shown in Figure 10-1. As we change the price level, we have different aggregate expenditure curves and different levels of GDP that bring the economy to equilibrium. Since we derive the aggregate demand curve by changing the price level, changes in the price level lead to movements along a given aggregate demand curve.

If one of many other variables change that is being held constant along a given aggregate demand curve, then the aggregate demand curve itself will shift. As with a market demand curve, it is important to distinguish between changes that lead to movements along the curve compared to changes that shift the entire curve.

*Changes in the price level lead to movements along a given aggregate demand curve.*

As implied in Figure 10-1, if any other variable that affects aggregate expenditures changes besides the price level then the aggregate expenditure function will shift up or down, and the aggregate demand curve will change. For example, assume that there is an increase in autonomous consumption spending that leads to an increase in aggregate expenditures. At the same price level, the equilibrium level of real GDP will be greater, so the aggregate demand curve must have shifted to the right, leading to an increase in aggregate demand. The effects of an increase in consumption spending are shown in Figure 10-2. The increase in consumption spending leads to an increase in both aggregate expenditures and aggregate demand.

An increase in consumption spending leads to an increase in aggregate expenditures and aggregate demand. Since aggregate expenditures are now greater at the same price level $P_1$, the aggregate demand curve has shifted to the right. Spenders in

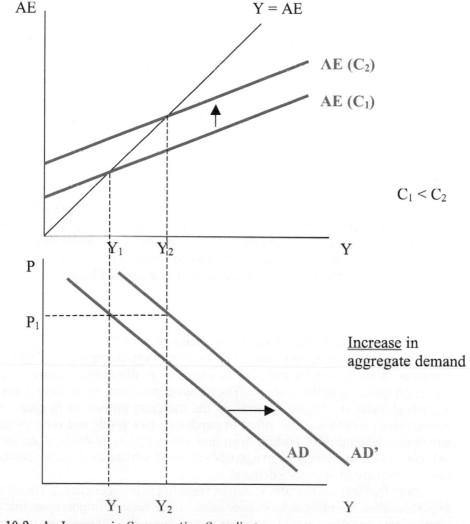

Figure 10-2   An Increase in Consumption Spending

the economy now want to purchase more output at any price level. Aggregate demand increases.

Not only will increases in consumption spending lead to increases in aggregate demand, so will increases in any other type of spending. Remember that aggregate expenditures consist of consumption, investment, government, and net export spending. Changes in any of these variables will lead to changes in aggregate expenditures which will lead to changes in aggregate demand. Except for a change in the price level, when aggregate expenditures increase aggregate demand will increase. When aggregate expenditures fall, aggregate demand will decline. Aggregate demand and aggregate expenditures move in the same direction. The determinants of aggregate expenditures (except for the price level) are also the determinants of aggregate demand. These are shown in Table 10-1.

*Any variable that causes a change in aggregate expenditures (except for a change in the price level) will also cause a change in aggregate demand.*

Since aggregate expenditures consist of consumption, investment, government, and net export spending, any change in these categories of spending not caused by a change in prices will lead to a change in both aggregate expenditure and aggregate demand. Table 10-1 summarizes these determinants of aggregate demand besides the price level.

**Table 10-1**   Determinants of Aggregate Demand

| Consumption | Investment | Government | Net exports |
|---|---|---|---|
| Consumer income | Interest rates | Fiscal policy | Income |
| Wealth | Cost of capital | Monetary policy | Foreigners' income |
| Expectations | Business confidence | Social policy | Foreign prices |
| Demographics | Capacity utilization | Wars | Exchange rates |
| Personal taxes | Business taxes | Natural disasters | Protectionism |
| Interest rates | Regulations | | |
| | Technology | | |

As shown in Table 10-1, there are at least 20 variables that are held constant along a given aggregate demand curve. In constructing the aggregate demand curve, we make a very large *ceteris paribus* assumption. There are many variables being held constant when we draw an aggregate demand curve. A change in any of these variables will lead to a change in aggregate demand, as described below.

## Consumption Spending

The variables that influence consumption spending include:

*Consumer Income:* As shown by the consumption function in the last chapter, increases in consumer income lead to increases in disposable income and consumption spending in the economy. The increase in consumption that results from a given increase in income depends on the marginal propensity to consume. As income rises, consumers can afford to purchase more goods and services so consumption spending rises, leading to an increase in aggregate demand. An increase in income leads to an increase in aggregate demand, while a decrease in income will cause a decrease in aggregate demand.

Note that income also affects import spending in the economy. As shown by the import function, an increase in income causes an increase in import spending. Since imports are a negative entry in aggregate expenditures (X – M) the increase in import spending by itself would cause a decrease in aggregate demand. But as long as the marginal propensity to consume is greater than the marginal propensity to import, then the increase in aggregate expenditures that results from an increase in consumption spending will outweigh the decrease in aggregate expenditures that results from the increase in import spending. An increase in income will lead to an increase in aggregate demand, *ceteris paribus*.

*Wealth:* Household wealth is the stock of all assets owned by a household minus its liabilities, or the difference between what is owned and what is owed. Wealth is different from income in that wealth is a stock variable, what you own at a given point in time, while income is a flow variable, what you earn over a given period of time. Wealth for most households consists of the house owned, stocks and bonds, the contents of the home, and other assets such as jewelry, gold or silver coins, antique automobiles, or paintings. Increases in wealth, say from a rise in housing or stock prices, will lead to increases in consumption spending as consumers feel richer and spend more. Decreases in wealth will lead to declines in consumption spending, or at least reduce the rate of growth of consumption. This wealth effect was evident during the latter part of 2008, when declines in stock and housing prices led to declines in consumption spending in the U.S. economy. This is illustrated in Figure 10-3. A decrease in wealth will lead to a decrease in aggregate demand, *ceteris paribus*.

**Consumption**

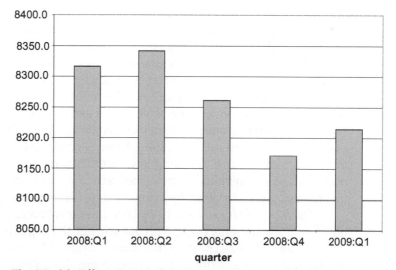

Figure 10-3    The Wealth Effect: Personal Consumption Expenditures, 2008–2009

*Expectations:* Consumer expectations about the future can influence consumption spending today. In particular, expectations of future prices and future income can affect consumption spending today.

If households expect prices to increase in the future, they may increase consumption spending today. The rate of expected inflation will help to determine how much is spent today compared to how much is saved for future consumption. If inflationary expectations increase, households will consume more today before the price level is higher and money is worth less. The opposite happens with expected deflation. If households expect the price level to fall, they may postpone current consumption and wait until prices are lower. The lack of spending may have recessionary effects on the economy, as the recent deflationary experiences in Japan have shown. If households anticipate an increase in the price level, they will increase current consumption.

Expectations of future income can also influence consumption spending today. If consumers expect their income to increase in the future, they will spend more today. For example, I originally obtained my job at Binghamton University on December 23, 1997, for the spring 1998 semester. That day I went and did more Christmas shopping, even though I would not have an increase in pay until the next February. I knew I would have more income to pay off the bills. Increases in expected income increase consumption spending. On the other hand, if consumers expect declines in income due to greater probabilities of job losses in the future, then current consumption spending will decline as households save more for an uncertain future. Income may be saved for rainy day rather than spent today. This is another reason for the declines in consumption spending shown in Figure 10-3.

*The Permanent Income Hypothesis:* is a model suggested by Milton Friedman that consumption spending depends on permanent income, not current income. Friedman is the founder of the Chicago school of economics that supports the power of free markets. He believed that households made consumption decisions based on their lifetime stream of income, or permanent income, not on the income earned in a given period. For example, college seniors may increase their spending, even with no increase in current income, as their expectations of future income become greater.

An increase in expectations of future prices or an increase in expectations of future income will lead to an increase in aggregate demand, *ceteris paribus.*

*Demographics:* Changes in the composition of the population can affect consumption spending in an economy in several ways. There are two important factors, the age distribution and the income distribution.

First, if the permanent income hypothesis is correct, then consumers are aware of their lifetime income and will try to spread their spending evenly throughout their lifetimes. Households spend more relative to income when young and old, and save more relative to income when middle-aged and have to save for children's college expenses and for retirement. When young, individuals may be in college or early years of employment when income is low relative to consumption spending. When young, dissaving may occur if spending is greater than income. The same phenomenon occurs when an individual retires. Once retired, the household no longer has earned income and starts dissaving by living off of its lifetime savings and Social Security.

*The life cycle hypothesis* is the idea that saving tends to be greatest in the middle of a household's life cycle, with dissaving at the beginning and end of the cycle.

Holding income constant, the more young or old people in the population, the greater will be the amount of consumption spending. The more middle-aged people, the less will be consumed out of a given amount of income.

Second, differences in income distribution can affect the level of consumption spending in an economy. To show this, ask yourself the following question: Who has a higher marginal propensity to consume (MPC), poor people or wealthy people? Before you answer, consider who has to spend more of their income. The poor have to spend more of their income in deciding which bills to pay each month. Wealthy people can afford to save more of their income, so the wealthy have a lower MPC. This means that differences in income distribution can influence the amount of consumption spending in an economy. The more income received by the poor, the more will be consumed.

Differences in the MPC between rich and poor provide a macroeconomic rationale for redistributing income from rich to poor in the economy. If we transfer one dollar from a rich person to a poor person, we take a dollar that might have been saved and give it to someone who will spend it. Increases in income equality will increase consumption spending from a given amount of income in an economy.

Demographics affect consumption spending and aggregate demand in two major ways. An increase in the number of young or old people will lead to an increase in aggregate demand, *ceteris paribus*. An increase in income equality will lead to an increase in aggregate demand, *ceteris paribus*.

*Personal Taxes:* affect the level of disposable income in the economy. An increase in taxes will reduce disposable income, while a tax cut will lead to an increase in disposable income. Consumption spending moves directly with changes in disposable income. As disposable income increases, consumption spending increases depending on the MPC. If disposable income falls then consumption spending declines. As we will explore in the next chapter, tax policy is a common means of stimulating the economy when policy makers fear a recession. For example, George W. Bush cut taxes three times, in 2001, 2003, and 2008, in attempts to avoid recession. Barack Obama's American Recovery and Reinvestment Act of 2009 also contained provisions for tax cuts to stimulate the economy.

A decrease in personal taxes will lead to an increase in aggregate demand, *ceteris paribus*.

*Interest Rates:* influence the level of consumption spending on durable goods in the economy. *Durable goods* are usually defined as goods that last longer than one year. Examples include items such as washers and dryers, dishwashers, refrigerators, furnaces, home entertainment equipment, etc. When interest rates decline, it is less expensive for households to borrow the funds to pay for such durable goods, and consumption spending increases.

A decrease in interest rates will lead to an increase in aggregate demand, *ceteris paribus*.

In sum, an increase in consumption spending leads to an increase in aggregate demand. An increase in consumption spending may be caused by increases in income or wealth, higher expected prices or income, increases in young or old households, increases in income equality, or a decrease in personal taxes or interest rates. All of these events will lead to rightward shifts of the aggregate demand curve.

## Investment Spending

Remember that investment spending consists of the purchases of capital by firms in the economy. Capital is the machinery, factories, tools and equipment used in production processes. Similar to consumption spending, an increase in investment will increase the aggregate demand curve as aggregate expenditures in the economy increase. The effects of an increase in investment spending are similar to those shown in Figure 10-2. The aggregate expenditure function shifts upward and the aggregate demand curve shifts to the right. The determinants of investment spending that influence aggregate demand include:

*Interest Rates:* The cost of borrowed funds influences the cost of investment decisions made by firms. Suppose that a firm needs to buy a new machine. It can use its own funds, in which case it sacrifices the interest it could have earned in an interest-bearing asset such as a bank account or bond. If it borrows the funds, it has to pay interest to the lender. In either case, the opportunity cost of the funds used for the investment expenditure is the interest that is paid or foregone. As interest rates decline, more and more investment opportunities become profitable for firms.

**Table 10-2** Investment Opportunities for Catskinners, Inc.

| Machine Type | Cost | Rate of Return |
|---|---|---|
| A | $4000 | 5% |
| B | $3000 | 7% |
| C | $2000 | 9% |
| D | $1000 | 11% |

As an example, consult Table 10-2, which shows the different investment opportunities available for Catskinners, Inc.

Suppose that there are four different machines available for skinning cats, and Catskinners, Inc. can only purchase one of each machine. For each machine A, B, C or D, the cost and rate of return are listed in Table 10-2. The rate of return is the net profit earned on each machine as a percent of the cost or amount invested in the machine. For example, if machine A costs $4000 with a rate of return of 5%, then it will earn a net profit for Catskinners of .05 × 4000 = $200 per year.

When should Catskinners buy a machine, and which should they purchase first? It all depends on nominal interest rates. Suppose that interest rates are 12%. Then Catskinners is better off keeping its money in the bank than buying any machines. If it keeps $1000 in the bank, it can earn $120 in interest. If it buys machine D, it will only earn $110 in profit with an 11% rate of return. It is better off keeping its money in the bank than spending any money on machines. As long as interest rates are at 12% or higher, investment spending will be 0. The firm is better off keeping its money in the bank than purchasing any machines.

Suppose instead that interest rates are 10%. Now, machine D becomes profitable. The firm can earn $110 per year by spending $1000 on machine D, but only $100 per year if it keeps that $1000 in the bank. If interest rates are 10%, investment spending will be $1000 as the firm purchases machine D only.

If interest rates fall to 8%, then both machines D and C become profitable because they have a rate of return greater than that interest rate. If $3000 is kept in the bank, the interest earned in a year is equal to .08 × 3000 = $240. If machines D and C are purchased, then Catskinners has a net income of $290. (0.09 × 2000 + 0.11 × 1000). It is not profitable to purchase machine B, since it still has a rate of return that is less than the interest rate. So if interest rates are 8%, investment spending will be $3000 as the firm purchases machines C and D.

Similarly, if interest rates are 6%, then machines D, C and B all have rates of return greater than the interest rate so the firm will purchase those 3 machines. Investment spending will be $6000. Finally, if interest rates are 4% or less, than all four machines will be purchased since all four will have a rate of return greater than the interest rate. Investment spending will be $10,000. Note that as interest rates decline, more and more investment projects have rates of return greater than the interest rate and investment spending increases. The investment function is shown in Table 10-3.

*An Investment Function:* is a model that shows the relationship between interest rates and investment spending in the economy. As interest rates decline, investment spending increases as the opportunity cost of the funds used for capital purchases becomes less. As interest rates decrease more and more investment opportunities become profitable. The investment function for Catskinners, Inc. is illustrated in Figure 10-4.

**Table 10-3**   An Investment Function for Catskinners, Inc.

| Interest rate | Investment spending | Machines purchased |
|---|---|---|
| 12% | 0 | None |
| 10% | 1,000 | D |
| 8% | 3,000 | D, C |
| 6% | 6,000 | D, C, B |
| 4% | 10,000 | D, C, B, A |

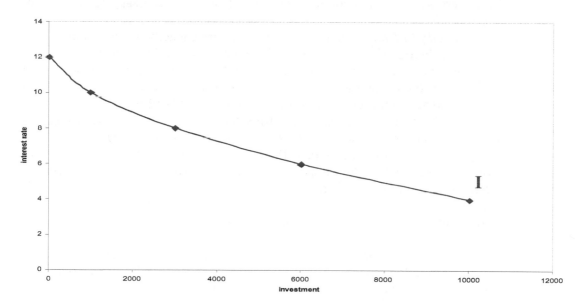

Figure 10-4   An Investment Function for Catskinners, Inc.

As shown in Table 10-3 and Figure 10-4, there is an inverse relationship between the interest rate and the amount of investment spending. Lower interest rates make more investment opportunities profitable. If there is an inverse relationship between interest rates and investment for a single firm, the same will be true for all of the firms producing in the economy. If interest rates decline, the overall quantity of investment spending in the economy will increase. The increase in investment spending will lead to an increase in aggregate demand.

As shown in Figure 10-4, the investment function is downward sloping. A decrease in interest rates leads firms to spend more on capital purchases. This increase in investment spending will cause an increase in aggregate demand.

Overall, a decrease in interest rates will lead to an increase in aggregate demand, *ceteris paribus.*

*Cost of Capital:* The cost of capital will influence the ability of firms in the economy to purchase capital. If the cost of capital declines, then capital becomes relatively less expensive compared to labor and firms will hire more capital as a result. If hammers are inexpensive, carpenters can afford to purchase more hammers. If steel rollers are less expensive than a steel mill can afford to purchase more steel rollers. A decrease in the cost of capital will lead to an increase in investment spending and an increase in aggregate demand, *ceteris paribus.*

*Business Confidence:* Investment spending may also depend heavily on business confidence, or firms' expectations about the future of the economy and their own profit opportunities. If firms believe that the economy will be prosperous in the future and that their own profits are likely to be high, they are more likely to invest in capital expenditures today such as new factories or machinery. If, as in the Great Depression or the recession of 2008–2009, business confidence is so low that firms believe that the economy will be declining in the future, they are much less likely to make investment expenditures today. There is no sense in building new factories or purchasing new equipment if the firm does not believe that it can sell its output in the future.

An increase in business confidence will lead to an increase in investment spending. The increase in investment spending will cause an increase in aggregate demand. So an increase in business confidence will lead to an increase in aggregate demand, *ceteris paribus*.

*Capacity Utilization:* is the amount of factory capacity in the economy that is currently being utilized, or how much factory space and time is being used up compared to the maximum that could be used. For example, if the economy could produce 200 billion pounds of output in a year, and if it produces 160 billion pounds instead, then capacity utilization is 80%. Capacity utilization is important because it determines whether or not firms need to build new factories. If capacity utilization is low, so that there is excess capacity, then current factories are not being used to their full potential, so there is not much sense in building new factories if there is still a lot of space in the old factories. As capacity utilization increases, current factories begin to get used up, so it is more likely that firms will need to build new factories. An increase in capacity utilization will lead to an increase in investment spending and an increase in aggregate demand, *ceteris paribus*.

*Business Taxes and Regulations:* are included among of the costs of production for firms in the economy. The more firms have to spend in business taxes or the more resources that are devoted to meeting regulatory requirements, the greater are the costs of production. If governments are able to reduce costs to businesses through reductions in business taxes or regulations, there will be more resources available for investment spending. A cut in business taxes or regulations will lead to an increase in investment spending in the economy.

In the 1980s, the election of Ronald Reagan as president ushered in era of economic policy known as "Reaganomics" or "supply-side economics." The policy was essentially a return to the classical model of the economy that was dominant before the Great Depression. One important belief was the idea that tax cuts and deregulation could help to spur investment spending and trigger movements in the aggregate supply curve for the economy. But for our purposes, the increase in investment spending from business tax cuts or deregulation will also lead to an increase in the aggregate demand curve for the economy. We will discuss these ideas of supply-side economics further in the next chapter.

A reduction in business taxes or business regulations will lead to an increase in aggregate demand, *ceteris paribus*.

*Technology:* is the state of a society's knowledge and practical arts of industrial and agricultural production. The technology available at the time influences the range of investment opportunities available for firms. For example, as computers became less expensive and more readily available, many firms made investment expenditures in computer hardware and software. These computer purchases represented a significant portion of investment spending in the 1990s and 2000s. As new technology becomes available, investment spending will grow and aggregate demand will increase.

An increase in technology will lead to an increase in aggregate demand, *ceteris paribus*.

Overall, an increase in investment spending leads to an increase in aggregate demand. An increase in investment spending may be caused by a decline in interest rates, a decrease in the cost of capital, an increase in business confidence, an increase in capacity utilization, a decrease in business taxes or regulations, or an increase in technology.

## Government

The federal, state and local governments can influence aggregate demand through their spending and tax policies, or fiscal policy. The federal government can also influence aggregate demand through monetary policy and social policy, as well as through its reactions to wars and natural disasters.

*Fiscal policy:* As we will see in the next chapter, fiscal policy consists of changes in government spending or taxes to influence some macroeconomic variable. The most common form of fiscal policy is expansionary fiscal policy, or actions meant to increase the aggregate demand curve and expand GDP. Increases in government spending will increase aggregate expenditures and lead to an increase in aggregate demand. Reductions in personal taxes will lead to an increase in disposable income, which will then increase consumption spending and aggregate demand.

An increase in government spending will lead to an increase in aggregate demand, *ceteris paribus.*

A decrease in personal taxes will lead to an increase in aggregate demand, *ceteris paribus.*

*Monetary policy:* consists of changes in the money supply and interest rates to influence some macroeconomic variable. As we will see in Chapter 13, an increase in the money supply will lead to lower interest rates, which will increase investment spending and thus cause an increase in aggregate demand. Changes in the money supply that are meant to increase aggregate demand are known as expansionary monetary policy.

An increase in the money supply will lead to an increase in aggregate demand, *ceteris paribus.*

*Social policy:* The public's attitude toward issues such as poverty, health care, education and space exploration can have profound effects on the level and growth of government spending. For example, during the 1960s, the federal government increased spending dramatically through the War on Poverty and the Apollo manned mission to the moon. These programs led to increases in aggregate demand, and inflation was higher by the end of the decade. In 1996, the Clinton Administration introduced welfare reform, which decreased government spending on public assistance programs. If the Obama Administration decides to put a person on Mars, government spending will increase.

Increases in spending on social programs will lead to an increase in aggregate demand, *ceteris paribus.*

*Wars and natural disasters:* Government spending on wars and natural disasters also has effects on aggregate demand. For example, as of this writing (May 2009) the U.S. government has spent $671 billion, or $341 million per day, on the War on Iraq *(www.costofwar.com).* Increases in war spending lead to increases in the overall level of government spending and increases in aggregate demand. In fact, the federal government spending on World War II is widely credited with ending the Great Depression due to the increase in aggregate demand that resulted from the war. Also, natural disasters, such as Hurricane Katrina, can also lead to increases in government spending.

Increases in spending on wars or natural disasters will lead to an increase in aggregate demand, *ceteris paribus*.

In sum, increases in government spending, through fiscal policy, social policy, or wars or natural disasters, or decreases in personal taxes, will lead to increases in aggregate demand, *ceteris paribus*.

## Net Exports

The final category of aggregate expenditures is net export spending, which is the difference between exports and imports. Aggregate demand will increase with an increase in exports or a decrease in imports, either of which will lead to an increase in net exports.

*Income:* As we saw in the import function, increases in household income will lead to an increase in import spending. Since imports are subtracted from aggregate expenditures, then an increase in imports will reduce aggregate expenditures and aggregate demand. A decrease in income will reduce import spending and increase aggregate demand. Remember that income also affects consumption spending. So an increase in income will increase consumption spending and reduce import spending. As long as the marginal propensity to consume is greater than the marginal propensity to import, the net effect of an increase in income will be an increase in aggregate demand. The positive effects of income on consumption will swamp the negative effects of income on import spending in the economy.

An increase in income will lead to an increase in import spending, which causes a decline in aggregate expenditures, *ceteris paribus*. But an increase in income will also lead to an increase in consumption spending, so the net effect of an increase in household income is an increase in aggregate expenditures and aggregate demand.

*Foreigners' income:* Incomes earned by foreigners in the rest of the world affect their abilities to purchase U.S. exports. As foreigners earn more income, they gain the purchasing power to buy more products from other countries including the United States. In fact, one rationale for free trade is that the increase in incomes earned around the world will help to foster world trade as consumers in each country purchase more foreign goods with their higher incomes. As foreigners become more wealthy, export spending will increase.

An increase in foreigners' income will lead to an increase in aggregate demand, *ceteris paribus*.

*Foreign prices:* influence the relative cost of U.S. goods and services compared to foreign products. If the price of Russian wheat increases, for example, then European and Asian consumers will now find American wheat relatively less expensive and exports of U.S. wheat will increase. The increase in exports will increase aggregate demand. Alternatively, if Russian wheat becomes less expensive, then U.S. exports of wheat will decline, and aggregate demand will decrease.

An increase in foreign prices will lead to an increase in aggregate demand, *ceteris paribus*.

*Exchange rates:* Changes in the value of the dollar, along with changes in the values of other currencies, can influence foreign demand for U.S. exports and U.S. demand for foreign imports. As the value of the dollar declines, U.S. exports become less expensive to foreigners, so exports increase from the U.S. Also as the value of the dollar declines, foreign goods become more expensive to U.S. consumers, so imports into the United States will decrease. The increase in exports and decline in imports leads to an increase in net exports and in aggregate demand.

A decrease in the value of the dollar will lead to an increase in aggregate demand, *ceteris paribus*.

*Protectionism:* is a trade policy that prevents the free flow of goods and services between countries through tariffs or quotas. A tariff is a tax on imports, while a quota is a restriction on the quantity of a product that can be imported into a country. By reducing import spending, tariffs and quotas are meant to reduce imports and increase aggregate demand. But more often than not the opposite occurs as countries retaliate and the volume of world trade shrivels up. If foreigners do not earn dollars by importing their goods into the United States, they do not have the currency to purchase our exports. A reduction in protectionist policies will lead to an increase in net exports as the volume of world trade increases. As countries around the world reduce their trade barriers, the United States can sell more exports around the world.

A reduction in protectionist policies will lead to an increase in aggregate demand, *ceteris paribus.*

## SUMMARY—AGGREGATE DEMAND

In the last few pages, we have examined the variables that are the determinants of aggregate demand.

A change in the price level leads to a change in the quantity of aggregate demand, or a movement along a given aggregate demand curve.

A change in aggregate demand results from a change in one of the variables being held constant along a given aggregate demand curve. This is a shift of the entire curve. Any variable that leads to a change in aggregate expenditures, except for a change in the price level, will also change aggregate demand.

An increase in aggregate demand will result from any of the following events:

- An increase in consumer income
- An increase in household wealth
- An increase in expectations of future prices
- An increase in expectations of future income
- An increase in the number of young or old people
- An increase in income equality
- A decrease in interest rates
- An increase in business confidence
- A decrease in the cost of capital
- An increase in capacity utilization
- A decrease in business taxes
- A decrease in business regulations
- An increase in government spending
- A decrease in personal taxes
- An increase in the money supply
- An increase in spending on social programs
- An increase in spending on wars or natural disasters
- An increase in foreigners' income
- An increase in foreign prices
- A decrease in the value of the dollar
- A decrease in protectionism

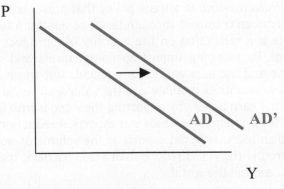

Figure 10-5   An Increase in Aggregate Demand

An increase in aggregate demand is a rightward shift of the aggregate demand curve as shown in Figure 10-5. An opposite change in any of these variables would lead to a decrease, or leftward, shift of the aggregate demand curve. All of these variables are held constant along a given aggregate demand curve.

In the next section we turn our attention to the other half of the model, the aggregate supply curve.

## MODELS OF AGGREGATE SUPPLY

There are several different models of aggregate supply depending on the assumptions made about the flexibility of wages and prices and the existence of money illusion in the economy. We have already examined two models of aggregate supply, the classical model and the fixed-price Keynesian model. From these we will derive three other models of aggregate supply, for a total of five models of aggregate supply all together. Depending on the assumptions made, the aggregate supply curve may be vertical, horizontal, or upward-sloping, or some combination in between. The five models we will study are:

    a.   the classical aggregate supply curve
    b.   the fixed-price Keynesian aggregate supply curve
    c.   the ordinary upward-sloping aggregate supply curve
    d.   the neo-Keynesian aggregate supply curve
    e.   the neo-classical aggregate supply curve

Remember that the aggregate supply curve shows the amount of desired output that firms and workers in the economy are willing and able to produce at different price levels. The way that desired output responds to changes in the price level depends on the assumptions made about the economy, especially whether wages are flexible or fixed, and how long it takes workers to learn about price changes in the economy.

We will look at each of the five models of aggregate supply in turn.

## THE CLASSICAL AGGREGATE SUPPLY CURVE

We have already derived the classical aggregate supply curve in Chapter 8, so we will briefly review the highlights here. The classical aggregate supply curve is vertical at the level of full employment GDP for the economy. In the classical model it is assumed

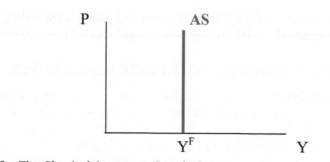

**Figure 10-6**   The Classical Aggregate Supply Curve

that wages, prices, and interest rates are flexible so that markets always clear and that there is no money illusion. An increase in the price level leads to a decrease in real wages and a potential shortage in the labor market. But since markets always clear, nominal wages must rise to eliminate the shortage in the labor market. As the labor market returns to equilibrium at the same real wage rate, the quantity of labor and real GDP produced also remains constant. So an increase in the price level has no effect on the quantity of real GDP produced, and the classical aggregate supply curve is vertical.

The classical aggregate supply curve is vertical due to the assumptions of market-clearing and the lack of money illusion. For convenience and comparison with the other models of aggregate supply, the derivation of the aggregate supply curve from Figure 8-7 is reproduced in Figure 10-7.

In the classical model, an increase in the price level leads to a reduction in real wages that is recognized by workers because of the assumption of no money illusion. Because markets always clear, nominal wages must increase to eliminate the shortage in the labor market. Real wages return to $W_0$ and the quantity of labor remains constant at $L_0$, so real GDP remains at $Y_0$. An increase in the price level has no effect

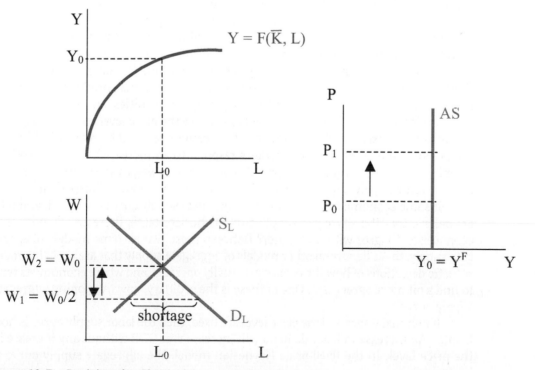

**Figure 10-7**   Deriving the Classical Aggregate Supply Curve

on the quantity of real GDP that firms and workers are willing and able to produce. In the classical model, the aggregate supply curve is vertical.

## THE FIXED-PRICE KEYNESIAN AGGREGATE SUPPLY CURVE

By definition, in the fixed-price Keynesian model prices are assumed to be fixed, so the aggregate supply curve is horizontal. Firms and workers are willing to produce whatever output is necessary to meet the demands of spenders in the economy at the going fixed price level. Output produced will adjust until it is just sufficient to match the quantity of desired spending in the economy. Since prices cannot adjust to bring the economy to equilibrium, output adjusts instead along the horizontal aggregate supply curve until desired output is equal to desired spending.

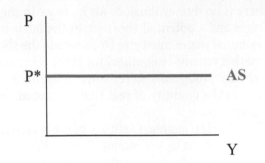

Figure 10-8   The Fixed-Price Keynesian Aggregate Supply Curve

In the fixed-price Keynesian model, the aggregate supply curve is horizontal. Firms and workers are willing and able to produce any level of real GDP at the going price level.

The derivation of the aggregate supply curve in the fixed-price Keynesian model is shown in Figure 10-9. If the price level is fixed and nominal wages are fixed, then real wages must be fixed. Workers will be willing to supply whatever quantity of labor is demanded by employers at the going fixed real wage rate. If real wages are fixed, then the labor supply curve is horizontal at the going real wage rate.

Suppose the economy starts in equilibrium at $Y_0$ and $P_0$. Since the real wage is fixed, the labor supply curve is horizontal. Now assume that producers decide to increase their output, perhaps due to new profit opportunities, an increase in capital, or an increase in the productivity of labor. Since the price level and real wages are assumed to be fixed, workers know that they cannot respond by requesting higher wages from employers. Instead, workers respond to an increase in the demand for labor by increasing the quantity supplied of labor. In this way, as shown in Figure 10-9, the aggregate supply curve in the fixed-price Keynesian model is horizontal.

If some economists believe that the aggregate supply curve is vertical, and others believe that the aggregate supply curve is horizontal, is there any wonder that economists disagree with each other? Between these two extreme models of aggregate supply, there lie several other models of aggregate supply that are probably more realistic depictions of how the economy actually operates, and where economists tend to find a bit more agreement. One of these is the ordinary, upward-sloping aggregate supply curve.

If nominal wages and the price level are fixed, then the labor supply curve is horizontal. An increase in labor demand will increase real GDP without any increase in the price level. In the fixed-price Keynesian model, the aggregate supply curve is horizontal.

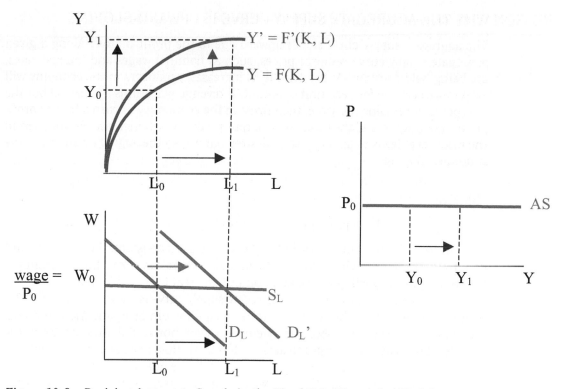

Figure 10-9   Deriving Aggregate Supply in the Fixed-Price Keynesian Model

## THE ORDINARY, UPWARD-SLOPING AGGREGATE SUPPLY CURVE

As a compromise between the extreme versions of the aggregate supply curve, economists developed a model where the aggregate supply curve slopes upward as real GDP is increased. We will call this the "ordinary" aggregate supply curve for lack of a better term. As the price level in the economy increases, firms and workers will desire to produce a greater quantity of real GDP. The ordinary aggregate supply curve is shown in Figure 10-10.

The ordinary aggregate supply curve is upward-sloping. As the price level increases, the quantity of desired output that firms and workers are willing and able to produce will also increase. The reasons why are described in the next section.

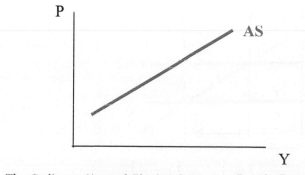

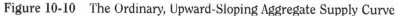

Figure 10-10   The Ordinary, Upward-Sloping Aggregate Supply Curve

## REASON WHY THE AGGREGATE SUPPLY CURVE IS UPWARD-SLOPING

The aggregate supply curve slopes upward due to the profit motive. Along a given aggregate supply curve resource prices, such as nominal wages and interest rates, are being held constant. As the price level increases, producers in the economy will earn more revenue for each unit of output. If revenue per unit is increasing but the cost per unit remains the same, then firms in the economy will earn a higher profit per unit of output, and the quantity of output produced will increase. An increase in the price level leads to an increase in desired output, so the aggregate supply curve is upward-sloping.

### The Profit Motive

$$P \uparrow \rightarrow \text{profit per unit} \uparrow \rightarrow \text{units produced} \uparrow \rightarrow Y \uparrow$$

As the price level increases, holding resource costs constant, the profit per unit of output for the firm will increase. If firms and workers can earn a higher profit per unit of output, they will produce more output and real GDP will increase.

The derivation of the ordinary aggregate supply curve is shown in Figure 10-11. Again we assume that the economy starts in equilibrium at $P_0$ and $Y_0$. If nominal wages are fixed, then the labor supply curve is again horizontal. An increase in the price level will cause real wages to decline. If money illusion exists, workers will not realize that real wages have fallen. As real wages fall, the quantity of labor with a marginal product greater than the real wage will increase, so the quantity of labor demanded by producers will rise. With money illusion and fixed nominal wages workers will be willing to increase the supply of labor as a result of the greater hiring by producers. As the quantity of labor increases, real GDP increases along the production function. An increase in the price level leads to an increase in profit opportuni-

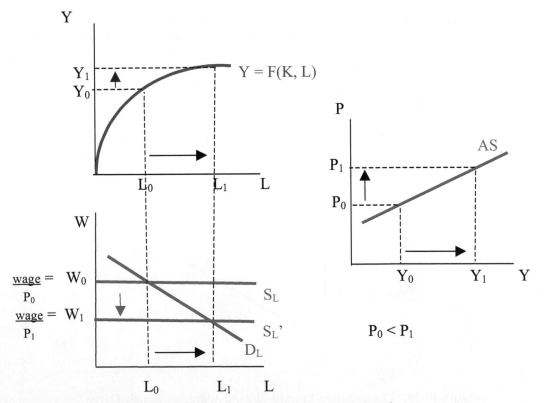

Figure 10-11   Deriving the Ordinary Upward-Sloping Aggregate Supply

ties as more workers become profitable, so desired output increases. The ordinary aggregate supply curve is upward-sloping.

In the ordinary model the aggregate supply curve slopes upward. An increase in the price level reduces real wages, but with money illusion workers are not aware of the price increase. They are willing to increase their labor effort in response to the increase in the quantity of labor demanded by firms. As the price level increases, workers and firms are willing and able to produce more output.

## THE DETERMINANTS OF AGGREGATE SUPPLY

In the ordinary aggregate supply model, there are several variables being held constant along a given aggregate supply curve. As mentioned earlier, one of these is resource prices. A change in resource prices will lead to a shift of the aggregate supply curve. A change in the price level will lead to a movement along a given aggregate supply curve. Besides the price level, the determinants of aggregate supply include resource prices, technology, business confidence, the quantity of resources, capacity utilization, the value of the dollar, and business taxes and regulations. Note that some of these variables, such as technology and business confidence, may also affect investment spending and the aggregate demand curve.

*Changes in the price level lead to movements along a given aggregate supply curve, or a change in the quantity of aggregate supply.*

*An increase in aggregate supply is a rightward shift of the aggregate supply curve.*

The determinants of aggregate supply include:

*Resource Prices:* The costs of land, labor, and capital are important determinants of aggregate supply. Resource prices help to determine how much firms must charge to cover the costs of production, and thus they are critical to the overall price level in the economy and how much firms are willing to produce at different price levels. If resource prices increase, then the costs of production rise and firms must charge higher prices to cover the increase in costs. The aggregate supply curve would decrease or shift to the left. On the other hand, if resource prices decline then firms can lower their prices and the aggregate supply curve will increase or shift to the right.

In Figure 10-11, an increase in nominal wages would lead to an upward shift of the horizontal labor supply curve. The quantity of labor and real GDP would decrease at a given price level, so the aggregate supply curve would shift to the left. An increase in other resource prices would reduce the quantity of resources employed and lead to a downward shift of the production function. Again less GDP would be produced at a given price level and the aggregate supply curve would shift to the left. As an exercise, try to draw both cases.

A decrease in resource prices will lead to an increase in aggregate supply, *ceteris paribus.*

*Technology:* An increase in technology will cause an increase in aggregate supply in the economy. Technological improvements enable firms to become more efficient so that they can produce more output at any given price level. For example, the introduction of computers has enabled both small and large firms to adopt new production methods and lower the costs of production. This means that the firms are willing to sell any given level of output at a lower price level or to produce more at a given price level. The aggregate supply curve shifts to the right.

In Figure 10-11, changes in technology would affect the shape of the production function, which would then change the position of the aggregate supply curve.

An increase in technology will lead to an increase in aggregate supply, *ceteris paribus.*

*Business Confidence:* can be affected by anything from macroeconomic news to global geopolitical events. When firms have high business confidence, they are more likely to invest in improving efficiency and building more capital for the future. On the other hand if business confidence declines, then firms are more likely to rely on old production methods and the real GDP produced will be less at any price level. For example, during the Great Depression business confidence was so low that firms were willing to produce less output at any price level and aggregate supply declined. The recession of 2008–2009 also witnessed significant declines in investment spending due to declines in business confidence.

In Figure 10-11, changes in business confidence would affect the demand for labor and the production function. An increase in business confidence will lead to more investment in capital and a greater perceived productivity of labor, both of which will influence the demand for labor and the production function.

An increase in business confidence will lead to an increase in aggregate supply, *ceteris paribus.*

*The Quantity of Resources:* available in an economy can also influence the height and shape of the aggregate supply curve. As the availability of resources increases, firms can produce more at any price level. For example, immigration has led to increases in aggregate supply and economic growth in many countries such as the United States and Israel. Middle Eastern countries have seen economic growth as a result of their vast oil reserves. Asian countries have grown through infusions of international capital. Historically wars have often been fought to allow a country to gain more land resources. Increases in resources often accompany economic growth through increases in the aggregate supply curve.

In Figure 10-11, the quantity of labor is represented by the labor supply curve. The quantity of other resources influences the shape of the production function.

An increase in the quantity of resources will lead to an increase in aggregate supply, *ceteris paribus.*

*Capacity Utilization:* can affect the amount that is being produced at any given price level. Capacity utilization is the percent of current factory space that is used in production. As firms increase capacity utilization, they can produce more at any given price level.

In Figure 10-11, capacity utilization is represented by the position on the production function. As we move along the production function, capacity utilization increases.

An increase in capacity utilization will lead to an increase in aggregate supply, *ceteris paribus.*

*The Value of the Dollar:* will also influence the aggregate supply curve through its effect on the prices of foreign inputs. If the value of the dollar falls, U.S. firms will require more dollars to purchase foreign resources such as Saudi oil, Canadian lumber, or Brazilian steel. The increases in the prices of foreign inputs will increase the costs of production for firms throughout the economy and cause a decrease in aggregate supply. If instead the value of the dollar rises, then the costs of foreign inputs will decline and the costs of production will decrease. In such a case the aggregate supply curve would increase, since firms would be willing to sell any level of real GDP at a lower price level than previously.

In Figure 10-11, the price of foreign inputs can influence the availability of foreign inputs and the shape of the production function.

An increase in the value of the dollar will lead to an increase in aggregate supply, *ceteris paribus.*

*Business Taxes and Regulations:* may affect aggregate supply since they affect the costs of production. An increase in business taxes or regulations will increase the costs of production for firms throughout the economy and lead to a decrease in aggregate supply. On the other hand, a decrease in business taxes or regulations will reduce production costs and lead to an increase in the aggregate supply curve. In fact, a major tenet of Reaganomics in the 1980s was that deregulation of business, as well as cuts in business and personal taxes, would lead to increases in aggregate supply so that real GDP would increase while inflation was reduced. This is why the policy was often referred to as "supply-side economics."

In Figure 10-11, business taxes and regulations may affect both the labor demand and labor supply curves.

A decrease in business taxes or regulations will lead to an increase in aggregate supply, *ceteris paribus*.

## SUMMARY—THE ORDINARY AGGREGATE SUPPLY CURVE

The ordinary supply curve is upward-sloping due to the profit motive. As the price level increases workers become more profitable and profit per unit of output increases, so firms in the economy want to produce more output.

A change in the price level leads to a movement along a given aggregate supply curve. A change in any other variable that is held constant along a given aggregate supply curve will cause a change in aggregate supply.

An increase in aggregate supply may result from:

- A decrease in resource prices
- An increase in technology
- An increase in business confidence
- An increase in the quantity of resources
- An increase in capacity utilization
- An increase in the value of the dollar
- A decrease in business taxes or regulations

An increase in supply is represented as a rightward shift of the aggregate supply curve, as shown in Figure 10-12. At any price level, firms and workers in the economy are willing and able to produce more real GDP then they were before, so the supply curve shifts to the right. On the other hand, if there was a decrease in aggregate supply, then firms and workers would be willing and able to produce less at any price level, and the aggregate supply curve would shift to the left.

If we put the two halves of the model, aggregate demand and aggregate supply together, we can illustrate the concept of equilibrium in this model. This is done in the next section.

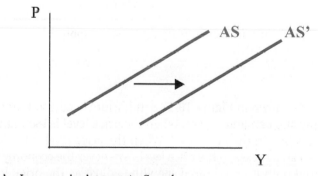

Figure 10-12    An Increase in Aggregate Supply

# EQUILIBRIUM IN THE ORDINARY AGGREGATE SUPPLY/AGGREGATE DEMAND MODEL

As you may imagine, equilibrium in the ordinary aggregate supply/aggregate demand model occurs at the intersection of the aggregate supply and aggregate demand curves. At that price level, the quantity of desired spending is just equal to the quantity of desired output, or spenders in the economy are purchasing just the quantity of output that firms and workers want to produce, and the economy is in equilibrium. If the price level is too high, desired output will be greater than desired spending and overproduction would result. Firms and workers in the economy would want to produce more output than spenders in the economy desire to purchase. In this situation the price level will fall as firms lower their prices to try to attract new customers. If the price level is too low then the amount of desired spending in the economy will be greater than the amount of desired output. Spenders in the economy would want to purchase more output than firms and workers in the economy are willing and able to produce. With overconsumption the price level will increase as consumers try to bid the output away from each other. It is only in equilibrium at the intersection of the aggregate supply and aggregate demand curves where desired spending is equal to desired output and there is no reason for the price level to change.

In the classical model the price level was variable so prices and spending adjusted to the fixed amount of output produced in the economy. In the fixed-price Keynesian model the price level was fixed so output adjusted to spending in the economy. In the ordinary aggregate supply/aggregate demand model, both prices and output adjust to bring the economy to a new equilibrium. This is shown in Figure 10-13.

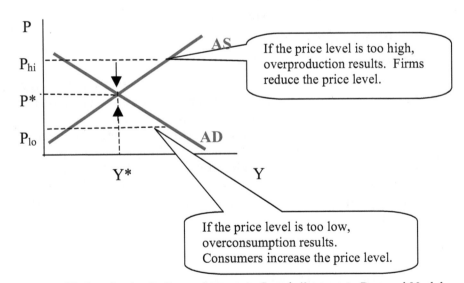

Figure 10-13   Equilibrium in the Ordinary Aggregate Supply/Aggregate Demand Model

As shown in Figure 10-13 equilibrium occurs at Point E, the intersection of the supply and demand curves. When the price level is too high overproduction will lead in a decline in the price level. When the price level is too low overconsumption will lead in an increase in the price level. Whenever the economy is not in equilibrium both desired output and desired spending adjust as the price level changes to bring the economy back to equilibrium.

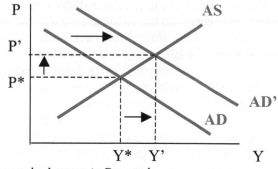

Figure 10-14   An Increase in Aggregate Demand

## AN INCREASE IN AGGREGATE DEMAND

An increase in aggregate demand leads to a rightward shift of the aggregate demand curve. As long as the aggregate supply curve is upward-sloping the increase in aggregate demand will lead both to an increase in the price level and in real GDP. This is shown in Figure 10-14. As we discussed in the last section, any event that leads to an increase in aggregate expenditures, except for a decrease in the price level, will also lead to an increase in aggregate demand. Increases in aggregate demand can help to stimulate the economy since real GDP increases. The macroeconomic cost is that inflation may increase as a result.

An increase in aggregate demand leads to an increase in the price level and an increase in real GDP. Conversely, a decrease in aggregate demand will cause a reduction in the price level and in real GDP.

## INCREASE IN AGGREGATE SUPPLY

An increase in aggregate supply is represented by a rightward shift of the aggregate supply curve. As long as the aggregate demand curve is downward-sloping the increase in aggregate supply will lead to a decline in the price level and an increase in real GDP. An increase in aggregate supply is shown in Figure 10-15.

As shown in Figure 10-15 an increase in aggregate supply leads to economic growth with a lower price level. This is one reason why politicians have often sought supply-side changes in the economy as with Reaganomics. An increase in aggregate supply puts downward pressure on inflation while real GDP grows at the same time. The opposite occurs with a decrease in aggregate supply. In that case inflation occurs while real GDP is declining at the same time. The case of declining aggregate supply

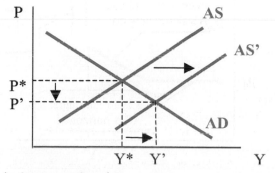

Figure 10-15   An Increase in Aggregate Supply

is known as stagflation, where the economy is stagnating with inflation at the same time. Such stagflation occurred in the 1970s during the Arab Oil Embargo and many observers believe that the same effects may have occurred in the summer of 2008 due to high oil prices and the falling value of the dollar.

The ordinary aggregate supply/aggregate demand model is probably the most useful and simplest model in explaining changes in the macro economy. The model is more realistic than the first two we examined in that both spending and output are allowed to adjust at the same time in response to a change in the price level. The model has some limitations in that occasionally the price level may not adjust to changes in aggregate supply or aggregate demand, or there may be a tendency for the economy to return to full employment given enough time. These limitations are addressed in the next two models of aggregate supply known as the neo-Keynesian model and the neo-classical model.

## THE NEO-KEYNESIAN AGGREGATE SUPPLY CURVE

The neo-Keynesian aggregate supply curve consists of three ranges depending on how far the economy is from full employment. Each of the three aggregate supply curves that we looked at above is represented in the neo-Keynesian aggregate supply curve. When the economy is in recession so that real GDP is far below full employment the aggregate supply curve is horizontal. As the economy approaches full employment the aggregate supply curve becomes upward-sloping. Once the economy is beyond full employment the aggregate supply curve becomes vertical as the economy reaches its limits of production.

The neo-Keynesian aggregate supply curve is shown in Figure 10-16. The horizontal range is known as the Keynesian range. The upward-sloping portion is known as the intermediate range. And finally, the vertical portion is known as the classical range. As the economy comes closer to full employment the aggregate supply curve becomes steeper.

In the Keynesian range real GDP is far below full employment. If the economy is in recession then unemployed resources exist that can be put to work without having to raise resource prices. If unemployed workers are sitting idle at home they can be put to work without having to raise the wage rate. If empty factories are idle it is not necessary to raise interest rates to bid these factories away from alternative uses. When resources are idle output can be increased without raising the price level since putting those resources to work does not require an increase in their compensation. In this range the aggregate supply curve is horizontal since increases in real GDP can be forthcoming without an increase in the price level.

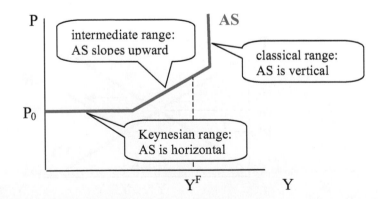

Figure 10-16   The Neo-Keynesian Aggregate Supply Curve

In the intermediate range the aggregate supply curve is upward-sloping. Firms are willing to increase output only with an increase in the price level. There are several reasons for the upward slope in this region. First, bottlenecks may cause shortages in critical inputs that begin to raise the cost of production as firms have to turn to more expensive inputs. Second, firms may anticipate wage increases in the future and raise the price level in anticipation of higher wages in the future. Finally, the law of diminishing returns will eventually set in so that it takes greater and greater increases in resources to obtain equal increases in real GDP. For these reasons the aggregate supply curve is upward-sloping in the intermediate range.

In the classical range the aggregate supply curve is vertical since the economy has reached its limits in terms of resources and technology. No matter how much the price level is increased firms and workers are incapable of producing any more output. The aggregate supply curve becomes vertical at a level of real GDP greater than full employment because it is possible to temporarily produce beyond full employment by working resources overtime. But eventually the economy reaches its limits and the aggregate supply curve becomes vertical.

Due to the distinct ranges of the neo-Keynesian aggregate supply curve the effects of an increase in aggregate demand depend on how far the economy is from full employment. During recession increases in aggregate demand can increase real GDP without causing much inflation in the economy. But once the aggregate supply curve becomes upward-sloping then an increase in aggregate demand is more likely to cause an increase in the price level.

Equilibrium in the neo-Keynesian model is shown Figure 10-17. As usual the equilibrium price level and real GDP occur at the intersection of the aggregate supply and aggregate demand curves. The same factors will lead to shifts in the curves as those of the ordinary model. The aggregate demand curve depends on all those variables that affect consumption, investment, government spending, or net exports. A shift in any of these variables (except for the price level) will still shift the aggregate demand curve. The determinants of aggregate supply are still the same as in the ordinary case, such as resource prices, technology, business confidence, capacity utilization, the quantity of resources, the value of the dollar, and business taxes and regulations.

As usual the equilibrium occurs at the intersection of the aggregate supply and aggregate demand curves. The effects of the change in aggregate demand depend on the range of the aggregate supply curve.

A variant of the neo-Keynesian model is to smooth out the kinks of the aggregate supply curve, as shown in Figure 10-18. In this model, the aggregate supply curve starts out horizontal but then becomes steeper as real GDP increases. The more

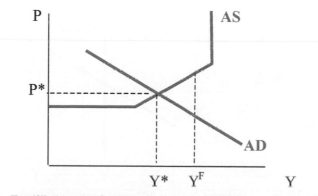

Figure 10-17   Equilibrium in the Neo-Keynesian Model

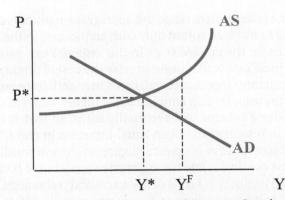

**Figure 10-18** A Variant of the Neo-Keynesian Aggregate Supply Curve

real GDP produced in the economy, the greater the increase in the price level necessary to bring forth another increase in real GDP.

## THE NEO-CLASSICAL AGGREGATE SUPPLY CURVES

In the neo-classical model there are two distinct aggregate supply curves, one for the short run and one for the long run. In the short run wages are fixed and workers in the economy suffer money illusion so that they are unaware of price changes in the economy. In the long run the economy is similar to the classical model in that wages are flexible and there is no money illusion. In the long run wages have enough time to adjust to changes in contracts and workers have enough time to learn about price changes in the economy. In the long run the aggregate supply curve is vertical, similar to the classical model. In the short run, on the other hand, the aggregate supply curve is upward-sloping similar to the ordinary model.

The neo-classical model of aggregate supply is shown in Figure 10-19. It shows that the long run aggregate supply curve is vertical at the level of full employment, while the short run aggregate supply curve is upward-sloping.

The short run aggregate supply curve shows how desired output responds to changes in the price level when wages are fixed and when workers suffer from money illusion. If the price level increases then real wages fall, and firms are aware that their profit per unit has risen and will increase their labor demand to produce more output. If workers are unaware of the price increase in the economy they will not realize that real wages have fallen and will be willing to increase the quantity of labor supplied so that output will increase. Alternatively, if workers believe that wages are fixed in the short run then they will increase their labor effort in response to the increase in labor demand. In either case an increase in the price level will lead to an

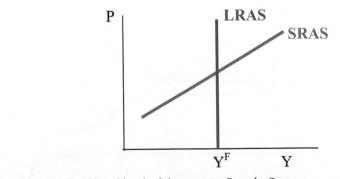

**Figure 10-19** The Neo-Classical Aggregate Supply Curves

increase in the quantity of real GDP that firms and workers are willing and able to produce, so that the short run aggregate supply curve is upward-sloping.

The determinants of the short-run aggregate supply curve are similar to the ordinary aggregate supply curve. In the short run the aggregate supply curve is affected by both real and nominal variables. The quantity of desired output is affected by real variables such as technology, real wages, and labor supply and demand. It is also affected by nominal variables such as the price level, nominal wages, and nominal interest rates. Increases in technology or declining resource prices, for example will lead to rightward shifts of the aggregate supply curve. Higher resource prices will lead to declines in the short-run aggregate supply curve.

The long-run aggregate supply curve is similar to that of the classical model; it is vertical at the level of full employment. In the long run wages are flexible so the labor market always clears, and there is no money illusion so that workers have enough time to learn about price changes in the economy. Given enough time an increase in the price level will lead to a proportionate increase in nominal wages so that real wages return to equilibrium and the economy returns to full employment. The long-run aggregate supply model is similar to the dynamics of the classical model except that the process is not instantaneous since the economy will take time to adjust to a new long-run equilibrium.

## EQUILIBRIUM IN THE NEO-CLASSICAL MODEL

In the short-run in the neo-classical model the economy may or may not be in equilibrium at full employment. Equilibrium occurs at the intersection of the aggregate demand and the short-run aggregate supply curves. If the intersection occurs to the left of the long run aggregate supply curve then the economy is in recession since the equilibrium level of real GDP is less than the full employment level of real GDP. The case of recession is shown in Figure 10-20a. If the intersection occurs at the long-run aggregate supply curve, then the economy is in long-run equilibrium. This is shown in Figure 10-20b. And finally if the intersection occurs to the right of the long-run aggregate supply curve the economy is likely to experience inflation. This case is shown in Figure 10-20c.

In the neo-classical model the economy adjusts to long-run equilibrium through changes in the aggregate supply curve. If the economy is in a recession as in Figure 10-20a, there will be downward pressure on resource prices in the economy. As resource prices fall the short-run aggregate supply curve will shift to the right until the economy returns to full employment at a lower price level. If the economy is in long-run equilibrium where the short-run aggregate supply curve and aggregate demand curve intersect at the long-run aggregate supply curve then there is no reason for the short-run aggregate supply curve or price level to change. If the intersection of the aggregate demand curve with the short-run aggregate supply curve occurs to the right of the long-run aggregate supply curve then the economy is producing beyond full employment. As resources become scarce there will be upward pressure on resource prices in the economy. As resource prices rise the short-run aggregate supply curve will shift to the left until the economy returns to full employment at a higher price level and is again in long-run equilibrium. These adjustment processes are shown in Figure 10-21.

If the intersection of aggregate demand and short run aggregate supply occurs to the left of the long run aggregate supply curve, then $Y^* < Y^F$ and the economy is in a recession. If the intersection occurs at the long run aggregate supply curve, then $Y^* = Y^F$ and the economy is in long-run equilibrium. If the intersection occurs to the right of the long run aggregate supply curve, then $Y^* > Y^F$ and the economy is likely to experience inflation since the real GDP being produced is greater than full

## a. Economy is in recession $(Y^* < Y^F)$

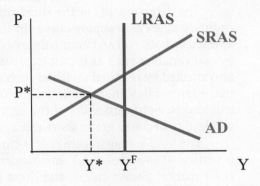

## b. Economy is in long-run equilibrium $(Y^* = Y^F)$

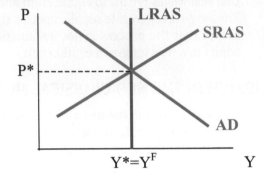

## c. Economy will experience inflation $(Y^* > Y^F)$

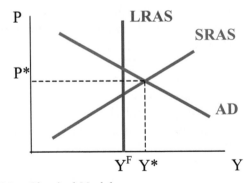

Figure 10-20    Equilibrium in the Neo-Classical Model

employment. As resources become scarce, there will be upward pressure on resource prices in the economy.

As shown in Figure 10-21a if the economy is in a recession an increase in aggregate supply will bring the economy back to full employment. The increase in aggregate supply occurs as resource prices decline.

As shown in Figure 10-21b if the economy is at full employment there is no reason for aggregate supply to change and the economy is in long-run equilibrium.

As shown in Figure 10-21c if the economy is producing above full employment then a decrease in aggregate supply will bring the economy back to full employment and inflation will result.

As shown in the above figures changes in the short run aggregate supply curve provide the adjustment mechanism to bring the economy to full employment in the

**a. Economy is in recession $(Y^* < Y^F)$   SRAS increases.**

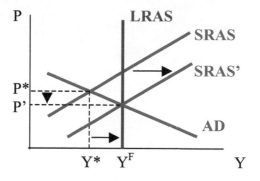

**b. Economy is in long-run equilibrium $(Y^* = Y^F)$   SRAS is constant.**

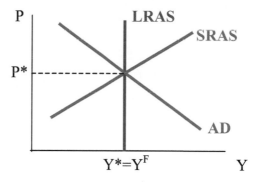

**c. Economy will experience inflation $(Y^* > Y^F)$   SRAS will decrease.**

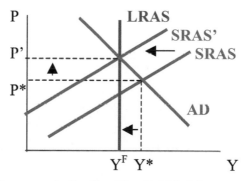

Figure 10-21   Adjustment Processes in the Neo-Classical Model

long run. If the economy is not in full employment, then resource prices and the short run aggregate supply curve will adjust until the economy returns to long run equilibrium at full employment.

Once again the aggregate demand curve in the neo-classical model is similar to that of the Keynesian model. Changes in the price level lead to movements along a given aggregate demand curve. Any other variable that changes aggregate expenditures will also change aggregate demand.

So concludes our journey through aggregate demand and aggregate supply analysis. We will use these models extensively in the next three chapters on fiscal and monetary policy.

# 11

# FISCAL POLICY

In the next three chapters we explore the economic policy tools available to the federal government. When the economy is in a recession, the government may exercise expansionary policy in an attempt to increase aggregate demand. When the government fears inflation, it may exercise contractionary policy to reduce the rate of growth of aggregate demand. The two types of tools available to the government include fiscal policy and monetary policy.

Fiscal policy is at the discretion of the president and Congress, and consists of attempts to influence aggregate demand through changes in government spending or taxes. Monetary policy is conducted through the Federal Reserve System, the central bank of the United States. Most monetary policy is implemented through the daily interventions in bond markets by the Federal Reserve Bank of New York. Fiscal policy occurs less frequently and requires active intervention on the part of the president and Congress. The recession of 2008–2009 and the election of Barack Obama as president have brought about historic changes in the exercise of both fiscal and monetary policy in the U.S. economy, as described in the following chapters.

*Fiscal policy* is a change in government spending or taxes meant to influence some macroeconomic variable such as real GDP growth, the unemployment rate, or inflation.

There are two ways that government spending and taxes can affect the economy. First, automatic stabilizers provide supplemental income during times of economic decline so that fluctuations in income will be reduced. Automatic stabilizers are passive; the existence of the policy or program helps to reduce fluctuations in income without the government doing anything more. *Automatic stabilizers* are government policies or programs that moderate fluctuations in real GDP in the economy (or reduce the spending multiplier) by reducing the volatility of income changes for households and firms. Automatic stabilizers do not require any action on the part of the government to be effective.

Second, discretionary fiscal policy is active; it occurs when the government recognizes an economic problem and actively passes legislation to try to correct the problem. *Discretionary fiscal policy* occurs when the government decides to change government spending or taxes through changes in legislation or regulation to influence the macroeconomy. Discretionary fiscal policy requires action by the government. We will discuss each of these types of government influence below.

## AUTOMATIC STABILIZERS

As stated above automatic stabilizers consist of government policies and programs that reduce the volatility of the business cycle by moderating fluctuations in income.

Examples of automatic stabilizers include:

- Progressive income taxes
- Unemployment insurance
- Welfare programs
- Agricultural price supports
- The stability of government spending

### Progressive Income Taxes

There are three types of tax systems that governments may impose on their taxpayers. These are called progressive, proportional, and regressive tax systems.

A *progressive tax system* means that average income tax rates increase as income increases, so that high income people pay a higher percentage of their income in taxes than do low income people.

In a *proportional tax system* the average tax rate is constant as income increases. All income classes pay the same percentage of their income in taxes.

In a *regressive tax system* the average tax rate declines as income increases so that the poor pay a higher percentage of their income in taxes then do the rich.

An example of a progressive tax is the U.S. federal income tax system where marginal tax rates increase as taxpayers' incomes increase and they move to higher tax brackets. An example of a proportional tax would be a flat tax without income exemptions so that everybody pays the same percentage of their income in taxes. Sales and property taxes tend to be regressive since the poor pay a higher percentage of their income in these taxes compared to wealthier people who do not have to spend as much of their income.

With progressive income taxes as household incomes increase they move to higher tax brackets and the government takes more of their income in taxes. This means that the increase in income is not as great as it would be without the tax system. Similarly, as income is falling taxpayers move to lower tax brackets so that the government takes less of their income in taxes and the reduction in income is moderated. In this way a progressive income tax system automatically stabilizes fluctuations in income in the economy.

### Unemployment Insurance

In the United States unemployment insurance programs are administered by state labor departments with financial assistance and guidance from the federal government. Unemployment insurance helps to moderate fluctuations in income especially when the economy is in recession. When workers lose their jobs their incomes would fall much more dramatically without the help of unemployment insurance. Generally, if workers are employed for twenty-six weeks they become eligible for unemployment insurance so that if they lose their jobs they still receive some income in unemployment benefits. This means that the reduction in income is less and spending in the economy will not fall as much as it would without unemployment insurance. When workers have jobs with incomes their employers pay premiums into the unemployment insurance system so increases in income are not as great as they would be otherwise. In this way, unemployment insurance acts as an automatic stabilizer to moderate fluctuations in income in the economy.

## Welfare Programs

Welfare programs are similar to unemployment insurance in their effects on income changes in the economy. Welfare programs include Temporary Assistance for Needy Families (TANF), food stamps, section 8 housing assistance, Women, Infants and Children food program (WIC), and energy assistance programs. When households lose their jobs, they may first become eligible for unemployment insurance benefits. But these usually last only for six months, unless the economy is in recession and the federal government extends the duration of unemployment benefits. After that, a family may collect TANF benefits for two years. By providing income to the poorest families in our economy, welfare programs act as an automatic stabilizer in the economy. They allow households to receive subsistence income when there is a lack of employment so that declines in income are not as great as they would be otherwise. Because of the spending multiplier, if income and spending are less volatile in the economy, then there will be smaller fluctuations in GDP. When households lose income and decrease spending, there is a multiplied effect on GDP in the economy. By acting as an automatic stabilizer, welfare programs reduce fluctuations in income in the economy, leading to more stable GDP growth and a less erratic business cycle for the economy.

## Agricultural Price Supports

Even though less than two percent of the U.S. population consists of farmers, total income in the economy is stabilized when farmers' income is more constant. Agricultural price supports, such as price floors on corn or soybeans or subsidies for production, marketing, or export, all help to stabilize farmers' incomes in times of agricultural price declines, and thus help to automatically stabilize fluctuations of income in the economy. When farmers' incomes are decreasing, agricultural price supports help to moderate the decline in income, providing farmers with additional income when food prices are low. If income earned in the agricultural sector is more stable, then overall income in the economy will also be more stable.

## The Stability of Government Spending

As shown in Figure 11-1, government spending for all levels of government tends to be relatively stable over time. Throughout the 2000s, government spending has consistently been averaging about 17–18% of GDP. Since 1947 after World War II, the period of time with the highest percentage of government spending was during the Korean War in 1953 when government spending made up 34% of GDP. Government spending as a percentage of GDP declined throughout the 1960s and 1970s. In the 1980s it averaged 20% of GDP, and then declined slightly so that it has been less than 20% from the late 1990s into the 2000s. Note also that government spending has been trending upward lately as the federal government responds to the challenges of recession by employing expansionary fiscal policy. The stability of government spending, about 18–20% of GDP, contributes to the overall stability of GDP as a whole. If government spending was more erratic, the changes in spending would be multiplied into even larger changes in GDP. So the stability of government spending acts as an automatic stabilizer to keep the economy as a whole more constant.

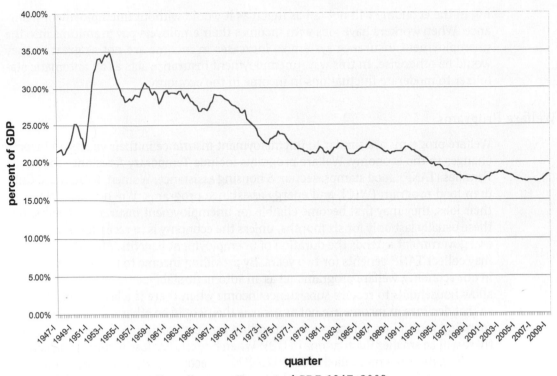

Figure 11-1   Government Spending as a Percent of GDP 1947–2009
Source: Bureau of Economic Analysis

## Summary

Automatic stabilizers are government programs and policies that stabilize the economy automatically without any active intervention on the part of government. Their very existence helps to moderate income swings in the economy. Examples of automatic stabilizers include progressive income taxes, unemployment insurance, welfare programs, agricultural price supports, and the stability of government spending itself. Automatic stabilizers are passive. Discretionary fiscal policy, on the other hand, is active. The government recognizes a problem and decides to change government spending or taxes to address the problem. We turn to discretionary fiscal policy in the next section.

## DISCRETIONARY FISCAL POLICY

Discretionary fiscal policy occurs for two reasons: either the government wants to speed up the economy by increasing aggregate demand or it wants to slow down the economy by reducing aggregate demand. Fiscal policy works by influencing the aggregate demand side of the economy. Increases in government spending or tax cuts will increase aggregate demand, while decreases in government spending or tax increases will reduce aggregate demand. There is also a segment of the profession known as supply-side economics which believes that income tax policy can also influence the aggregate supply side of the economy through its effects on labor effort.

The most famous examples of discretionary fiscal policy in U. S. history are Franklin D. Roosevelt's New Deal programs of the Work Project Administration and Civilian Conservation Corp, John F. Kennedy's 1963 tax cuts, Lyndon Johnson's tax increases in 1967, George W. Bush's tax cuts of 2001, 2003, and 2008, and Barack Obama's American Recovery and Reinvestment Act of 2009. In each of these cases

Figure 11-2   FDR and the CCC. Franklin D. Roosevelt meets with workers from the Civilian Conservation Corp in Shenandoah National Park in August 1933.

Source: Shenandoah National Park Archives

the federal government attempted to use its taxing and spending powers to affect aggregate demand in the economy. Discretionary fiscal policy is the result of Keynesian economics. Classical economists believe that changing government spending or taxes would have no effect on the economy. A photograph of Franklin D. Roosevelt (F.D.R.) meeting with workers from the Civilian Conservation Corp at Shenandoah National Park is shown in Figure 11-2.

## THE AMERICAN RECOVERY AND REINVESTMENT ACT OF 2009

The grandest experiment yet in the history of U.S. fiscal policy may be the American Recovery and Reinvestment Act of 2009 that was passed into law by Congress on February 13, 2009 and signed by President Obama four days later at a ceremony in Denver. The act contains tax cuts and increases in government spending to stimulate the economy that are unprecedented in scope and magnitude, approximately $789 billion combined. According to the legislation, the act has five major purposes:

1. "To preserve and create jobs and promote economic recovery"
2. "To assist those most impacted by the recession"
3. "To provide investments needed to increase economic efficiency by spurring technological advances in science and in health
4. "To invest in transportation, environmental protection, and other infrastructure that will provide long-term economic benefits"
5. "To stabilize State and local government budgets, in order to minimize and avoid reductions in essential services and counterproductive state and local tax increases"

(*http://frwebgate.access.gpo.gov/cgibin/getdoc.cgi?dbname=111_cong_bills&docid=f:h1enr.pdf,* accessed May 21, 2009)

The act distributes funds to various sectors of the economy in the government's attempt to increase spending and stimulate aggregate demand. In general, the act targets funds in the following ways:

- $357 billion, or 45%, of the funds are directed to federal spending and entitlement programs.
- $288 billion, or 37%, of the funds are targeted towards tax relief for individuals and businesses.
- The remainder of the funds, $144 billion or 18%, is devoted to assistance for state and local governments.

*(http://appropriations.house.gov/pdf/PressSummary02-13-09.pdf,* accessed May 21, 2009)

Between the bailout bill in 2008 and the recovery package in 2009, the federal government has devoted over $1.5 trillion to fiscal and monetary stimulus.

The Obama Administration has even established a web site, *www.Recovery.gov,* to enable the public to track how the fiscal stimulus money is being spent. Not since the Great Depression have we witnessed such a large attempt at expansionary fiscal policy, and never before has fiscal policy been so transparent to the public. Figure 11-3 shows the website's report on funds available and paid out from the stimulus package each week from March 27 to May 8, 2009. For example, by May 8, 2009 $102.9 billion had been made available to agencies, but only $36.8 billion of the funds had actually been spent. Figure 11-3 illustrates the concept of fiscal policy lag, that it takes a significant amount of time between when a fiscal policy measure is introduced and when it is actually implemented.

The American Recovery and Reinvestment Act of 2009 represents a significant change in U.S. fiscal policy. The White House predicts that the act will create 3.5 million jobs for the U.S. economy once the provisions take effect *(http://www.whitehouse.gov/assets/documents/Recovery_Act_Overview_2-17.pdf).* The models we explore in this

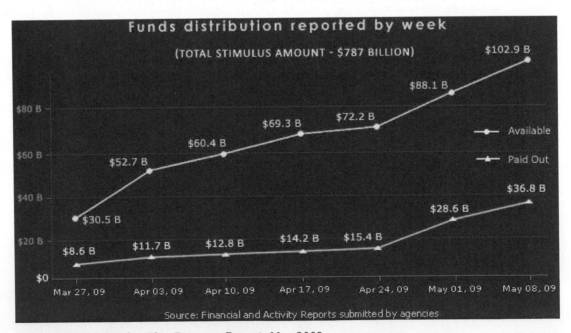

Figure 11-3   Stimulus Plan Progress Report, May 2009

Source: www.Recovery.gov

chapter will relate how different economic theories view these attempts to stimulate the economy. For the sake of all of us, let us hope that the White House is right.

In the rest of this chapter we will explore how fiscal policy works in the five different models we have examined in the last three chapters. First we will review fiscal policy in the classical model. Next, we examine the effects of changes in government spending or taxes in the fixed-price Keynesian model. Finally we will look at the three different models of aggregate supply and aggregate demand, the ordinary model, the neo-Keynesian model, and the neo-classical model.

## FISCAL POLICY IN THE CLASSICAL MODEL

The effects of changes in government spending or taxes in the classical model were covered extensively in Chapter Eight, so we will only summarize the results here. In the classical model expansionary fiscal policy leads to complete crowding out. Any increase in government spending is exactly offset by declines in consumption and investment spending so that there is no effect on aggregate supply or aggregate demand overall. Fiscal policy is completely ineffective in changing the level of spending in the economy. The composition of spending changes since higher real interest rates reduce the amount of investment and consumption spending in the economy. With the decline of investment spending there is less capital formation and a decreased potential for economic growth in the future.

Figure 11-4   Obama Signs Stimulus Package. On February 17, 2009, Barack Obama signed the American Recovery and Reinvestment Act of 2009 in Denver as Vice-President Joe Biden looked on. The legislation represented the most significant initiative in U.S. fiscal policy since the Great Depression.
(*http://denver.bizjournals.com/denver/stories/2009/02/16/daily11.html*, retrieved May 21, 2009)

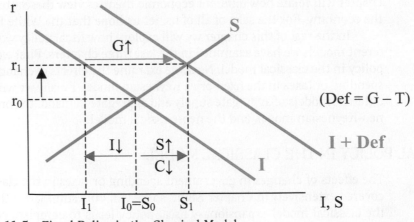

Figure 11-5   Fiscal Policy in the Classical Model

The classical model graph from Figure 8-19 is reproduced in Figure 11-5. An increase in government spending without any change in taxes creates a deficit that must be financed through the issuance of bonds. As the demand for loanable funds increases real interest rates will rise. The increase in real interest rates leads to decreases in investment and consumption spending equal to the increase in government spending, so there is no overall effect on aggregate demand. Again complete crowding out means that any increase in government spending is exactly offset by declines in private spending so fiscal policy has no effect on overall spending in the economy.

An increase in government spending leads to an increase in the demand for loanable funds. The higher real interest rates cause investment spending to decline and saving to increase. The increase in saving is equivalent to an equal decline in consumption spending. Since the increase in government spending leads to offsetting declines in consumption and investment spending there is no change in aggregate demand in the economy.

When economic policy makers were guided by the classical model there was little role for government to play in resolving economic recessions or inflations. As in the Hoover Administration from 1929 to 1933, classical economic advisors believed that the economy would correct itself and that government intervention would only make the economy worse. When F.D.R. took office in 1933 he ushered in the era of Keynesian economics with his New Deal policies. The relationship between the federal government and the national economy has since been radically changed as a result.

To classical economists the American Recovery and Reinvestment Act will only serve to make the recession worse. The increases in government spending will crowd out private spending from higher real interest rates. The resulting deficits will reduce the potential for economic growth in the future and impose immoral burdens on future generations. These classical ideas are still in the background of conservative arguments against the 2009 stimulus package.

## FISCAL POLICY IN THE FIXED-PRICE KEYNESIAN MODEL

Remember that in the fixed-price Keynesian model the aggregate supply curve is horizontal because the price level is assumed to be fixed. Since the only variable in the model is the quantity of real GDP, real interest rates are also assumed to be constant. Under these assumptions, changes in government spending or taxes will be very effective in changing real GDP due to the concepts of the spending and tax multipliers. In

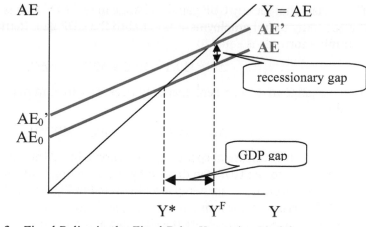

**Figure 11-6**   Fiscal Policy in the Fixed-Price Keynesian Model

this model the government can increase aggregate expenditures and aggregate demand through increases in government spending or reductions in taxes, and it can reduce aggregate expenditures and aggregate demand through decreases in government spending or increases of taxes. We will use the Keynesian-cross diagram of Chapter Nine to illustrate the effects of fiscal policy in the fixed-price Keynesian model

We will begin by assuming that the economy is in a recession so that equilibrium real GDP is less than potential real GDP. The GDP gap is the difference between potential GDP, $Y^F$, and actual GDP, $Y^*$. If the GDP gap is positive then the economy faces recession. To eliminate the GDP gap the government can use its fiscal policy tools to increase aggregate expenditures and bring the economy back to full employment. The recessionary gap shows how much aggregate expenditures must be increased in order to eliminate the GDP gap. The recessionary and GDP gaps are shown in Figure 11-6. First we will provide some definitions.

> *Recessionary Gap* is the increase in aggregate expenditures required to bring the economy to full employment when actual real GDP is less than potential real GDP.

> *Inflationary Gap* is the decrease in aggregate expenditures necessary to return the economy to full employment when actual real GDP is less than potential GDP.

> *GDP Gap* is the difference between potential real GDP and actual real GDP.

Suppose that the economy is currently in equilibrium at $Y^*$ which is less than full employment GDP (or potential GDP) $Y^F$. The GDP gap shows the difference between the two. The recessionary gap shows the increase in aggregate expenditures necessary to bring the economy to full employment.

If the government desires to increase aggregate expenditures in this situation it has three options. First it could increase government spending by the amount of the recessionary gap. Second it could decrease taxes to increase aggregate expenditures. Third, it could have a balanced budget change where both government spending and taxes are increased by the same amount at the same time. We will examine each of these cases in turn.

## An Increase in Government Spending

The spending multiplier for an increase in government spending is equal to

$$1 / (1 - MPC + MPIM).$$

This means that for any GDP gap the change in real GDP that is necessary to restore the economy to full employment is equal to the GDP gap. Remember the spending multiplier formula is equal to

$$\Delta Y = [1 / 1 - MPC + MPIM)] \times \Delta G.$$

So the change in government spending necessary to eliminate the GDP gap will be equal to

$$\Delta G = \Delta Y / [1 / (1 - MPC + MPIM)].$$

The change in government spending necessary to bring the economy to full employment is equal to the GDP gap divided by the spending multiplier. The effects of an increase in government spending are illustrated in Figure 11-7.

An increase in government spending leads to an upward shift of the aggregate expenditure curve. To eliminate the GDP gap and bring the economy to full employment, the increase in government spending necessary is equal to the recessionary gap, where

$$recessionary\ gap = GDP\ gap / spending\ multiplier.$$

As we will see, a change in government spending is the most effective means of implementing fiscal policy in that it leads to the largest increase in real GDP for a given change in the budget deficit.

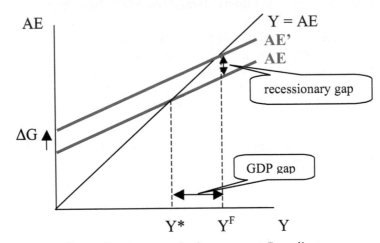

Figure 11-7   The Effects of an Increase in Government Spending

## A Decrease in Taxes

A second way that the government can increase aggregate expenditure is through a decrease in personal taxes that increases disposable income and consumption spending in the economy. Remember from Chapter Nine that the tax multiplier is equal to

$$(-MPC + MPIM) / (1 - MPC + MPIM)$$

This means that the tax multiplier formula is equal to

$$\Delta Y = [(-MPC + MPIM) / (1 - MPC + MPIM)] \times \Delta T$$

To eliminate a certain GDP gap equal to $\Delta Y$ the necessary change in taxes is equal to

$$\Delta T = \Delta Y / [(-MPC + MPIM) / (1 - MPC + MPIM)]$$

Tax changes have a smaller effect on real GDP than changes in government spending since the tax multiplier is smaller in magnitude than the government spending multiplier. In fact, as we will see, the relationship between the tax and the spending multipliers is that

$$\text{tax multiplier} = 1 - \text{spending multiplier}.$$

For example, if the spending multiplier is equal to 5 then the tax multiplier is equal to –4. An increase in government spending will have a larger impact on real GDP than a tax cut of equal magnitude.

## A Balanced Budget Change

*A balanced budget change:* occurs when an increase in government spending is exactly matched by an increase in taxes so that the fiscal policy action has no effect on the government budget. If the budget was balanced it will remain balanced. If the government had a deficit the deficit will stay the same. Similarly any surplus would remain constant. Balanced budget changes are changes in both government spending and taxes that will increase or decrease GDP with no effect on the government budget.

Since a balanced budget change consists of changes in both government spending and taxes the effects will depend on both of the multipliers. The two multipliers combined will be equal to

$$\frac{1}{(1 - \text{MPC} + \text{MPIM})} + \frac{(-\text{MPC} + \text{MPIM})}{(1 - \text{MPC} + \text{MPIM})} = \frac{1 - \text{MPC} + \text{MPIM}}{1 - \text{MPC} + \text{MPIM}} = 1$$

As shown above, the balanced budget multiplier in the fixed-price Keynesian model is equal to 1. In any model such as this without income taxes the sum of the spending and tax multipliers is equal to 1. For example, if government spending is increased by $100 billion and taxes are increased by $100 billion, then real GDP will increase by $100 billion in this model. The balanced budget multiplier is equal to 1.

## An Inflationary Gap

If equilibrium real GDP is greater than potential real GDP, then an inflationary gap is said to exist. This is the opposite of a recessionary gap. If the economy is producing above full employment, shortages of resources will begin to push up resource prices and inflation may result. To deal with an inflationary gap, the government may reduce aggregate expenditures to decrease real GDP in the economy. In the real world, the government seldom uses fiscal policy to reduce aggregate demand in the case of an inflationary gap. Inflationary gaps are not viewed as crucial problems to economic policymakers in the ways that recessionary gaps may be.

## A Numerical Example of the Fixed-Price Keynesian Model

Suppose that the economy of Macroland currently has an equilibrium level of real GDP of $625 million and potential real GDP of $1000 million. The marginal propensity to consume for Macroland is 0.75, and the marginal propensity to import is 0.15. How can the economy of Macroland use fiscal policy to achieve full employment? The economy faces a GDP gap.

$$\text{The GDP Gap} = \text{potential real GDP} - \text{actual real GDP}$$
$$= \$1000 - \$625 = \$375 \text{ million}$$

First, the government can use an increase in government spending to eliminate the GDP gap. There is a recessionary gap, since actual real GDP is less than potential real GDP. Since the MPC is 0.75 and the MPIM is 0.15, the spending multiplier is

$$1/(1 - MPC + MPIM) = 1/(1 - 0.75 + 0.15) = 2.5$$

Since $\quad\quad\quad\quad\quad\quad \Delta Y = \text{spending multiplier} \times \Delta G,$

then $\quad\quad\quad\quad 375 = 2.5 \times \Delta G,$ so $\Delta G = 375/2.5 = 150$ million.

The recessionary gap is $150 million. An increase in government spending of $150 million will increase real GDP by $375 million and eliminate the GDP gap. Graphically,

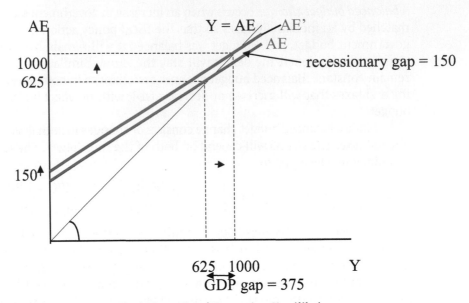

Figure 11-8    A Numerical Example of Keynesian Equilibrium

Second, the government can cut taxes to increase aggregate expenditures. To find the effects of a change in taxes, we need to use the tax multiplier formula. The tax multiplier is equal to

$$(-MPC + MPIM) / (1 - MPC + MPIM) =$$
$$(-0.75 + 0.15) / (1 - 0.75 + 0.15) = -0.6/0.4 = -1.5.$$

So $\quad\quad \Delta Y = \text{tax multiplier} \times \Delta T \quad$ or $\quad 375 = -1.5 \times \Delta T \quad\quad$ so
$$\Delta T = 375/-1.5 = -250.$$

A $250 million decrease in taxes will increase GDP by $375 million. A tax decrease is necessary to increase real GDP since the tax multiplier is negative.

Note that the magnitude of the tax decrease necessary to restore full employment, $250 million, is greater than the magnitude of the required government spending increase, $150 million. The government spending increase can achieve the desired result with less of an impact on the budget deficit than a decrease in taxes. The reason is that the magnitude of the tax multiplier, 1.5, is less than the magnitude of the government spending multiplier of 2.5. Dollar for dollar, increases in government spending have a greater effect on the economy than do tax cuts. Changes in government spending affect aggregate expenditures directly. An increase in government spending of one dollar increases aggregate expenditures by one dollar. Changes in

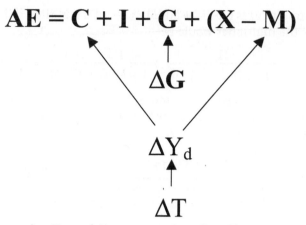

$$AE = C + I + G + (X - M)$$

$$\Delta G$$

$$\Delta Y_d$$

$$\Delta T$$

Figure 11-9   Comparing Tax and Government Spending Changes

taxes only affect aggregate expenditures indirectly. First, the change in taxes will influence disposable income, and then the change in disposable income affects consumption and import spending. This idea is illustrated in Figure 11-9.

A change in government spending affects aggregate expenditures directly. A one dollar increase in government spending will increase aggregate expenditures by one dollar. A change in taxes, on the other hand, only affects aggregate expenditures indirectly. The change in taxes affects disposable income, and then the change in disposable income affects consumption and import spending.

For example, in the case above the tax cut of $250 million will increase disposable income by the same amount. Since the MPC is 0.75 an increase in disposable income of $250 million will increase consumption spending by $0.75 \times 250 =$ $187.5 million. Since the MPIM is 0.15, an increase in disposable income of $250 million will increase import spending by $0.15 \times 250 = \$37.5$ million. Since imports are subtracted from aggregate expenditures, the net effect on aggregate expenditures from the change in both consumption and import spending is $187.5 - 37.5 =$ $150 million, the same as the increase in aggregate expenditures from the increase in government spending. These results are summarized in Table 11-1.

**Table 11-1**   Comparing Tax Cuts and Government Spending Increases

Given: GDP Gap = $375 million, MPC = 0.75, MPIM = 0.15

$\Delta G$ = $150 million leads to $\Delta AE$ = $150 million.

$\Delta T$ = –$250 million leads to $\Delta Y_d$ = $250 million.

$\Delta Y_d$ = $250 million leads to $\Delta C$ = 0.75 × 250 million  = + $187.5 million
$\Delta Y_d$ = $250 million leads to $\Delta M$ = 0.15 × 250 million = –  $37.5 million
net $\Delta AE$ =   $150 million

An increase in government spending of $150 million has the same effect on aggregate expenditures as a tax cut of $250 million. In both cases, aggregate expenditures increases by $150 million and real GDP increases by $375 million.

Third, the government could use a balanced budget change to increase aggregate expenditures and bring the economy to full employment. The balanced budget multiplier occurs when any increase in government spending is financed through an equal increase in taxes. Since the spending multiplier is 1/ (1 – MPC + MPIM) and the tax multiplier is (−MPC + MPIM)/ (1 − MPC + MPIM), if they both change at the same time the multiplier would be:

$$\frac{1}{1 - MPC + MPIM} + \frac{-MPC + MPIM}{1 - MPC + MPIM} = \frac{1 - MPC + MPIM}{1 - MPC + MPIM} = 1.$$

Since the balanced budget multiplier is 1, then $\Delta Y = \Delta G = \Delta T = \$375$ million. So if G and T are both increased by \$375 million, then GDP will increase by \$375 million. This is shown in Table 11-2.

**Table 11-2**  A Balanced Budget Change

| | |
|---|---|
| increase of G by \$375→Y increases by 2.5 × 375 = +937.50 | |
| increase of T by \$375→Y decreases by −1.5 × 375 = −562.50 | |
| net ΔY = +375.00 | |

An increase in both government spending and taxes of \$375 million will increase real GDP by \$375 million. This result occurs because the sum of the spending and tax multipliers is equal to one.

## Summary

In the fixed-price Keynesian model the government has three options to increase aggregate expenditures and real GDP. It can increase government spending, cut taxes, or conduct a balanced budget change where both government spending and taxes are increased by the same amount at the same time. Increases in government spending are more effective in eliminating a GDP gap than are tax cuts or balanced budget changes.

A limitation of the Keynesian model lies in the assumptions that are made concerning the price level and interest rates. Since the price level is fixed, the model assumes away the inflationary effects of fiscal policy. Since interest rates are fixed, the model assumes away the crowding out effect of fiscal policy. These issues are addressed in the ordinary aggregate supply / aggregate demand model of fiscal policy.

For the recession of 2008–2009 the American Recovery and Reinvestment Act of 2009 provided the Keynesian prescription of tax cuts and government spending increases to bring the economy out of recession. As we discussed earlier the act provides for deficit increases of almost \$800 billion through tax cuts and spending initiatives. If the multiplier concepts work in the real world then this \$800 billion in deficit spending should increase real GDP by a multiple of that amount. The problem is that this model assumes away the two most important potential problems associated with expansionary fiscal policy. Since the price level is fixed an increase in government spending will not cause inflation. If interest rates are fixed, an increase in deficit spending will not cause any crowding out effect. We address these issues in the next three models, where the aggregate supply curve may be upward-sloping. Once we allow prices and interest rates to vary, fiscal policy becomes less effective.

## FISCAL POLICY IN THE ORDINARY AGGREGATE SUPPLY/AGGREGATE DEMAND MODEL

In the ordinary aggregate supply/aggregate demand model, the aggregate demand curve is downward-sloping and the aggregate supply curve is upward-sloping. In most cases an increase in government spending or tax cut will lead to an increase in aggregate demand and higher real GDP and prices. The effects of fiscal policy in this model depend on the assumptions made about the determinants of the aggregate supply curve and the way in which any increase in government spending is financed.

There are three ways of financing any increase in government spending:

1.  Increasing taxes to pay for the increase in government spending
2.  Issuing bonds to borrow the money to pay for the increase in government spending
3.  Printing money to obtain the currency necessary to pay for the increase in government spending

Since printing money often causes hyperinflation in an economy, governments tend to shy away from printing money as a means to finance increases in government spending. One exception is monetary policy in 2009, as discussed in the next chapters, when the Fed effectively printed money by purchasing Treasury bonds directly from the Treasury. We will discuss increases in the money supply in Chapter 13. This leaves the first two methods, increasing taxes or issuing bonds. The effects on aggregate demand, and the economy overall, depend on which method the government uses to finance any increase in government spending.

First, once we recognize that the aggregate supply curve is upward-sloping, the spending and tax multipliers are reduced in magnitude. Instead of an entire increase in aggregate demand being translated into output increases, some of the increase in aggregate demand will lead to inflation instead. The steeper is the aggregate supply curve the greater is the increase in the price level that will result from any increase in aggregate demand. These are shown in Figure 11-10, which shows the effects of an increase in aggregate demand in the fixed-price Keynesian and ordinary aggregate supply/aggregate demand models.

In the fixed-price Keynesian model, it is assumed that prices are fixed, so that an increase in government spending will lead to the full multiplier effect increase in GDP:

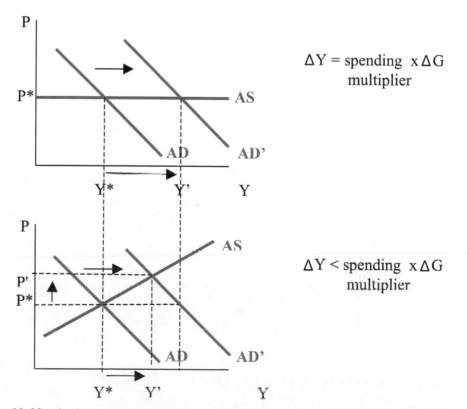

Figure 11-10   An Increase in Aggregate Demand through Expansionary Fiscal Policy

An increase in government spending causes an increase in aggregate demand. When the aggregate supply curve is upward-sloping there is less of an increase in real GDP from the same increase in aggregate demand. The effective spending multiplier is less since the economy does not achieve the full increase in real GDP that would result in the fixed-price model where the aggregate supply curve is horizontal. In this model, a possible consequence of expansionary fiscal policy is inflation. The effects on real GDP will depend on the method used to finance the increase in government spending.

## An Increase in Government Spending Financed through Issuing Bonds

When the government increases spending, aggregate demand will increase. The extent of the horizontal shift of the aggregate demand curve depends on the sizes of the government spending increase and the spending multiplier. The issuing of bonds, however, will cause a partial crowding out effect. As the government issues bonds, nominal interest rates will increase as the government must bid funds away from private investment. The increase in interest rates will reduce investment spending and cause a partial shift back of the aggregate demand curve. The effects of expansionary fiscal policy financed through bonds are shown in Figure 11-11.

If an increase in government spending is financed through an increase in the sale of bonds, interest rates may rise and cause a partial crowding out effect. The increase in government spending will cause an increase in aggregate demand, while the increase in interest rates will cause a partial shift back of the aggregate demand curve. The net effects are increases in the price level and real GDP, but these increases are less than what would occur without the partial crowding out effect.

The effects of tax cuts would be similar graphically. If a tax cut is financed through the issuing of bonds, a partial crowding out effect may result that will lead to a decrease in aggregate demand that will reduce the effects of the initial increase in aggregate demand from the increase in disposable income.

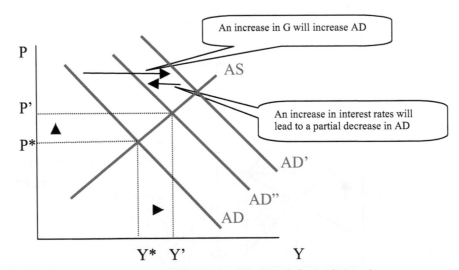

Figure 11-11   Expansionary Fiscal Policy Financed through Bonds

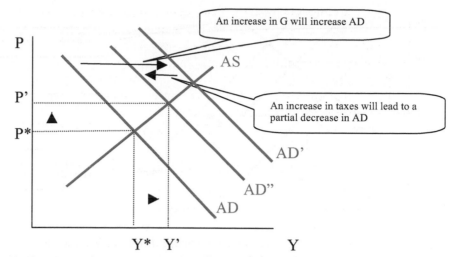

Figure 11-12   Expansionary Fiscal Policy Financed through a Tax Increase

## An Increase in Government Spending Financed through a Tax Increase

If an increase in government spending is financed through an equal increase in taxes, a balanced budget change results. As shown in the last section, since the balanced budget multiplier is equal to one, the net effect of a balanced budget change is an increase in real GDP. The increase in aggregate demand that results from an increase in government spending will be partly offset by a decrease in aggregate demand that results from the increase in taxes. Since the government spending multiplier is greater than the tax multiplier, the net effect will be an increase in aggregate demand, real GDP, and the price level. The effects of a balanced budget change are shown in Figure 11-12.

If an increase in government spending is financed through an equal increase in taxes, the increase in aggregate demand through an increase in government spending is partly offset by a decrease in aggregate demand caused by higher taxes. The net effect is an increase in real GDP and the price level.

In this model, the increases in aggregate demand from the provisions of the American Recovery and Reinvestment Act of 2009 will still increase GDP, but an unintended consequence may be higher rates of inflation in the economy. Since the resulting deficits are financed through issuing bonds, the stimulus package may also serve to increase the crowding out effect in the economy. Overall the expansionary fiscal policy initiatives of the act will still increase real GDP, but the effects are less than they would be in the fixed-price Keynesian model.

## Supply-Side Economics

A caveat must be introduced here to acknowledge the role of supply-side economics. During the Reagan Administration of 1981 to 1989, many of Reagan's economic advisors favored the idea of supply-side economics, which was also known as Reaganomics. The idea was that government could influence the supply side of the economy through income tax cuts and deregulation to help to stimulate the economy. It was believed that income tax cuts would increase labor supply by raising after-tax wages. Deregulation could help to spur investment and employment by reducing costs to businesses. These increases in the aggregate supply curve would help to increase real GDP while inflation was brought under control at the same time.

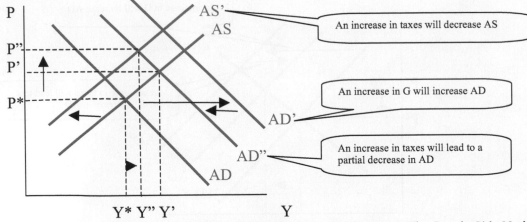

Figure 11-13   Expansionary Fiscal Policy Financed through a Tax Increase: The Supply-Side Model

## Tax Increases

In terms of a tax increase, supply-side economists believed that a tax increase would lead to a reduction in labor effort and a decrease in the aggregate supply curve. The decrease in the aggregate supply curve will offset the expansionary effects of fiscal policy and lead to even more inflation. The effects on real GDP depend on the relative shifts of the aggregate supply and aggregate demand curves. The case where real GDP increases slightly as the price level increases is shown in Figure 11-13.

If an increase in government spending is financed through an increase in taxes, supply side economists believed that the tax increase would cause a reduction in aggregate supply as labor effort decreased due to a reduction in after-tax wages. The results are more inflation, and less real GDP growth, than would occur without the supply-side effects.

## Tax Cuts

If the government wants to stimulate the economy, supply-side economists believed that increases in aggregate supply were superior to increasing aggregate demand since there is less inflationary pressure. With increases in aggregate supply the price level falls, while with increasing aggregate demand the price level rises. Income tax cuts and deregulation would help to increase the aggregate supply curve for the US economy in the 1980s, and reduce the inflationary expectations that had become so high in the late 1970s. If income tax cuts helped to stimulate work effort and real GDP, then tax revenues may rise as income tax rates fall in the economy. The effects of a tax cut in the supply side model are shown in Figure 11-14.

In a supply side model, the effects of income tax cuts and deregulation will increase the aggregate supply curve. As the aggregate supply curve increases, real GDP will rise and the price level will fall. If the income tax cuts also increase disposable income, then aggregate demand will rise as a result. Real GDP will increase in the economy, but the effects on the price level are indeterminate. As shown in Figure 11-14, the price level may fall as a result if the supply-side effect is large enough. In the supply-side model, an income tax cut will increase both aggregate demand and aggregate supply. Real GDP will increase, while the price level may rise or fall. As shown, the price level declines slightly since the aggregate supply curve shifts more than the aggregate demand curve.

Those who favored tax cuts were successful in getting such legislation included in the American Recovery and Reinvestment Act of 2009.

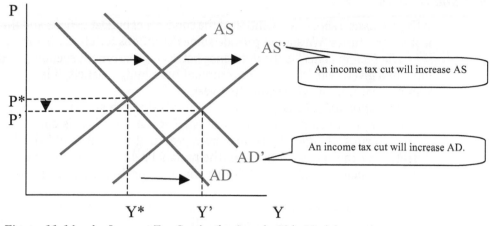

Figure 11-14   An Income Tax Cut in the Supply-Side Model

## The Laffer Curve

One of the underpinnings of Reaganomics was the Laffer Curve. Arthur Laffer was a Berkeley economist and an advisor to Ronald Reagan during his 1980 presidential campaign. Laffer theorized that there must be a relationship between tax revenue and tax rates that for some ranges, cuts in tax rates would increase tax revenue as work effort increased. The increase in tax revenue from increased income would more than compensate for the decrease in tax revenue from lower tax rates. Laffer believed that at income tax rates of 0% and 100%, the government would not earn any tax revenue. Between these tax rates, tax revenue would first rise, but eventually fall as the higher tax rates discouraged work effort. A typical Laffer Curve is shown in Figure 11-15.

A Laffer Curve shows that as income tax rates (t) increase, tax revenue (T) first rises and then falls. At 0% tax rates there is no tax revenue because there are no taxes. At 100% tax rates there is no tax revenue because no one is willing to work. In between these two extremes lies an optimal tax rate, t*, that will maximize the tax revenue for the government. Laffer believed that t* was likely to be small. Unfortunately, he was wrong. When Reagan reduced income tax rates in the 1980s, tax revenue did not increase. Instead, we ended up with the largest budget deficits that the federal government had ever known up to that time. The United States national debt tripled during the years of the Reagan Administration. The tax cuts led to reductions in tax revenue, not the increases predicted by the Laffer Curve.

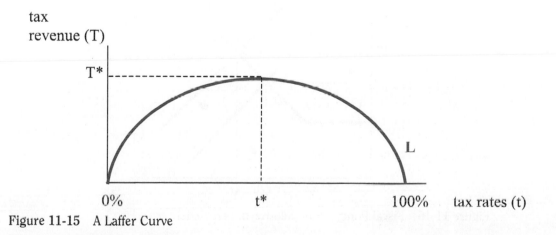

Figure 11-15   A Laffer Curve

## Debts and Deficits

In the discussion above, we mentioned the concepts of budget deficits and the national debt several times. We should provide some definitions for clarity before we go on.

*The budget deficit* is the difference between government spending and tax revenue for a given year. When the government has a budget deficit, it is spending more than it is earning in tax revenue that year.

*The national debt* is the sum of all funds that the government owes to all of its creditors that has not yet been paid off. The national debt is cumulative. When the nation runs a budget deficit in a given year, that amount is added to the national debt. Over the course of the year, the national debt increases as the government borrows money to fund a deficit during that year, or declines as debt from previous deficits is paid off.

Briefly, the national debt increased dramatically during the Reagan Administration, fell with the surplus of the Clinton years, and then increased again when George W. Bush increased federal deficit spending. The national debt represents the sum total of the tax burden we are passing on to future generations. The American Recovery and Reinvestment Act of 2009 created new records for both deficits and the national debt in the years following the passage of the act.

## FISCAL POLICY IN THE NEO-KEYNESIAN MODEL

The neo-Keynesian model assumes that there are three ranges of aggregate supply, and that aggregate supply becomes steeper as GDP increases. The effect of an increase in government spending is to increase aggregate demand, but the effects on GDP and prices depend on where the change occurs on the aggregate supply curve.

In the Keynesian range, an increase in aggregate demand will lead to an increase in real GDP but no increase in the price level since the aggregate supply curve is horizontal in this range. When the economy is in a recession, expansionary fiscal policy can be successful in stimulating GDP without causing inflation. The closer that the economy gets to full employment, the more likely it is that inflation will result.

In the intermediate range the aggregate supply curve is upward-sloping. An increase in aggregate demand raises both real GDP and the price level. Fiscal policy is effective in increasing real GDP in this range, but the cost is higher inflation.

In the classical range, when the economy is beyond full employment, the aggregate supply curve is vertical because the economy has reached its limits. Real GDP

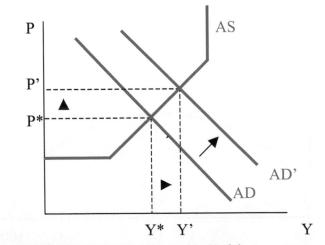

**Figure 11-16**   Fiscal Policy in the Neo-Keynesian Model

cannot be increased no matter how high prices are raised. In this range, an increase in aggregate demand will only cause inflation in the economy with no increase in real GDP. An increase in aggregate demand in the intermediate range is shown in Figure 11-16.

In the intermediate range, an increase in aggregate demand will lead to an increase in both real GDP and the price level. When the economy is in a recession, increases in aggregate demand will increase real GDP without causing inflation. As the economy gets closer to full employment, increases in aggregate demand become more and more inflationary. In the classical range, increases in aggregate demand only cause inflation in the economy.

In terms of the American Recovery and Reinvestment Act of 2009, in the neo-Keynesian model the effects of the tax cuts and increases in government spending will at first lead to increases in real GDP without inflation because during a recession the economy is operating in the Keynesian, or horizontal range of aggregate supply. But this model suggests that the more we use fiscal and monetary policy to increase aggregate demand, and the closer the economy is to full employment, the more likely it is that inflation will occur as a result of expansionary fiscal policy.

## FISCAL POLICY IN THE NEO-CLASSICAL MODEL

Finally, we examine fiscal policy in the neo-classical model. Here there are two aggregate supply curves, one in the short run when wages are fixed, and one in the long run when wages are variable. An increase in government spending will lead to an increase in aggregate demand. If the economy starts in a recession, then the increase in aggregate demand leads to an increase in both price and quantity until the economy returns to full employment at a higher price level. This is shown in Figure 11-17.

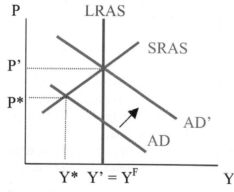

Figure 11-17    Fiscal Policy in the Neo-Classical Model When the Economy Is in Recession

When the economy starts in a recession, the increase in aggregate demand can bring the economy back to full employment with an increase in the price level and real GDP.

Suppose instead that the economy starts at full employment. An increase in government spending may lead to a temporary increase in GDP, but in the long run the result is inflation as resource prices increase, as shown in Figure 11-18. Here, the increase in government spending leads to an increase in AD and a temporary increase in real GDP. But since output is above full employment real GDP, in the long run resource prices will increase as workers learn about price increases and wages become flexible, and as there are shortages in other resource markets such as land and capital.

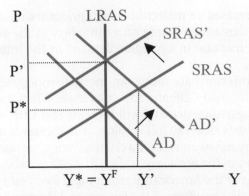

Figure 11-18    Fiscal Policy in the Neo-Classical Model When the Economy Is at Full Employment

The increase in resource prices causes a decrease in aggregate supply until the economy returns to full employment at a higher price level.

In this model, the American Recovery and Reinvestment Act of 2009 should be effective in increasing real GDP as long as the economy is in a recession, but the cost is an increase in the inflation rate. Once the economy reaches full employment, further expansionary policies would only lead to inflation. Once again, we see that fiscal policy is more effective when the economy is in recession compared to when the economy is at full employment.

## Summary: Policy Choices in the Neo-Classical Model

The neo-classical model can be used to explore the policy options available to those who attempt to influence the macroeconomy. Suppose that the economy starts in a recession as in Figure 11-17. The equilibrium level of real GDP, Y*, is less than the full employment level of real GDP shown by the long run aggregate supply curve. From here, the government has two basic choices, what we will call the classical response and the Keynesian response.

First, policymakers can use the classical response as shown in Figure 11-19. If the economy is in recession, eventually resource prices will fall. The fall in resource prices will lead to increases in the short run aggregate supply curve, and the economy returns to full employment.

When the economy starts in a recession, unemployed resources will place downward pressure on resource prices and aggregate supply will increase. Given enough

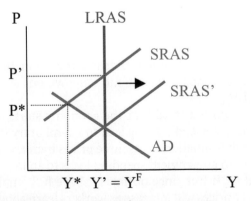

Figure 11-19    The Classical Response to Recession

time, the increase in the aggregate supply curve will lead to an increase in real GDP with a lower price level.

While the classical response is elegant in its simplicity, many critics, especially Keynesian economists, believe that the increase in aggregate supply that will bring the economy out of recession may take a very long time. In the meantime, the economy must suffer from the high rates of unemployment that occur during recession. Neo-classical economists rely on the idea of the long run where variables are flexible enough for the economy to bring itself back to full employment. But a favorite saying of Keynes comes from a 1920's book in monetary policy. "In the long run, we're all dead." Keynesian economists believe that it is better to be active in stimulating aggregate demand to bring the economy out of recession more quickly than the economy can adjust itself. The costs of unemployment should not be borne for long periods of time. The Keynesian response to a recession is shown in Figure 11-20. Rather than waiting for the aggregate supply curve to adjust through changes in resource prices, Keynes believed that a better response was active fiscal and monetary policies to increase aggregate demand.

When the economy starts in a recession, the increase in aggregate demand will increase real GDP and the price level. Keynesian economists are willing to sacrifice some inflation for the benefit of having a quicker reduction in unemployment in the economy. They believe the long run is just too long of a time to wait.

This apparent tradeoff between inflation and unemployment is often summarized in a model known as the *Phillips Curve*, which posits an inverse relationship between inflation and unemployment rates. The Phillips Curve is the topic of Chapter 14.

These controversies between the different types of policy responses to recession have been evident in the Congressional debates surrounding the recession of 2008–2009. In 2008 a credit crisis threatened the entire U.S. banking system. Rather than let the banks fail as in the Great Depression, the Bush Administration under Treasury Secretary Henry Paulsen provided capital to banks through the Troubled Assets Relief Program (TARP). Also, in 2009 the automobile industry received federal funds in an unsuccessful attempt to avoid bankruptcy for Chrysler and General Motors.

Republicans and other conservative pundits have argued that these bail outs for banks and car companies will only reward previous mistakes and encourage risky behavior in the future. Bail outs create moral hazard problems as the costs of bad decisions are transferred to taxpayers. These arguments represent the classical response to recession. Rather than having active fiscal policies to try to stimulate the economy, in the long run we are all better off if we allow these companies to fail. What will rise from the ashes will be stronger and more efficient companies.

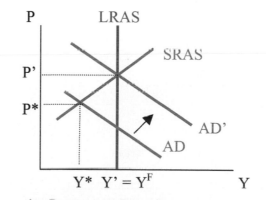

Figure 11-20   The Keynesian Response to Recession

Government assistance only perpetuates bad corporate decision-making. Rather than having government interference in markets, markets should be able to police themselves and punish those who are inefficient. The economy in the long run will be stronger as a result. By employing market mechanisms, eventually wages and interest rates will fall in response to recession and the economy can return itself to full employment without government interference.

The Keynesian response to recession has been represented by the policies of both the Bush and Obama Administrations. The phrase "too big to fail" has been mentioned in the media extensively. Inaction on the part of government would only lead to a deepening recession. Allowing banks or car companies to fail would create ripple effects throughout the entire economy, and may then lead to even greater declines in real GDP and higher costs of recovery. The interconnections between different institutions in the economy would lead to systemic risk if one of these institutions was allowed to fail. The social and economic costs of high unemployment rates should not be allowed to persist for significant periods of time. Rather than waiting for the economy to correct itself in the long run, we are better off using expansionary fiscal and monetary policies to stimulate aggregate demand in the short run. The government's response to the current recession has been a Keynesian response.

This concludes our chapter on fiscal policy. We now turn to the other important tool of economic policy known as monetary policy.

# 12

# MONEY AND BANKING

We often take the importance of money for granted. I don't mean personally. Most of us know the difference between having money in our pockets and not. What I mean is that we often fail to appreciate the social, cultural, political, and economic importance of money. Throughout history, the type of payment system in effect at the time has had profound impacts on the character of civilization. We will explore these ideas in this chapter. In addition, we will examine the functions of money and how the Federal Reserve measures the amount of money in circulation at a given point in time.

In this chapter, we will first look at the definition of money and then describe the functions of money. Next, we will briefly explore the history of money and banking and the evolution of the payments system. Then we will show how the Federal Reserve measures money using the concepts of M1, M2, and M3. Finally we will examine the structure of the U.S. banking system. In the next chapter we will then explore the different models of monetary policy and the monetary policy tools of the Federal Reserve System.

## MONEY

*Money* is any asset that is generally acceptable in exchange for goods and services or as payment for debt.

Money is any asset that everyone is willing to accept. This idea of acceptability is known as liquidity. Dollar bills are liquid because we are all willing to take them in payment, even though they have no intrinsic value. Throughout history many items have functioned as money, from clam shells to cigarettes, as we will discuss below.

*Liquidity* is the acceptability of an asset as a medium of exchange.

## FUNCTIONS OF MONEY

Generally, money has four functions, but some authors of economics texts only list the first three. They are:

1. a medium of exchange
2. a unit of account
3. a store of value
4. a standard of deferred payment

We will discuss each in turn.

### Medium of Exchange

Perhaps the most important function of money is to act as a medium of exchange, or to facilitate trade by reducing the transaction costs of exchange. It is often said that money acts as a lubricant in the economy. In the same way that oil acts as a lubricant to help an engine run more smoothly, money acts as a lubricant to help the economy run more smoothly. It does this by reducing the necessity for barter. (As we will see, there are many automobile analogies in monetary policy.)

*Barter* is the direct exchange of one good or service for another good or service. Barter is often difficult and time consuming. By acting as a medium of exchange, money helps to avoid the necessity of bartering. Barter exchange requires a double coincidence of wants. In order to be willing to barter, you must have what I want and I must have what you want. If I cannot find someone that is willing to trade with me, then I am stuck with what I have got.

Let us look at two examples. First, I have a friend who installs carpet who had a toothache. He prefers barter exchange to using money in order to avoid income taxes. In order to heal his toothache through barter, he could not just go to any dentist and pay him with the money he earned from installing a carpet for someone else. Rather, he has to find a dentist who is both willing to fix his toothache and who needs new carpet. It may be difficult to find the right dentist, and in the meantime he still has a toothache. The ability to use money would allow him to find a dentist much more easily.

Second, let us imagine trying to put together a regular college class without money. Students would only be able to take classes from those professors who want what they have, and are teaching the courses that the student wants to take. Professors would only be willing to teach to those students who have what they want, but the only students willing to take their classes may not have what the teacher needs.

For instance, suppose your family consists of chicken farmers. You come to campus with a bunch of chickens and eggs. The only teachers willing to teach you would be those who want or need chickens and eggs. But these teachers may not teach the courses that interest you. If all biology teachers were vegans, you would not be able to take any biology classes.

Suppose that as a teacher, my family needs toilet paper and toothpaste that day, and my family would like to have steak and potatoes for dinner. I would probably not be willing to teach you with your chickens. But I may not be able to find students with toilet paper, toothpaste, steak or potatoes who are willing to learn economics that day. So my family would have to do without. I hope you can see that money makes it much easier to put together a college class. You do not have to negotiate with your professor to arrange payment for each class; you pay your money to the college and the college pays your professor. You do not have to argue over how many eggs an accounting class would be worth. You know what classes to take each day and your professor knows what classes to teach each day. By reducing transaction costs in this way, money helps to create wealth in the economy because more trades are able to be accomplished. Money acts as a medium of exchange because money is liquid.

## Unit of Account

Money allows the measurement and comparison of the value of different goods and services. Money acts as a yardstick, or a common measure of the value of goods, services, and income, so that revenues and costs can be measured through accounting procedures. It would be much more difficult if a farmer had to express her revenues in terms of corn, wheat and soybeans, and her costs in labor hours, pounds of fertilizer, and gallons of water for irrigation. It is much easier to calculate profits when revenue and costs can be expressed in terms of money.

Another function of money that we take for granted is that, by acting as a unit of account, money reduces the number of relative prices that we all must keep in our heads. For example, imagine an economy without money as a numeraire good (good used to measure the value of everything else). Without money, the value of each good has to be measured in terms of all of the other goods in the economy, which becomes an impossible mental feat as the number of goods in the economy increases.

For example, let us assume we have an economy without money but with different types of food. What happens as we increase the types of food available? We will take each case in turn.

1. Suppose that there is an economy with only one good, apples. Then prices are impossible, since there is no other good to be used for measurement. There is nothing to compare to, so there is no way to express the price of apples in terms of some other good.

2. With two goods, apples and bananas, there is only one relative price, the price of apples compared to the price of bananas, or $P_A/P_B$. Once we know $P_A/P_B$, we also know $P_B/P_A$.

3. Suppose there are three goods, apples, bananas and cherries. Then we have three relative prices to consider:
    $$P_A/P_B \qquad P_B/P_C$$
    $$P_A/P_C$$

4. With four goods, apples, bananas, cherries and dates, we have six possible sets of relative prices:
    $$P_A/P_B \qquad P_B/P_C \qquad P_C/P_D$$
    $$P_A/P_C \qquad P_B/P_D$$
    $$P_A/P_D$$

5. With five goods, apples, bananas, cherries, dates, and eggs, the number of relative prices is now ten:
    $$P_A/P_B \qquad P_B/P_C \qquad P_C/P_D \quad P_D/P_E$$
    $$P_A/P_C \qquad P_B/P_D \qquad P_C/P_E$$
    $$P_A/P_D \qquad P_B/P_E$$
    $$P_A/P_E$$

Do you notice a pattern here? As the number of goods increases, the number of relatives prices increases exponentially. The formula is actually:

$$\# \text{ relative prices} = [N(N-1)] / 2$$

So the existence of money makes it much easier to think! Rather than having to carry around thousands of sets of relative prices, we only need to know the price of each good and then we can compare from there. We are able to have room in our brains for much more important things, like taking this course!

Money can act as a unit of account because money is standardized. Every dollar bill has the same value as all others. It provides a common measuring stick of value.

## Store of Value

Since money is durable, it acts as a store of value. By doing so, it allows the accumulation of wealth to take place. It is much easier to store money than it is to store goods or services. Many goods, such as farm produce, are perishable. Many services, such as baby-sitting hours, cannot be stored.

For example, suppose that I am a fisherman and that my daughter is getting married. I want to save up so that my daughter can have the wedding of her dreams. Also assume that no money exists. In order to save for my daughter's wedding, I take my boat out an hour early each day and stay for an hour later each night, and catch lots of extra fish which I then throw in my backyard. I diligently do this until my daughter's wedding day.

Will my daughter have a nice wedding? Of course not! All we will have is a pile of smelly fish in the backyard. But, if I can take my fish to the market each night and sell them for money, then I can save up and my daughter will have a wonderful wedding. Money allows me to accumulate wealth in a way that fish cannot.

While some types of commodity money such as maize and tobacco leaves may not have been very durable, the more durable a commodity is, then the more easily it could be used as money.

Money acts as a store of value because money is durable.

## Standard of Deferred Payment

Money also allows debts to be expressed and paid back with items similar in quality to what was borrowed. Money is fungible, or substitutable or replaceable. If I lend you a nice, crisp, brand new dollar bill, it does not matter if I get paid back with the same dollar bill, an old crumply dollar bill, two half dollars, or four quarters. All have the same value as what I lent, as long as inflation does not reduce the purchasing power of money during the term of the loan.

For instance, if I lend you a dollar, and then you rip it in half and give it back to me, then I am really no worse off. I just have to scotch tape the bill together. But if I lend you a banana, then you cut the banana in half and return it to me, now I am worse off. I have to eat the banana right away before it rots. It is much easier to lend dollars than bananas. So the existence of money facilitates the process of borrowing and lending in our economy. When you lend someone ten dollars, you do not expect to receive the same ten dollar bill in repayment. But if you lend someone your car, you expect to receive the same car when the loan is paid back. Because money is fungible, it reduces the transaction costs of borrowing and lending.

Money acts as a standard of deferred payment because money is fungible.

In essence, money is a cultural phenomenon. Money is any asset that a culture defines as having value and acceptability. Without culture to give money value, dollar bills would be merely worthless pieces of paper. But because the global culture has faith in the stability of the U.S. government, then U.S. dollars have value and are accepted around the world. In fact, almost 70% of the currency issued by the federal government is held outside the United States (New York Fed). U.S. dollars are held as a store of value across the globe.

## A BRIEF HISTORY OF MONEY

One could probably spend a lifetime and still not learn all there is to know about the history of money. I will try to be as brief as possible. Much of this argument comes from Jack Weatherford, *A History of Money*.

While there have been many different types of commodities that have functioned as money over time, we have witnessed an evolution of the payments system over time that has enabled us to reduce the transaction costs of exchange. A brief synopsis may look as follows:

BARTER → COMMODITY → COINS → FIAT → CHECKS → ELECTRONIC
            MONEY                    MONEY                      MONEY

### Barter

We have already discussed barter. Trade may occur, but the transaction costs will be high.

### Commodity Money

The origins of commodity money are lost in antiquity. As far back as you go in recorded history, you see some forms of commodity money. Commodity money is an asset that has an intrinsic value apart from its use as money: it is a commodity that has another use. Many items have functioned as commodity money over time. Here is a brief list:

Babylon, Assyria—barley
India—almonds
Greece—iron nails
Aztecs—cocoa beans
Nicobar Islands—coconuts
Yap Islands—large stone wheels
Mongolia—bricks of tea
Asia—rice, cowrie shells
Norway—butter, dried cod
Roman Empire, China, North Africa—salt (This is the origin of the word *salary*.)
Siberia—reindeer
Borneo—buffalo
Hittites—sheep
Europe—cattle (This is the origin of the words *capital* and *chattel*.)
Russia, North America—furs
Ireland—slave girls
American colonies—tobacco leaves, maize
German Prisoner of War camps in WW II—cigarettes

As you can see, many different items have functioned as money over time. Obviously, some types of commodities make better money than others. Some goods may perish easily, may be difficult to carry around, or may not be suitable for small payments.

To function well as commodity money, an item should be:

• in limited supply

• durable

• divisible

• have value apart from its use as money, especially if high demand by
  wealthy

- portable
- fungible

The less that a form of commodity money met these characteristics, the higher were the transaction costs of exchange. Agricultural products, for instance, may not be durable or fungible. Large stone wheels are not very portable. Cattle and sheep, or slaves, may run away. Even though many items functioned as commodity money throughout history, over time gold and silver nuggets became the dominant form of commodity money. But gold and silver nuggets were still difficult to weigh and assay (test the purity), so eventually these became gold and silver coins.

## Coins

As gold and silver nuggets became more common as form of exchange, they were cumbersome because the nuggets would have to be weighed and assayed. Eventually the need for weighing and assaying was eliminated through the development of coins. With a coin the government could attest to the weight and purity of the metal in the coin, and the transaction costs of exchange using precious metals were greatly reduced. As we will see, the first coins were minted by the country of Lydia in the 600 B.C.s, which were made of electrum, a naturally occurring alloy of gold and silver, and were called "staters." The idea of coins soon spread throughout Greece and Rome, and Western Civilization has not been the same since.

## Fiat Money

Gold and silver coins were still difficult to carry in large quantities, and may not have been appropriate for small purchases. Fiat money evolved over time to further reduce the transaction costs of exchange. Fiat money is an asset that is acceptable because the government says it is, or by government fiat. It is also known as fiduciary money. At first, paper currency may have represented a certain value of a commodity, such as tobacco or silver. Over time, this practice ceased so that now most paper currencies are true fiat money, having no other intrinsic value. If you examine the front of a dollar bill, it says "This note is legal tender for all debts, public and private." That means that we are all obligated to accept those pieces of paper in payment. Figure 12-1 is a copy of the newest $20 bill issued by the Federal Reserve Bank. It describes the various security features meant to prevent counterfeiting. Note that the front says "This note is legal tender for all debts, public and private." It does not promise to redeem the bill in $20 of gold or silver. It is fiat money.

## Checks

One problem with fiat money was that there was no protection against theft. This problem became more acute as the distance between buyer and seller increased. One way of solving this problem is through the use of a check, which can only be cashed by one person and so is more difficult to steal. Checks began to grow as a means of payments in the United States after the Civil War.

## Electronic Money

We are in the midst of another step in the evolution of the payments system, the gradual movement toward electronic money. Electronic money includes such payment

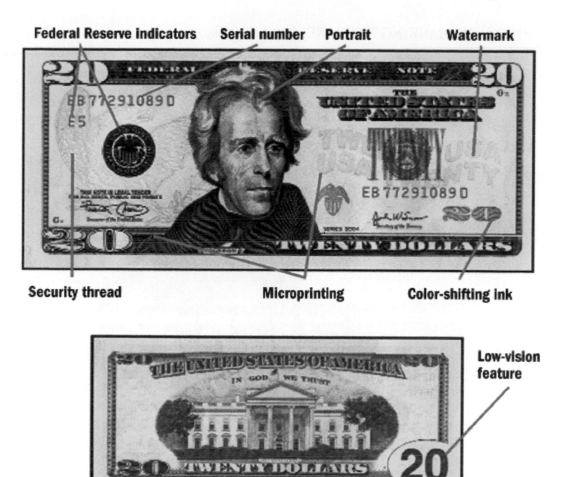

**Figure 12-1** Fiat Money: A $20.00 Bill. The newest $20 bill issued by the Federal Reserve Bank. It describes the various security features meant to prevent counterfeiting. Note that the front says "This note is legal tender for all debts, public and private." It does not promise to redeem the bill in $20 of gold or silver. It is fiat money.

systems as ATFs (Automatic Transfer of Funds), debit cards, stored value cards, Pay-pal, and electronic checks. Electronic money frees the buyer and seller from the necessity of geographically transferring the payment. Funds can be transferred electronically between any two points in the world instantaneously. One example of electronic money is JPay, which is used to transfer funds to inmates in the U.S. penal system. Inmates never see cash, only electronic accounts where their funds to spend are stored (*www.jpay.com*).

Electronic money frees exchange from the restrictions of time and place. Once again we see an evolution which helps to reduce the transaction costs of exchange. We are only beginning to grasp the importance and implications of the shift toward electronic money. In the way that the automobile changed the 20th century, electronic money and the internet will change the 21st century. One implication is a reduction in population density as households no longer need to be physically close to stores and work. The effects on our society, politics, culture and environment remain to be seen.

## A MONEY AND BANKING TIMELINE: 640 B.C.–2008 A.D.

Here is a brief timeline in the history of money and banking:

| | |
|---|---|
| 640 B.C. | Lydia introduces the first coins, known as staters, made of electrum, a natural alloy of gold and silver. Lydia lies between Turkey and Greece. |

**Stater of Croseus (Lydia)**
Source: Federal Reserve Bank of Richmond

| | |
|---|---|
| 630 B.C. | Greek city-states begin to follow Lydia's lead as commerce begins to flourish. Aegina begins to mint its own staters. |
| 600 B.C. | Aethenian tetradrachma is introduced. Worth "four handfuls" of iron nails. First Evidence of Chinese coins during Chou dynasty. |
| 500s B.C. | As more and more coins become acceptable and standardized, commerce thrives in the Greek city-states. People are freed from the land and tributary systems, or having to pay their taxes in tribute or what they produced. A merchant class could develop, along with culture, the arts, and science. |
| 490 B.C. | Corinthian "ponies" are the first with denominations. |

**Athenian Tetradrachma**
Source: Federal Reserve Bank of Richmond

| | |
|---|---|
| 350s B.C. | Greek city-states are conquered by Macedonia. Phillip sets an exchange rate of ten silver to one gold. Alexander the Great then standardizes money from the Indus River to Naples. |
| 323 B.C. | When Alexander the Great dies, his image becomes the first of a mortal man on a coin. |
| 320s B.C. | Rome begins minting silver coins and expanding its empire. |

| | |
|---|---|
| 200s B.C. | Rome issues the silver Denarius, which followed it as it expanded into the Italian Peninsula, Spain and Gaul. As Rome expanded, they melted down Greek coins and other symbols of external power. |
| 100s B.C. | Rome accumulates a large gold reserve. |
| 68 B.C. | The first Jewish Shekel is created in revolt to Roman rule. |
| 50s B.C. | Julius Caesar mints gold Aureus, at a weight of 40 coins to a pound of gold. |
| 31 B.C. | Augustus begins rule until 14 A.D. The Aureus spreads as far as India. Augustus creates the Denarius, a silver coin worth about a day's pay. He takes authority to mint the coin away from the Roman Senate. |

**Denarius of Tibirius Caesar (14–37)**

Source: Federal Reserve Bank of Richmond

| | |
|---|---|
| 20s A.D. | As the Roman Empire expands from present-day Belgium to India, it has a difficult time in supplying enough coins. This led to deflationary pressures, and the re-emergence of commodity money such as blocks of salt as pay for Roman soldiers. |
| 64 A.D. | Rome burns. In the preceding years, Caligula and Nero had spent excessively because of the high value of coins due to deflation. As the rulers became greedier, Nero began to reduce the silver content of coins. Over time, rulers begin to reduce the silver content of the Denarius, from 100% to eventually 5%. This leads to catastrophic inflation. |
| 200 A.D. | By this time, there has been so much inflation due to silver dilution of coinage that all faith in the Roman monetary system is lost. The former Roman Empire returns to a barter system and the weighing of gold and silver. The Dark Ages ensue. |
| 618 A.D. | Chinese are the first to use paper money. |
| 1000s A.D. | Without money and effective commerce, Europe is stuck in a feudalist system known as the Dark Ages. People must work the land to pay tribute to the lord (or landowner). Without money as a dominant means of exchange, it was difficult for a merchant class to develop, or for people to have the time to develop arts and sciences. |
| 1200s A.D. | Rumblings of modern money. European countries begin to mint coins. |
| 1400s A.D. | First developments of paper currency or fiat money in the West. In Italian provinces, such as Venice, bankers begin to issue bank notes redeemable for a certain amount of specie (gold or silver). As these circulate, they function as paper money. The bankers (such as the |

Medicis) also make loans and charge interest. With the development of a banking system, the Renaissance was able to flourish.

In Amsterdam, goldsmiths become important as a means of weighing, assaying, and storing gold nuggets used for transactions. Deposits slips of the goldsmiths become a form of paper currency. Fractional reserve banking begins as the goldsmiths make loans with some of the gold held in deposit.

1558 A.D.   Elizabeth I becomes Queen of England. The Henry's before her had debased the coins by reducing silver content, and the populace "clipped" the coins by filing them down. In an attempt to improve the coinage, the Queen mints new coins. They disappear from circulation as people spend the old coins and hoard the new coins, as predicted by the queen's financial advisor, Thomas Gresham. Gresham becomes famous through *"Gresham's Law,"* the idea that "bad money drives out good money." If two coins are circulating at the same time, one of high quality and one of low quality, then people will spend the low quality coins and hoard the high quality coins. Examples in the United States include silver quarters (those minted before 1964) and Delaware quarters. Why don't we see any quarters before 1964? Why do we still see so many quarters from 1965 and 1966? Gresham's Law also helps to explain why we have ridges (or milled edges) on many coins such as dimes and quarters. The ridges enable the holder to determine whether or not a coin had been filed down.

**English Crown (1689–1691)**
Source: Federal Reserve Bank of Richmond

1700s       Europe strengthens and standardizes its coinage system. China has a well-developed paper currency with increasing security features. The American colonies have many types of money, including wampum and furs, maize and tobacco, tobacco notes, state coins such as the Massachusetts Pine Tree Shilling, and foreign coins such as the Spanish dollar and British pound.

1775–1781   In the American colonies, the Continental Congress issues a paper currency, known as continentals, to finance the American Revolution. As more and more continentals are printed, hyperinflation results. This causes the currency to become worthless, or "not worth a continental." By 1781, continentals cease to be issued.

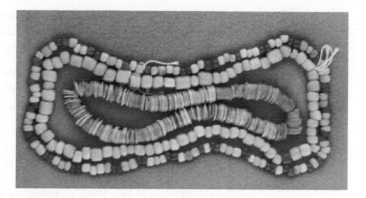

**wampum**

Source: Federal Reserve Bank of Richmond

| | |
|---|---|
| 1781 | The first national bank, The Bank of North America, is chartered in Philadelphia by the Continental Congress. It begins operations on January 7, 1782. It is a private bank founded by Robert Morris, who deposits large amounts of gold and silver, and then issues new paper currency backed by these specie after the continental fails. |
| 1791 | The United States' first central bank, The Bank of The United States, is chartered by Congress with a 20-year charter. (We now call it the First Bank of the United States, but they didn't know it would have to be called the first bank at the time. Kind of like World War I.) The main drive to establish a central bank came from Alexander Hamilton. While it was a private corporation, it had responsibility for the supply of money and credit in the newly formed United States, and acted as a central bank for other banks and the government. It soon became the largest corporation in the country. |
| 1792 | Supported by Alexander Hamilton, Congress passes the United States of America Money Act (Coinage Act) of 1792. The act establishes a national currency based on the decimal units of the Spanish dollar and a bimetallic standard of both silver and gold coins. The act defines the value of a dollar in terms of gold and silver. State bank notes are not prohibited (*http://www.ripit4me.org/Subjects/MoneyBanking/Money/LegHistory/LegHistoryMoney.htm*). |
| 1811 | Due to distrust of centralized power, large banks, and large corporations in general, the 20-year charter of the Bank of the United States is allowed to expire. Congress refuses to renew the charter by one vote, so the charter lapses. The Bank of the United States ceases to be. |
| 1816 | After the difficulties in financing the War of 1812 and a change in political circumstances, the Second Bank of the United States is established with a 20-year charter from Congress. It is similar in purposes and functions to the First Bank of the United States. |
| 1828 | Andrew Jackson, an ardent enemy of central banks, is elected president. He vows to destroy the Second Bank of the United States in opposition to the concentration of economic and financial power inherent in a central bank. |

| 1832 | Andrew Jackson vetoes the re-chartering of the Second Bank of the United States. |
|------|-------------------------------------------------------------------------------|
| 1836 | After twenty years, the charter for the Second Bank of the United States expires. The United States enters a period of 77 years without a central bank. Without a central bank or nationally chartered banks, state banks dominate the U.S. financial landscape. |
| 1836–1865 | This time period is known as the "Era of Free Banking." With no central bank or nationally chartered banks, state-chartered banks, and unchartered "free banks," control the money supply. There are many different types of bank notes, some backed by gold or other specie, in circulation at the time as forms of paper currency. Also, demand deposits become a form of payment. |
| 1863 | The first elements of modern banking are established when the *National Banking Act of 1863* is passed by Congress. The act has several important provisions, including the creation of the Office of the Comptroller of the Currency. The OCC is empowered to charter national banks, which can only issue notes backed by U.S. government securities. It allows national bank notes to circulate freely, while state bank notes are taxed to drive them out of circulation and to encourage a uniform currency. One consequence is not that state banks are eliminated, but they are forced to develop other types of payments systems. In this way, checks become a more popular form of payment. |
| 1873, 1884, 1890, 1893 | Even though the Banking Act of 1863 helps to stabilize the money supply, there remain frequent financial crises and panics, such as the bank panics that occur in these years. Runs on banks are common. The depression in 1893 becomes so severe that it takes the intervention of J. P. Morgan, a prominent banker and financier, to restore confidence in the financial markets. |
| 1896 | The election of 1896 pits William McKinley, the Republican candidate, against William Jennings Bryan, a populist and the Democratic candidate. One of the major campaign issues is whether or not the country should adopt a silver standard or a gold standard for currency. McKinley favors the gold standard to keep the value of money high and to enhance financial stability. Bryan favors the silver standard to make credit easy and to keep interest rates low, so it is easier for working-class industrialists and farmers to borrow. He gives a famous speech before the Democratic National Convention on July 9, 1896. It ends with this famous phrase: |

> Having behind us the producing masses of this nation and the world, supported by the commercial interests, the laboring interests and the toilers everywhere, we will answer their demand for a gold standard by saying to them: You shall not press down upon the brow of labor this crown of thorns, you shall not crucify mankind upon a cross of gold. (*historymatters.gmu.edu/d/5354*)

McKinley wins, so the U.S. keeps the gold standard. Money and credit remain scarce in the country. (*The Wizard of Oz* is often viewed as a political fable about this election.)

| | |
|---|---|
| 1900 | As a result of the election of 1896, the United States adopts a gold standard through the Gold Standard Act of 1900. The gold standard continues until it is suspended by Franklin Roosevelt in 1933. Many coins are made of gold and paper currency is backed by gold. |
| 1907 | A major financial crisis known as the Panic of 1907 occurs. There are many bank and business failures, and stock prices plummet. J. P. Morgan once again bails out the financial markets, with less success than in 1893. The gold standard, by keeping money and credit tight, exacerbates the problem. |
| 1908 | As a result of the Panic of 1907, the *Aldrich-Vreeland Act* is passed. This act establishes the National Monetary Commission, which is charged to explore proposals for a new central bank to help provide more stability in financial markets. After studying the issue for several years, Sen. Nelson Aldrich devises a central bank plan that is controlled by bankers. William Jennings Bryan and other populists strongly oppose the plan, favoring a central bank under public control rather than under banker control. The debate goes back and forth for several years, until Woodrow Wilson is elected president. |
| 1912 | Woodrow Wilson is elected president. He selects Senator Carter Glass and Economist Parker Willis to devise a new plan for a central bank. By December, they submit a plan that forms the origins of the Federal Reserve Act. From December 1912 to December 1913, the Federal Reserve Act is debated and revised in Congress. |
| 1913 | *The Federal Reserve Act of 1913* is passed. The act creates the Federal Reserve System, combining the interests of both the public sector and of bankers. It is crafted in the typical fashion of American compromise, with twelve regional banks instead of one central bank, a Board of Governors with long, staggered terms, and district bank directors that are chosen from both the banking and the public sectors. We will focus much more closely on the structure of the Federal Reserve in the next section. |
| 1929 | In October 1929, the stock market crashes. The Great Depression follows. By 1933, almost 10,000 banks have failed. When he takes office in March 1933, Franklin Roosevelt (FDR) declares a bank holiday. A significant amount of legislation, still affecting us today, then follows as FDR tries to grapple with the Great Depression. When FDR eliminates the gold standard, the United States effectively has a silver standard until the redemption of silver certificates is suspended in 1971. |
| 1933 | *The Glass-Steagall Act* is passed. The act provides the basis for banking regulation for the next 66 years, until it is repealed by the Gramm-Leach-Bliley Act of 1999. Also known as the Banking Act of 1933, the Glass-Steagall Act <ul><li>separates the commercial banking, investment banking, and insurance industries.</li><li>provides for interest rate ceilings on time deposits (implemented through Regulation Q).</li><li>requires that banks pay 0% interest on checking accounts, and checking account services are limited to commercial banks.</li></ul> |

- creates the Federal Deposit Insurance Corporation (FDIC) to increase consumer confidence in the banking system and avoid runs on banks. Originally, deposits are insured up to a value of $2500.

A silver certificate of 1934

Source: Federal Reserve Bank of Buffalo

| | |
|---|---|
| 1934 | Still in response to the Great Depression, several other acts with important implications for the financial system are passed. One is the *Federal Home Loan Bank Act of 1934,* which establishes the savings and loan industry as a means of promoting home ownership. The act limits savings and loans associations to consumer and residential loans, and prevents them from offering checking account services. It creates the Federal Savings and Loan Insurance Corporation (FSLIC) to insure deposits. The system provides for a large regulatory divide between the savings and loans and commercial banks, which persists until the 1980s. A second act that passes in 1934 is the *Securities and Exchange Commission Act.* This act establishes the Securities and Exchange Commission to promote stability in equity markets. It also makes the FDIC the primary regulator of state nonmember banks, and gives the FDIC responsibility to monitor the securities holdings of insured banks. |
| 1964–1971 | The United States gradually abandons the silver standard. First, silver quarters and dimes are replaced by copper and nickel coins after 1964. (See the previous discussion on Gresham's Law.) For the Kennedy half dollars, the silver content was reduced until by 1971 there were no longer any silver coins minted for general circulation in the United States. Since 1971 the United States has had a true fiat money system. The only asset backing dollars are Treasury bonds, which are just promises by the government to pay more pieces of paper in the future. |
| 1975 | The *Home Mortgage Disclosure Act* requires banks to report on their lending activity to low income and minority individuals. |
| 1977 | In an attempt to prevent redlining, the *Community Reinvestment Act* is adopted. Banks are required to make loans in areas where they have branches. |

| 1980 | The era of traditional banking comes to an end as the depression-era regulations are slowly unraveled. Deregulation of the banking system begins with DIDMCA, or the *Depository Institutions Deregulation and Monetary Control Act of 1980*. This act changes the financial universe by deregulating the savings and loan industry. Thrift institutions are now allowed to invest in other assets besides consumer and residential loans, such as speculative real estate ventures and junk bonds. Savings and loans are able to offer checking account services for the first time. The act also eliminates interest rate ceilings for banks and savings and loans, so now banks and thrifts can pay any interest rate on deposits that they desire. DIDMCA also enables the Fed to set reserve requirements for all banks, and allows all banks to borrow from the discount window. |
|------|------|
| 1982 | *The Depository Institutions (Garn- St. Germain) Act of 1982* is passed. This act increases FDIC insurance from $40,000 to $100,000 overnight, it allows banks and thrifts to offer Money Market Deposit Accounts, and gives the FDIC and FSLIC emergency powers to merge banks and thrifts if insolvency may otherwise occur. The moral hazard created by the 1980 and 1982 acts contributed greatly to the excesses of the savings and loan crisis. |
| 1980s | The savings and loan crisis leads to the failure of almost 10,000 thrift institutions. |
| 1989 | *The Financial Institutions Reform, Recovery, and Enforcement Act (FIRREA) of 1989* is passed as bailout to the savings and loan industry. The act provides funds for S & L bailouts, eliminates the FSLIC and the Federal Home Loan Bank Board, and creates the Office of Thrift Supervision (OTS) to regulate thrifts and the Resolution Trust Corporation (RTC) to manage and liquidate insolvent thrifts. The RTC dissolves on December 31, 1995. FIRREA also raises deposit insurance premiums to help cover the costs of the bailout, and re-imposes many of the restrictions that Congress gave up in the 1980 and 1982 laws. Even with the provisions to increase funding for the FDIC, the bill still does not provide enough funds for the bailout. |
| 1991 | The regulatory hammer falls with the *Federal Deposit Insurance Corporation Improvement Act (FDICIA) of 1991*. This act re-capitalizes the FDIC, and increases revenues by allowing the FDIC to set risk-based premiums. It increases the frequency of examinations, and also provides more stringent capital requirements and reporting requirements. Most importantly, it creates the policy of "prompt corrective action," where the degree of regulatory scrutiny received by a bank is determined by the level of capitalization. The more capital a bank has compared to assets, then the more lenient are the regulatory authorities in judging the safety and soundness of the institution. |
| 1999 | After prodding by financial executives, Congress passes the *Gramm-Leach-Bliley Financial Services Modernization Act of 1999*. By repealing the Glass-Steagall Act, Gramm-Leach-Bliley allows commercial banks to provide investment services and insurance services, much as they could before the Great Depression. In 1998, Citibank merges with Traveler's Insurance to form Citigroup, despite the prohibitions |

of the Glass-Steagall Act. Alan Greenspan agrees to allow Citigroup's leader Sandy Weil a temporary waiver to form the mega-company. The deal is that as long as Weil is able to get Congress to repeal the Glass-Steagall Act, then Greenspan would continue to allow the waiver for Citigroup. If Congress disagrees, then Citigroup would be disbanded. If Congress agrees, then the waiver would no longer be necessary. Of course, the financial industry has enough money to convince Congress, so Glass-Steagall is repealed in 1999 and a new financial industry is born.

2002     *The Sarbanes—Oxley Act* is passed in response to the corporate accounting scandals of 1998–2002. The act requires that CEOs sign off on financial statements, creates a new oversight board for the SEC, and extends the SEC's powers over auditing and investigating corporate malfeasance.

2003     Congress passes *the Check Clearing for the 21st Century Act,* also known as Check 21. The law allows banks to substitute electronic copies of checks for paper checks, so that paper checks no longer have to be transferred to clear. This law may eventually be viewed as the real birth of electronic money in the United States.

2007     Financial markets begin to unravel as home foreclosures top 1 million per year in the United States. The Fed responds by opening up Term Auction Facilities as an alternative to the discount window to provide loans to banks. In the Term Auction Facility, the Fed announces a certain quantity of funds to be auctioned off, and then the interest rate charged is determined by the bids received.

2008     The financial crisis of 2008 begins as the investment banking industry is changed forever. In March, Bear Stearns fails and is bailed out by having the Fed subsidize its purchase by JP Morgan. As mortgage-backed securities, collateralized debt obligations, and credit default swaps begin to default, more and more financial institutions around the world face mounting losses. The investment banking industry disappears as the last four major investment banks are taken over by commercial banks or go bankrupt. In September, Lehman Brothers is allowed to go bankrupt, Merrill Lynch is purchased by Bank of America with subsidies from the Fed, and the remaining two investment banks, Goldman Sachs and Morgan Stanley, decide to become commercial bank holding companies. Congress responds with the bail out bill, "The Emergency Economic Stabilization Act of 2008," that provides $700 billion to the Treasury for the Troubled Assets Relief Program (TARP). When the first version of the bill fails to pass Congress on September 29, the Dow Jones Industrial Average has its largest one-day point decline of 777 points. The Fed responds with new types of loan facilities and by reducing the target for the federal funds rate to historic lows of 0 to .25% in December.

## THE IMPACT OF MONEY

From the above discussion I hope you have gained an appreciation of the importance of money in the development of civilization. Without money trade is more difficult, so people are forced to be more self-sufficient. There is little time for leisure. The government must raise its taxes in-kind through the taking of tribute, or taking a portion of the farmer's product. Transfer of wealth and property is difficult except through heredity.

Money facilitates trade and fosters commerce, allowing markets to develop, a merchant class to arise, leisure to become possible, and arts and culture to prosper. We have seen this throughout history, from Lydia, Greece, Rome, Venice, Amsterdam, to the American Colonies.

It is difficult to underestimate the impact of money on society. And it is not all bad!

## MEASURING MONEY

Since money is liquidity or acceptability, then money can be measured differently depending on the standard of liquidity which is employed. Because of this, the Fed uses several measures of money to reflect different levels of liquidity in assets. These are known as M1, M2, and M3, often called monetary aggregates. As we move from M1 to M2 to M3, the liquidity of assets declines as more assets are included in the measure of money.

### M1

M1 is the most liquid measure of money.

    M1 = currency and coins
        + checking account deposits (demand deposits)
        + travelers' checks
        + other checkable deposits

Other checkable deposits include share draft accounts at credit unions and Negotiable Order of Withdrawal (NOW) accounts at commercial banks. M1 includes the assets that most everyone is willing to accept in exchange for goods and services or as payments for debts. In dollar terms, it is the smallest measure of money since it includes the fewest categories.

### M2

M2 is the second measure of money. It includes more assets than M1 so is a larger measure.

    M2 = M1
        + small denomination time deposits (< $100,000) (CDs)
        + savings deposits
        + money market deposit accounts
        + non-institutional money market mutual fund shares

M2 includes everything in M1 plus personal savings.

### M3

M3 is the broadest measure of the money supply, in that it includes the most assets and is the largest number of the three.

    M3 = M2
        + large denomination time deposits (>$100,000)
        + institutional money market mutual funds
        + repurchase agreements
        + term Eurodollars

Here, $100,000 is used as the dividing line between large and small time deposits because that was the limit of FDIC insurance before the changes in monetary policy that occurred in 2008. "Institutional" refers to large investors such as corporations, municipal governments, and pension plans. A repurchase agreement (or repo) is a loan where a security is used as collateral. If a borrower needs temporary funds, they will sell a security at a certain price to obtain funds, and then buy back (or repurchase) the security at a slightly higher price once the funds are no longer needed. The lender profits due to the price differential. Eurodollars are dollars held in foreign banks outside the United States or in foreign branches of U.S. banks.

The Federal Reserve discontinued the publication of M3 statistics in March of 2006 because it felt that the costs of measuring the statistics were not worth the additional information provided by the series.

While the measurement of M1, M2 and M3 is fairly technical, it is easy to remember a simplified version:

M1 = cash and checks
M2 = M1 + personal savings
M3 = M2 + institutional savings

On May 11, 2009, the Federal Reserve reported that M1 was $1593.4 billion, and M2 was $8312.8 billion. M3 statistics are no longer reported.

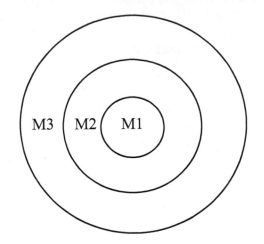

Figure 12-2   M1, M2 and M3

## THE STRUCTURE OF THE FEDERAL RESERVE SYSTEM

The structure of the Fed mimics that of the U.S. national government, with features such as the separation of powers and federalism. Rather than having one central bank located in New York City, the Fed consists of 12 regional banks spread out throughout the country, much the same way that state power is spread throughout the country. This is meant to avoid the concentration of political and economic power. The President selects the Board of Governors, but they are appointed to fourteen-year, staggered terms to provide a separation of powers and political insulation. Supreme Court justices also serve long (lifetime) terms to provide political insulation. Member commercial banks play a role by purchasing equity capital (stock) in the regional Federal Reserve Banks, providing free reserve funds, and helping to select the Board of Directors of their regional Federal Reserve Banks. The Federal Open Market Committee (FOMC) guides the monetary policy decisions of the Fed, which are implemented by the Federal Reserve Bank of New York.

That, in a nutshell, is the structure of the Federal Reserve.

The creation of the Fed was an extremely political process replete with much debate and compromise. The Panics of 1893, and especially 1907, had highlighted the need for a central bank to stabilize the financial system. The National Monetary Commission, under the direction of Senator Nelson Aldrich, had recommended a strong central bank with headquarters in New York City, which would be controlled by prominent bankers. Many progressives, led by William Jennings Bryan, were against a central bank controlled by banking interests. They felt that citizens appointed by the government would do a much better job in serving the public interest than elite bankers. When Woodrow Wilson was elected President, the debate continued for another year until the Federal Reserve Act of 1913.

The structure of the Federal Reserve, as we will see, is very much a result of the compromises between these two factions, those who wanted banker control vs. those who wanted public control.

## CENTRAL BANKS AROUND THE WORLD

The United States was fairly late to adopt a central bank compared to most other countries. The first attempts at central banking in the United States, the First Bank of the United States in 1791 and the Second Bank of the United States in 1816, were not able to outlast their original twenty-year charters. For most of the 1800s, the United States was without a central bank.

Most other countries, on the other hand, adopted a central bank much earlier, as shown by Table 12-1. Note that compared to most countries, the United States was relatively late in establishing a central bank. Generally, most other countries have central banks that are more centralized, with one primary bank rather than the twelve

**Table 12-1**   Central Banks of Selected Countries

| Country | Name of Bank | Year of Origin |
|---|---|---|
| Sweden | Riksbank | 1668 |
| Great Britain | Bank of England | 1694 |
| Spain | Banco de España | 1782 |
| France | Banque de France | 1800 |
| Holland | De Nederlandsche Bank | 1814 |
| Norway | Norges Bank | 1816 |
| Denmark | Nationalbanken i Kjøbenhavn | 1818 |
| Japan | Bank of Japan | 1882 |
| Italy | Banca D'Italia | 1893 |
| Argentina | Banco Central de la República Argentina | 1899 |
| Switzerland | Swiss National Bank | 1906 |
| Australia | Reserve Bank of Australia | 1911 |
| United States | Federal Reserve System | 1913 |
| Columbia | Banco de la República | 1923 |
| Greece | Bank of Greece | 1927 |
| New Zealand | Reserve Bank of NZ | 1934 |
| Canada | Bank of Canada | 1934 |
| Thailand | Bank of Thailand | 1942 |
| Germany | Bundesbank | 1948 |
| China | People's Bank of China | 1948 |
| Ethiopia | National Bank of Ethiopia | 1963 |
| Brazil | Banco Central do Brasil | 1964 |
| European Union | European Central Bank | 1999 |

Source: central bank websites

regional banks of the Federal Reserve System. (The European Central Bank, which is modeled after the Fed, is an exception.) Despite the differences, the goals of most central banks are the same: to control the nation's money supply, to maintain financial and price stability, and to provide an efficient payments system. These are common goals for many of the world's central banks.

A common trend that we can witness recently is a move toward greater central bank independence in most of these countries. Central banks are more effective at promoting financial stability when they can act independently of political pressures.

## THE FEDERAL RESERVE SYSTEM

The Federal Reserve System was established in 1913 to provide a pool of reserve funds for member banks. The Panic of 1907 caused many runs on banks, and when banks ran out of funds for depositors, they were forced to close their doors. A pool of reserve funds would help to avoid this problem. Each bank would contribute to the reserve fund by depositing a sum of money into a Federal Reserve Account at its district Federal Reserve Bank. If a bank faced a sudden demand for deposit withdrawals, it could borrow from the pool of reserve funds at its district bank. The Federal Reserve System was primarily meant to increase the liquidity of the banking system.

Even though the Fed was originally meant to prevent runs on banks, without deposit insurance runs continued, reaching a height during the Great Depression. Besides the practical purposes of providing a pool of reserve funds, the original legislative purpose of the Federal Reserve System was to provide "a safer, more flexible, and more stable monetary and financial system." (The Federal Reserve Act of 1913)

In the *Federal Reserve System: Purposes and Functions,* four general functional areas of the Fed are listed:

1. conducting monetary policy
2. bank supervision and regulation
3. maintaining financial stability
4. providing financial services to the U.S. government, financial institutions, and the public, and operating the nation's payments system

The rest of the chapter will be devoted to exploring how the Fed organizes and implements these tasks within the Federal Reserve System.

## THE STRUCTURE OF THE FEDERAL RESERVE SYSTEM

The structure of the Federal Reserve System was greatly influenced by economic and political history. The Panic of 1907 provided the impetus for a central bank, but the recurrent distrust of the concentration of economic power led to a decentralized system with 12 central banks. To keep the Fed insulated from political pressures, the Board of Governors was selected with staggered terms, and by 1935 the Board did not have representation from the Comptroller of the Currency as it originally did, and each governor was elected to a fourteen-year term. The goal of political independence was well established early in the history of the Fed. Finally, the need to balance the interests of bankers and the public led to a structure for each district bank, where some of the directors of each Federal Reserve Bank are chosen by bankers, and others are chosen by the Board of Governors to represent the public interest. Our American political system of Federalism and the separation of powers are mimicked in the structure of the Federal Reserve System.

Essentially, the Federal Reserve System consists of the following institutions:

1. The Board of Governors of the Federal Reserve System
2. The Federal Open Market Committee
3. The Federal Advisory Council
4. 12 regional (or district) Federal Reserve Banks
5. About 2,800 member commercial banks

The relationships between each of these organizations are listed in Figure 12-3. It also shows the functional responsibilities for each of the structural elements. We will decipher this diagram by looking at each of the institutions and how they are connected with the rest.

## The Board of Governors

The Board of Governors is the most important institution, in that it sets the general direction of monetary policy and it oversees the other parts of the system. The Board consists of seven members with staggered, 14-year terms. One of the seven members is generally appointed once every two years, so that the president only gets to choose two Governors in a four-year term. Once the Governor is appointed by the President, he or she must be confirmed by the Senate. Once approved, they serve terms of fourteen years to keep the Fed independent and insulated from political pressures.

The Board of Governors meets in Washington, D.C. The term of one Governor expires on January 31 of each even-numbered year. The chair and vice chair are appointed by the President and confirmed by the Senate for four-year terms. Alan Greenspan was Chairman of the Board of Governors from 1987 to 2006. The current (2009) Governors of the Federal Reserve System include:

Ben S. Bernanke, Chairman
Donald L. Kohn, Vice Chairman
Kevin M. Warsh
Elizabeth A. Duke
Daniel K. Tarullo

Ben S. Bernanke replaced Alan Greenspan as Chair on February 1, 2006. Duke was appointed in 2008 and Tarullo was appointed in 2009, both to fill unexpired terms. There are currently two vacancies *(www.federalreserve.gov)*.

The responsibilities of the Board of Governors include:

- analyzing current domestic and international economic and financial developments
- supervising and regulating Federal Reserve Banks
- maintaining the nation's payments system
- protecting consumers
- conducting monetary policy

In terms of Figure 12-3, the Board of Governors controls the system in many ways. First, the Board of Governors makes up seven of twelve members of the Federal Open Market Committee (FOMC). The Board also chooses three of each of the Federal Reserve Bank's Directors, known as Type C Directors who are meant to protect the public interest. Finally, the Board of Governors has responsibility over

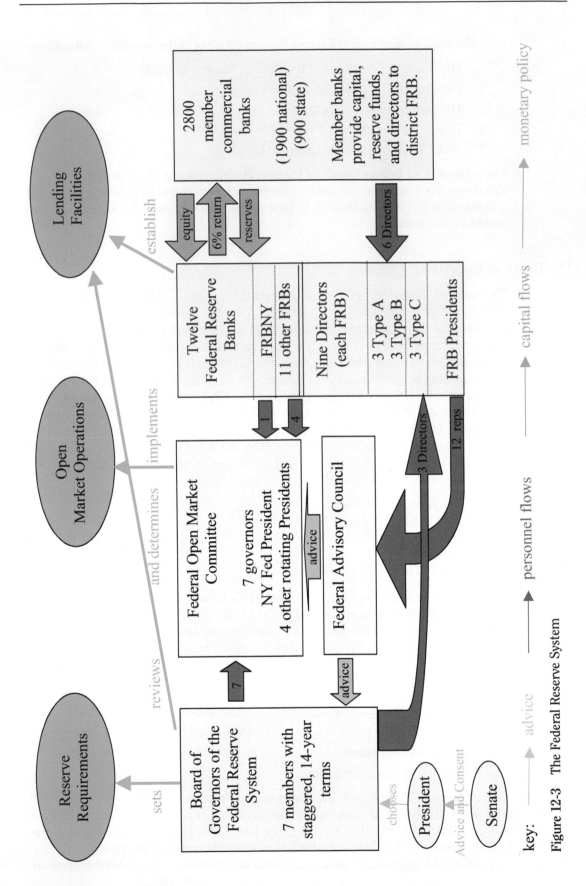

**Figure 12-3** The Federal Reserve System

monetary policy. It directly sets reserve requirements, it reviews and determines the discount rate after it has been established by the Federal Reserve Banks (a technicality; in reality the Board sets discount rates, as we will see), and it influences open market operations through its seats on the FOMC. These tools of monetary policy will be a frequent topic of the next chapter.

## The Federal Open Market Committee

The Federal Open Market Committee (FOMC) consists of the seven members of the Board of Governors, the New York Fed President, and four other Federal Reserve Bank presidents who rotate among themselves. All bank presidents participate, but only five are allowed to vote at any meeting. The reason for the special treatment of the New York Fed is because New York City is where the actual buying and selling of bonds takes place, in the bond markets of Wall Street. The New York Fed, near these markets, actually implements the open market operations each day.

The FOMC meets every six weeks (or eight times per year) to assess the economy and set a direction for monetary policy. At each meeting, the FOMC will set a target for the Federal Funds Rate for the next six weeks, and then send a directive to the New York Fed instructing it to conduct open market operations consistent with its objective. For instance, the current target for the Federal Funds Rate is 0 − .25%. The Fed sends a directive to the New York Fed instructing it to conduct open market operations consistent with a federal funds rate of 0 − .25%. Each morning, the New York Fed predicts changes in the demand for bank reserves for the day. It then uses open market operations, most usually purchasing securities from banks, to increase the supply of bank reserves just enough to match the anticipated increase in demand for the day, to keep the Federal Funds Rate on target. More on this in the next chapter.

## Federal Advisory Council

The Federal Advisory Council consists of twelve representatives, one from each of the Federal Reserve Bank presidents. The Federal Advisory Council meets periodically to advise the Board of Governors and FOMC on issues involving the Federal Reserve Banks. Although it is included in all of the organization charts, in my twelve years of studying the Fed I have not heard of the Federal Advisory Council doing a single thing.

Other advisory councils include the Consumer Advisory Council and the Thrift Institutions Advisory Council.

## Twelve Federal Reserve Banks

As we pointed out earlier, the United States does not have a single central bank, like most other countries, but rather has a decentralized system of twelve regional "central" banks spread throughout the country. This system was a political compromise to avoid the concentration of political and economic power among bankers and financiers in New York City known as the "Money Trusts." The twelve regional banks help to diffuse economic power throughout the country, though ironically New York continues to play a special role.

The distribution of the Federal Reserve Banks throughout the country was a subject of intense competition between cities in 1914, and it was a result of the interplay between politics and geography. The districts were divided up into twelve, so that each district had roughly the same number of banks in 1914. Three cities, New York, Chicago, and St. Louis, were already financial centers and considered essential sites for reserve banks. For the other nine reserve bank sites, cities from around the country were invited to apply. A survey was then taken among banks to see which cities were preferred. Some of the greatest contests were between New Orleans and Atlanta, Baltimore and Richmond, Cincinnati and Cleveland, and Denver and Kansas City. In each case, the latter city won.

By the way, Missouri ended up with two Federal Reserve Banks, St. Louis and Kansas City. Again, this was due to both politics and geography. Two members of the selection committee, the Secretary of the Navy and the Speaker of the House, were Missourians. Also, many of the banks between Kansas City and Denver preferred Kansas City as a site. (It was downhill.)

The Federal Reserve Bank districts are shown in Figure 12-4.

## The Federal Reserve Board

Figure 12-4   The Twelve Federal Reserve Districts

If you examine a one-dollar bill (or really old fives, tens or twenties), you see a circle on the left front side with a letter inside of it. This letter, A through L, represents the Federal Reserve Bank that printed the piece of currency, as shown by the letters above to the left.

Along with the twelve district banks, there are also 25 Federal Reserve Branches. For example, The Federal Reserve Bank of New York has a branch in Buffalo. These banks and branches are quasi-private, quasi-public institutions owned by the member banks.

### Directors

As a compromise between those who favored a central bank controlled by bankers, and those who wanted a central bank molded in the public interest, the Federal Reserve Banks were organized with three classes of directors.

*Type A Directors* are elected by member banks to represent professional bankers. *Type B Directors* are elected by member banks to represent industry and commercial interests. *Type C Directors* are appointed by the Board of Governors to represent the public interest. They are not involved in banking.

For each of the Twelve Federal Reserve Banks, the Board of Directors consists of three Type A Directors, three Type B Directors, and three Type C directors. This assures that directors reflect all constituencies of the American public. By choosing three of the directors for each Federal Reserve Bank, the Board of Governors is able to exercise some influence over the banking system throughout the country. Overall, the Federal Reserve represents the true spirit of American compromise.

## Functions

There are many functions of the Federal Reserve Banks, including:

- clearing checks
- issuing new currency
- withdrawing damaged currency
- administering discount loans
- evaluating mergers and expansions
- acting as a liaison between businesses and the Board of Governors
- examining bank holding companies and state member banks
- collecting data on local business conditions
- conducting economic research for monetary policy
- assisting with the implementation of monetary policy

Federal Reserve Banks assist with monetary policy in several ways. They establish the discount rate in each region, in consultation with the Board of Governors. They decide which banks in their region can obtain discount loans. They select one commercial banker to serve on the Federal Advisory Council. Finally, the twelve presidents participate in the FOMC meeting to report on their region's economic conditions, although only five of them may vote at any given meeting. The New York Fed president has a permanent vote, while the other four votes rotate around the other eleven presidents. Economic research staff from each district also attends to assist the committee in understanding regional economic conditions.

## The Special Role of the Federal Reserve Bank of New York

As we have seen throughout this chapter, the New York Fed plays a special role in the Federal Reserve System. This is ironic given the attempts of the founders to create a decentralized financial system.

1. The New York Fed holds the world's monetary gold, about $160 billion worth depending on current prices. I have had the opportunity to bring students there twice. The gold vaults are five stories down, on the bedrock of Manhattan. It's a LOT of gold. Each country has its own jail-cell-full of gold. You can touch the blocks.

2. The New York Fed supervises and regulates some of the country's largest banks, with about a quarter of all bank assets.

3. The New York Fed is geographically close to Wall Street and the New York Stock Exchange, on Liberty Street in the financial district.

4. Because of its proximity to the bond markets, the New York Fed conducts the day-to-day open market operations of buying and selling bonds to keep the federal funds rate at its target level.

5. The New York Fed is the source of foreign exchange interventions since it houses the Foreign Exchange Desk.
6. The New York Fed is the only Federal Reserve Bank that is a member of the Bank for International Settlements.
7. The New York Fed is the only permanent member of the FOMC.
8. The New York Fed is in New York City.

## Member Commercial Banks

The number of commercial banks that are members of the Federal Reserve has declined in recent years, from about 5400 in 1990 to less than 2600 today. This is mainly the result of mergers, but also some re-chartering from federal to state charters to avoid the costs of Federal Reserve membership. By law, nationally chartered banks are required to be members of the Federal Reserve System, while state banks can opt into the system if they so desire.

The costs of joining the Fed can be high. Member banks are required to hold 3% of their bank capital as stock in their district Federal Reserve Bank. These equity investments are limited by law to a return of 6%. Also, the bank is required to hold a certain percentage of its reserves in its district bank's Federal Reserve Account, which pays no or little interest. The opportunity cost of funds devoted to membership in the Federal Reserve System may be excessive.

Some benefits of joining the system include a guaranteed 6% return on equity invested in the district bank, and the opportunity to vote for Type A and Type B directors.

DIDMCA (Depository Institutions Deregulation and Monetary Control Act) of 1980 required that all banks hold reserve requirements, so part of the costs to membership was eliminated. Nonetheless, the costs of membership have been prohibitive to many banks, as shown by the following chart:

**Table 12-2**   Structure of Commercial Banks
December 31, 2006

| | |
|---|---|
| Number of Commercial Banks | 7,368 |
| Total Member | 2,593 |
| National | 1,696 |
| State | 897 |
| Total Nonmember | 4,775 |

Source: Federal Reserve, 93rd Annual Report

One reason why these member banks are important is because of the money creation process. When banks make loans, they create deposits in other banks. These other banks can then make loans which creates even more deposits. Through this process of making loans from the deposits provided by loans from other banks, the banking system is able to create money.

Figure 12-3 also lists the tools of monetary policy at the top of the diagram. These include open market operations, lending facilities, and setting reserve requirements. We will discuss these tools of monetary policy, and different theories of monetary policy, in the next chapter.

# 13

# MONETARY POLICY

In the present chapter we examine the role of monetary policy in the United States economy. First, we continue our discussion of banks from Chapter Twelve by looking at balance sheets and how we can keep track of flows of money through the banking system. One important concept is that of money creation, that banks can create money in the economy through the process of making loans. Next we discuss the tools of monetary policy. These have been increased dramatically since the ascension of Ben Bernanke to the Chair of the Board of Governors and his attempts to rescue the financial system after the credit crisis of 2008. We then finish the chapter with a review of the three major theories of monetary policy and a discussion of the Fed's attempts to combat the recession of 2008–2009.

## THE MONEY CREATION PROCESS

To understand the money creation process in the banking system first we must take a brief detour through banking finances. We start with the idea of a bank balance sheet.

## THE BANK BALANCE SHEET

The balance sheet starts with a simple identity:

$$\text{Net Worth} = \text{Assets} - \text{Liabilities}$$

This can be rearranged to get:

$$\text{Assets} = \text{Liabilities} + \text{Net Worth}$$

This equation defines the two sides of a balance sheet. On the left side, assets are listed. On the right side, liabilities and net worth are listed. (In banking parlance, net worth is often known as "capital," "bank capital," "equity capital," or "equity.") The table is called a balance sheet because the left and right sides must always balance, or be equal to each other.

> *Balance sheet:* A record of financial position at a given point in time. On the left side assets are listed, and on the right side liabilities and bank capital are listed, where Assets = Liabilities + Bank Capital. It shows the uses and sources of bank funds.
>
> *Assets:* What you own. Property or financial instruments that are subject to ownership.
>
> *Liabilities:* What you owe. The financial claims on an institution.
>
> *Bank capital:* A bank's net worth or equity. Bank Capital = Assets – Liabilities.

## A Typical Bank Balance Sheet

For a typical U.S. commercial bank, the balance sheet looks something like the one listed in Table 13-1. Assets are listed on the left, while liabilities are put on right-hand side of the balance sheet along with net worth. The two sides of the balance sheet must always balance, or be equal to each other.

**Table 13-1**  A Typical Bank Balance Sheet

| Assets | Liabilities |
|---|---|
| Reserves<br>  Vault cash<br>  Federal Reserve Account | Checkable deposits |
| Cash items in process of collection | Non-transactions deposits<br>  small time deposits<br>  savings deposits<br>  large time deposits |
| Deposits at other banks | |
| Securities<br>  U.S. Treasury<br>  U.S. government agency<br>  Municipal<br>  Other | Borrowings<br>  Federal Funds<br>  Discount loans<br>  Other borrowing |
| Loans<br>  Commercial and industrial<br>  Real estate<br>  Consumer<br>  Interbank<br>  Other loans | Bank Capital<br>  (including Loan Loss Reserve) |
| Other assets<br>  (including physical capital) | |

The major categories of bank assets include reserves and other cash, securities, loans, and physical capital. Liabilities include checking and savings accounts, time deposits, borrowings, and bank capital. Because of the definition of bank capital, the balance sheet must always balance. The left side must be equal to the right side. Any transaction will either affect both sides of the balance sheet equally, or there will be a counteracting change in one column so that both columns remain the same.

For an example of a balance sheet for a financial institution, see *www.alternatives.org.* Click on "about us" and then on "financial statements." Look at page 4 of the 2008 audit. Alternatives is the credit union where I serve as Treasurer of the Board of Directors.

For an example of the balance sheet of all commercial banks for 2008, see *www.federalreserve.gov/releases/h8/current*. Or start at the Fed, and follow the links to—all statistical releases—assets and liabilities – latest date. The categories are combined in a slightly different way, but you can get the idea.

We now look some of the components of the balance sheet.

## ASSETS

As we have seen, the major types of assets include reserves, securities, loans and other assets. Reserves are the most liquid, while physical capital is the least liquid. In general, reserves do not pay interest, and loans provide higher returns than do securities.

## Reserves

*Reserves* are the sum of vault cash and funds in a bank's Federal Reserve account. Reserves are held to provide a cushion for deposit outflows. If many depositors all try to withdraw funds at the same time, banks have to have the cash on hand to satisfy the demand. Federal Reserve accounts, or accounts held at the regional Federal Reserve Bank to which the commercial bank belongs, also help to provide a cushion for deposit outflows. Each member bank is required to hold a Federal Reserve Account. This provides a pool of reserve funds that are lent and borrowed through what is known as the Federal Funds market. The rate charged is the Federal Funds rate.

While reserves do not pay interest, banks are required to hold a certain percentage of their demand deposits in reserve in order to provide liquidity services to their customers. The amount of required reserves is determined by the reserve ratio, which is set by the Federal Reserve Board of Governors. This is perhaps most easily expressed mathematically:

Let

$RR$ = required reserves
$r$ = reserve ratio
$D$ = demand deposits
$R$ = actual reserves
$ER$ = excess reserves

Then

$$RR = r \times D$$
$$R = RR + ER \qquad \text{so} \qquad ER = R - RR$$

The first equation states that required reserves are a certain percentage, $r$, of a bank's demand deposits. The second equation states that reserves are made up of required reserves and excess reserves, so excess reserves are the difference between actual reserves and required reserves. (Sorry about all of the Rs.) This provides some of the rudiments to understanding monetary policy.

## Cash Items in Process of Collection

*Cash items in process of collection* are proceeds from checks that have been deposited into a bank but not yet cleared. This occurs when a check is deposited into a checking or savings account, and before the check "clears" or when payment is received from the issuing bank. The check is still considered an asset because payment is expected in the near future. When payment is received from the issuing bank, the amount is subtracted from "cash items in process of collection" and added to "reserves." This will be shown in detail later.

## Deposits at Other Banks

Small banks may keep accounts at larger banks in exchange for liquidity services such as check collection, foreign exchange, securities purchases, or correspondent banking. As another example, our credit union holds CDs in many other credit unions around the country, both for investment purposes and also to help assist other Community Development Credit Unions.

These first three items, reserves, cash items in process of collection, and deposits at other institutions, are often known as "cash assets." Collectively, the two categories of securities and loans are often called "bank credit."

## Securities

Since banks are not allowed to own stocks, government securities provide an important source of investment income. These include Treasury securities, government agency bonds such as Fannie Mae or Freddie Mac, state and local municipal bonds, and other bonds such as school districts or transportation districts (such as Port Authority). Securities provide a lower return compared to loans, but they are also a much safer investment. Banks hold securities as a means of diversifying their portfolios, and providing a guaranteed flow of income, even at a lower return than available from loans.

## Loans

Banks are in the business of making loans. Almost two-thirds of all bank assets are held in loans. The reason is simple—bank loans are profitable. Bank loans provide the largest source of profits for most financial institutions. The cost of making bank loans, however, is a lack of liquidity and a greater default risk on assets. The extra risk is compensated for by a higher return.

For example, at the credit union, we are constantly trying to develop new loan products in order to keep as much of our assets in loans as possible. The reason is that loans are our most profitable asset, and loans also help us to meet our mission of helping the disadvantaged in our community.

## Other Assets

*Other assets* include mostly physical capital, such as the building, counters, chandeliers, computers, desks, chairs, and equipment.

## LIABILITIES

Liabilities are what the bank owes to its depositors and others. They provide the sources of funds that banks are able to transform into assets.

## Checkable Deposits

*Checkable deposits* allow checks to be written to third parties, providing a convenient and safe method for transferring funds. These include demand deposits (or checking accounts), which historically by law had been prohibited from paying interest; NOW accounts (or Negotiable Order of Withdrawal), which were the first to pay interest; and money market deposit accounts, which are not considered as part of M1 and are not subject to reserve requirements. Checkable deposits are assets for the depositors, but liabilities for the banks.

## Non-Transaction Deposits

*Non-transaction deposits* are those where checks cannot be written on the account. In return for less liquidity, non-transaction deposits pay higher interest. One type is savings accounts (sometimes known as passbook accounts), where deposits or withdrawals can be made at any time. A second type is time deposits (or certificates of deposit or CDs), which have fixed maturity dates, higher interest payments, but substantial penalties for early withdrawal. Time deposits are divided between small (<$100,000), which are usually purchased by personal investors, and large (>$100,000), which are generally purchased by institutional investors. Until 2008, the limit for FDIC insurance on any depository account was $100,000. As a result of the bail out bill of 2008, the limit was raised to $250,000 to help avoid a flood of funds away from banks as depositors lost faith in the banking system.

*Negotiable CDs,* which are CDs that can be traded in the secondary market, have provided an important source of bank funds since their introduction by Citibank in 1961.

## Borrowings

The main sources of borrowing for banks include other banks, the Fed, and corporations. Banks borrow overnight-to-fourteen-day reserves from other banks through their Federal Reserve accounts, charging what is known as the Federal Funds rate. Banks borrow discount loans from the Fed through something known as the discount window. The rate charged for discount loans is . . . surprise . . . the discount rate. In 2008, the Fed expanded its type of lending facilities in response to the credit crisis. Finally, banks can borrow from their parent corporations (holding companies) or other corporations through repurchase agreements or eurodollar markets.

*Federal Funds rate:* the rate that one bank charges to another for loans from its Federal Reserve account.

*Discount rate:* the rate the Federal Reserve charges directly to banks for discount loans from the Fed's discount window.

## Bank Capital

*Bank capital* is also known as net worth or equity capital. It is the difference between assets and liabilities. Bank capital is what the bank owes to the owners of the firm, which is one explanation for why it is listed as a liability. In many accounting procedures bank capital includes loan loss reserves, or funds that are put aside to compensate for the revenue lost due to the inevitable failed loans.

## BANK OPERATIONS

In a very basic sense, banks function to undertake a process of asset transformation. They start with assets with one set of characteristics, such as risk, return, or maturity, and transform them into other assets with a different set of characteristics. For instance, banks may take a series of short-term savings deposits that are safe, liquid, and mature quickly, and transform these into a 30-year mortgages that are less safe, less liquid, and mature much more slowly. In the process of asset transformation, banks find profit opportunities.

*Asset transformation* is the process of taking assets with one set of characteristics and transforming them into assets with a different set of characteristics. One way of illustrating the process of asset transformation, and analyzing the flow of funds through the financial system, is through the use of T-Accounts.

*T-Accounts* are simplified balance sheets that show only the changes in financial position for each transaction.

## ACCOUNTING FOR BANK TRANSACTIONS

We can use T-accounts to analyze many types of banking transactions. In using T-accounts, we must always remember a simple rule: *A balance sheet must always balance, or the two sides must always be equal.*

Deposits

We will start with a $100 cash deposit into a checking account at FirstBank. The T-account would record the transaction like this:

### FIRSTBANK

| Assets | | Liabilities | |
|---|---|---|---|
| reserves (vault cash) | + 100 | demand deposits | +100 |

Both reserves (specifically vault cash) and demand deposits increase by $100.

Let us say instead that there is a $100 deposit of a check drawn on SecondBank. The initial change in the T-account would look like this:

### FIRSTBANK

| Assets | | Liabilities | |
|---|---|---|---|
| cash items in process of collection | + 100 | demand deposits | +100 |

Cash items in process of collection originally increase by $100, since the check has been deposited but payment has not yet been received from the issuing bank. Also, demand deposits increase and the bank has $100 more in liabilities. Again, the balance sheet balances.

Once the check clears, the payment will have been received from the issuing bank. The payment by the issuing bank is recorded as follows:

### FIRSTBANK

| Assets | | Liabilities |
|---|---|---|
| reserves | + 100 | |
| cash items in process of collection | − 100 | |

Here there is no change in liabilities, only counteracting changes in assets.

The final position of the bank as a result of the $100 check deposit is as follows:

### FIRSTBANK

| Assets | Liabilities |
|---|---|
| reserves + 100 | demand deposits +100 |

Note that in the end, the effects of a cash deposit are the same as a check deposit once the check clears.

For SecondBank, the bank that issued the check, the final position is the opposite:

SECONDBANK

| Assets | | Liabilities | |
|---|---|---|---|
| reserves | – 100 | demand deposits | – 100 |

So the overall effect on reserves in the total banking system is 0, since FirstBank's reserves increase by $100 and SecondBank's reserves decrease by $100.

## MONEY CREATION

The money creation process? Does this sound too good to be true? How can I get in on the action?

While it is not possible for individuals to create money (Doh!), it is possible for the banking system as a whole to create money through the process of the lending of excess reserves. The Fed can influence the money creation process through the mechanism of open market operations. If the Fed purchases securities from a bank, then the reserves of the bank increase by the amount of the purchase. Since demand deposits are unaffected, these reserves are excess reserves which can be lent out by the bank. This lending may create a deposit in a different bank, which then gains additional excess reserves. By influencing the quantity of bank reserves, open market operations can have effects on the money supply process and interest rates.

## OPEN MARKET OPERATIONS

A common tool of monetary policy is open market operations, or the buying and selling of securities by the Fed to influence the quantity of money in circulation. Very often, open market operations are conducted with large commercial banks to influence the quantity of bank reserves. We will explore an example below.

In its most basic form, *open market operations* are the sale and purchase of securities by the Fed to influence the quantity of bank reserves. Changes in bank reserves can lead to multiplied changes in the money supply. In its simplest form, open market operations between the Fed and a bank will affect the level of bank reserves. If the Fed buys securities from a bank, then reserves increase. If the Fed sells securities to a bank, then reserves decrease. This can be shown in Figure 13-1:

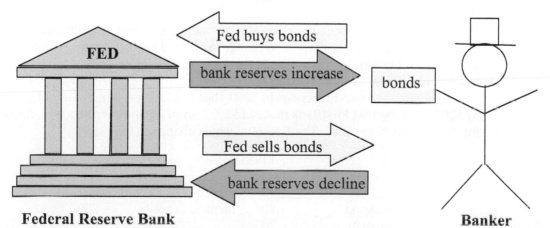

**Federal Reserve Bank**                                    **Banker**

Figure 13-1   Open Market Operations

The effects of selling bonds to the non-bank public would be different because it would affect cash and not bank reserves, but the initial effects on the money supply would be the same.

## Open Market Purchase from a Bank

Let us look at the effects of an open market purchase from a bank in a simple model. For now, we will assume that banks hold no time deposits, and that net worth is equal to zero. We will also assume that the reserve ratio is 0.10 (10%), so that banks are required to keep ten percent of demand deposits in reserve. There is no cash drain in the system, so that all loan proceeds are deposited back into the banking system. Banks desire to hold no excess reserves.

Suppose that the Fed buys $200 worth of bonds from FirstBank, paying with a check. Once the check clears, the Fed's and Firstbank's balance sheets will be affected in the following ways:

| FIRSTBANK | | | FEDERAL RESERVE BANK | | |
|---|---|---|---|---|---|
| Assets | | Liabilities | Assets | | Liabilities |
| reserves | + 200 | | securities | + 200 | reserves | + 200 |
| securities | − 200 | | | | |

Here, since reserves increase by $200, then these reserves can be lent out, since there has been no increase in demand deposits or required reserves.

To review: An open market purchase from a bank increases reserves by the amount of the purchase.

## A SIMPLE MODEL OF MULTIPLE DEPOSIT CREATION

We will finish up this section by looking at a simple model of multiple deposit creation.

Suppose that the Fed purchases $200 of securities from FirstBank as above:

| FIRSTBANK | | |
|---|---|---|
| Assets | | Liabilities |
| reserves | + 200 | |
| securities | − 200 | |

The first effect is that, once the check clears, reserves increase by $200 and securities decline by $200. Since there is no change in demand deposits, there is no change in the amount of required reserves. So the $200 increase in reserves is all in excess reserves which can then be lent out.

Since excess reserves increase by $200, then FirstBank can increase its lending by $200. Let's say that FirstBank makes a $200 loan to Al, and then sets up a checking account for Al for $200. The T-account would change as follows:

| FIRSTBANK | | |
|---|---|---|
| Assets | | Liabilities |
| reserves | + 200 | demand deposits  + 200 |
| securities | − 200 | |
| loans | + 200 | |

The act of lending increases checkable deposits in the banking system, so it creates money. Let us now assume that the $200 is spent by Al writing a check that is deposited into SecondBank. For FirstBank, the final position is:

### FIRSTBANK

| Assets | | Liabilities |
|---|---|---|
| securities | − 200 | |
| loans | + 200 | |

So the initial effect of the open market purchase is to reduce FirstBank's securities holdings by $200 and to increase the amount of loans by $200.

Al spends his $200 by writing a check to Betty for $200. Betty does her banking at SecondBank, so assume now that a $200 check is deposited into SecondBank:

### SECONDBANK

| Assets | | Liabilities | |
|---|---|---|---|
| reserves | + 200 | demand deposits | + 200 |

If SecondBank's demand deposits increase by $200, then required reserves increase by $0.1 \times 200 = \$20$. Since reserves increase by $200, and required reserves increase by $20, then excess reserves increase by $200 - 20 = \$180$. Since SecondBank has an increase in excess reserves of $180, it can now increase its lending by $180. The final position would be:

### SECONDBANK

| Assets | | Liabilities | |
|---|---|---|---|
| reserves | + 20 | demand deposits | + 200 |
| loans | + 180 | | |

Assume that SecondBank makes a loan to Charlie, who does his banking at Thirdbank. As Charlie deposits his $180 loan into Thirdbank, then Thirdbank has to keep $18 in reserves, and can lend out the rest:

### THIRDBANK

| Assets | | Liabilities | |
|---|---|---|---|
| reserves | + 18 | demand deposits | + 180 |
| loans | + 162 | | |

ThirdBank can then make a loan to Donna, who does her banking at FourthBank.

Do you notice a pattern here? Each time a bank receives a deposit, it has to keep a certain portion in reserve and can then lend out the rest. This loan becomes a deposit at a different bank, which must then keep a certain portion in reserve and can lend out the rest. The process continues until there is nothing left to lend out. So in the simple model, an initial deposit leads to an infinite series of deposit expansions in the banking system. This is the process of money creation.

## Money Creation

In this example, we saw the following increases in deposits:

| Bank | Change in deposits |
|------|--------------------|
| FirstBank | + $200 |
| SecondBank | + $180 |
| ThirdBank | + $162 |
| FourthBank | + $145.80 |
| FifthBank | + $131.22 |

. . .

Once the initial change in reserves has been lent out, how much will the money supply have increased by? In the simple model, the money multiplier is given by

$$\Delta M = (1/r) \cdot \Delta R$$

So in this simple example, an increase in reserves of $200 will lead to an increase in the money supply of $2,000.

## DERIVING THE MONEY MULTIPLIER

There are several ways to derive the money multiplier. An easy version is provided by Mishkin (Mishkin, *The Economics of Money, Banking and Financial Markets*):

If banks hold no excess reserves, then RR = R.

By definition, $RR = r \times D$.

So $r \times D = R$.

then $D = (1/r) \times R$ or

$\Delta D = (1/r) \times \Delta R$.

Since a change in demand deposits leads to a change in the money supply, then $\Delta M = (1/r) \times \Delta R$.

This is the formula for deposit expansion in the simple model. The money multiplier is $1/r$. The equation can also be derived by finding and solving an infinite series.

## TOOLS OF MONETARY POLICY

Now that we have explored the ways in which money flows through the banking system, we can now discuss the tools of monetary policy available to policymakers at the Federal Reserve. The Fed can change the money supply, $M^s$, in several ways.

## Open Market Operations

Open market operations affect the money supply by influencing the quantity of reserves held by banks. With an open market purchase, the amount of bank reserves increases. An open market sale causes the opposite effect—the quantity of bank reserves declines. As we discussed in the last section, the initial increase in bank reserves through an open market purchase can lead to excess reserves which may be lent out. These changes in bank reserves then lead to multiplied changes in the money supply.

Open market operations are used to maintain a target for the Federal Funds rate. The Federal Funds rate is the rate that banks charge each other for loans from their Federal Reserve accounts. If the Fed anticipates an increase in the demand for reserves in the banking system, it will conduct an open market purchase to increase the supply of reserves to maintain the Federal Funds rate at its target level. From December 2008 to the time of this writing in May 2009, the Fed has kept the Federal Funds target rate at a historically low range of 0 − .25%. This is another indication of its attempts at expansionary monetary policy in response to the current credit crisis and recession.

*The Federal Funds rate* is the rate that banks charge each other for loans from their Federal Reserve accounts. The FOMC sets a target for the Federal Funds rate, and the New York Fed then conducts open market operations in an effort to maintain the Federal Funds rate at its target level.

In March of 2009, the Fed began to use open market operations not only to purchase Treasury securities, but also to purchase agency debt and mortgage-backed securities. "Agency" refers to Fannie Mae, Freddie Mac, Ginnie Mae, and the Federal Home Loan Bank, four government-sponsored enterprises (GSEs) that purchase mortgages throughout the country. The purpose of the Fed purchases of agency debt and securities is to increase liquidity in housing markets throughout the country.

## Lending Facilities

Historically, the Fed traditionally lent funds to banks in the form of discount loans. *Discount loans* are loans that the Fed makes directly to member commercial banks from a lending facility known as the discount window. The rate charged for these loans is known as the discount rate. The *discount rate* is the rate that the Fed charges for loans to member banks from its discount window.

A decrease in the discount rate will cause an increase in discount loans, as borrowing becomes cheaper. The increase in discount loans leads to an increase in the money supply. Discount loans are now categorized as primary, secondary, and seasonal credit facilities. Since Ben Bernanke became Chair of the Fed in 2006, and especially since the credit crisis and housing crunch that began in 2007, the Fed has introduced many new types of lending facilities, first to banks and then to other types of financial institutions as the credit crisis spread.

Before 2008, the Fed only lent to depository institutions. The major source of loans from the Fed came through the discount window. Bernanke extended lending to banks through Term Auction Facilities in December of 2007. Once the credit crisis began to take its toll in financial markets, starting in March of 2008 and the Bear Stearns collapse, Bernanke created many types of new lending facilities to provide liquidity in threatened markets besides banks. First, lending facilities were extended to primary securities dealers such as Bear Stearns and Merrill Lynch through the Term Securities Lending Facility and Primary Dealer Credit Facility in March of 2008. In September and October, lending was extended to money markets and commercial paper markets. Finally, in November 2008 the Term Asset-Backed Securities Loan Facility was created to lend to "All U.S. persons that own eligible collateral." This extension of credit to non-depository institutions in this way during 2008 was unprecedented in the history of U.S. monetary policy (*http://newyorkfed.org/markets/ Forms_of_Fed_Lending.pdf,* retrieved May 27, 2009).

Besides the lending facilities discussed above, the Fed introduced Reciprocal Currency Arrangements in December 2007 to lend dollars to foreign central banks, and Transitional Credit Extensions in September 2008 to U.S. and London broker-dealer subsidiaries of Goldman Sachs, Morgan Stanley, and Merrill Lynch. AIG has its own loan program.

A summary of the different types of Federal Reserve lending facilities is provided in Table 13-2. Along the top, borrowers can be either depository institutions, primary dealers, or others such as commercial paper, money market, or term asset-backed securities dealers. Along the left side, standing facilities are those where borrowers can receive funds on demand at a set interest rate at any time, similar to the traditional borrowing from the discount window. In standing facilities the Fed sets

**Table 13-2**  Federal Reserve Lending Facilities

| | **Depository Institutions** | **Primary Dealers** | **Other Borrowers** |
|---|---|---|---|
| *Standing Facilities* | Primary Credit Facility (discount window) (1914) | Primary Dealer Credit Facility (March 2008) | Asset-Backed Commercial Paper Money Market Fund Liquidity Facility (Sept 2008) |
| | | | Commercial Paper Funding Facility (Oct 2008) |
| | | | Money Market Investing Funding Facility (Oct 2008) |
| *Auction Facilities* | Term Auction Facility (Dec 2007) | Term Securities Lending Facility (March 2008) | Term Asset-Backed Securities Loan Facility (November 2008) |

Source: James McAndrews, New York Fed, *http://newyorkfed.org/markets/Forms_of_Fed_Lending.pdf*, retrieved May 27, 2009

the interest rate and the market determines the quantity of funds lent. In auction facilities, on the other hand, the Fed periodically sets the quantity of funds to be auctioned and the market determines the interest rate. These are the newer types of lending facilities introduced in 2007 and 2008.

As shown in Table 13-2, the Fed greatly expanded its role of lending to different types of financial institutions during the credit crisis and recession that began in 2007. Before 2007, the only type of lending was through the discount window. Since that time, the complexity of lending facilities has increased dramatically as different types of financial markets faced meltdown, and the Fed responded with new types of loans.

## Reserve Requirements

A change in the required reserve ratio (r) will lead to a change in the money multiplier. For example, if the reserve ratio declines, then the money supply increases. A decrease in the reserve ratio means that banks have more excess reserves, so they can make more loans. The increase in loans leads to multiple deposit creation, and the money supply increases.

Even though changes in reserve requirements can be powerful tools in changing the money supply, the Fed has been reluctant to use this tool in recent years, even during time of recession as in 2008–2009.

## Informal Powers

A fourth tool of monetary policy consists of the informal powers of the Fed, or what some textbooks have called "moral suasion." The Fed has many carrots and sticks that it can employ with member banks. On the carrot side, the Fed can invite bankers to fancy luncheons, international conferences, and educational meetings. I've been to the New York Fed many times, but the first time I was there, I remember eating fancy jumbo Gulf shrimp on a gold-rimmed plate in a large, ornate, mahogany-paneled dining room. It was the fanciest lunch I have ever had! The Fed can offer such treats to those bankers that follow the desired policies of the Fed. In this way, the Fed can have some informal control over other variables in the model. For example, the Fed might provide better treatment to those who hold high levels of excess reserves, or it may want to discourage the use of discount loans.

The Fed also has many "sticks." If a bank does not hold excess reserves, or uses the discount window too often, then the Fed has the ability to punish the bank through more frequent or more stringent regulations. Capital requirements, for instance, may influence a bank's choices concerning excess reserves or discount loans.

A now-famous use of informal powers occurred on October 15, 2008, when then Treasury Secretary Henry Paulson and Fed Chair Ben Bernanke summoned the CEOs of the nine largest banks to Washington D.C. for a meeting. While the executives may have been flattered to receive such attention, they were also forced to sell to the government equity shares in their banks valued at $125 million. Paulson felt that having the largest banks receive these bail out funds would remove the stigma of accepting the funds for the smaller banks. The bankers were given no choice. If they refused to accept the funds the government would not provide any assistance in the case the institution collapsed. The Fed has both carrots and sticks *(http://online.wsj.com/article/SB122402486344034247.html)*.

In summary, the Fed can increase the money supply through open market purchases, lowering the discount rate, providing liquidity through other lending facilities, reducing reserve requirements, or using its informal powers.

## MODELS OF MONETARY POLICY

To end this chapter, we will briefly explore the different models of monetary policy. If the Fed changes the quantity of money in circulation, what are the effects on the economy as a whole? There are three primary models of monetary policy: the classical model, the monetarist model, and the Keynesian model. We will explore each of these in the paragraphs below.

## The Classical Model of Monetary Policy

Interestingly enough, around the turn of the last century similar models of money demand were being developed on both sides of the Atlantic. In the United States, Irving Fisher was analyzing money demand based on the quantity of transactions in the economy. In Great Britain, Alfred Marshall and others at Cambridge University were exploring models of money demand based on the volume of transactions, or nominal GDP. Since the models were so similar, in modern macroeconomics the two models have been combined to form the classical model of money demand.

### *The Cambridge Model—The Equation of Exchange*

Rather than using the value of transactions as the basis for money demand as did Irving Fisher, the Cambridge model uses the value of nominal GDP. Since nominal GDP is much more easily measurable, the Cambridge model of money demand has become the basis for the classical model of the macroeconomy. The Fisher model, over time, has been subsumed by the Cambridge model, since the two models start with similar assumptions and have similar results, but the Cambridge model is easier to measure.

We start with this notation:

M = quantity of money
V = income velocity of money (or just velocity)
P = price level
Y = real GDP
PY = nominal GDP

The equation of exchange is given by:

$$M \cdot V = P \cdot Y$$

Or, the money supply times velocity is equal to the price level times real GDP.

This essentially says that the money supply must turn over enough times to purchase the nominal GDP produced in the economy. For example, suppose we have roughly a $2 trillion money supply and a $14 trillion economy in terms of nominal GDP. Then the velocity must be 7: Each piece of currency must turn over seven times if $2 trillion in money will be sufficient to purchase $14 trillion worth of output.

## The Velocity of Money

*The velocity of money* is the average number of times that a unit of currency must be used in a year for the quantity of money in circulation to be sufficient to purchase the quantity of nominal GDP produced in that year. Another definition is the turnover rate of money based on nominal GDP. The velocity of money is given by

$$V = (P \times Y)/M$$

This equation states that money must turn over enough times (the velocity) to purchase the quantity of nominal GDP produced.

## The Demand for Money in the Cambridge Model

Alfred Marshall and other Cambridge economists posited that the demand for money is a constant proportion of nominal income. This is described in the following equation:

$$M^d = k \times P \times Y$$

where "k" is known as the Cambridge k, or the percentage of nominal income that households desire to hold as money. The classical model assumes that k is constant. This also implies that V is constant. To see this, we have

$$M^d = k \, (P \times Y)$$
$$M = (P \times Y) / V$$

If the money market is in equilibrium, them $M = M^d$, or the money supply is equal to the money demand. This then gives us

$$k \, (P \times Y) = (P \times Y) / V$$

or

$$k = 1/V$$

From the quantity theory of money we can derive an equation for the aggregate demand curve in the classical model

If $$MV = PY$$

then $$P = MV / Y$$

The above formula provides the equation for the aggregate demand curve in the classical model. The formula shows the relationship between the price level and the amount of GDP purchased in the economy. If velocity is fixed, then an increase in the money supply will lead to an increase in aggregate demand in the classical model.

The equation of exchange states that $MV = PY$, or that the money supply × velocity must equal the price level × real GDP (Y) (where PY = nominal GDP). The quantity the-

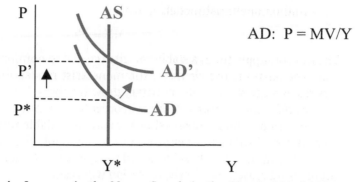

Figure 13-2   An Increase in the Money Supply in the Classical Model Money Neutrality

ory of money is based on the equation of exchange, but believes that both velocity and real GDP are constant, so that an increase in the money supply will lead to a proportionate increase in prices. The only effect of monetary policy is to change the price level, since real GDP is fixed at the level of full employment in the classical model.

It is assumed that the aggregate supply curve is vertical in the classical model. In the classical model an increase in the money supply leads to an increase in aggregate demand. As discussed in Chapter Eight, this shows the idea of *money neutrality*. Changes in the money supply only affect nominal variables such as the price level, but not real variables such as real GDP. Since the aggregate supply curve is vertical the increase in the aggregate demand curve has no effect on real GDP, only the price level. Due to the quantity theory of money the change in the price level will be proportionate to the change in the money supply. If the money supply doubles, the price level will double. If the money supply triples, the price level will triple. If the money supply is halved, the price level will be cut in half. In the classical model, inflation is a monetary phenomenon.

## The Monetarist Model of Monetary Policy

The modern monetarist model still uses the quantity theory, (MV = PY) but relaxes the assumptions that velocity and real GDP are constant. If velocity is stable, then a stable rate of growth in real GDP can be achieved through a stable rate of growth in the money supply. If the money supply increases too quickly then inflation will result; if the money supply grows too slowly then recession may result.

The monetarist position is laid out in the historical volume of Milton Friedman and Anna Schwartz, *A Monetary History of the United States,* published in 1950. In it, they analyze the rate of change in the money supply in the United States economy from the Civil War to the 1940s. They argue that the most important economic variable in understanding United States economic history is the rate of growth of the money supply. In fact, Friedman and Schwartz argue that the Great Depression of the 1930s was caused when the Fed decreased the money supply too drastically in the late 1920s in a misguided attempt to curb borrowing for stock speculation. Monetarists believe that the rate of growth of the money supply is the key to controlling other macroeconomic variables.

The monetarist model begins with the equation of exchange, as in the classical model. The difference with the classical model is that it relaxes the assumption that real GDP is fixed, and it assumes that velocity is stable enough that it can be treated as a constant.

In the monetarist model,

$$M\tilde{V} = PY$$

The money supply times a stable velocity is equal to nominal GDP. This equation provides the basis for the claims of the monetarist model. First and foremost, monetarists advocate for a stable monetary growth rule:

*Stable monetary growth rule:* In order to maintain a stable rate of growth of real GDP, monetary policy makers should maintain a stable rate of monetary growth. To increase real GDP by N% per year, the money supply should be increased by N% per year. If the money supply is increased too quickly, *inflation* will result. If the money supply is increased too slowly, *recession* will result.

These statements provide the essence of the monetarist view of monetary policy. The neo-classical model of the economy is often associated with the monetarist view. Imagine an economy where the long run and short run aggregate supply curves are both increasing over time due to increases in resources and technological progress. As long as the money supply increases at the rate of economic growth, then the aggregate demand increases can keep pace with aggregate supply and the price level will be stable with gradual increases in real GDP over time. If the money supply grows too quickly aggregate demand will grow too quickly and inflation will result. If the money supply grows too slowly aggregate demand will not keep up with aggregate supply and a recession may result. The case of stable monetary growth is shown in Figure 13-3.

In order to support a stable rate of GDP growth, monetarists believe that monetary policy should support a stable monetary growth rule. To achieve stable rates of GDP growth and leftward shifts of LRAS at a stable price level, the money supply should be increased at the same rate of GDP growth. If GDP grows by 3% per year, the money supply should be increased by 3% per year. The increases in AD from increases in the money supply will match the increases in SRAS and LRAS from increases in resources and technology and the price level will remain stable. If the money supply increases too quickly, AD increases more quickly then SRAS and inflation will result. If the money supply increases too slowly, then AD will not keep up and a recession would result. In the monetarist model, the rate of growth in the money supply is the most important determinant of inflation and recession.

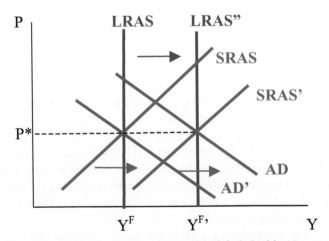

Figure 13-3    Monetary Policy in the Monetarist Model: A Stable Monetary Growth Rule

## The Keynesian Model of Monetary Policy

A Keynesian economist would respond to these last two views of monetary policy with several points. First, velocity and real GDP are not constant or stable, especially in the short run. Second, the demand for money plays a greater role in determining real GDP than suggested by the classical model. Also, the classical model ignores the effects of interest rates and investment in determining the level of real GDP.

### *Money Supply*

For now we assume that the supply of money is fixed by the central bank and is independent of interest rates. The money supply curve is vertical.

### *Money Demand*

Keynes believed that the demand for money depended on three factors. Households hold money due to the transactions motive (for planned purchases), the precautionary motive (for unplanned purchases), and the speculative motive (for investment purposes). The first two depend on the price level and real income, while the latter depends on interest rates. We focus on the speculative demand for money.

In the Keynesian model, the motives for holding money are

1.  Transactions demand—Households demand money for planned purchases. This depends on the price level (P) and real GDP (Y).

2.  Precautionary demand—Households hold money for unplanned purchases. This also depends on P and Y.

3.  Speculative demand—Households hold money to take advantage of changes in the prices of financial assets. This depends on nominal interest rates (i), and sets the Keynesian model apart from the classical model of money demand.

For example, when my children were little, I saw these principles at work in the way that they used Beanie Babies. My daughters would play with them, talk to them, and use the Beanie Babies to cheer themselves up. This would be similar to the transaction and precautionary demands. My son, on the other hand, held Beanie Babies such as Sammy Sosa and Mark McGuire in the hope that the value of the Beanie Babies would increase. He never played with them, just kept them in his room. This is an example of speculative demand. People may want to hold money to enjoy it, or people may want to hold money to earn more money.

Assume that households can hold a fixed amount of financial wealth (F) in either money (M) or bonds (B). Money earns no interest but provides liquidity. Bonds represent all those assets that do pay interest but provide less liquidity compared to money. The tradeoff here is between interest income and liquidity.

Given our assumptions, then

$$F = M + B \quad \text{and} \quad \Delta F = \Delta M + \Delta B \text{ where } \Delta = \text{change in}$$

Households hold a fixed amount of wealth in money and bonds. Any change in financial wealth must come from either a change in money holdings or a change in bond holdings.

If F is fixed, then what is $\Delta F$ equal to? . . . . . . . . . . . . . . . . . $\Delta F = 0$!
If $\Delta F = 0$, then $0 = \Delta M + \Delta B$ and

$$\Delta M = -\Delta B$$

In order to increase their money holdings, households must decrease their bond holdings. The demand for money is what is left over when households have met their demand for bonds. In this way, the money market is the residual of the bond market.

The total demand for financial wealth is limited by the total supply of financial wealth. This can be expressed as

$$B^s + M^s = B^d + M^d$$

where $B^s$ = bond supply
$M^s$ = money supply
$B^d$ = bond demand
$M^d$ = money demand.

Then

$$B^s - B^d = M^d - M^s$$

If the bond market is in equilibrium, then the money market is in equilibrium. (Both sides would equal 0.) An excess supply of bonds ($B^s > B^d$) means there is an excess demand for money ($M^d > M^s$), and vice versa.

To derive the money demand curve, start with the assumption that interest rates are unexpectedly high compared to the past trend. In this situation, households will expect interest rates to fall closer to average. As interest rates fall, the price of bonds will increase. Households will want to take advantage of these potential capital gains by increasing their bond holdings and reducing their holdings of money. So when interest rates are unexpectedly high, households will want to increase bond holdings and money demand will be less.

Similarly, when interest rates are unexpectedly low, households will expect interest rates to be increasing in the future. This means that the price of bonds will be falling, and households will want to sell their bonds to avoid capital losses as bond prices fall. As they sell their bonds, households hold more money. So at low interest rates households want to hold less bonds and more money. All of this means that the demand for money is downward-sloping, like most other demand curves, as shown in Figure 13-4.

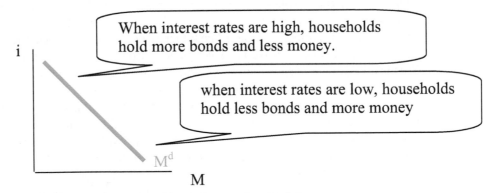

Figure 13-4   Money Demand in the Keynesian Model

## Equilibrium in the Liquidity Preference Model

Once again, equilibrium occurs at the intersection of the supply and demand curves. Remember we started talking about interest rates? In this model interest rates adjust so that money supply equals money demand, or so that households are satisfied holding the quantity of money in circulation. Interest rates will change with changes in either money supply or money demand. Equilibrium is displayed in Figure 13-5.

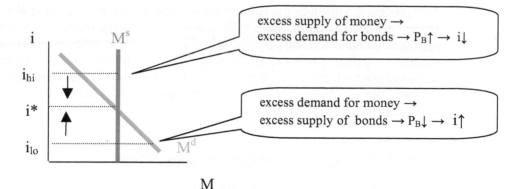

Figure 13-5   Equilibrium in the Fixed-Price Keynesian Model

If interest rates are not in equilibrium, then forces are put into motion to bring interest rates back into equilibrium.

## Changes in Money Demand

In the fixed-price Keynesian model, changes in money demand are caused by

- changes in real income
- changes in the price level
- changes in household preferences for holding money

An increase in money demand leads to higher interest rates. A decrease in money demand leads to lower interest rates.

To analyze the effects of changes in the money supply we can use the concept of the Keynesian Monetary Policy Transmission Mechanism, which traces through the changes that occur throughout the economy from some initial change in the money supply. First, the changes in the money supply will change interest rates so that the money market can return to equilibrium. Along an investment function, the change in interest rates will lead to a change in investment spending. The change in investment spending will lead to changes in aggregate demand, the price level, and real GDP. The effects of an increase in the money supply are shown in Figure 13-6.

In the Keynesian model, an increase in the money supply will increase real GDP through the following process:

| increase in money supply | $\rightarrow$ | decrease in interest rates | $\rightarrow$ | increase in investment | $\rightarrow$ | increase in aggregate demand |
|---|---|---|---|---|---|---|

$\rightarrow$ increase in real GDP and P

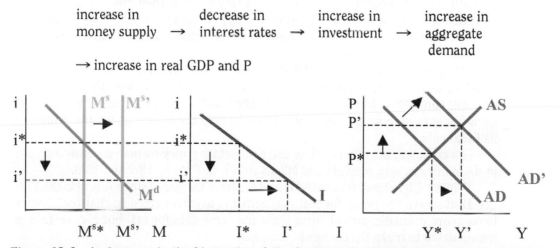

Figure 13-6   An Increase in the Money Supply in the Keynesian Model: The Keynesian Monetary Policy Transmission Mechanism

This process is known as the Keynesian Monetary Policy Transmission Mechanism. In the Keynesian model increases in the money supply can be successful in stimulating aggregate demand and real GDP, but as in the other models inflation may result from expansionary monetary policy. In this model the effects of monetary policy depend on many factors, such as the sensitivity of household money demand to changes in interest rates, the sensitivity of investment spending to changes in interest rates, the size of the spending multiplier, and the shape of the aggregate supply curve.

## MONETARY POLICY IN THE RECESSION OF 2008–2009

As discussed earlier, the Fed and Treasury responded to the current crisis and recession that began in 2007 by making unprecedented changes to monetary policy. Before 2007, the discount window provided loans at a fixed interest rate to depository institutions only. Beginning in December 2007, the Term Auction Facility was introduced to provide auctions of funds to depository institutions at market interest rates. After the Bear Stearns debacle in March of 2008, the Fed introduced, for the first time ever, lending facilities for primary securities dealers to avoid further collapse of the investment banking sector. When Lehman Brothers was allowed to collapse in September, the entire financial system faced a meltdown. The Fed responded by lending to other financial markets such as commercial paper, money, and asset-backed securities markets.

The Treasury Department, under Secretary Henry Paulson, convinced Congress to provide funds to financial institutions through the Emergency Economic Stabilization Act of 2008, passed on October 3, 2008 and commonly known as the "bail out bill." The act provided $700 billion in funds to provide liquidity to financial institutions through the Troubled Assets Relief Program (TARP). The first $350 billion was used to purchase equity stakes in troubled banks and provide funds for the takeover of failing investment banks. In 2009, some of the funds were used to help bail out the automobile industry (*money.cnn.com*).

Besides all of this lending and direct infusion of capital into the financial system, the Fed was active in expanding the money supply through reductions in the target for the federal funds rate and the discount rate. In August of 2007, the target for the federal funds rate was 5.25% and the discount rate was 6.25%. At that time the discount rate was kept at one percentage point above the federal funds rate target. On August 17, the Fed changed its policy and lowered the discount rate so that it is now one-half percent above the federal funds rate target. Since then, the Fed consistently lowered both rates until now the target for the Federal Funds rate is 0 – 0.25% and the discount rate is 0.5%, both historic lows (*http://newyorkfed.org/markets/ statistics/dlyrates/fedrate.html*).

In 2009, the Fed announced that it would start to purchase Treasury securities directly from the Treasury in an attempt to keep interest rates low so the federal government can borrow funds to support its deficit. In this way, the Fed's monetary policy is being used to keep treasury yields low to help the federal government finance its fiscal policy.

As expected, the effect of all of these monetary policy maneuvers is an increase in the money supply, both M1 and M2, as shown in Figures 13-7 and 13-8.

Figure 13-7 shows that both M1 and M2 have increased since July of 2008. Figure 13-8 shows the graph for just M1, with the axis truncated so that the change looks more dramatic. Both figures show the same data for M1, but Figure 13-8 is manipulated to make the change look bigger.

Unfortunately, all of the models that we have examined in this chapter suggest that increases in the money supply may lead to inflation. As the Fed and Treasury

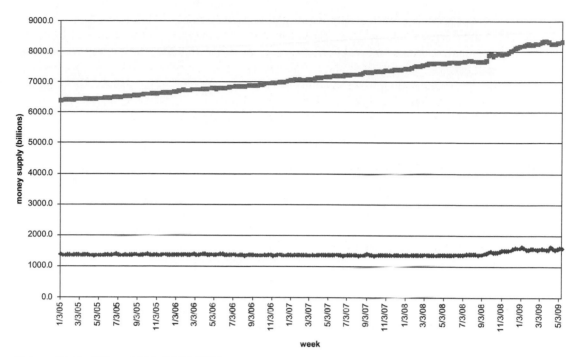

Figure 13-7    M1 and M2, 2005–2009

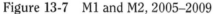

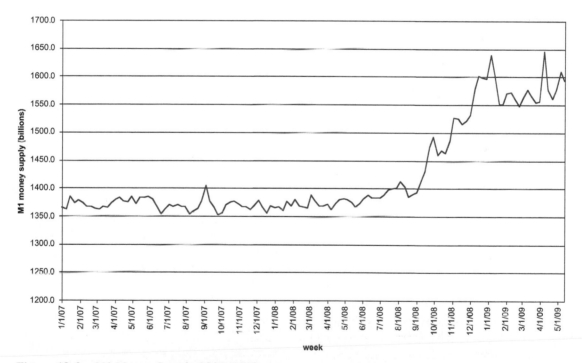

Figure 13-8    M1 Money Supply 2007–2009

increase the money supply in attempts to restore financial and economic stability, the increases in aggregate demand may be inflationary. Our only hope against inflation is that once the economy has expanded sufficiently, the Fed can put on the monetary brakes and slow down growth in aggregate demand before inflation begins to rear its ugly head. As of this writing, only time will tell.

# 14

# PHILLIPS CURVES AND THE ROLE OF EXPECTATIONS

A Phillips Curve is a model that compares the rates of inflation to the rates of unemployment for a given time period in an economy. The theory that lies behind the Phillips Curve suggests that there should be an inverse relationship between unemployment rates and inflation rates. The Phillips Curve describes policy options available to lawmakers and the Fed. If the government tries to reduce unemployment rates it can do so by stimulating aggregate demand, but it may cause inflation as a result. If the government tries to reduce inflation by slowing down growth in aggregate demand, then higher rates of unemployment may result. Generally, the Phillips Curve inverse relationship between unemployment and inflation holds in times of aggregate demand changes in the economy. When the aggregate supply curve is changing, on the other hand, then the Phillips Curve relationship falls apart.

While the Phillips Curve provided a decent model for the 1960s when aggregate demand was changing, in the 1970s the relationship disintegrated as the economy witnessed changes in aggregate supply instead. By the 1990s many observers had heralded the Phillips Curve as dead. However, the model has experienced resurgence in the 2000s when again the tradeoffs between unemployment and inflation appear relevant. In fact, a January 2009 article in the *Wall Street Journal* spoke of the comeback of the Phillips Curve:

> The central idea of the theory named for economist Alban William Phillips is that there's an inverse relationship between unemployment and inflation. It was shelved by some in the 1990s when unemployment fell to historically low levels without the expected uptick in inflation. But the relationship appears to have reinserted

itself, something households are being reminded of in painful ways via job and salary cutbacks almost daily.

The national unemployment rate already increased over two percentage points in the final eight months of 2008 to 7.2%, and that's before the recent flood of corporate layoffs. Meanwhile, inflation has fallen off sharply.

In a one-day bloodbath for the economy, companies from across the economic spectrum, including Caterpillar Inc., Sprint Nextel Corp., Pfizer Inc., Home Depot Inc. and General Motors Corp., all announced layoffs on Monday alone.

And as the Phillips Curve would predict, the effects are being felt not just by the unemployed but the employed, too. Companies from Home Depot to Yahoo Inc. and Eddie Bauer Holdings Inc. have recently launched salary freezes for at least some of their staffs. Even the Obama Administration has instituted pay freezes for top White House positions.

Predictably, households fearful of job or at least income cuts are reporting record-low levels of confidence, according to the latest Conference Board survey released Tuesday. And inflation has come down drastically even when energy prices are excluded, reflecting the reluctance of consumers to spend.

"The Phillips Curve was out of vogue for a while, but now it's back," said Sung Won Sohn, a professor at California State University.

*(http://blogs.wsj.com/economics/2009/01/27/phillips-curve-makes-ugly-comeback/)*

## THE ORIGINS OF THE PHILLIPS CURVE

Alban William Housego (Bill) Phillips was born in New Zealand in 1914. Originally trained in electrical engineering while working at an Australian mine from the age of sixteen, he immigrated to Britain in 1937. His involvement in World War II caused him to be taken prisoner by the Japanese. After the war he enrolled in the sociology department of the London School of Economics (LSE), where his interests soon turned to economics and statistics. With his engineering background he developed a mechanical model of the Keynesian economy, known as a Phillips Machine, which he described in a 1950 paper. He soon joined the statistics faculty at LSE where he stayed until 1967, when he left for Australian National University. He died in 1975 after becoming immortalized for a paper he wrote in 1958 which introduced the model of the Phillips Curve *(http://homepage.newschool.edu/het//profiles/phillips.htm)*.

Phillips' famous 1958 paper examined the relationship between the rate of change of money wages and unemployment rates in Great Britain between 1861 and 1957. Primarily an empirical paper, Phillips showed an inverse relationship between wage growth and unemployment rates. When unemployment rates were low, wages rose more quickly as employers had to compete for labor. When unemployment rates were high, wage growth was sluggish due to a lack of competition in labor markets. In this way, Phillips' paper demonstrated an inverse relationship between wage growth and unemployment, and the Phillips Curve was born. The Phillips Curve that was derived in the 1958 paper for the baseline period of 1861–1913 is shown in Figure 14-1 *(http://encyclopedia.farlex.com/Phillips+Curve*; A W H Phillips, "The Relationship Between Unemployment and the Rate of Change of Money Wage Rates in the United Kingdom, 1861–1957," *Economica NS*, vol. xxv, November, 1958, 283–99).

While Phillips' original paper looked at the relationship between unemployment rates and wage changes, on the other side of the Atlantic United States economists took Phillips' ideas and examined price inflation rates rather than wage inflation. The logic is that wage increases should lead to price increases as producers pass on the higher resource costs in the economy. Soon after its publication the Phillips Curve transformed from a model of wage inflation to a model of price inflation.

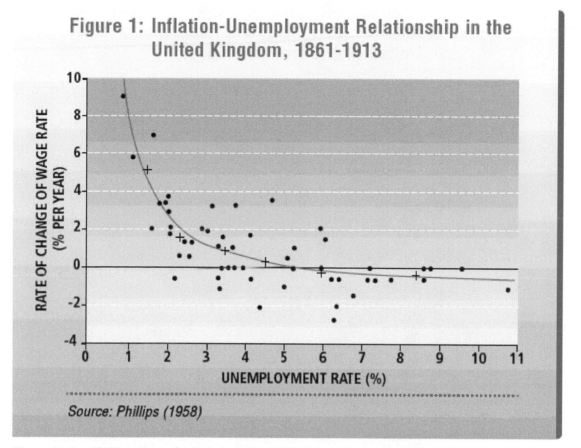

Figure 1: Inflation-Unemployment Relationship in the United Kingdom, 1861-1913

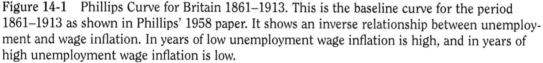

Source: Phillips (1958)

Figure 14-1   Phillips Curve for Britain 1861–1913. This is the baseline curve for the period 1861–1913 as shown in Phillips' 1958 paper. It shows an inverse relationship between unemployment and wage inflation. In years of low unemployment wage inflation is high, and in years of high unemployment wage inflation is low.

(*http://www.richmondfed.org/publications/research/annual_report/2006/pdf/article.pdf,* retrieved 06.02.09)

The *Phillips Curve* is a model that shows an inverse relationship between inflation rates and unemployment rates in an economy over a certain period of time. Early advocates of the Phillips Curve believed it provided a menu of inflation/unemployment combinations that could be chosen by policy makers. In the 1970s the model was revised by neo-classical economists to include both long run and short run curves. By the 1990s the model had fallen into disrepute, but it seems to be making a comeback in the late 2000s.

## THE AMERICAN CONVERSION

In the United States, it was Richard Lipsey in 1960 who first conceived of a broader model of the Phillips Curve using price inflation as a proxy for wage inflation. Later in that same year, Paul Samuelson and Robert Solow published a paper showing the inflation-unemployment tradeoffs for the U.S. economy from 1900 to 1958, and derived a Phillips Curve for the 1960s. It was Samuelson and Solow who first suggested the policy implications of the Phillips Curve. Policy makers could choose to fight inflation at the risk of higher rates of unemployment, or they could choose to reduce unemployment rates at the expense of higher inflation rates. But in this model it was

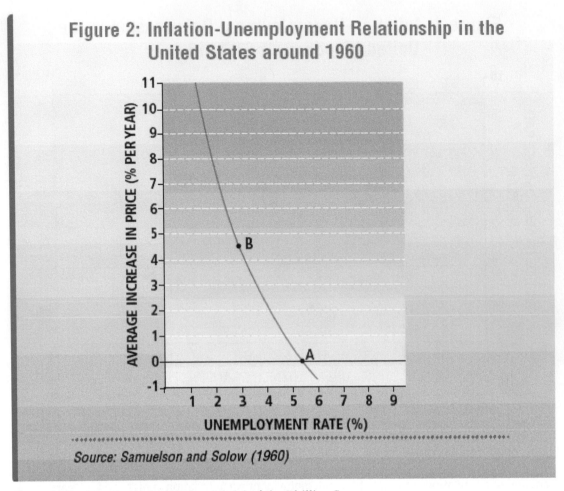

Figure 2: Inflation-Unemployment Relationship in the United States around 1960

Source: Samuelson and Solow (1960)

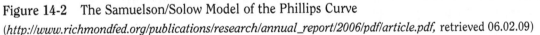

**Figure 14-2**    The Samuelson/Solow Model of the Phillips Curve
(*http://www.richmondfed.org/publications/research/annual_report/2006/pdf/article.pdf,* retrieved 06.02.09)

not possible for policy makers to achieve both low rates of unemployment and low rates of inflation at the same time. Both Solow and Samuelson went on to win Nobel prizes for their work in mathematical economics *(http://homepage.newschool .edu/het//profiles/phillips.htm)*.

The Samuelson/Solow model of the U.S. Phillips Curve is shown in Figure 14-2. They labeled the curve for the 1960s, in the belief that these tradeoffs between inflation and unemployment would only be short-lived. A change in economic conditions may lead to a change in the tradeoffs involved along a Phillips Curve. But for the time being, in the early sixties policy makers could feel comfortable in their choices between low unemployment and low inflation rates.

Samuelson and Solow viewed the Phillips Curve as a menu of policy options. For example, at point A price stability could be achieved with an unemployment rate of 5%. Or unemployment rates could be reduced to 3% at point B, if policy makers were willing to accept an inflation rate of 4.5%. In this view economic policy making becomes merely choosing a point on the Phillips Curve.

## THE 1960s: AGGREGATE DEMAND CHANGES

In the 1960s, many economists believed that the tradeoffs implied by the Phillips Curve between unemployment and inflation were real. The data for the U.S. economy

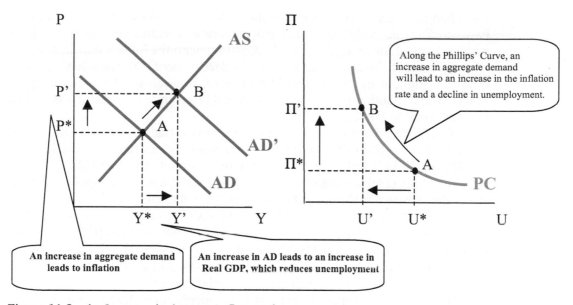

Figure 14-3    An Increase in Aggregate Demand

in the 1960s displayed a clear inverse relationship between inflation and unemployment, as shown in Figure 14-7 (b). Since the data so closely supported the inverse Phillips Curve, the model began to gain credence, especially among American economists.

The reason why the Phillips Curve was a valid model in the 1960s is because the economy was experiencing changes in aggregate demand during that time period. Because of rising incomes consumption spending was increasing. Business optimism led to increases in investment spending. The Vietnam War, War on Poverty, and the moon mission all led to large increases in government spending in the 1960s. These increases in spending all contributed to increases in aggregate demand in the economy. As shown in Figure 14-3, an increase in aggregate demand leads to a tradeoff between inflation and unemployment. Here, the inflation rate is denoted by $\Pi$ and U stands for the unemployment rate. As aggregate demand increases real GDP increases so the unemployment rate falls, but the increase in aggregate demand also leads to an increase in the price level. Unemployment falls as the rate of inflation increases.

As shown in Figure 14-3, an increase in aggregate demand leads to a leftward movement along the Phillips Curve from Point A to Point B. Unemployment is reduced as real GDP increases, and the inflation rate increases as the price level rises. On the other hand, a decrease in aggregate demand would lead to a rightward movement along the Phillips Curve as unemployment increased and inflation fell. Changes in aggregate demand are consistent with the tradeoffs implied by the Phillips curve. Because of this, in the 1960s economists believed that the Phillips Curve provided important policy prescriptions concerning the tradeoffs between inflation and unemployment. When aggregate demand changes, there is a tradeoff between inflation and unemployment. Economists could believe in the Phillips Curve. This was all soon to change with the economic events of the 1970s.

## THE 1970s: AGGREGATE SUPPLY CHANGES

In the late 1960s, several neo-classical economists began to question the validity of the trade-offs implied by the Phillips Curve. Milton Friedman began to criticize the Phillips Curve model for ignoring the concept of money neutrality. If money is neutral, then changes in the money supply only affect nominal variables. Inflation rates should have no effect over real GDP or unemployment rates. Friedman proposed the idea of a natural rate of unemployment, a rate consistent with the full employment level of GDP. Edmund Phelps also contributed to the development of the neoclassical model by suggesting that the theory should distinguish between short run and long run Phillips Curves. Both men went on to win Nobel Prizes in economics, at least in part for their work on Phillips Curves.

Their ideas were vindicated in the 1970s when the tradeoffs of the Phillips Curve fell apart. During the 1970s the United States economy experienced several supply-side shocks. In 1974 and 1979, the world suffered through the Arab Oil Embargoes. When the price of oil and gasoline increased drastically, aggregate supply decreased. When the increases in the price of oil and gasoline led to increases in other resource prices, aggregate supply decreased further. By 1980, the rate of inflation was 14% and the unemployment rate was up to 7.8% *(www.bls.gov)*. As shown in Figure 14-4, these declines in the aggregate supply curve led to reductions in real GDP and increases in the price level. This is a situation known as stagflation, where real GDP is declining (stagnation) with a rising price level (inflation).

Note that with changes in the aggregate supply curve, there are no tradeoffs between inflation and unemployment. When the aggregate supply curve declines, both inflation and unemployment increase. When aggregate supply increases, both unemployment and inflation decline. In this situation, either the Phillips Curve is upward-sloping, or the curve has shifted for some reason.

The data for the U.S. economy in the 1970s is shown in Figure 14-7 (c). Note that the Phillips Curve points for this period are very erratic, and do not show a clear relationship at all, much less a tradeoff between inflation and unemployment. When economic events are dominated by aggregate supply changes as they were in the 1970s, there is no tradeoff between inflation and unemployment and the Phillips Curve fails to provide any guidance for policymaking. Figure 14-4 shows the Phillips Curve and aggregate demand/aggregate supply analysis when the economy experiences a decrease in aggregate supply.

Figure 14-4 shows the effects of a decrease in aggregate supply. When AS shifts to the left, real GDP is reduced so unemployment increases, and the price level rises so inflation is increased. The economy moves from Point A to Point B. In the AS/AD

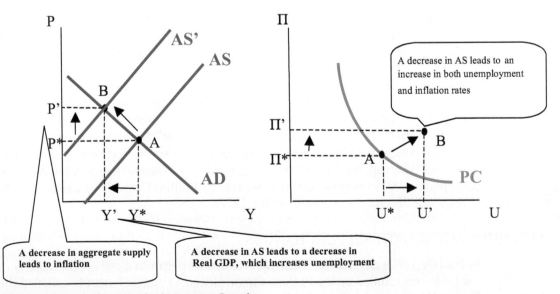

Figure 14-4   A Decrease in Aggregate Supply

graph, the movement is along the aggregate demand curve as the aggregate supply curve shifts to the left. In the Phillips Curve the movement from Point A to Point B represents a shift away from the Phillips Curve, not a shift along the Phillips Curve. With changes in aggregate supply the economy does not face a tradeoff between inflation and unemployment. Both either increase or decrease at the same time.

## THE NEO-CLASSICAL MODEL OF THE PHILLIPS CURVE

As mentioned earlier, in the late 1960s neo-classical economists such as Milton Friedman and Edmund Phelps began to question the validity of the Phillips Curve because it ignored the concepts of money neutrality and the long run. In the 1970s the neo-classical view gained popularity as the supply-side changes in the economy obliterated the tradeoff between inflation and unemployment. As shown in Figure 14-7 (c), in the 1970s the data did not fit to a nice downward-sloping curve as it did in the 1960s. As the data points no longer fit the Phillips Curve, a new theory became necessary to match the model to the data.

In the neo-classical model a distinction is made between the short run and the long run, similar to the distinction made in the neo-classical aggregate supply model. In the long run wages, prices, and interest rates are flexible and there is enough time to learn about real variables so that no money illusion exists. Similar to the classical model in the long run the economy returns to full employment. There are self-correcting mechanisms that, given enough time, markets will clear, workers will learn about price changes, and the economy will be producing at its potential.

In the short run market imperfections may exist. Wages and other resource prices may be inflexible due to union contracts, minimum wage laws, or other fixed-price contracts such as leases or rental agreements. Money illusion may exist if there is not enough time to learn about price changes in the economy. In the case of money illusion economic decisions are based on nominal variables instead of real variables. In the short run the economy may not be at the full employment level of GDP.

An important concept in the neo-classical model of the Phillips Curve is that of the natural rate of unemployment. The natural rate of unemployment is analogous to full employment or potential GDP. It is the rate of unemployment that exists when the economy is operating at full employment GDP. Remember that full employment (or potential) GDP is the amount of output produced in the absence of cyclical unemployment.

The *Natural rate of unemployment* is the rate of unemployment that exists when the economy is producing at full employment (or potential) GDP. It is the sum of frictional, structural, and seasonal unemployment. The natural rate of unemployment is denoted by $U^N$.

In the neo-classical model, there are two separate Phillips Curves, one for the short run and one for the long run. The reasoning is similar to the neo-classical aggregate supply curves. In the long run the economy adjusts to full employment, so the Long-Run Phillips Curve (LRPC) is vertical at the natural rate of unemployment. In the long run wages, prices and interest rates adjust, and workers learn about price changes, so the economy operates at full employment and the unemployment rate is at its natural rate. In the long run, changes in the inflation rate have no effect on unemployment.

In the short run, the Phillips Curve is downward-sloping as usual. In the short run there may be a policy tradeoff between inflation and unemployment. It may be possible to temporarily reduce unemployment rates in exchange for higher rates of inflation, but eventually people will begin to expect higher rates of inflation and the tradeoffs will change. Neo-classical economists believe that the Short-Run Phillips Curve (SRPC) depends on inflationary expectations. In fact, Friedman called the

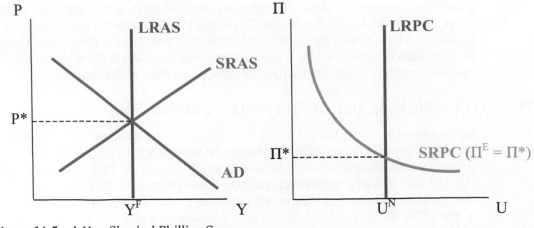

Figure 14-5   A Neo-Classical Phillips Curve

short-run curve the "Expectations Augmented Phillips Curve." For simplicity, we will just call it the Short-Run Phillips Curve. The Short Run Phillips Curve depends on expectations of future inflation rates in the economy. At a given level of inflationary expectations, there is a temporary tradeoff between inflation and unemployment. But if inflationary expectations change then the Short Run Phillips Curve will shift. An increase in inflationary expectations will lead to an upward shift of the SRPC. At the natural rate of unemployment along the Long Run Phillips Curve, the expected rate of inflation ($\Pi^E$) is equal to the actual rate of inflation ($\Pi$). In long run equilibrium, inflationary expectations are correct so that $\Pi^E = \Pi$.

Figure 14-5 illustrates the neo-classical Phillips Curve model alongside the neo-classical aggregate demand/aggregate supply model. The vertical Long Run Phillips Curve at the natural rate of unemployment is analogous to the vertical Long Run Aggregate Supply curve at the level of full employment GDP. Both occur when there is enough time to eliminate market imperfections in the economy. The Short Run Phillips Curve is similar to the Short Run Aggregate Supply Curve. In the short run market imperfections such as inflexible wages or money illusion may exist.

In Figure 14-5 the neo-classical AD/AS model is shown on the left and the neo-classical Phillips Curve model is shown on the right. The LRAS is vertical at the level of full employment ($Y^F$), and the LRPC is vertical at the natural rate of unemployment ($U^N$). The price level P* is consistent with the rate of inflation $\Pi^*$. At the natural rate of unemployment, the actual rate of inflation ($\Pi^*$) is equal to the expected rate of inflation ($\Pi^E$). Along the SRPC, the expected rate of inflation is equal to the actual rate of inflation at the natural rate of unemployment. The SRPC intersects the LRPC at the actual rate of inflation. At the natural rate of unemployment inflationary expectations are correct, and there is no reason for the SRPC to change.

The Short Run Phillips Curve depends on inflationary expectations. An increase in inflationary expectations will lead to an increase (upward shift) in the Short Run Phillips Curve. A decrease in inflationary expectations will lead to a decline in the SRPC. The Long Run Phillips Curve depends on the natural rate of unemployment. A decline in the natural rate of unemployment, through increases in technology or changes in labor demographics, will shift the LRPC to the left. Increases in the natural rate of unemployment will shift the LRPC to the right.

## Expansionary Policy in the Neo-Classical Model

As we saw in Chapter Ten, in the neo-classical model expansionary fiscal or monetary policy may increase aggregate demand, but the effects on real GDP will be temporary

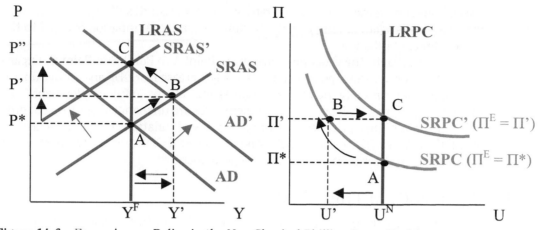

Figure 14-6    Expansionary Policy in the Neo-Classical Phillips Curve Model

as the Short Run Aggregate Supply curve adjusts. Similar results hold in the neo-classical Phillips Curve model. Expansionary policies may temporarily reduce unemployment along the SRPC, but as inflationary expectations adjust to the higher rates of inflation the SRPC will shift to the right and we will return to the natural rate of unemployment but with higher rates of inflation.

The effects of expansionary fiscal or monetary policies that increase aggregate demand are shown in Figure 14-6. In the left hand graph, an increase in aggregate demand will lead to an increase in real GDP and the price level. The higher price level means that inflation has increased. The increase in real GDP means that unemployment has declined. The result is a leftward movement along the Short Run Phillips Curve on the right hand graph. The economy, for the time being, has higher inflation rates and lower unemployment rates. But in the long run, inflationary expectations in the economy will adjust to the higher rate of inflation. As inflationary expectations increase, the Short Run Phillips Curve shifts upward to the right. The economy returns to the natural rate of unemployment, but now at a higher level of expected inflation and actual inflation.

In the AD/AS graph, the increase in expected inflation eventually leads to higher resource prices as resource owners must be compensated for the higher expected rates of inflation. As wages, rents and nominal interest rates increase, the Short Run Aggregate Supply curve shifts to the left. The economy returns to full employment at a higher price level, the same way it returns to the natural rate of unemployment at a higher rate of inflation.

In Figure 14-6 the effects of expansionary fiscal or monetary policy are shown. Assume that the economy starts at full employment at Point A in both graphs. Expansionary policy will increase aggregate demand so that real GDP increases to Y'. The increase in real GDP leads to a temporary decrease in the unemployment rate to U'. The increase in aggregate demand leads to an increase in the price level. As the unemployment rate declines, inflation increases as the economy moves upward along the original SRPC. The economy moves to Point B in both graphs.

At Point B the economy is no longer in long-run equilibrium. Real GDP is greater than potential GDP so the economy faces an inflationary gap. As the economy produces above its potential resources become scarce. The resulting upward pressure on resource prices leads to a decline in SRAS until the economy returns to long run equilibrium at Point C.

Meanwhile, over in the Phillips Curve graph, at Point B the actual rate of inflation, $\Pi'$, is greater than the expected rate of inflation, $\Pi^E = \Pi^*$. Eventually people will learn about the higher rate of inflation, and inflationary expectations adjust to the new level of inflation. As expected inflation rates increase, the SRPC shifts to the right, until the economy is again at long run equilibrium where actual inflation is equal to the expected rate of inflation.

In both graphs the economy moves from Point A to Point B to Point C. Expansionary fiscal or monetary policy can temporarily increase real GDP and reduce unemployment, but eventually the economy adjusts and returns to full employment GDP. In the long run, real GDP and unemployment rates are unchanged, but the economy suffers from a higher price level and higher rates of inflation. In the neo-classical model the effects of fiscal and monetary policies on real GDP are only temporary, but their effects on the rate of inflation can be permanent.

## EMPIRICAL EVIDENCE OF PHILLIPS CURVES

Before we move on to look at Phillips Curve models in the decades of the 1980s, 1990s, and 2000s, it is useful to observe the actual graphs of inflation and unemployment rates in the United States for these decades. This is displayed in Figure 14-7. The graphs plot monthly data for the United States economy for the periods shown. In Figure 14-7 (a), the data for the entire period 1960–2009 is shown. Note that for this long of a time series, no discernable pattern between inflation and unemployment is obvious. Figure 14-7 (b) shows a clear tradeoff between inflation and unemployment in the 1960s. It was these data in the decade after Phillips' paper that lent popularity to the concept of the Phillips Curve. In the 1970s, as shown in Figure 14-7 (c), the relationship shown by the Phillips Curve fell apart due to the supply-side changes in the economy at the time. This was when the neoclassical ideas of Long Run and Short Run Phillips Curves began to take credence. Changes in the Phillips Curve were the only way to explain the data. By the end of the 1970s, the public's experience with inflation had led to increasing inflationary expectations in the economy as a whole, and the Phillips Curve began to shift upwards.

In the 1980s, as shown in Figure 14-7 (d), the role of expectations became obvious. Note that it is possible to discern two patterns of Phillips Curves, and it is clear that the Phillips Curve decreased over time. In the early 1980s, high rates of inflation created high rates of inflationary expectations, and the Phillips Curve shifted upward. High inflation rates became embedded in the economy, almost as a self-fulfilling prophesy. If everyone expects high rates of inflation, then wages, interest rates, and rents will increase and then prices have to rise to pay the higher resource costs. When Paul Volcker became Chair of the Fed in 1979, he exercised contractionary monetary policy to bring inflation rates, and expected inflation, under control. The two different Phillips Curves in the 1980s, representing the different sets of inflationary expectations, are evident in Figure 14-7 (d).

In Figure 14-7 (e), the data for the 1990s is shown. Notice that most of the points are closer to the horizontal axis here. During this time the Phillips Curve became flatter as inflationary expectations stabilized at lower levels. The 1990s was a period of balanced growth in the United States economy. Real GDP increased and unemployment rates fell without much of a threat of inflation throughout the latter part of the 1990s.

In the 2000s, the data suggest a possible return to the tradeoffs of the original Phillips Curve. The points for the decade of the 2000s again display an inverse relationship between inflation and unemployment, especially for the most recent data points toward the bottom of the graph. As mentioned in the Wall Street Journal quote in the front of the chapter, during 2007–2009 unemployment increased as inflation rates fell so low that the economy actually saw moderate deflation for the first time since the Great Depression. The tradeoffs implied by the Phillips Curve again became relevant.

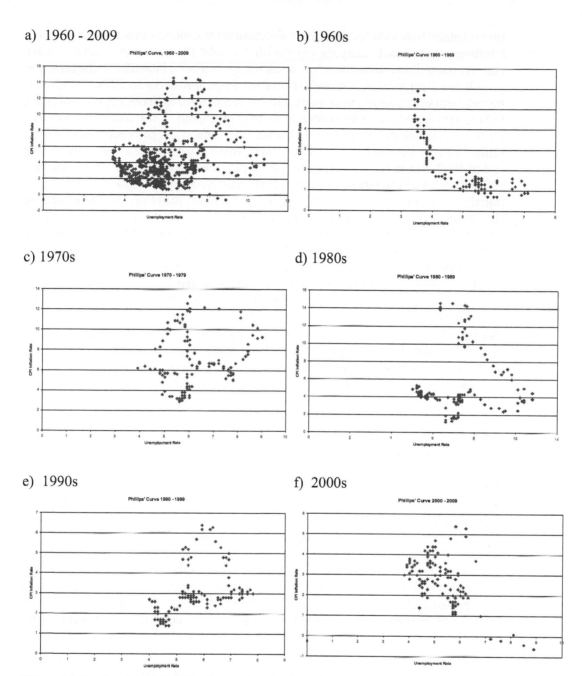

**Figure 14-7** Empirical Phillips Curves for the United States (monthly data)
Source: Bureau of Labor Statistics

## THE 1980s: CHANGES IN EXPECTATIONS

As shown in Figure 14-7 (d), in the 1980s there was a clear change in the position of the Phillips Curve. The graph displays a case of declining inflationary expectations. In the early part of the decade, inflation rates were high, had been high for several years, and therefore inflationary expectations had swelled in the economy. The increases in inflationary expectations during the 1970s led to upward shifts of the Short Run Phillips Curve, so that by the early 1980s high inflationary expectations meant that the SRPC intersected the LRPC at high rates of inflation, perhaps as high as 10%. Once the increase in inflationary expectations becomes embedded in the economy, there is a tendency for these higher rates of inflation to become institutionalized. Again, high rates of inflationary expectations may create self-fulfilling prophecies. If everyone expects higher inflation, then higher rates of inflation will occur. It becomes difficult to break the cycle of price increases in the economy.

When Paul Volcker became Chair of the Federal Reserve in 1979, the ideas of monetarism were coming into vogue. He was determined to break the cycle of rising inflationary expectations by reducing the rate of growth of the money supply. The contractionary monetary policy had the intended effects. As the economy entered a prolonged recession in 1981–1982, unemployment rates increased to 10.8% by the end of 1982. But at the same time, inflation rates declined from 14.6% in March of 1980 to 3.5% by February of 1983. As actual inflation declined in the economy, inflationary expectations eventually decreased, and the Short Run Phillips Curve began to shift down. The monetary policy actions of Volcker were successful in reducing inflationary expectations in the economy, but the cost was a prolonged recession with high rates of unemployment (*www.bls.gov*).

Figure 14-8 shows the effects of a contractionary monetary policy. By reducing the money supply, the Fed can decrease aggregate demand in the economy. The decline in aggregate demand leads to a decline in real GDP and a decline in the price level. The decline in real GDP means that the economy enters a recession and unemployment increases. The decline in the price level means that the inflation rate has declined. Along the Short Run Phillips Curve the economy moves to the right with higher rates of unemployment and lower rates of inflation. Eventually, as people get used to the lower rates of inflation, inflationary expectations subside and the SRPC shifts downward. The economy returns to the natural rate of unemployment with a lower inflation rate. The resulting downward pressure on resource prices leads to an increase in the Short Run Aggregate Supply curve at the same time as the economy returns to full employment.

In Figure 14-8 the effects of contractionary fiscal or monetary policies are shown. Assume that the economy starts in equilibrium at Point A in both graphs. A contractionary economic policy would lead to a decrease in aggregate demand, so the price level falls and real GDP declines. As the economy moves into a recession, unemployment rates increase. The economy moves to Point B in both graphs. Along the Short Run Phillips Curve, the rate of unemployment increases and the inflation rate falls. When households begin to anticipate the lower rate of inflation the SRPC will shift downward to the left. The reduction in inflationary expectations leads to downward pressure on resource prices and the Short Run Aggregate Supply curve shifts to the right. In both graphs the economy returns to full employment at Point C with

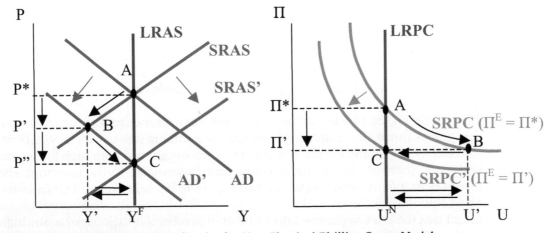

Figure 14-8  Contractionary Policy in the Neo-Classical Phillips Curve Model

a lower price level and a lower rate of inflation. In this way inflationary expectations can be reduced in the economy, but the cost is the high rates of unemployment in the meantime.

Figure 14-8 does a decent job of describing the effects of the Reagan/Volcker recession of the early 1980s. In 1980 inflationary expectations were exceedingly high. When Volcker applied the monetary brakes aggregate demand fell, and the recession of 1981–1982 was a result. But the benefit of the recession was that it was successful in reducing inflationary expectations in the economy. By the middle 1980s the American economy returned to a path of economic growth with much lower rates of inflation. The two Short Run Phillips Curves with the different rates of inflationary expectations is evident in the empirical data shown in Figure 14-7 (d). The data points clearly show two separate Phillips Curves for that decade. In the 1980s the inflation—unemployment tradeoff seemed to return.

While the importance of expectations seemed to grow in the United States economy during the 1980s, the role of expectations in economic theory also began to increase. Notice that in the past few discussions we mentioned how changes in inflationary expectations will change the location of the Short Run Phillips Curve. But we never discussed how these expectations are actually formed. How do households calculate their anticipated rate of future inflation? What data and evidence is used in the decision-making process? As usual, economists have different ideas about the processes involved in forming expectations about future economic variables. Two important theories of expectations formation are adaptive expectations and rational expectations.

## THE ROLE OF EXPECTATIONS

The adaptive expectations model was originally used by Pigou and Keynes to explain changes in stock prices and business cycles. In adaptive expectations models expectations are based on knowledge of past and current data. To estimate the future rate of inflation, for example, households will examine past and current rates of inflation. For example, if past inflation is 5%, and current inflation is 5%, then a reasonable estimate of future inflation is 5%. If the inflation rate was 4% last year and 5% this year, then a reasonable estimate is an inflation rate of 6% next year. In this way, people's forecasts of future inflation are based on current and past inflation rates.

One problem with adaptive expectations is that people may guess wrong. It assumes that economic forecasters have no knowledge of economic theory or anticipate no future fiscal or monetary policy changes. For example, suppose that the Fed finds a 6% rate of inflation unacceptable. Then it may take contractionary monetary policy actions before inflation gets that high. The monetary policy actions will reduce the rate of inflation. With this knowledge, a forecast of 6% is unreasonable and irrational. Many economists believe instead that forecasts of future economic variables will be rational, or take advantage of all available information at the time, including knowledge of future policy actions and macroeconomic theory. These models are known as rational expectations models.

*Adaptive expectations* are forecasts of future economic variables based on past and current values of the variable. *Rational expectations* are forecasts of future economic variables based on past and current values of the variable, knowledge of policy actions, and the relevant macroeconomic theory. With rational expectations, forecasts are made using all available information, not just past and current values.

The first paper to use the idea of rational expectations was by John Muth in 1961 who used the idea to explain changes in hog prices. The price that hog farmers expect to occur was generally the price that did occur. Farmers were able to guess correctly about future hog prices. Muth reasoned that expectations had an effect on future prices. If farmers expect hog prices to rise, they may withhold their supply of hogs until prices actually do rise. If investors anticipate that a stock price will rise, the demand for the stock will increase and the price will rise. In these ways expectations of future prices can affect future prices as a self-fulfilling prophecy. "The concept of rational expectations asserts that outcomes do not differ systematically (i.e., regularly or predictably) from what people expected them to be." If predictions are wrong, people change their expectations *(http://www.econlib.org/library/Enc/RationalExpectations.html;* Muth, John A. "Rational Expectations and the Theory of Price Movements." *Econometrica* 29, no. 6 (1961): 315–335).

The strongest proponents of rational expectations theory in the United States have been Robert Lucas of the University of Chicago and Thomas Sargent of the University of Minnesota. Starting in 1972, they began to publish papers exploring the implications of rational expectations theory for macroeconomic policy. They believed that fiscal and monetary policy were ineffective because people would anticipate the policy changes, so by the time the policy changes occurred they would have no effect. If the government tried to use expansionary fiscal policy to increase aggregate demand, households and firms would anticipate the effects on higher prices and interest rates, and adjust their labor effort and aggregate supply accordingly. If the Fed increases the money supply, workers will anticipate the resulting inflation and seek higher nominal wages, again decreasing the aggregate supply curve. In this way, fiscal and monetary policies are ineffective in changing real GDP in the economy, and only lead to price changes.

By the late 1980s, rational expectations models began to gain a foothold in mainstream macroeconomic thought. Many economists began to apply ideas of rational expectations to different economic problems, from agricultural commodity prices to stock markets to exchange rates. Both Sargent and Lucas published popular textbooks on rational expectations in 1986 and 1987 respectively. As changes in inflationary expectations became more important to the economy as a whole, many economists turned their attention to the role of expectations in economic decision-making. The models of rational expectations became more and more important to macroeconomic theory. (Lucas, Robert E. Jr. *Models of Business Cycles.* Oxford: Basil Blackwell, 1987. Sargent, Thomas J. *Rational Expectations and Inflation.* New York: Harper and Row, 1986).

While the models of Lucas and Sargent are very complicated mathematically, we can provide a brief review and a simplified model here. Basically, rational expectations models believe that economic forecasts are based on the predictions of an economic model. Specifically, the economic model is determined by the author, and is usually a complicated mathematical formula to predict the value of some future variable. Everybody makes forecasts using the model specified in the theory, and then uses those forecasts to make economic decisions. These decisions then affect further forecasts and the model is updated with new data. People continually update their forecasts based on new information, and these expectations affect future values of the variables being forecasted. If a forecast is wrong it is revised the next time using new information or a new model. In this model expectations are not systematically wrong.

A simplified version of the rational expectations model can be illustrated using the framework of the aggregate demand/aggregate supply and Phillips Curves of this chapter. In the rational expectations model, both aggregate demand and aggregate supply depend on expectations. The aggregate demand curve depends on expectations of future income, inflation rates, economic conditions, money supply and gov-

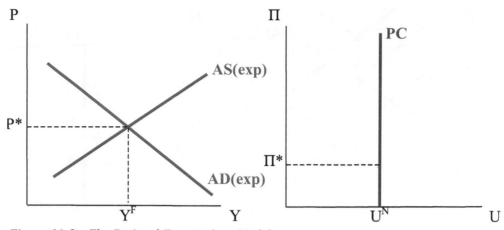

Figure 14-9    The Rational Expectations Model

ernment policies. All available information is used in determining the levels of aggregate expenditure in the economy. Changes in expectations will lead to changes in aggregate demand. For example, if fiscal policy can lead people to expect higher future incomes, then aggregate demand will increase. Similarly, the aggregate supply curve depends on expectations of future wages, prices, interest rates, labor and capital stocks, and taxes and regulations.

In Figure 14-9 the rational expectations model of the Phillips Curve and AD/AS is shown. The aggregate demand curve is labeled AD(exp) because aggregate demand depends on expectations of future income, prices, and money growth. The aggregate supply curve is denoted AS(exp) because aggregate supply also depends on expectations of future labor market conditions, business profitability and technology. If expectations are rational then the Phillips Curve is vertical. There is no trade-off between inflation and unemployment, even in the short run. Any attempts by the government to reduce unemployment rates will be anticipated by households before they have a chance to have any effect. The economy is always at the natural rate of unemployment. Expectations of future wages, prices, and interest rates adjust to keep the economy at full employment.

For example, suppose that the Federal Reserve attempts to stimulate the economy by increasing the money supply. The policy action will be anticipated by households in the economy. Through economic theory households know that inflation will result, so nominal resource prices increase. As resource prices increase, the aggregate supply curve declines. In the rational expectations model, these changes in aggregate demand and aggregate supply occur simultaneously, so the economy remains at full employment and the natural rate of unemployment.

If the government employs expansionary fiscal policy through increases in government spending or tax cuts, then aggregate demand will increase with higher expectations of future incomes and prices. Households and firms are able to anticipate the policy change before it happens. Because workers and producers are knowledgeable of economic theory, they know that the fiscal policy move will cause inflation and crowding out. The changes in expectations of future income and wages will cause the aggregate supply curve to shift to the left. Again these changes occur simultaneously so the economy stays at full employment. In the rational expectations model, the only way fiscal or monetary policies can have any effect is by fooling people. As long as households anticipate policy changes then those policy changes have no effect on real GDP and the rate of unemployment in the economy. The Phillips Curve is vertical. In the rational expectations model, the different data points observed in

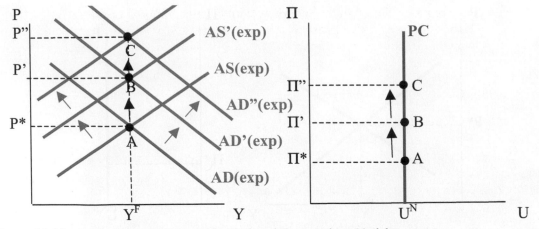

Figure 14-10    Expansionary Policy in the Rational Expectations Model

Figure 14-7 are due to changes in the natural rate of unemployment and actual inflation rates over time.

The effects of expansionary policy in the rational expectations model are shown in Figure 14-10. Suppose the government makes repeated attempts to expand the economy and reduce unemployment rates through expansionary fiscal or monetary policies. Every time the government increases aggregate demand, households and firms rationally expect the policy change to occur and change their expectations in ways that shift the aggregate supply curve to counteract the shift in aggregate demand. The result is the policy changes have no effects on real GDP or unemployment in the economy. Expansionary policies only lead to inflation as expectations adjust to the policy change. Under these circumstances the Phillips Curve is vertical. The rate of unemployment is always at the natural rate. The only way that policy has any effect on real variables is when that policy change is unexpected.

In the rational expectations model, any attempts to increase aggregate demand through expansionary fiscal or monetary policies will be met by counteracting changes in the aggregate supply curve as households and firms anticipate the policy change and adjust their expectations accordingly. The increases in aggregate demand have no effects on output or employment, only the price level and inflation rate. The economy moves from Point A to Point B to Point C with no change in real GDP or the unemployment rate. In the rational expectations model the Phillips Curve is vertical.

Note that at this point we have covered two hundred years of economic theory in the textbook beginning with the classical model, and in some sense we have now come full circle. We started in Chapter Eight discussing the classical model, where changes in government spending, taxes or the money supply had no effect on real GDP. After reviewing the evolution of economic thought we return to the same basic ideas of the classical model in rational expectations theory, that changes in fiscal or monetary policy have no effects on real GDP or employment rates in the economy. Once again we have the classical dichotomy ideas that changes in nominal variables have no effect on real variables in the economy. The only difference is that in rational expectations theory, policy changes can have temporary effects only if people are fooled into having the wrong expectations. Otherwise, the results of rational expectations are similar to the classical model we started with. The economy stays at full employment due to the flexibility of the various markets involved.

Throughout the 1980s, the rational expectations model provided some of the theoretical underpinnings of Reaganomics and supply-side economics. If agents acted rationally, then decreases in government spending would not affect real variables but only reduce inflation in the economy. With tax cuts, rational workers would increase labor effort with an increase in after tax wages, and increases in expected income would lead to increases in the aggregate supply curve without much effect on aggregate demand.

## THE 1990S: BALANCED GROWTH

As shown in Figure 14-7(e) a few pages back, during most of the 1990s the economy experienced economic growth without high rates of inflation. By the late 1980s inflation rates had come under control, so into the 1990s inflationary expectations were well-contained. After a mild recession in 1991, the economy experienced 10 years of economic growth, the longest period of economic expansion in American history. As income and wealth increased in the economy and business confidence grew, the aggregate demand curve in the economy expanded. As the internet and personal computers introduced new technological production efficiencies, aggregate supply also grew. During the Clinton Administration the federal government developed a budget surplus for the first time since the early 1960s. This enabled total saving in the economy to increase, and the decline in interest rates encouraged investment spending and capital formation. During the 1990s the U.S. economy experienced balanced growth, with increases in aggregate demand and aggregate supply at the same time. The result was steady economic growth with little threat of inflation.

The process of balanced growth is illustrated in Figure 14-11. As aggregate demand increases in the economy aggregate supply does so as well. Increases in income, wealth, and business confidence led to increases in aggregate demand in the 1990s. As technology increased, both the Short Run and Long Run Aggregate Supply curves shifted to the right. The economy was able to grow without inflation, as shown in Figure 14-7 (e). In the 1990s unemployment rates fell to low levels without any accompanying increase in inflation. This means that the natural rate of unemployment declined, and the Long Run Phillips Curve shifted to the left. The decline in the natural rate of unemployment had several causes. Computers and the internet made it easier for workers to find jobs or to become self-employed, so the duration of unemployment declined. By the 1990s women had become absorbed into the workforce, so there were not a lot of new women entering the labor market without experience as in the 1970s. Most of the baby boomers had already entered the labor force and found jobs, while their children were too young to be entering the labor force yet. Temporary job agencies made it easier to find work. All of these factors made the

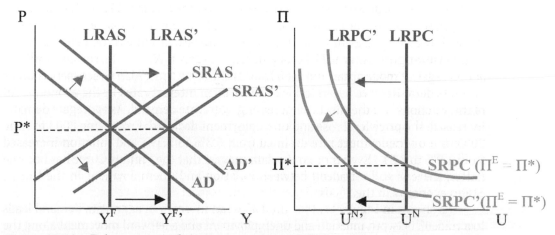

Figure 14-11   Balanced Growth in the Neo-Classical Phillips Curve Model

natural rate of unemployment decline, and the Long Run Phillips Curve to shift to the right, during the 1990s, as shown in Figure 14-11.

With balanced growth, increases in aggregate demand are matched with increases in Short Run Aggregate Supply so that real GDP increases while the price level remains constant. Increases in technology increase the Long Run Aggregate Supply curve so the economy remains at full employment with a higher level of potential GDP. In the Phillips Curve graph, declines in the natural rate of unemployment cause the Long Run Phillips Curve to shift to the left. At the new natural rate of unemployment inflationary expectations would be too high, so the Short Run Phillips Curve shifts to the left at the same time as inflationary expectations return to the actual rate of inflation. With balanced growth, it is possible to achieve increases in real GDP and reductions in the unemployment rate without causing inflation. This is the story of the United States economy in the 1990s, especially after the recession of 1991.

In the 1990s and into the next decade macroeconomic theory continued to evolve. Rational expectations models were applied in many contexts, both in macroeconomics and microeconomics. Once rational expectations theory was applied extensively, it was found that the predictions of the model did not always hold in the real world. Economic decision-makers did not always have the information and knowledge assumed by the models. Neo-classical economists turned their attention to growth theory, time inconsistency problems of policy, real business cycles, and dynamic general equilibrium models of the macroeconomy. Neo-Keynesian economists began to explore models of wage and price rigidity and money illusion in the economy, some based on the rational formation of expectations. Search theory became more widely applied to economic problems. Greg Mankiw at Harvard began to champion the idea of a macroeconomic synthesis between the competing models. As long as the economy continued to grow at a steady pace with low inflation, there were little crises for macroeconomic theory to solve, and much academic effort was devoted to revising current models of the economy rather than developing new ones. This economic complacency would be short-lived as economic policy makers faced the problems and challenges of the 2000s.

## THE 2000s: THE RETURN OF THE PHILLIPS CURVE

In the early 2000s, the economy was still enjoying the tail end of the longest economic expansion in U.S history. GDP continued to grow, and inflation and unemployment rates were low. But by early 2001 the economy entered a recession, brought about by the crash of the telecommunications stock bubble that began in 1995. The problems were made worse by the terrorist attacks of September 11, 2001, that caused disruptions in financial markets and a general decline in confidence. When George W. Bush became president in 2001, he moved quickly to address the pending recession with tax cuts. After 9/11 President Bush began a War on Terror and military actions against Afghanistan and then Iraq. At the same time, Alan Greenspan as Chair of the Federal Reserve began to lower short-term interest rates in the economy. All of these actions had the effects of increasing aggregate demand. As aggregate demand increased, the price level rose and unemployment declined. From June 2003 to June 2005, the unemployment rate declined from 6.3% to 5.1%, and inflation increased from 1.9% to 2.5%. Even though the data suggest that the Phillips Curve has become flatter, there is still a tradeoff between inflation and unemployment in the United States economy in the 2000s.

As shown in Figure 14-3 for the 1960s, an increase in aggregate demand leads to a tradeoff between inflation and unemployment and a leftward movement along the

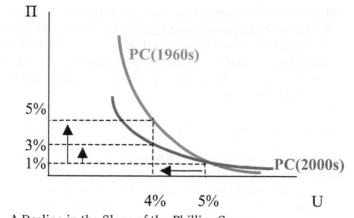

Figure 14-12   A Decline in the Slope of the Phillips Curve

Phillips Curve. The increase in real GDP leads to a decline in the unemployment rate, while the increase in the price level causes an uptick in inflation. In many ways, from a macroeconomic perspective the 2000s were similar to the 1960s. Both decades began with recessions, and then had tax cuts, wars, and expansionary monetary policies to increase aggregate demand. The increase in aggregate demand led to an increase in real GDP so unemployment rates declined. As unemployment rates decline there is a leftward movement along the Phillips Curve so that inflation rates increase. One difference between the 1960s and 2000s is that in the 2000s the Phillips Curve was flatter, so that the reduction in the unemployment rate did not cause as large of an increase in the rate of inflation. As inflation rates approach 0, the Phillips Curve becomes flatter as inflationary expectations become stabilized. As shown in Figure 14-12, when the Phillips Curve becomes flatter then a given decline in the unemployment rate will cause less of an increase in the rate of inflation. In the 1960s for example, when unemployment was reduced from 5% to 4%, inflation increased from 1% to 5%. But in the 2000s when unemployment was reduced from 5% to 4%, inflation only increased from 1% to 3%. The Phillips Curve had become flatter, especially during the declines in inflationary expectations of the 1980s. But during the 2000s the U.S. economy once again faced the tradeoffs of the Phillips Curve because once again macroeconomic events were dominated by demand-side changes in the economy.

The tradeoffs of the Phillips Curve were even more pronounced during the economic downturn in the latter part of the decade from 2006–2009. As the housing bubble burst and stock prices fell, declines in wealth led to declines in aggregate demand. As aggregate demand fell, unemployment increased and the economy actually witnessed deflation in the last few months of 2008. As unemployment grew the inflation rate decreased, and the economy moved to the right along the Phillips Curve. As unemployment increased inflation fell. As shown in Figure 14-7 (e), during the 2000s two distinct patterns of Phillips Curves are discernable. Over the course of the decade inflationary expectations continued to stabilize at even lower rates of inflation, and the Phillips Curve shifted downward.

## SUMMARY: THE POLICY IMPLICATIONS OF THE PHILLIPS CURVE

With the Obama Administration and Federal Reserve's attempts to bring the economy out of the current recession, the policy implications of the Phillips Curve must be kept in mind. As we saw in the last few years, the Phillips Curve is not dead yet. The increases in unemployment during 2008 and 2009 led to lower rates of inflation and even deflation. But as expansionary policies try to increase aggregate demand and reduce unemployment rates, policy makers must be wary of the growing threats of inflation in the economy. As we saw in the 1970s and 1980s, if inflationary expectations begin to grow out of control, then it may require an even more severe recession to rein these inflationary expectations back in again. Policy makers would be wiser to not let inflation rear its ugly head to begin with, even if that means a longer time to economic recovery.

## CONCLUSIONS: MACROECONOMIC POLICY AND THEORY

These last few paragraphs bring us to the end of our journey through macroeconomics. (Yea!) In Chapters 5–7 we explored the different variables used to measure the performance of the economy, and in Chapters 8–10 we examined three important theories of macroeconomics, the classical model, fixed-price Keynesian model, and different models of aggregate supply and aggregate demand. In these last four chapters we analyzed how these models can be applied to problems of economic policy-making. I hope that in the process, you have gained an appreciation for the variety of models and theories used in macroeconomics. People have different ideologies and convictions, with different models to support their ideas. Just about any argument can be supported with some economic model out there some where. The point is to be aware of the models that others are using, and to know the models that help to support your own views of the world. Over time, hopefully those models that do not work so well will be discarded and those with a great deal of explanatory power will stand the test of time. Economics as a social science becomes stronger as a result.

One reason for throwing so many models at you in the text is because you never know what models will be useful in the future, and I want to be sure that my students and readers are well prepared for what may come at them later on. The classical model had resurgence in the 1980s, and the Phillips Curve is making a comeback today. There tend to be cycles in the popularity of economic models over time. With conservative administrations classical models are more popular, while with liberals Keynesian models are more popular. Keynesian models provide a greater role for government to play in the economy. Classical models provide a greater role for markets. If you only learn one type of theory you only learn half of the story. It is no accident that the Obama Administration is relying on Keynesian economics; it goes along with his politics.

Throughout your study of macroeconomics, I hope you have realized the important connections between theory, policy and economic events. Often a crisis will cause economists to study new problems and develop new theories. From these theories the government develops economic policies, which in turn influence economic conditions and the development of new theories, which then again influence policy and economic events. For example, before the 1930s the classical model was dominant, which relied on microeconomic concepts of efficient markets. This made sense when most markets were regional, there were many panics in individual markets, and the transportation and communication technology did not yet exist for a truly national economy. During this time much of the action was in individual markets.

With the development of the automobile, telegraph, and telephone, technology made national markets possible and macroeconomics in general became more meaningful. In a sense the Great Depression was the first macroeconomic crisis because markets had been connected nationally like never before. During this time Keynesian models came into vogue, reaching their pinnacle with the Kennedy Administration in the early 1960s. The demand-side changes at the time lent validity to the Phillips Curve model published in 1958 (the year I was born!), and the Phillips Curve model came into vogue. With the supply-side changes in the 1970s, the Phillips Curve and Keynesian economics in general fell into disrepute, and in the 1980s we witnessed a return to classical principles in the form of supply-side economics, the neo-classical model, and rational expectations. Since that time we have seen a return to Keynesian economics as again demand-side changes became more relevant to the economy. The Bush II and Obama Administrations both used Keynesian principles in their attempts to get the economy out of recession. This is entirely appropriate when the administration is engineering aggregate demand changes in the economy.

In this way, theory and policy influence economic events, and economic events affect theory and policy. Generally, new economic theories are developed in times of economic crisis. Who knows what theories will arise from the current recession? Who knows which one of you readers will develop them?

So concludes our exploration of macroeconomics. I sincerely hope that the costs of the book and the time spent reading and studying it were worth the benefits of the knowledge gained. In short, I hope you learned a lot that was both useful and interesting, and that your understanding of the world has increased. You now have the economic tools to make better choices, to begin to comprehend our current economic mess and to have some idea of what the government can do about it. You can now contribute to economic debates and participate more fully in civic life. You now have a better awareness of the economy around you and your place in it.

Go out and make the world a better place.

# INDEX

# Student Comments from the Preliminary Edition

Textbook was affordable! Also, I liked that we used the whole book.

I like the textbook because it is comprehensive and tends to be clear.

No index, also a lot of concepts are repeated or are hard to find, hidden in blocks of text.

Like it because it is easy to follow. Any time I didn't understand something while reading, there was always an example to describe it more.

Some concepts were oversimplified.

The textbook simplified macroeconomics to text that was easily understandable and relatable to.

Too boring, dull, over-repetitive.

I like how the textbook keeps bringing up the same point from previous paragraphs and chapters.

Sometimes ideas are repetitive and I waste my time reading the <u>very long</u> chapters.

What I didn't like was that it was written as if the author was speaking.

I liked how the textbook didn't sound like a textbook. It was colloquial language, and it made it easy to understand. Like you were actually in class learning about macroeconomics.

The textbook explains everything well.

The book was very easy to read and follow, and information was easy to discern.

The class, professor, and book all suck.

It does a good job explaining the context of the class.

Testbook is seem very helpful for me. The words is not hard, easy to read, explain detailly.

Didn't buy.

The book should be in color.

The textbook was very easy to understand. It also provides real life examples that I was able to analyze and found interesting.

It is a very well written textbook! Congratulations!

Some chapters were too long.

I really like the new textbook, and feel it helps and is actually worthwhile reading. I would urge you not to jump to a 2nd edition, because none of us could resell our books, and many of the mistakes are minor. Its soft cover and eventually a demand will arise for the newer version as older versions deteriorate.

The text was easy to read and very focused. Any question I had on the problem set was answered.

Very basic, simple language that is easy to understand. Good examples and illustrations. It's a very very good book.

Textbook very easy to understand. I loved the textbook.

It was very straightforward and easy to read.

It was not thick but explains everything.

It's very long and complicated to read.

It is not useful when you have it. It's very helpful when you don't have it.

Very easy to read. Confortable and familiar language. Included great examples which allows readers to understand material better.

Very clear and informative with lots of examples.

I liked that the textbook used examples that made some of the difficult topics easier to understand.

I liked the affordability and the fact that whatever was taught in class was in the textbook (examples and all) in case I missed a lecture—I could always catch up. Also the little comments were funny. The size of the book was good.

It's cheap and easy to understand. helpful!

I actually really liked the textbook. It was very helpful.

The price was great.

Extremely helpful, easy to read, graphs made sense.

The textbook was too long.